TRACES OF THE ANIMAL PAST

CANADIAN HISTORY AND ENVIRONMENT SERIES

SERIES EDITOR: Alan MacEachern
ISSN 1925-3702 (Print) ISSN 1925-3710 (Online)

The Canadian History & Environment series brings together scholars from across the academy and beyond to explore the relationships between people and nature in Canada's past.

Alan MacEachern, Founding Director
NiCHE: Network in Canadian History & Environment
Nouvelle initiative canadienne en histoire de l'environnement
http://niche-canada.org

No. 1 · *A Century of Parks Canada, 1911–2011*
Edited by Claire Elizabeth Campbell

No. 2 · *Historical GIS Research in Canada*
Edited by Jennifer Bonnell and Marcel Fortin

No. 3 · *Mining and Communities in Northern Canada: History, Politics, and Memory*
Edited by Arn Keeling and John Sandlos

No. 4 · *Canadian Countercultures and the Environment*
Edited by Colin M. Coates

No. 5 · *Moving Natures: Mobility and the Environment in Canadian History*
Edited by Ben Bradley, Jay Young, and Colin M. Coates

No. 6 · *Border Flows: A Century of the Canadian-American Water Relationship*
Edited by Lynne Heasley and Daniel Macfarlane

No. 7 · *Ice Blink: Navigating Northern Environmental History*
Edited by Stephen Bocking and Brad Martin

No. 8 · *Animal Metropolis: Histories of Human-Animal Relations in Urban Canada*
Edited by Joanna Dean, Darcy Ingram, and Christabelle Sethna

No. 9 · *Environmental Activism on the Ground: Small Green and Indigenous Organizing*
Edited by Jonathan Clapperton and Liza Piper

No. 10 · *The First Century of the International Joint Commission*
Edited by Daniel Macfarlane and Murray Clamen

No. 11 · *Traces of the Animal Past: Methodological Challenges in Animal History*
Edited by Jennifer Bonnell and Sean Kheraj

 UNIVERSITY OF CALGARY Press

Traces OF THE Animal Past

METHODOLOGICAL CHALLENGES IN ANIMAL HISTORY

EDITED BY
Jennifer Bonnell
AND Sean Kheraj

Canadian History and Environment Series
ISSN 1925-3702 (Print) ISSN 1925-3710 (Online)

© 2022 Jennifer Bonnell and Sean Kheraj

University of Calgary Press
2500 University Drive NW
Calgary, Alberta
Canada T2N 1N4
press.ucalgary.ca

All rights reserved.

This book is available in an Open Access digital format published under a CC-BY-NCND 4.0 Creative Commons license. The publisher should be contacted for any commercial use which falls outside the terms of that license.

LIBRARY AND ARCHIVES CANADA CATALOGUING IN PUBLICATION

Title: Traces of the animal past : methodological challenges in animal history / edited by Jennifer Bonnell and Sean Kheraj.
Names: Bonnell, Jennifer, 1971- editor. | Kheraj, Sean, editor.
Series: Canadian history and environment series ; 11.
Description: Series statement: Canadian history and environment series ; 11 | Includes bibliographical references and index.
Identifiers: Canadiana (print) 20220280940 | Canadiana (ebook) 20220281041 | ISBN 9781773853840 (softcover) | ISBN 9781773853833 (hardcover) | ISBN 9781773853857 (open access PDF) | ISBN 9781773853864 (PDF) | ISBN 9781773853871 (EPUB)
Subjects: LCSH: Human-animal relationships—History—Research—Methodology. LCSH: Animals—Social aspects—History—Research—Methodology. | LCSH: Animals—History—Research—Methodology.
Classification: LCC QL85 .T73 2022 | DDC 590.7—dc23

The University of Calgary Press acknowledges the support of the Government of Alberta through the Alberta Media Fund for our publications. We acknowledge the financial support of the Government of Canada. We acknowledge the financial support of the Canada Council for the Arts for our publishing program.

  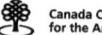

The editor and publisher would like to thank the Faculty of Liberal Arts & Professional Studies, York University, Toronto, Canada, the Avie Bennett Historica Chair in Canadian History at York University, and the University of Stavanger for the financial support they provided to this work.

Copyediting by Michael Gollner
Cover image: Aelbert Cuyp, *Young Herdsmen with Cows*, ca. 1655–60, oil on canvas, 112.1 x 132.4 cm, Courtesy of the MET Collection API, https://www.metmuseum.org/art/collection/search/436064
Cover design, page design, and typesetting by Melina Cusano

Contents

Introduction: Traces of the Animal Past . . . 1
    Jennifer Bonnell and Sean Kheraj

Part I: Embodied Histories . . . 17

1. Kicking over the Traces? Freeing the Animal from the Archive . . . 19
    Sandra Swart

2. Occupational Hazards: Honeybee Labour as an Interpretive Device in Animal History . . . 49
    Jennifer Bonnell

3. Hearing History through Hoofbeats: Exploring Equine Volition and Voice in the Archive . . . 73
    Lindsay Stallones Marshall

Part II: Traces . . . 89

4. Who is a Greyhound? Reflections on the Non-Human Digital Archive . . . 91
    Susan Nance

5. Accessing Animal Health Knowledge: Popular Educators and Veterinary Science in Rural Ontario . . . 117
    Jody Hodgins

6. Animal Cruelty, Metaphoric Narrative, and the Hudson's Bay Company, 1919–1939 . . . 137
    George Colpitts

Part III: The Unknowable Animal — 155

7. Vanishing Flies and the Lady Entomologist — 157
   Catherine McNeur

8. Guinea Pig Agnotology — 175
   Joanna Dean

9. Tuffy's Cold War: Science, Memory, and the US Navy's Dolphin — 199
   Jason M. Colby

10. The Elephant in the Archive — 217
    Nigel Rothfels

Part IV: Spatial Sources and Animal Movement — 233

11. Making Tracks: A Grizzly and Entangled History — 235
    Colleen Campbell and Tina Loo

12. Spatial Analysis and Digital Urban Animal History — 269
    Sean Kheraj

13. Visualizing the Animal City: Digital Experiments in Animal History — 291
    Andrew Robichaud

14. What's a Guanaco? Tracing the Llama Diaspora through and beyond South America — 315
    Emily Wakild

Part V: Looking at Animals — 337

15 Hidden in Plain Sight: How Art and Visual Culture Can Help Us Think about Animal Histories — 339
    J. Keri Cronin

16 Creatures on Display: Making an Animal Exhibit at the Archives of Ontario — 357
    Jay Young

17 Portraits of Extinction: Encountering Bluebuck Narratives in the Natural History Museum — 371
    Dolly Jørgensen

Epilogue: Combinations and Conjunction — 389
    Harriet Ritvo

Contributors — 403
Index — 409

Introduction: Traces of the Animal Past

Jennifer Bonnell and Sean Kheraj

In July 1624, Gabriel Sagard held his own farewell party in the Recollet convent in Quebec. He had recently learned that his order was recalling him to France after he had spent nearly a year living in Wendake, the territories of the Wendat, one of the largest confederacies of Indigenous people in North America. The news was unexpected. His Wendat hosts had brought him back to Quebec to obtain supplies and trade furs. Instead of returning to Wendake, Sagard was ordered to sail on the first ship back to France. He prepared a feast at the convent to say goodbye and he wanted to leave his Wendat hosts with a meaningful, precious gift. He gave them a cat.[1]

Domestic cats are not indigenous to North America. In 1624, they were a rarity. The cats that French colonists brought with them to New France in the early seventeenth century were novel species introductions. They travelled with European people aboard ships on months-long journeys across the Atlantic. Cats were useful on such voyages as they hunted the rats that stowed away aboard ships and feasted on the provisions people brought with them to survive the difficult passage to the so-called New World.

French Catholic missionaries used cats as gifts, gestures of friendship in their encounters with Indigenous peoples of the Americas. Sagard used this cat for this very purpose. It was a tool of diplomacy, an improbable

1

"creature of empire," in a mission to bring Christianity to Wendake.[2] He made note of this small moment on the frontlines of the Columbian Exchange:

> Before my departure we took [the Wendat] into our convent, feasted them, and showed them all the civility and friendliness that we could, and gave each of them some small present, and to the captain and chief of the canoe in particular a cat to take back to his country as a rarity unknown to them. This present gave him infinite pleasure and he made much of it; but when he saw that the cat came to us when we called it he concluded that it was possessed of reason and understood all we said to it. Therefore, after having humbly thanked me for so rare a gift, he begged us to tell this cat that when it should be in his land it must not behave badly nor be running into the other lodges nor in the woods, but remain always in his abode to eat the mice, and that he would love it like his own son and not let it be in want of anything. I leave you to think and reflect upon the candour and simplicity of this good man, who supposed that just the same understanding and the same power of reason belonged to the rest of the animals of the settlement, and to judge if it was unnecessary to detach him from this idea and set him in the path of reason himself, since he had already put the same question to me respecting the ebb and flow of the sea, which he believed on that account to be alive, to understand and to have volition.[3]

This translated passage from Sagard's 1632 book, *Le grand voyage du pays des Hurons*, is a complicated text to interpret. Sagard describes his Indigenous hosts as expressing a childlike wonder at a simple domestic cat, confusing the cat's behaviour for human reason. Still, for the Wendat, the cat was an utterly novel creature, unknown in Wendake but perhaps connected to other aspects of the non-human world. Historians could spend years pulling apart the layers of meaning from this text to explore the different ways in which French and Wendat people might have understood animals in the early decades of the seventeenth century. Did this cat bring joy to the Wendat men who received it? What does this encounter reveal about the place of non-human animals in Wendat cosmologies? How did Sagard perceive the sentience of a cat or other animals or the ebb and flow of the sea?

But what can a text like this tell us about this cat? How did it feel about playing such a role in the emergence of the alliance between the French and the Wendat in the early years of the French empire in North America? What was its experience of the environments of New France? How did it adapt to the new setting? Where did it sleep?

Gabriel Sagard's gift of a cat to the Wendat illustrates the methodological challenge at the heart of animal history. Non-human creatures have been present at every major event in human history.[4] Animals have even shaped and influenced that history. And yet historical scholarship about animals is often limited to these glimpses or traces of animals in the past. Most evidence of animals in the past comes from people who wrote about animals, drew pictures of animals, photographed animals. They often documented animals as peripheral or background objects. Non-human animals themselves leave different kinds of traces, ones not necessarily meant for historical interpretation and difficult, if not impossible, to decipher. Seeing the past through the eyes of an animal is a treacherous exercise replete with opportunities for wrong turns, misinterpretation, and clumsy ventriloquism. Still, the same might also be said of efforts to tell the histories of marginalized people who leave few traces of their own. How then do historians tell stories about animals?

These are questions that we and other animal historians face as we approach the archives and other repositories of historical evidence to try to understand animals as historical actors. In late 2018, the Archives of Ontario opened its *ANIMALIA: Animals in the Archives* exhibit, which highlighted the role of animals in Ontario history by showcasing sources related to various species that stood out in its collections (see Young, Chapter 16). The exhibit raised issues for us as historians about how we use such sources in our work. What methods and theories do we employ when trying to understand animal history? We invited an international group of animal historians to participate in a two-day conference at the Archives of Ontario on precisely this question.[5] The response was immediate and enthusiastic. Scholars in the field of animal history were eager to share their methodological challenges from their ongoing research projects.

They were also eager to extend that conversation to a broader community of readers. The result is this book.

Ours is certainly not the first work to pose these questions about methods in animal history research. Indeed, some of these questions have been persistent in the field of animal history from its inception. Harriet Ritvo, a founding scholar in the field of animal history, noted the neglect of the study of animals in nineteenth-century English cultural history in her 1987 book, *The Animal Estate: The English and Other Creatures in the Victorian Age*. Ritvo explores changing discourse about the mammals with which English people interacted most frequently by examining the written texts of organizations concerned with breeding, veterinary medicine, agriculture, and natural history. Hers is a study of human ideas and perceptions of animals in the past, but as she notes, in these sources "Animals ... never talk back."[6] Nigel Rothfels' early collection of essays on animal representations proposes that the human depiction of animals "is in some very important way deeply connected to our cultural environment, and that this cultural environment is rooted in history."[7] Sandra Swart refuses the impossibility of animal history and the limits of text by looking at new "texts" and new materialities. She suggests methods by which historians can interpret the ways that animals indeed "talk back" by biting, bucking, and otherwise "kicking against the traces." For Swart, the materiality and biology of animals as living creatures in her sources provide a way of seeing history through the eyes of animals.[8] Etienne Benson also challenges the so-called impossibility of animal history—that is to say, the limits to seeing animals mediated solely through human texts. These texts embody both humans and non-human creatures, Benson argues, because they are the result of an interdependence between people and other animals, "a collection of traces of the animal who writes through the human as well as of the human who writes about the animal." Historical documents, then, are co-constructed more-than-human texts that are both material and discursive simultaneously.[9]

In 2013, the journal *History and Theory* published a special issue on animal history, edited by David Gary Shaw, in which eight historians in the field explored some of the theoretical and methodological challenges to the study of animal history. Shaw noted the changes in history as a discipline that began largely as a social concern to understand people and their actions over time to one broad enough in focus to include aspects of the non-human world, including animals.[10] Most recently, Susan Nance's *The Historical Animal* included essays that explore a variety of themes in animal history, including a section dedicated specifically to considering "Archives and the Animal Trace." The authors confronted the challenges of finding the animal in the archive, a historical figure that is often peripheral in sources and marginal to the processes of creating archival collections. Nevertheless, as Zeb Tortorici contends, "[e]ven if we consciously choose to limit ourselves to mainstream historical archives ... we find that animals do exist in such archives across material, textual, geographic, and temporal boundaries." He goes further to suggest that historians might need to go beyond the search for physical and textual traces of animal history and "open up our very notion of what an archive is," a task taken up by some of the contributors to this volume.[11]

This collection of essays focuses on those traces and builds upon these previous studies to push forward debates and questions about methods in animal history. In doing so, we seek to provoke new questions that advance the field and open new research possibilities for the study of historical human-animal relations. The chapters that follow make methodological processes transparent and situate the historian within the narrative; they are not historical case studies *per se*, but metanarratives of the animal historian and their subjects. In each case, the authors reflect upon current research and how they confront some of the main methodological challenges of animal history. They offer new approaches and new directions for a maturing field of historical inquiry. The chapters in this book go beyond making the case that animals mattered in the past and explore how historians can uncover and interpret traces of evidence of historical animals.

As the *ANIMALIA* exhibit at the Archives of Ontario reveals, non-human animals can be found throughout archival collections, if you know how to look for them. One of the primary methodological challenges of animal history has been a search problem. How do we find historical sources that capture the role of animals in the past? Because archival records are mainly produced by people, and preserved and organized for anthropocentric purposes, non-human animals are often marginal within traditional archival collections; they are incidental in the archives. Nance

Fig. 0.1 A dog and horse incidentally captured in a Toronto Engineering Department photograph, 1890. Source: City of Toronto Archives, F. W. Micklethwaite, Fonds 1661, Series 1037, Item 6.

argues that historians and archivists are typically trained "to edit animals out of our analysis," and as a result animals can be difficult to see in the records.[12] She uses photography as an example of the peripheral status of the non-human animal in the anthropocentric archive.

Nineteenth- and twentieth-century photographs in archival collections include numerous examples of historical animals, many of which are not the primary subject. For example, this 1890 photograph by F. W. Micklethwaite, commissioned by the Toronto Engineering Department, was part of a series of photos of bridges and street-level railway crossings (Fig. 0.1). Proudly standing on the sidewalk near the crossing on York Street was one such incidental animal in the archive, a small dog, and on the other side of the street one of the thousands of horses that pulled carts on the streets of nineteenth-century Toronto. The only label that appears at the bottom of the photo reads: "RR Crossing York St from N 45 yards distant." To "see" these animals requires a different perspective on the part of the historian, one that places non-human animals at the centre of one's view.

As many chapters in this collection show, there are other methodologies for finding animals in historical records and archives. Artwork and other documents of visual culture similarly capture elements of animal history that might not be immediately apparent without careful consideration, observation, and practice (Cronin, Chapter 15). In other sources, non-human animals are ostensibly invisible, nearly absent from the written record, even though they are known to have been present and crucial historical actors. In Chapter 8, Joanna Dean's re-examination of the guinea pigs of Connaught Laboratories seeks to make the silences in lab records about animal testing visible to historical analysis. Digital history methods provide new ways of finding animals in the archive, from the use of Geographic Information Systems (GIS) (Kheraj, Chapter 12 and Robichaud, Chapter 13) to the creation of digital archives from the ephemera of the Web (Nance, Chapter 4). And oral history holds some potential to explore the archive of animal history kept within the memories of people who lived, worked, and played with other creatures (Colby, Chapter 9). Each of these different methodologies for finding animals in historical sources operates as a lens that brings animal history into focus within those sources where they might otherwise have gone unnoticed. An animal-centric lens on the past can help historians find animals in the archives and acknowledge that animals mattered in the past.

Acknowledging that animals mattered in human histories involves moving beyond questions of the existence of animal agency. Unlike earlier studies in animal history, which pointed to the presence of animal agency—in the resistance demonstrated by the kicking mule, or the selective loyalty of the household pet—as a way of justifying the existence of the field, this collection proceeds from the assumption that historical animals had agency, however limited by the structures and circumstances they found themselves within.[13] Animal agency is not only self-evident from the numerous accounts of animal resistance and self-determination that historians have documented; it is also, as Linda Nash has shown, fundamentally insufficient as an analytical approach. Agency, Nash contends, is conceptually constrained by its anthropocentrism, taking as its point of departure "the self-contained individual confronting an external world." This works no less well for humans than it does for non-human animals. Human intentions, she argues, like non-human ones, do not emerge through "disembodied contemplation" but rather "through practical engagement with the world." Agency becomes in her analysis "too simple to describe" how human and non-human animals inhabited the world.

Instead, a more fruitful point of departure, particularly for environmental historians, lies in considering the "organism-in-its-environment."[14] Thus, changing ecosystems become an important context for writing animal history. Swart (Chapter 1) and Bonnell (Chapter 2) demonstrate the rich possibilities for this kind of analysis. Throughout, contributors position agency, with all of its complexity and limitations, as "the start of the analysis, rather than the conclusion of the argument."[15] They seek instead to comment on the process of writing histories that "take animals seriously" through the exercise of historical empathy.[16]

Several chapters in this collection strive to see history through the eyes of non-human animals. In some ways, this approach extends the methods of social history or histories "from the bottom up." The proposition of thinking about the past from the view of another species is one of the ways in which animal history has the potential to yield revisionist insights relevant to all fields of historical scholarship. As Swart suggests, these insights may not result in a fundamental rewriting of the past, but they change, "however slightly," how historians write history.

This approach comes with several risks. Animal historians who seek to write histories from the view of non-human animals run the risk of performing a form of ventriloquism, an awkward attempt to speak on behalf of animals.[17] This idea hearkens back to the original slogan of the Society for the Prevention of Cruelty to Animals: "We speak for those that cannot speak for themselves" (Figure 0.2). This is something that Susan Pearson has argued was the result of a long-standing perception of language as a distinguishing characteristic between people and other animals.[18] This way of thinking about language has been embedded in history as a discipline for much of the nineteenth and twentieth centuries as a way to exclude prehistory from history itself, "savagery" from "civilization." Embedded in the methodologies of animal history then are possibilities of new ways for all historians to think differently about the sources they use to understand the past.

Animal history can challenge this reductionist mode of thinking by broadening the ways that historians approach text and language. Sandra Swart (Chapter 1) and Lindsay Marshall (Chapter 3) both suggest ways of reading the bodies of animals as sources, forms of language and communication that only become readable to scholars through the adoption of various interdisciplinary lenses and (in Marshall's study) through Indigenous ontologies. This approach can even use the remains of animals as historical texts, one example of which is known as "osteobiography."[19] Finding the language of animals and the ways their bodies can be read as texts expands the range of sources available to historians and opens possibilities to tell the histories of other species besides our own. Neither scholar tries to speak on behalf of non-human animals; instead, they use interdisciplinary insights and historical empathy to situate the biology of non-human animals (in these cases, horses) in the past. At its best, the exercise of historical empathy for other species may also enhance our understanding of humans in other subfields of history. As Erica Fudge argues, "the history of animals is a necessary part of our reconceptualization of ourselves as human."[20]

In many ways, the methodological challenges that animal historians confront in this volume have much in common with the challenges that all historians face when trying to interpret and understand historical actors through the scant records and evidence left behind. There are, of course, differences, especially the chasm of language between humans and non-human animals. Nevertheless, the methods that animal historians use to interpret the past could be of value to all historical scholars seeking to understand the voices of those not readily apparent in the archives.

Many of the methodological challenges that the authors in this collection explore are, in fact, relevant to scholars in all fields of history. Emily O'Gorman and Andrea Gaynor argue that environmental history as a subfield has an opportunity for more explicit engagement with interdisciplinary more-than-human scholarship and multi-species studies. The same could be true for many other subfields. O'Gorman and Gaynor ask, "What does a more-than-human approach mean for the way historians actually go about their research?" The creative and imaginative methods used in animal history have application in other areas of historical scholarship. For instance, the GIS methods Kheraj and Robichaud explore in Chapters 12 and 13 of this volume are easily applicable to other areas of urban history. Jason Colby's (Chapter 9) engagement with the limitations of oral history present some difficulties that are unique to studying non-human animals, but the limitations are comparable to those of oral history methods in fields beyond animal history. The methods Susan Nance deploys to

Fig. 0.2 Cover of *Our Dumb Animals*, vol. 25, no. 8 (January 1893), the periodical of the Massachusetts Society for the Prevention of Cruelty to Animals with slogan, "We speak for those that cannot speak for themselves."

construct a digital archive of the history of racing greyhounds may have transferable relevance to social historians seeking to better understand marginalized people who left few traces in traditional textual archival sources. As animal historians struggle to make meaning from the remnants of evidence about animals found in traditional sources, the more-than-human methodologies they employ have the potential to support research in other fields of historical scholarship that face similar challenges concerning power, historical evidence, and the construction of archives.[21]

Navigating the pitfalls of anthropomorphism is another challenge animal historians face in their interdisciplinary explorations of animal pasts. Contributors not only encounter anthropomorphism in historical human relationships with animals (Colpitts' anti-cruelty advocates in Chapter 6 and Colby's dolphin trainers in Chapter 9 are good examples), but also wrestle with ways to avoid it in navigating the gap between human and non-human experience. Recognizing anthropomorphism for what it is, as a somewhat crude expression of historical empathy, is a good place to begin. Contributors move beyond this, however, to recognize the presence of an animal intelligence that we cannot fully grasp or comprehend. A readiness among environmental humanities scholars to adopt a position of humility in approaching the non-human world, combined with recent scholarship on animal intelligence among the animal behavioural sciences, has prompted animal historians to come some distance in recognizing historical animals as sentient creatures with motivations and forms of intelligence of their own. A growing recognition of animals as intelligent social beings departs from twentieth-century scientific representations, which tended to view animals as incapable of language or thought, to approximate what anthropologist Paul Nadasdy calls "human-animal sociality" in his ethnographic work with northern Indigenous hunters. For his Kluane interview subjects, non-human animals are not "like people"; rather, they "are people." As he points out, "there are many different kinds of people, and the social rules and conventions for dealing with human people are different from those governing social relations with rabbit people, which are different again from those governing relations between humans and moose people, and so on."[22] Animal historians are beginning to wrestle with the possibilities presented by these kinds of alternative relationships with non-human animals, as Marshall's work in Chapter 3 attests. Returning to Sagard's cat, we can appreciate it not only as an emissary between cultures, but also between different forms of human and non-human animal relationships.

* * *

The chapters in this volume represent specific geographic and interdisciplinary selections within the broader field of animal history; by no means do they neatly represent the field in its entirety. The authors draw from research on animal histories of North America with an emphasis on Canada. The volume also includes select cases from Europe, South America, and Asia. Together, they offer a range of methodological approaches to animal history. The scholars in this collection employ methodologies that are remarkably interdisciplinary. The chapters engage with research in natural sciences, historical geography, digital humanities, ethnography, Indigenous studies, labour studies, gender studies, environmental history, and more. These are merely samples of the vast interdisciplinarity of the field of animal history. There are other valuable methodologies that rely upon scholarship in literary studies, critical theory, discourse analysis, and environmental humanities that do not appear in this volume.

This examination of methodological challenges in animal history is organized into five sections. Each section is based on different methodological approaches and problems in the field of animal history. Section 1, "Embodied Histories," demonstrates different methods for centring animals in historical research with an emphasis on the materiality of animal bodies. In Chapter 1, Sandra Swart uses the body of the horse as an archive to explore alternative approaches to the history of human-horse relationships. Physical traces, corporeal memory, and Indigenous knowledge converge in this piece to offer possibilities for a more horse-centred history. The result is a provocative challenge to the rigid boundaries between animal and human, wild and tamed. Jennifer Bonnell turns our attention to a different working animal in Chapter 2, where she employs honeybee labour as an interpretive device to consider the effects of changing working environments upon honeybee health and resilience. As working animals who formed a nexus between industrializing environments and human producers and consumers, honeybees emerge in this study as important indicators of environmental change. In Chapter 3, Lindsay Marshall takes a different approach to centring horses in human histories. Drawing upon the traditional ecological knowledge of two Indigenous nations known for their horsemanship, she examines the epistemological divide between settler and Indigenous representations of human-horse interactions in the nineteenth-century US West. For Marshall, writing a horse-centred history of settler-Indigenous conflicts becomes a powerful tool for decolonizing historical research.

Section 2, "Traces," brings together three essays that explore the challenges of uncovering historical evidence of animal experiences, knowledge of animal health, and ideas of animal ethics. Susan Nance recounts her struggles to find histories of greyhound racing dogs in Chapter 4. Traditional archives of racing associations and other collections failed to keep records that capture this history. Instead, Nance turns to the vast Web archives of the Internet to compile her own digital archive of the history of greyhounds and the culture of greyhound racing. Jody Hodgins plumbs popular animal health manuals that circulated among settler farmers in rural nineteenth-century Ontario for evidence of changing settler knowledge about animal health. Animal health manuals, she finds, provided rural livestock owners with access to scientific information at a time when veterinary services were out of reach for many. Locating traces of animal history becomes an exercise of reading between the lines in George Colpitts' analysis of the polarizing discourses surrounding the fur trade and its anti-cruelty opponents in Chapter 6. Both the fur industry and its protesters in interwar Britain and America, Colpitts argues, presented wild animals with an eye to consumer purchasing decisions rather than the reality of animal experience.

The challenges of working with fragmentary, often conflicting evidence and unconventional sources is the subject of Section 3, "The Unknowable Animal." The authors in this section each confront the problem of constructing stories of animal pasts from sometimes disjointed and even unreliable sources. As Catherine McNeur shows in Chapter 7, the history of the Hessian fly, a tiny creature that found itself at the heart of an agricultural and economic crisis in 1830s America, is also implicated in a history of science and gender. In the writings of Margaretta Hare Morris, a revealing story of how human ideas about gender came to shape knowledge of the existence of this species of fly that was so consequential to the Panic of 1837. In Chapter 8, Joanna Dean examines the relative invisibility of guinea pigs in the history and subsequent memorialization of the development of diphtheria and tetanus antitoxins at the University of Toronto's Connaught Laboratories in the 1910s and 1920s. The emergence of a powerful antivivisection movement in the early twentieth century played an important role, Dean suggests, in elevating the antitoxin-producing laboratory horses to equine stardom while obscuring the unpleasant fate of the guinea pigs used to calibrate serum dosage. Animal historians can also create archives of evidence from oral history interviews, as Jason Colby does in his study of Tuffy, the famed US Navy–trained bottlenose dolphin. But his interviewees remind Colby that oral history relies upon the frailty of human memory. The stories he gathers must be read through the imprecision of recollection. While memory can be unreliable, so too can written texts, as Nigel Rothfels shows in his chapter on elephants in the archives. The habit of embellishment and exaggeration so common in the literature and records surrounding circus elephants presents a whole different set of challenges for historians looking to piece together the history of these animals.

Section 4, "Spatial Sources and Animal Movement," builds upon the previous section's discussion of methods for finding animals in historical sources and considers approaches to the study of animal history that draw from different techniques of spatial analysis. In Chapter 11, Colleen Campbell and Tina Loo use a different kind of spatial data to understand the life histories of specific bears in Canada's Banff National Park and the surrounding Kananaskis country: radio-telemetry tracking data. They examine the Eastern Slopes Grizzly Bear Project, a long-term study of grizzly bear movements in Alberta that ran from 1994 to 2004. The results of that study told life histories of specific bears, where they lived and how they moved through a changing park environment over time. Sean Kheraj (Chapter 12) shows how developments in GIS software provide sole researchers with the ability to reveal and interpret animal geographies without the need for expensive computer equipment and large teams of technicians. Web-based GIS software and crowd-sourced digitized documents and mapping layers are readily available to animal historians to remix and reuse to generate new insights and understandings of how animals and people lived together in nineteenth-century cities. Andrew Robichaud (Chapter 13) recounts his experience in leading a team of GIS researchers to transform disparate sources on San Francisco's history into spatial visualizations. He argues that GIS visualizations can be used as tools of analysis for understanding animal histories that might not be readily apparent from textual sources alone. Space and movement inform Emily Wakild's analysis of the history of camelids in South America in Chapter 14. She employs the concept of diaspora for the study of llamas, alpacas, guanacos, and vicuñas and shows how diasporic thinking can shift categories for understanding animals and their histories.

The final section of the book, "Looking at Animals," presents reflections on visual analysis and the exhibition of animal history with an emphasis on gallery display and public history. In Chapter 15, J. Keri Cronin examines the hidden histories of non-human animals in art and visual culture, applying analytical tools from art history to decipher the complex relationships between material animal bodies and visual imagery. In Chapter 16, Jay Young considers the challenges and opportunities of using animals as a thematic pathway into the collections of the provincial Archives of Ontario. Designed to engage a wide audience, from visiting school groups to university researchers, the resulting *ANIMALIA: Animals in the Archives* exhibit explores the ways animals appear in the archives and other memory institutions, as accidental subjects, family members, valued resources, physical specimens, and pests. In the final chapter, Dolly Jørgensen analyzes representations of extinction at three European natural history museums. She shows how human encounters with animal traces are mediated through museum display practices and the meanings they communicate to visitors.

Readers surveying the breadth of topics—and species—in this collection may wonder: has the burgeoning field of animal history become too large? How is it that studies of organisms as divergent as honeybees and elephants, dolphins and bears, appear in the same collection? The field of animal history brings all these species together under the broader framework of human-animal relations, collapsing under its tent a mammoth range of creatures with unique biologies, life cycles, modes of cognition, and intelligences that we as humans have only begun to comprehend. Certainly, as Harriet Ritvo proposes in the epilogue of this volume, the field's use of the word "animal" to characterize such a startling diversity of form and experience risks reinforcing a human-animal binary that blunts and diminishes that diversity. Perhaps, as the field continues to mature, scholars will propose subfields for histories of cetaceans, histories of primates, or insects, or birds. As the essays in this volume attest, however, there is as much to bind us as to pull us apart. Historians of bees, like those of horses or beavers or guinea pigs, encounter shared methodological challenges of agency and ventriloquism, anthropomorphism and absence. Likewise, they draw energy and insight from new approaches to these challenges. In these ways, the field may find its coherence in its various methodologies. How we come to understand people and their relationships to other species remains at the heart of animal history.

NOTES

1. Father Gabriel Sagard, *The Long Journey to the Country of the Hurons*, ed. George M. Wrong, trans. H. H. Langton (Toronto: Champlain Society, 1939), 269–70.
2. Virginia DeJohn Anderson has written about the role of livestock animals as "creatures of empire" that provoked property disputes between English settlers and Indigenous peoples in early New England history. See Virginia DeJohn Anderson, *Creatures of Empire: How Domestic Animals Transformed Early America* (Oxford: Oxford University Press, 2004).
3. Sagard, *The Long Journey to the Country of the Hurons*, 270–71.
4. Consider, for instance, the many different micro-organisms that live within the human body. See Peter J. Turnbaugh et al., "The Human Microbiome Project," *Nature* 449 (2007): 804–10, https://doi.org/10.1038/nature06244.
5. This conference was generously supported by Professor Marcel Martel, Avie Bennett-Historica Chair in Canadian History at York University. Details about the conference can be found here: http://niche-canada.org/tracesoftheanimalpast/.

6   Harriet Ritvo, *The Animal Estate: The English and Other Creatures in the Victorian Age* (Cambridge, MA: Harvard University Press, 1987), 5.

7   Nigel Rothfels, "Introduction," in *Representing Animals*, ed. Nigel Rothfels (Bloomington, IN: Indiana University Press, 2002), xi.

8   Sandra Swart, "'The World the Horses Made': A South African Case Study of Writing Animals into Social History," *International Review of Social History* 55 (2010): 252.

9   Etienne Benson, "Animal Writes: Historiography, Disciplinarity, and the Animal Trace," in *Making Animal Meaning*, ed. Linda Kalof and Georgina M. Montgomery (East Lansing, MI: Michigan State University Press, 2011), 5.

10 David Gary Shaw, "A Way With Animals," *History and Theory* 52 (December 2013): 5.

11 Zeb Tortorici, "Animal Archive Stories: Species Anxieties in the Mexican National Archives," in *The Historical Animal*, ed. Susan Nance (Syracuse: Syracuse University Press, 2015), 96–97.

12 Nance, *The Historical Animal*, 4.

13 Erica Fudge, Jason Hribal, and Virginia Anderson, for example, draw upon illustrations of animal agency to make the case that animals warrant inclusion as historical actors in shaping human histories. See Erica Fudge, "Milking Other Men's Beasts," *History and Theory* 52, no. 4 (December 2013): 13–28; Jason Hribal, "Animals, Agency, and Class: Writing the History of Animals from Below," *Human Ecology Review* 14, no. 1 (2007): 101–12; Anderson, *Creatures of Empire*.

14 Linda Nash, "The Agency of Nature or the Nature of Agency?," *Environmental History* 10, no. 1 (2005): 67–69.

15 Joshua Specht, "Animal History after Its Triumph: Unexpected Animals, Evolutionary Approaches, and the Animal Lens," *History Compass* 14, no. 7 (2016): 332.

16 Swart, "'The World the Horses Made'," 250.

17 Donna Haraway warns against assuming an ability to speak for other species before listening. Benson has also called attention to this risk. See Donna J. Haraway, "The Promises of Monsters: A Regenerative Politics for Inappropriate/d Others," in *The Haraway Reader* (New York: Routledge, 2003), 309; Benson, "Animal Writes," 4.

18 Susan Pearson, "Speaking Bodies, Speaking Minds: Animals, Language, History," *History and Theory* 52, no. 4 (December 2013): 104.

19 E. Tourigny et al., "An Osteobiography of a 19th-Century Dog from Toronto, Canada" *International Journal of Osteoarchaeology* 26 (2016): 818–29.

20 Erica Fudge, "A Left-Handed Blow: Writing the History of Animals," in *Representing Animals*, ed. Nigel Rothfels (Bloomington, IN: Indiana University Press, 2002), 5.

21 Emily O'Gorman and Andrea Gaynor, "More-Than-Human Histories," *Environmental History* 25, no. 4 (October 2020): 726.

22 Paul Nadasdy, "The Gift in the Animal: The Ontology of Hunting and Human-Animal Sociality," *American Ethnologist* 34, no. 1 (February 2007): 31, https://doi.org/10.1525/ae.2007.34.1.25.

PART I:

Embodied Histories

1

Kicking over the Traces? Freeing the Animal from the Archive[1]

Sandra Swart

The world thought it saw the last wild horse in 1969. A ghostly little group had been glimpsed three years before by an expedition into the desolate southern Altai range.[2] But the very the last wild horse, a solitary stallion, disappeared into the Takhiïn Shar Nuruu (the Yellow Wild Horse Mountains) and was never seen again. What made these horses special was that of all the caballine creatures, they were the only ones never tamed.

They were classified as Przewalski's horse (*Equus ferus przewalskii*) in honour of their "discoverer"—a Russian colonel, Nikołaj Przewalski (1839–88), who pursued the mysterious beasts on the steppes of Mongolia in the late 1870s.[3] But, of course, they had long been known to the local people, who called them *takhi*, meaning "free or spirit horse."[4] Eyewitnesses noted their atavistic air: their dun coats had *pangaré* qualities, with pale hair around their eyes, muzzle, and belly. They were robust but very short, with roman noses and large patrician heads. Their manes stood up like mohawks, with no forelock. A strange, dark dorsal stripe ran down their spines, and their legs were striped with primitive markings. They were cave paintings come to life.

It was a historical moment primed by widespread intellectual interest in Charles Darwin's work for there to be intrigue in the wild progenitors of domestic beasts. Scholars eagerly pieced together their past from travellers' records, like *The Secret History of the Mongols*, in which Chinggis Khan (ca. 1162–1227) was thrown from his horse when startled by the sudden appearance of a takhi.[5] Centuries later, a Manchurian dictionary from 1771 defined the takhi as the "wild horse from the steppe."[6] It was widely, almost automatically accepted that the takhi was the wild ancestor of the domestic horse. Indeed, many Mongolians called—and continue to call—the takhi the "father" of their own horses; perhaps the father of *all* domestic horses, some add.[7]

Following their "discovery," the takhi became a coveted consumer item: zoos begged collectors for this spectacular drawing card. While a few bred desultorily in captivity, their native population declined rapidly. Perhaps the capture of foals for collections was a factor, but larger causes were the increasing competition with livestock and hunting (factors that had wiped out another stocky, oddly marked equid on the other side of the world at the same time—the quagga[8]). By the mid-twentieth century, the takhi had all but disappeared; only small remnant populations survived in European and North American zoos. Inbreeding impacted fecundity and a genetic bottleneck resulted from the breeding stock descending from a few of the founder captives. Moreover, domestic horses were occasionally bred back into the so-called Przewalski population. Doomed expeditions in Mongolia failed to locate any remaining herds—the species was designated "extinct in the wild." The world took notice.

So a global program was initiated to stave off extinction. Zoos exchanged captive-bred beasts to promote genetic diversity. By 1965, there was a growing herd spread among about thirty zoos. By the late 1970s, there were almost four hundred horses, which grew to over 1,500 by the early 1990s. It was then that the takhi were released back into the "wild" in Mongolia—but actually into protected reserves: first in Khustain Nuruu National Park.

The horse that "came in from the cold" now had to find forage for themselves and survive the dreaded *dzud*—the "killing cold" that may follow an unseasonably hot, dry summer coupled with an icy winter.[9] They had to survive predators, both lupine and human, and even attacks from

Fig. 1.1 Takhi in Khustain Nuruu National Park at a salt lick. Photo by author, 21 July 2013.

other takhis. At the same time, a persistent and romantic rhetoric survived with them: "Przewalski's horse . . . is the ancestor of today's domestic horses. As a species, it was never domesticated and is therefore the world's last truly wild horse."[10]

A vast written archive materialized: paperwork on transport, on lineage, on zoo programs, on NGOs, governmental and military agreements. This archive offers us a panglossian tale of reversing extinction through heart-warming global efforts—"we" have saved the "last wild horse." Now there are at least 2,000, reintroduced into Mongolia's national parks and other places. Takhis even roam and breed in Chernobyl's ruined and poisoned wasteland as it is slowly reclaimed by the forest and grasslands, the bears and the lynx. The takhi are thus a mobile metaphor of nature's redemptive potential, despite anthropogenic despoiling: the horses of the (nuclear) apocalypse now roam a rewilded landscape.

In many ways, this is a powerful and redemptive story, reclaimed through meticulous and extensive archival work. It is rare that not only a species but individual animals are recorded in such fine detail—a studbook traces their lineage as eagerly as any royalist genealogist.[11] There are small stories in the written collections, telling, in almost unmatched details, about the individual lives of horses. We encounter a happy mare named Botania, frolicking with her foal, and an unhappy stallion, Roccol, doomed to pace his enclosure alone. A little racier, we learn about the aptly named Rousseau and his broadminded approach to recreational masturbation.[12] Drawing on this extensive paperwork, we learn about international efforts to save a species, the development of successful breeding programs, and the joyful reintroduction to the lands they once roamed: an infusion of national pride to Mongolia and a sustained boost to its incipient tourist industry. It is a hopeful corrective disrupting the two poles of the continuum of the stories that we all too often tell about the other animals: either the smug Whiggish complacency of the story of domestication or the Malthusian despair of the extinction narrative. It is a good story to tell.

But the archive can only tell one story: ours.

Thus, in this chapter, I try to find ways of telling other possible stories. Although histories of horses have existed for a long time and proliferated in the last decade there are other ways to tell them.[13] I offer three alternatives to the conventional narrative—by exploring the ways we can see the body of the horse as an archive. Firstly, I analyze the findings of fieldwork in Mongolia, drawing on embodied and embedded methodology—the corporeal dynamics of "humans being with horses." Secondly, I look at findings from the natural sciences and consider how these may be incorporated into the historical narrative. Thirdly, I think about including "oral history" drawing on a body of Indigenous knowledge, which has been largely ignored by animal historians. Now, the art of being a historian is knowing exactly how far to go and then going just a little further. So I also wish to suggest that there might even be a kind of oral history not only about horses—but *from* them.

Writing a New Horsetory?

Both the strengths and vulnerabilities of horses acted as a historiographic "unseen hand," shaping human history, from warfare to patterns of human movement. Thus, historians have discussed the material difference horses made to human settlements and society, transport networks and military capacity. Including horses in human history does more than simply complete the story—it changes it. What is much less clear is how we write that history. There is now a robust body of scholarship analyzing how to write history that takes animals seriously. Yet, as Andre Gide observed, "[o]ne does not discover new lands without consenting to lose sight of the shore for a very long time."[14] These historians, in pioneering this new territory, have used the conventional archive. Few have "left the shore" and engaged with any new methods in reaching the subject. This essay considers ways to lose sight of the shore (in the playful, adventurous sense suggested by Sean Kheraj in Chapter 12) and head for uncharted water.

Historians hunger for new ways to write history that engage with the lives of animals. Two things have hampered our understanding: finding "animal sources" and interpreting exactly what they mean. This essay suggests new primary sources, approaches, and techniques to help us locate and then understand these "interpreters." Efforts at writing biographies of some elite animals have already been essayed: Bucephalus, Marengo, and Seabiscuit, for instance, have had their "stories" told. But can the stories of ordinary animals be told? Some historians have experimented with new(er) kinds of primary sources—taxidermy and photography. Now, this essay looks beyond the archive at traces on the body: to understand the histories of "ordinary animals" and their humans.

The essay discusses horses' and riders' bodies as visceral—if sometimes ephemeral—archives. It probes the possibility of "riding" itself as a methodology—with examples from the field in a strongly equine society: Mongolia. I explore the possibility of an embodied methodology—based on the bodies of horses and humans—further opening up the archive of blood and bone, muscle and sweat. On the one hand, new sophisticated technological developments in mtDNA analysis are discussed. On the other, a kinetic methodology of learning to ride in new ways, learning new languages of the body from horses in different (non-Western) contexts—and in so doing, understanding the histories of these animals together with those of their humans. Part of the decolonizing intellectual imperative is the shift toward thinking beyond the human, beyond the written page, beyond the hegemonic message left by the colonizer, and even beyond the static to the dynamic and diachronic process of animal-human interaction.[15] This essay thus offers a synthesis of an expanded understanding of the past that is consciously attempting to decolonize itself, coupled with a more sensory grasp of history.[16] So the essay explores riding "beyond the archive" to a new kind of fieldwork.

It then explores primary sources outside the archives: archaeology and DNA analysis.[17] Material evidence of pastoralists is almost invisible in the archaeological record—because of the perishability of their material culture and the light footprint they and their animals left, in contrast to sedentary peoples involved with cultivation. Moreover, in writing the history of humans who left no written records, instead of relying on external descriptions by travellers with only a shallow understanding or by hegemonic colonial officials, we now have access to a more impartial and authentic archive in animals.[18] The outsider view can be countered by—literally—an "insider view" from the animals' very bodies.

Horse-Sense and Sensory History

A half century ago, Levi-Strauss reminded us of how animals afford humans an important conceptual resource (animals, he argued, are good things to think with).[19] Thinking *about* animals is a historiographical imperative. Thinking *with* them is a methodological possibility. But thinking *like* them is hard. In a way, horses see and sense a parallel world to ours. Of course, we share at least the five most common sensory modalities, but their ranges differ. Horses have developed sensory capacity aimed at predator recognition and escape. Equine eyes are on the side of the head with monocular vision so they can see separate objects with each eye at the same time, permitting a grazing horse almost panoptic vision. Horses' nasal acuteness allows them a longer temporal understanding than ours; through smell they travel through time. Pheromone signals allow them to smell past mêlées, allies and enemies, births and death, emotions, and sexuality.[20] A horse's own sense of smell is acute—like their hearing, their sense of smell has evolved as a vital part of their defence system. There is ongoing production and reception of pheromone signals (smell messages produced by skin glands). Members of a herd even have a shared odour. Moreover, horses' hearing is far more sensitive than ours, perhaps to allow the horse to detect stalking carnivores. With our very different sensory experiences of the place, space, and time, horses and humans would thus write very different histories.

Yet, historically, humans have tried harder to understand the world from the horse's point of view than that of any other animal. It was necessary in domesticating, training, and riding them—dangerous and intimate processes that historically have compelled humans to see the world through horses' eyes far more than, say, the eyes of a tapir or a hippopotamus. Compellingly, on the issue of agency, humans historically involved with horses *recognized* their horses' efforts as resistance, so they contemporaneously acknowledged (animal) agency—by executing rogue horses, for instance. Horses also displayed the "weapons of the weak."[21] They disobeyed commands, destroyed equipment, escaped, physically retaliated, and resisted by literally "bucking the system" or "kicking over the traces." In the end, it is impossible to deny their agency.

An experimental blurring of the genres of *history* and *natural history* with an exploratory *horsetory* could offer a hippocentric story, suffused with horses' physical pleasure, memory, intense fear, and cyclical sexuality and fecundity, and strongest traits (as grass-eating herbivores, vulnerable as prey, with a fatal tendency toward overeating and overheating). It might be a story of grass, foals, blood, sex, pain, fear—perhaps mainly grass.[22] But it would be a Rorschach test that would reveal more about the historian (and her own epoch) than about horses. So, instead, the history of horses can be to some extent compared to that of oppressed social groups, but at the same time, horses have been the animals of the colonizing elite and critical in colonization and oppression. Thus, to locate horses at the centre of the narrative, one has had to extend the directions suggested by social history radically while accepting that the parallels are analogous but not interchangeable. Historians have long confronted methods of discussing the silenced—the under-represented, unrepresented, or even wilfully misrepresented in the conventional archive. (But to draw parallels between animals and oppressed humans is neither to conflate nor to underestimate the suffering of any human subaltern.)

The first step is to demonstrate that animals *have* a history in the first place.[23] Just as "great women" or "labour heroes" were initially "reclaimed," historians recovered celebrated warhorses or racehorses who were well represented in the conventional archive. Secondly, historians reconstructed narratives of "massed horses," aggregated victims of society's oppression, who also generated vast reams of paperwork in the archive. So horses' lives can be discovered and these lifeways changed over time, although not in "circumstances of their own choosing," as Marx contended for our species.

Indeed, perhaps it is time to move beyond "agency" as the central concern.[24] Certainly, if one is to take animal agency seriously, one has to reassess the idea of agency itself. Indeed, the failure to question what "agency" means actually reproduces familiar forms of power. The call to move beyond merely "discovering agency in the animal past" parallels a cogent call in African history to move beyond merely asserting agency. As Lynn Thomas has observed, "[t]oo often agency slips from being a conceptual tool or starting point to a concluding argument. For example, in my subfield of African women's and gender history, statements like 'African women had agency' can stand as the impoverished punch lines of empirically rich studies."[25]

Thus, rather than simply asserting or repetitively demonstrating agency, we should ask how agency was understood contemporaneously and what kind of archive and methodology might yield this data. Historically, on the issue of agency, humans involved with horses have long *recognized* horses' agency—but in ways that differed in different historical moments. For example, agency has been seen as both unquestionable and useful by Mongolian herders. They accepted their horse living within a free-roaming social structure that they would adopt of their own, modelled on a long understanding of takhi.[26] In summer, horses graze on wild grass, and as winter comes hay is fed to other livestock, but horses continue to fend for themselves—able to dig up grass even under deep snow.[27] Moreover, only male horses are ridden—and even geldings (castrated in the second year) are ridden only two or three days a week and then released back into the herd, which largely cares for itself. The whole system is predicated on—indeed, depends on—accepting animal agency.

Moreover, the instruments of control—reins, whips, bits—always tell their own stories about how the particular society using it at particular times felt about equine agency. Acts of rebellion might be quotidian, like the horse's flattened ears and bared teeth as the saddle's girth was done up. Such routine rebellion or mundane mutiny might be reflected in efforts to contain it—like tethering on Mongolian *zel* lines—which could not always curb horses, who broke free and galloped to a kind of freedom. These

Fig. 1.2 A multi-species solution to sweat: horses tethered on the *zel* lines are licked clean of the day's salt by the ger's goats. Photo by author.

small protests can be overlooked easily by historians—but they offer an ephemeral archive of resistance.[28]

Oral historians would benefit by widening their range of "listening," becoming more attentive to other-than-human animals in their research. This section demonstrates that oral history can contribute valuable evidence about animal lives and human-animal relations to animal history. Oral historians have long reconstructed the history of the silenced, the marginalized and those unable to write. Is this possible for and, more interestingly, *from* the horse? Horses are quiet creatures. They do speak, but mainly through the body. But even then, horses lie. They need to, simply to stay alive. Horses are stoic because as prey animals they mask injury and illness to avoid making themselves a target for predators.

But a good historian is trained in the detection of deceit and misremembering and is also able to learn new languages. Reading the horse's body offers an unexpected archive. Firstly, it is clear that each animal has an individual history written on their bodies. The brands or tattoos on

Fig. 1.3 The body of the horse is an archive. Photo by author.

a horse are a rich archive, as I discuss below. A head-shy riding horse or the scarred knees of a cart horse and the saddle-sore scars of a pack horse all bear testimony to how horses have endured human needs. Moreover, their history might be revealed by their actions (and reactions). The dead-mouthed school master and the bolting ex-racehorse all reflect their *past* experiences through their reactions to *current* experience. Body and behaviour need to be observed as closely as possible—and the closeness may be accelerated by riding. As a methodology, it is perhaps best described as "embedded history" akin to embedded journalism or auto-ethnography. An attentive inter-species historian learns by listening, watching, touching, and *being with* the subject. Here horses' and riders' bodies may offer visceral—if ephemeral—archives. Riding is a conversation between two bodies. In essence, I am arguing that riding itself may be a methodology—based on the exchange between the bodies of the horse and human: opening up a different kind of archive of blood and bone, muscle and sweat.

The kinetic methodology of learning to ride in new ways, learning new languages of the body from horses in different (including non-Western) contexts helps understand their histories with humans.

From the Horse's Mouth?

This chapter proposes the first tentative steps toward the intersection of animal history, sensory history, and oral history. Historians of the senses, like Alain Corbin, lament that the historian is always a "prisoner of language."[29] We are captives to "verbocentrism" and "textualism." There have been calls (including this chapter) for oral historians to be more "attentive to other-than-human animals," interviewing humans to understand animal lives and human-animal connections.[30] However, as multi-species ethnographers have acknowledged, "to an even larger extent than other ethnographies, [we are] faced with the problem of representation. No horses were interviewed in our study; it is their humans that speak on their behalf."[31]

But what if the horses could be interviewed?

What if we could hear straight from them? If not from the horse's mouth, then at least from the horse's body? What if, in so doing, we could escape both the anthropocentric ventriloquism of the "animal Other" by human interpreters and Corbain's carcerality of words. In fact, as this chapter will contend, the advantage of history at the nexus of the oral, the sensory, and the animal is that it can reach across the barrier of "species."

Mongolia is a good context for such an experiment. In a new place, riding in a new style, host horsepeople usually tend to try make explicit the "tacit" knowledge of how to ride—but few Mongolians do this, as culturally they favour learning by experience or embodied learning.[32] This is actually a boon to an oral historian eager to try "interview" the horse without a (human) "translator."[33]

In riding, body-to-body connection establishes a tacit dialogue. In this process, horses tell you not only about their present, but their own individual past and their culture—just as in a (human) oral history interview. In a horse-human dyad, we see "talking bodies." Riding can be a shared inter-species "apprenticeship"—as Fijn and Argent suggest—where both humans and horses pass along their social knowledge.[34] Horse and human can only balance by "talking" to each other, feeling the micro-movements of the other, attuning their bodies to a conversation. (According to a Mongolian proverb, "[i]f [only] one finds the right touch, [one] can cope with an unmanageable horse."[35]) Significantly, as this chapter showcases, this embodied knowledge of how to ride is itself embedded in cultural and historical contexts.[36] Mongolian horses have come to expect that their humans not keep the "still seat" of my own horse-human culture. The pony I rode expected me to move more in the saddle and reminded me firmly that a sitting trot was alien to his culture; he explained (through micro-movements) that I should adopt a raised light seat, hovering above his back at a trot, and should mirror his movements to one side or the other as he moved.[37] Of course, partly this is to do with the technology historically adopted—Mongolian riders tilt to one side to avoid their jarringly rigid saddles. (My equine interlocutor reminded me to do that also—my faulty use of the technology irked him too.[38]) The saddle was interesting for a historian concerned with "agency" because it permitted less (human) control over gait and speed. It seemed as though the horse was expected to choose an appropriate gait, where necessary, so that the rider could focus on the job at hand like herding. Csordas calls these "culturally elaborated ways of attending to and with one's body in surroundings that include the embodied presence of others."[39] Bodies communicate not only biology, but also culture—and culture always has a history.

A decade ago, I called the debate over the "Real Animal" versus the "Represented Animal" "an internecine war—or rather policing action—that never ends and has no clear goal; it is the Vietnam War of animal studies."[40] Clearly, what is needed to effect an armistice is either simply letting a hundred historiographical flowers bloom or choosing to embrace a synthesis of analyzing the shifts in representation together with evidence of the material lives of animals in historical contexts. Mieke Roscher has recently argued that a good way to do this may be in drawing on the bodily turn.[41] Historians have embraced, as it were, the "bodily" turn since the 1980s and especially from the 1990s,[42] analyzing the (human) body as historically variable and shaped by context. While early constructionist approaches were influential, they often failed to address individual corporeal experience. The body has been at the centre of a number of recent animal histories, but none have (yet) looked at (let alone argued for *performing*) the physical interactions of humans and horses or indeed of bodies in motion—as my study does, albeit tentatively.[43]

In this historical method of "embeddedness and embodiment," one is effecting a cross-fertilization between animal histories, oral histories, and histories of the body.[44] The interaction of the two bodies brings to light cross-species dynamics. Riding (as well as saddling up, feeding, brushing away flies, and so on) requires physical contact and close intimacy with an "Other"—a different sentient and socialized species. Quite aside from learning from how the horse responds and initiates interaction, the very self-reflexivity in "the doing of riding, the doing of history" is useful—as Kim Marra has argued in a very different context.[45] Oral historians engaged in zooethnography[46] ask and receive different answers. As recently as 1900 in the industrializing West, and much more recently in places like Mongolia, it would not be unusual for many humans to be able to decipher the equine lexicon, and many humans (and horses) would have spoken an idiographic horse-human patois, observable by historians. While some domesticated animals, for example, could be taught highly idiosyncratic signals, horses could not—because horses were typically used by different riders or drivers concurrently and often had more than one rider in their lifetime. A horse that could not comprehend the local horse-human patois was of no (human) utility—and even dangerous. Thus, humans had to teach horses common idiographic signals and codes of behaviour—that potentially could reveal something about that human society at that historical moment.

Equally, humans had to learn and teach horse signals—or co-construct them. They were able to understand the non-verbal vernacular like a horse swishing a tail, or shaking a head, or moving its ears to convey its moods. Some humans were particularly familiar with the subtle nuances of the idiom—those engaged in the horse industry itself, like grooms, or communities that imposed horsemanship as a condition of manhood, as in Mongolia throughout the twentieth century, perhaps most vigorously post-democracy. Mongolian men do not brush or groom ("If we do, the [horse] will grow thin. Maybe lose their strength.") Here we learn from the soft moments of hard men: all they do by way of displaying affection is remove sleep and grit from their horses' eyes in the mornings. This is the only intimacy permissible—purportedly in at least the last few human

Fig. 1.4 A horse's body language not only conveys signals to its herd but also to the human historian. Photo by author.

generations too.[47] Gendered norms jump the species barrier: horses are conceived as patrilineal, like humans, and good qualities come from stallions rather than mares.[48] To "know" a horse requires human oral history, in any case. Mongolian horses have no papers. A horse's pedigree is local knowledge—a purchaser must ask locals, especially male elders. So much of Mongolian masculinity is invested in horsemanship—a man noted when watching motorbikes herding horses: "Makes me sad. Not real Mongolia."[49] (An interlocutor drolly dismissed my gift, after I offered him my riding helmet when I left the country, with the dead-pan: "If you fall off, you are not Mongolian."[50])

An "Archive on the Skin"?

Identity and masculine status are also inherent to branding horses. The *tamaga* (also *tamgha* or *tamga*; brand mark) has passed traditionally from father to son. The brands themselves are embedded in history.[51]

The branding ceremony, at least at certain historical moments, required privacy from women, and sometimes followed the gelding of the colts. Brands have long communicated more than the banal information of who is using which grazing grounds, but rather their spiritual leanings and even traditional wealth and authority. *Tamga* are already used as a local archive: from at least the 1950s, marks were gathered from all over Mongolia as a form of local knowledge to uncover patrimonial descent and determining the lineage of "tribes." The marks could change over time: for example, under the Soviets, some mystic signs were abandoned by newly anti-religious herders, some of whom embraced the hammer and sickle and the initials of their names written in Cyrillic. There are complicated but shifting historical rules about branding[52] (which space does not permit exploring), but Caroline *Humphrey*'s 1970s study of the rich semiotics of branding remains seminal and a useful point for historians interested in tracking change since then:

> The point is that the signs of the tamaga system are not simply addressed to a hypothetical stranger horseman riding through the steppe. They are also intended for the use of kinsmen in their relations with one another, and even, one might say, for an individual in his relation with his social role. . . . [The brand] with mystic power, is handed down unchanged from generation to generation, and this is what—it is believed—shows a man's ancestry and origin. Knowing this, it does not seem so surprising that even today Mongol historians are attempting to penetrate the unwritten ethnogenesis of their tribes by the patient study of horse-brands.[53]

A Body of Knowledge?

The national emblem showcases a horse as the unifying symbol said to capture the essence of Mongolia. Certainly, the horse has survived as national symbol when so many other symbols disappeared as new regimes came to power. Undeniably, rural families still live closely with horses—but the steppes change and horses are no longer at the core of every single homestead nor every man's identity. So in talking about "Mongolian horse culture" we are in danger of a romantic metanarrative imposed on a messy reality. To avoid such ahistorical flattening which elides change over time, we must remember the ruptures imposed by socialist *negdels*, free-market restructuring,[54] technological transition from horses to motorbikes, and the changes imposed by climate change,[55] as well as regional differences (for example, between Darkhad and Khalkha horseways.)[56] Horse bodies help resist teleological and ahistorical flattening and elision. This is illustrated by how their bodies have changed over the years. In different eras, the body of the horse was (probably) affected by the body politic: even in just the twentieth century, Soviet collectivization and then the post-socialist free market *zerleg kapitalizm* ("wild capitalism")[57] impacted the lived experience of horses—recoverable, at least in part, by using the body as a proxy for health and even day-to-day activity. New bodies are appearing as Arab and Thoroughbreds are introduced to create mixed breeds (*eerliiz mor'*), to improve the height and speed of horses over short distances.[58] The size and composition of the herd changed over time, and the manner of husbandry, which affected appearance. Not only do they change over the years, but bodies of horses change visibly over a single year. This is alien to Western horse keeping, which has long strived for bodily consistency, while Mongolian horses lose about thirty per cent of their weight in the spring and regain it in the summer.[59] Many horse activities are seasonal: gelding and branding in the spring, Nadaam races in the summer, (for some) branding in autumn.[60] Such changes—over the years or yearly—can be historicized through travellers' descriptions,[61] old paintings and photographs and archival reports. Oral tradition might augment oral history here—some of this might be reachable in changing idiom and proverb,[62] folklore,[63] traditional songs,[64] or epic poetry.[65]

The changing idiom, the changing horse-human world and the concomitantly changing equine bodies are recoverable through a history of the sensory. Through a variety of primary sources—some of which are breathing beings—one is reminded of the intimacies of knowing between human and horse. Even the smells generated by horses were an everyday part of life. Humans were able to interpret a horse's nervous farting, in contrast to the thunderous farting of a triumphant horse. Historians have long neglected the senses, mainly because of their apparent lack of an archive.[66] The story of the visceral, the sensual, the experiential in history includes how aural, olfactory, tactile landscapes change over time and how humans relate differently over time to sounds. For example, the healthy horse generates a reassuringly familiar flatulence. Our history tends to come deodorized, but a different kind of archive could change that.

Annals, Annales, and Anal History

Humans have long stared into horse dung as eagerly and anxiously as ancient augurs once peered into animal entrails to predict the future.[67] For humans, dung is an unmediated daily record of a horse's well-being—not unlike the concise, chronological annals of the medieval period. Its production is one of horses' vital signs, along with their temperature, heart, and respiratory rate. Quantity at a time, quantity of events, consistency, and colour are all clues to equine health and habits. Dung is a diary abandoned in the grass.

For horses, excrement is a richer archive still—it reveals current identity and past biography. Feces can provide horses with information about another herd's proximity, or an individual horse's social and reproductive status. Defecation is a ritual not only with a physiological but a social purpose: when one horse excretes, others often follow suit. In fact, the daily defecation rituals at a stud pile are one of the more striking ethologically observable features of herd life, taking up a substantial amount of a stallion's time. Stallions urinate over the manure of the females, while breathing in the communicative odours.[68] A mare coming across dung simply smells it. If lost, she sniffs *any* excrement she encounters to follow the trail back to her herd. In this way, a fecal record is a diary, a database, and a map for horses—but it can also be useful to historians.

Ancient coprolite—fossilized feces—offers clues into more than bodily being but also behaviour. Horses never travelled alone. They were long pursued by predators—but the fellow travellers of horses were not always wolves or us. Or even visible. Sometimes the ecosystem horses co-created was internal. We are now able to analyze part of the interior ecosystem of equids, including gut microbiomes and the parasites sustained and spread by horses. This helps tell a more complete story about where horses were at various times, what they were eating, how closely they lived with other livestock and people. For instance, a recent study looked at the fecal material from a medieval latrine in the coastal town of Riga (Latvia) in order to identify the intestinal parasites present within the (human) population.

They found two eggs of pinworm (*Oxyuris equi*), which proved the presence of this parasite and therefore that equids were in this region by the medieval period.[69]

Horse Tales from Horse Tails

An archive of consumption follows the horse. Their fecal remains, so casually dropped behind them, leave a record for us of what they ate, their parasites, and their health. But something that follows more closely, if less pungently, in their wake contains an equally rich and untapped seam of data to be mined: their tails.

Hair is made up of a protein complex formed from amino acids from sources that are from outside the body (food, environmental water) and sources from within (metabolic turnover of tissues). Tail hair is a neatly ordered chronological archive of ecological, physiological, and geographical data that can be decoded through isotopic analyses. A recent study used it as a primary source to discover how takhi food resources have changed in the Gobi since the end of the nineteenth century. Researchers measured the amount of stable[70] carbon-13 (^{13}C) in the tail's hair follicles.[71] This isotope occurs in the cells of grasses in different magnitudes than in woody plants. Thus, by measuring its quantity, it is possible to determine whether the animal was grass-eating or leaf-eating.

Here, conventional and unorthodox methodologies converge, human and horse archives intersect, and the living and the dead connect: archival samples of hair from the tails of adult takhi were taken from horses hunted in the Dzungarian Gobi in the nineteenth century and were compared to that of modern takhi reintroduced to the area. (For a control sample, museum specimens of Asiatic wild asses or khulans [also kulans] were compared to those now living in the area.) Tail hairs grow regularly and slowly and are also resistant to degradation, so they constitute a neat little archive (like tree rings in dendrochronology).

An intriguing change was evident over time: today's takhis feed on grass throughout the year, but in the nineteenth century, only in the summer months. Grass grows in the plains near water sources. But woody shrubs survived both in more arid areas of the plain and in the foothills—and it was these the takhis relied on in the long winters of the nineteenth century. Once this empirical story was uncovered and triangulated with archival primary sources, an explanation had to be found: perhaps the seasonality of past diet was caused by their periodic need to seek refuge from people and their livestock—thus seeking winter shelter in the semi-desert. Living in the arid shrubby scrubland helped them elude hunters and competition from grass-feeding *Aduu* (Mongolian riding horse).[72] This is supported by the more conventional historical sources of the narrative descriptions of takhi survival, as noted by the brothers Grumm-Grzhimaylo in the 1890s and a few accounts from locals from the 1930s to 1950s, recoverable by oral historians interested in local or vernacular knowledge.[73] Reintroduced takhis are differently understood now—it is safe for them to stay and eat grass because they are protected by law. Moreover, they are cherished as a generator of national pride and international currency. Yet the study found that there were no changes in how the khulans ate: they still ate seasonally like nineteenth-century takhis. This is perhaps because, unlike the reconstructed history and symbol of pride attached to fellow-equid takhis, asses were still illegally hunted so they strategically avoid humans. But this kind of archive calls us to action: history matters in policy making.[74] After all, the results suggest that, in the future, the growing populations of takhis will trigger clashes with local herders, as they did in the nineteenth century, and future reintroduction projects should eschew the grasslands and restore the takhi to areas once preferred for subsistence.[75]

Thus, if the daily dung over time offers us an annal, the measurement of their tail archives offers us an archive of the *longue durée*, which includes environmental factors, long-term trends, quantification, and paying special attention to geography, akin to the historiography of the *Annales* School.

Animal historians can learn from the methods used to understand animal histories in the natural sciences. These methods may reinforce one another (as in the case study above), but they can come into conflict, as in the study below. Certainly, fresh archives might engender reconsidering the equine past, and integral to that is rethinking the taxonomic position of the takhi. We must reconsider whether the takhi is a species or rather a feral variety of the domesticated horse that reclaimed wildness a long time ago. The contention is *not* that we suddenly have a definitive new version (nor that science trumps archives!). Genetic resources are not necessarily

Fig. 1.5 Over two decades ago, the pioneering environmental historian Donald Worster called for environmental historians to get mud on their shoes. In getting out of the orthodox archive and into "embedded history," you get a lot dirtier than that. Photo of author by Graham Walker, 26 July 2013.

more robust than our archives—in fact, they are contested. The contention is rather that competing stories will emerge from the bodies of other horses. This is a call to consider the body of the horse as an archive, rather than solely relying on textual references or even material archaeological excavations.

Blood and Bones

We saw how historians can use *tamaga* as an "archive on the skin," but beneath the skin lies another archive. It has long been thought that the Botai culture of hunters and herders in today's Kazakhstan first tamed horses about 5,500 years ago. Finding horse-meat fat and milk fat in Botai pottery, researchers surmised that they ate horses they bred (or perhaps merely hunted) and kept mares confined for milking. Moreover, evidence of tooth damage suggests that the Botai used bits—suggesting a mounted culture.[76] But new genetic analysis has problematized this generally accepted model: a study sequencing horse DNA at a Botai excavation site suggests that this is not where today's domestic horses originated. In fact, it hints that perhaps Botai horses contributed little to the lineage of modern domestic horses—so *their* ancestors might come from an as-yet-undiscovered stock.[77] (For a historian of horse-human connections, the heated debate over origins, the discourse of domestication, and so on prove just as interesting as the question of original domestication itself.) Maybe Botai horse culture migrated to other parts of Eurasia, cross-breeding their herds with so many wild equids that very little of the original Botai DNA remained or perhaps the Botai horses did not survive and were substituted by horses domesticated in another place, meaning there were (at least) two centres of domestication. In any event, it is likely that the grand metanarrative of a single domestication event was not the case and that horse domestication was probably a messy process with many experiments, many failures, and a few successes.

As this essay has argued, a lot rides on the takhi being the "last wild horses." However, recent research also shows that there are several ways to disrupt the takhi as truly "wild" and rethink conservation rhetoric. They might even be the feral escapees from domesticated Botai horses—it might be 1990s rewilding efforts were not the first time the takhi had gone back out into the snow. Moreover, takhis and ordinary Mongolian horses interbred.[78] In fact, one could even make an argument that it may be equally important to "preserve" the ordinary Mongolian horse and its varieties.[79] After all, the Mongolian horse is of an ancient line, historically integral to building the Khan Empire and thus spread out over a vast territory, and concomitantly key in the genetics of several modern Eurasian horse breeds.

Natasha Fijn has pointed out the absurdities (and Western bias) in simply labelling the takhi as "wild" and other horses as "domesticated"—if the latter category implies animals whose breeding, environment, and diet is totally controlled by humans. After all, Mongolian horses are not moved to human-constructed habitats—instead they freely wander the unfenced steppe grasslands that once accommodated their very own Pleistocene forebears. Just like their ancestors, they make their own choices about

Fig. 1.6 In the shadow of a reimagined Chinggis Khan, an incipient tourist industry is being created, predicated on selling a full-horse experience—seeing the "last wild horses" and riding in the vernacular style on Mongolian ponies. Photo of author by Graham Walker.

mobility, food, friends, and sometimes even sex.[80] The stallion is expected to guard the herd against wolves, and, in contrast to other livestock, horses are not herded to new grazing or water everyday. Yet, in stark contrast, the much vaunted "wild" takhi were a carceral population for many generations: captive in foreign lands, with no agency in food choice, territory, nor breeding. When they were finally released back into their homeland, they needed shelter and food.[81] Moreover, the dichotomous divide is further problematized because, as Bökönyi contended, "Mongolian animal breeders would capture Przevalsky [sic] foals, admit them to their herds and rear them there: that is to say, they domesticated them"—the hybrids do produce fertile progeny. Although, tellingly, Bökönyi still felt the need to insist that this "does not at all reduce their quality as *genuine wild horses*."[82]

Conclusion

This chapter has proposed the first tentative steps toward the intersection of animal history, sensory history, and oral history that can breach the borders of "species." The opening vignette focused on the last wild horse, increasingly remembered (indeed, marketed) as Mongolia's national pride. The chapter then delineated a redemptive story of successfully forestalling extinction. But this metanarrative was disrupted by asking: Can we free the animal from the archive, just as the captive "Przewalski's horse" was freed from zoos to become takhis again?

To do this, we historicized a relationship that is recoverable—at least in part—through the sensory, the bodily, and the remembered, in order to engage with the material and semiotic complexities of living with horses. The horse's body offers us many kinds of archive. If we look, we can find new histories of horses in unexplored places: in both the living and the dead—in untapped Indigenous archives of knowledge, in bodies (theirs and ours), both in muscle and movement, in skin and hair, in blood and bones. A new kinetic methodology may be found in "embedded history," building an archive of praxis through riding or *being* with horses and their humans, and thereby learning an idiographic human-equine patois. What becomes clear from taking the oral history of horses and humans seriously, as well as the bodies they left behind, is that it is unhelpful to divide the world so simply into diametrically opposed and hermetically sealed categories.[83] What is "wild" when all the living takhi come from stock that was incarcerated in zoos for generations? What is "wild" when so-called tame horses must fend and forage unfenced and for themselves? After all, as noted, in Mongolia geldings are ridden only two or three days a week and then released back into the herd, which largely cares for itself. It is hard to say what is "wild" when nuances of "wildness" exist, like the difference between *agsam mor'* and *khangal*—roughly "unbroken and rebellious, either fierce or fearful" versus "untamed, undamaged, complete."[84] Moreover, stallions (*azrag*) kept for breeding and to be part of the milk production process[85] have long manes[86]—and as one interlocutor observed: "[Of course, we] [n]ever ride a stallion. It is like a wild animal. It is proud like a takhi."[87] Words that are used in categorizing display a different understanding from the stark binary of "wild" or "domestic," "tamed" or "untamed."[88] For example, a *khangal* refers to a horse that has not yet been trained but only "touched by the wind"—so it is not impossible to still train him. Wild and tame are on a continuum: not opposing categories, but palimpsestic and therefore full of possibilities.

Local or vernacular knowledge is a wildly under-utilized resource in writing human-animal histories and oral history is vital, for example in the cultural classification of significant animals. Turning to local knowledge can illustrate other linkages between people, animals and the environment—but so far, sensory and bodily histories as well as animal histories have merely genuflected in that direction.[89] A new archive of meaning may be found by foregrounding vernacular ideas. In a telling moment about different ways of knowing animals, I asked why Mongolian horses have no names. My guide answered: "Only colours." So I asked: "But what if you have two the same colour." He laughed gently and said: "They are never the same colour."[90]

NOTES

1. Warm thanks to Jennifer Bonnell, Sean Kheraj, and Nigel Rothfels for their comments.
2. Zoltán Kaszab, "New sightings of Przewalski Horses," *Oryx* 8, no. 6 (1966): 345–47.
3. The original name by Poliakof was *Equus prezewalksii*, with "*ferus*" added in the twentieth century.
4. Also "Przewalski's wild horse," "Asiatic wild horse," and "Mongolian wild horse."
5. Inge Bouman and Jan Bouman, "The history of Przewalski's horse," in *Przewalski's horse: The history and biology of an endangered species*, ed. Lee Boyd and Katherine Houpt (Albany: State University of New York Press, 1994).
6. N. Dovchin, "The Przewalski horse in Mongolia," trans. E. Geldermans, *Equus* 1 (1961): 22–27.
7. Fieldwork conversations, Ulaanbaatar, July 2013.
8. Sandra Swart, "Zombie Zoology: The quagga and the history of reanimating animals," in *The Historical Animal*, ed. Susan Nance (Syracuse: Syracuse University Press, 2015).
9. In fact, these "wild" animals are provided with roughage and salt licks. Fieldwork observations, July 2013.
10. Association pour le Cheval de Przewalski: TAKH, https://www.takh.org/en/the-horses/the-przewalski-s-horses-in-brief, accessed September 1, 2019.
11. Admittedly, the studbook was itself flawed, built from questionnaires that asked people to remember horses from decades earlier.

12 Following German zoologist Erna Mohr's 1959 monograph *The Asiatic Wild Horse: Equus Przevalskii Poliakoff, 1881* (London: J. A. Allen, [1959] 1971), a deluge of studies followed with at least twenty investigations by the early 1990s.

13 For a recent sampling, see Susanna Forrest, *The Age of the Horse—An Equine Journey Through Human History* (New York: Grove Atlantic, 2017); Ann Norton Greene, *Horses at Work: Harnessing Power in Industrial America* (Boston: Harvard University Press, 2008); Sandra Swart, *Riding High—Horses, Humans and History in South Africa* (Johannesburg: Witwatersrand University Press, 2010).

14 André Gide, *The Counterfeiters*, trans. Dorothy Bussy (London: Penguin, [1925] 1990).

15 The broader decolonization project that urges us to rethink how we study the past should include challenging insular anthropocentrism and the *Cartesian* dichotomy between animal and human, which several theorists are contesting now. See Alice Hovorka, "Animal geographies I: Globalizing and decolonizing," *Progress in Human Geography* 41, no. 3 (2017): 382–94; Kelly Struthers Montford and Chloë Taylor, eds., *Colonialism and Animality—Anti-Colonial Perspectives in Critical Animal Studies* (London: Routledge, 2020).

16 For the sensory turn, see Mark Smith, "Producing Sense, Consuming Sense, Making Sense: Perils and Prospects for Sensory History," *Journal of Social History* 40, no. 4 (2007): 841–58.

17 Of course, historians will access these at one remove being largely untrained in the methodology required—calling for interdisciplinary collaboration or merely reading research from zooarchaeological and cognate disciplines. Susan Nance has pointed out that writing animal history requires the willingness to be open to a range of methodologies and to learn from disciplines far removed from history, "from philosophy to veterinary medicine to find principles or theories with which to read historical sources for evidence." Susan Nance, "Animal History: The Final Frontier?," *The American Historian*, no. 6 (*2015*): 28–32.

18 Sandra Swart, "Settler Stock? Animals and power in the mid-seventeenth century contact at the Cape, c.1652–1662," in *Animals and Early Modern Identity*, ed. Pia F. Cuneo (Farnham: Ashgate, 2014).

19 Sandra Swart, "'But Where's the Bloody Horse?': Textuality and Corporeality in the 'Animal Turn'," *Journal of Literary Studies* 23, no. 3 (2007): 271–92.

20 Particular smells—like those of fire and blood—generate extreme but not excessive alarm in carnivore-fearing ungulates that evolved while roaming over highly combustible grasslands.

21 James C. Scott, *Weapons of the Weak: Everyday Forms of Peasant Resistance* (New Haven: Yale University Press, 1985). Scott showed how peasants who seemed utterly oppressed resisted their so-called "masters" with subtle, covert techniques of evasion and resistance, including daily acts of defiance. Fundamentally, like oppressed humans, horses also sometimes refuse to accept the terms of their subordination.

22 This section is drawn from Swart, *Riding High*, 217.

23 Drawn from Swart, *Riding High*.

24 Joshua Specht, "Animal History after Its Triumph: Unexpected Animals, Evolutionary Approaches, and the Animal Lens," *History Compass* 14, no. 7, (2016): 326–36

25   Lynn Thomas, "Historicising Agency," *Gender & History* 28, no. 2, (2016): 324–39.
26   This is reflected in the treatment of horses more dear to them. Like the takhi, these are not eaten but allowed to go into the wild and die naturally. Sometimes the skull is brought to an *ovoo* (the stone mounds in the shamanic tradition) to allow the horse to "go to the sky." A properly respected horse might bring good health to the living herd, while a restless soul might cause harm, like wolf attacks. Fieldwork, July 2013.
27   Fieldwork, July 2013.
28   Horses stay tied up with their saddles on until dusk—not from neglect, but because they are covered in salt from sweat. So if saddles were removed in sunlight their skin would burn. Fieldwork, 22 July 2013.
29   Alain Corbin, "Charting the Cultural History of the Senses," in *Empire of the Senses: the Sensual Culture Reader*, ed. David Howes (New York: Berg, 2005), 135.
30   Carrie Hamilton, "Animal stories and oral history: Witnessing and mourning across the species divide," *Oral History Review* 45, no. 2, (2018): 193–210; Jianxiong Ma and Cunzhao Ma, "The Mule Caravans of Western Yunnan: An Oral History of the Muleteers of Zhaozhou," *Transfers* 4 no. 3, (2014): 24–42.
31   Anita Maurstad, Dona Davis, and Sarah Cowles, "Co-being and intra-action in horse-human relationships: A multi-species ethnography of be(com)ing human and be(com)ing horse," *Social Anthropology* 21, no. 3 (2013): 324.
32   Children between four and five also learn to ride horses, and horses are ridden from as young as two. For children, teaching consists of "embodied showing," as they learn by doing. Richard Fraser, "Motorcycles on the Steppe: Skill, Social Change, and New Technologies in Postsocialist Northern Mongolia," *Nomadic Peoples* 22, no. 2 (2018): 330–68, see 352.
33   This communication was not only one-way—I tried to speak *Aduu* with a little leg pressure, reins in one hand and direction and pace changes suggested by the body, but my fieldnotes record how I inadvertently slipped into speaking "South African horse" and how rapidly the horse I was riding learned "some of my body language" in a matter of days until we spoke if not an international Esperanto, then at least a kind of shared equine pidgin. 22 July 2013.
34   The best ethnographic monograph we have on "living in multi-species herds" in Mongolia is *Natasha* Fijn, *Living with Herds: Human-animal Co-existence in Mongolia* (New York and London: Cambridge University Press, 2011). In a seminal study, Gala Argent focused on sacrificial horse burials two and a half millennia ago in the Altai Mountains, but, unconventionally, she explored the cooperative relationship between horse and human—demonstrating how archaeology can transcend the stereotype of animals as mere possessions. Gala Argent, "Inked: Human-Horse Apprenticeship, Tattoos, and Time in the Pazyryk World," *Society & Animals* 21 (2013): 178–93.
35   John Hangin et al., "Mongolian Folklore: A Representative Collection from the Oral Literary Tradition," *Mongolian Studies* 9, (1985–86): 34.
36   Lynda Birke and Kirrilly Thompson, *(Un)Stable Relations: Horses, Humans and Social Agency* (London: Routledge, 2018). Ethnographic studies that embrace the agentic possibility of the horse and communication between horse and human include Charlotte Marchina on lasso-pole horses, Robin Irvine on training racehorses, and Fraser on Mongolian livestock herding where it includes sheep and goats. Charlotte

Marchina, "Follow the horse: The complexities of collaboration between the lasso-pole horse (uurgach mor') and his rider among Mongolian horse herders," in *The Meaning of Horses: Biosocial Encounters*, ed. Dona Davis and Anita Maurstad (Abingdon: Routledge, 2016), 102–13; Robin Irvine, "Thinking with horses: troubles with subjects, objects and diverse entities in eastern Mongolia," *Humanimalia: A Journal of Human/Animal Interface Studies* 6, no. 1 (2014): 62–94; Fraser, "Motorcycles on the Steppe," 349.

37 My own horse in South Africa would have expressed *her* chagrin at these outrages to *her* human-horse culture.

38 Of course, sensory experience is transient, so offers a real challenge to historians, and while written descriptions of sensory experiences in the past can be used, we historians can go further by trying to recreate past sensory experiences, to better understand past ways. Thus even just riding in a "traditional saddle" is a method of experiential history: learning from trying to use technology of the past. Mongolian saddles sit high off the horse's back—perhaps herders ride half-standing and tilted to the side to offset not only the hard saddles but their small horses' short and concomitantly choppy gait?

39 Thomas Csordas, *Body/Meaning/Healing* (New York: Palgrave Macmillan, 2002), 7–8.

40 Sandra Swart, "Historians and Other Animals" (Review of D. Brantz, *Beastly Natures: Animals, Humans, and the Study of History*), H-Environment, November 2011, https://www.h-net.org/reviews/showpdf.php?id=31301.

41 Mieke Roscher, "New political history and the writing of animal lives," in *The Routledge Companion to Animal-Human History*, ed. Hilda Kean and Philip Howell (London: Routledge, 2019).

42 Roy Porter, "History of the Body Reconsidered," in *New Perspectives on Historical Writing*, ed. Peter Burke (Cambridge: Polity Press, 2001), 232–60; Iris Clever and Willemijn Ruberg, "Beyond Cultural History? The Material Turn, Praxiography, and Body History," *Humanities* 3, no. 4 (2014): 546–66.

43 Pascal Eitler, "Animal History as Body History: Four Suggestions from a Genealogical Perspective," *Body Politics* 2, no. 4 (2014): 259–74.

44 For our purposes, see Kathleen Canning, "The Body as Method? Reflections on the Place of the Body in Gender History," *Gender & History* 11, no. 3 (1999): 499–513.

45 For another kind of auto-ethnographic equine encounter, see Kim Marra, "Riding, Scarring, Knowing: A Queerly Embodied Performance Historiography," *Theatre Journal* 64, no. 4 (2012): 489–511.

46 Thus operating at the confluence of ethology and ethnography, but "reading" not only the present but extracting this data by reading past texts through this lens.

47 Fieldwork, July 2013. There is little verbal communication (other than shouting *khai!*—"stop that!" Or a soft *chu*—"go").

48 In the 1970s, the genealogies of stallions were remembered for about four generations—a useful project for a historian would be to plot how this has changed in the last fifty years. See Caroline Humphrey, "The Semiology of Horse Brands in Mongolia," *The Cambridge Journal of Anthropology* 1, no. 1 (1973): 23.

49 Fieldwork, July 2013.

50 Ironic given the great Chinngis' own fall (mentioned at the start of the essay). However, fieldwork etiquette required not pointing out this inconvenient archival truth.

51 Like the modified hammer or swastika brand (opinion was locally divided) on display at *Naran Tuul* ("The Black Market") in Ulaanbaatar. I first thought this brand referenced the new movement in Mongolia that embraces the trappings of German fascism, including a Nazi-themed bar in Ulan Bator (largely as an anti-Chinese gesture), but one must remember that the swastika was a Buddhist symbol long before Nazis adopted it and swastika brand-marks were around in Mongolia in at least the 1970s and probably long before. Fieldwork, July 2013.

52 For example, the elite branded the right flank and ordinary folk the left.

53 Humphrey, "The Semiology of Horse Brands in Mongolia," 33.

54 Andrei Marin, "Between Cash Cows and Golden Calves: Adaptations of Mongolian Pastoralism in the 'Age of the Market'," *Nomadic Peoples* 12, no. 2 (2008): 75–101.

55 Navchaa Tugjamba, Greg Walkerden, and Fiona Miller, "Adaptation strategies of nomadic herders in northeast Mongolia: climate, globalisation and traditional knowledge," *Local Environment* 26, no. 4 (2021): 411–30.

56 Since 1990, Mongolia has seen the creation of a democratic state and market economy, with the privatization of livestock—a radical change not only from Soviet-era collectives, but also from the pre-Soviet regime, when herders had access to grazing but under the authority of religious and aristocratic powers.

57 Rebecca Empson, "The Dangers of Excess: Accumulating and Dispersing Fortune in Mongolia," *Social Analysis* 56, no. 1 (2012): 117.

58 Irvine, "Thinking with Horses."

59 Bekhjargal Bayarsaikhan, *Travelling by Mongolian Horse* (Ulaanbaatar: Bit Press, 2005), 102.

60 "When Mongolia throws a party, the rest of Asia locks its doors," as Naadam celebrators boast of the traditional annual summer festival of wrestling, archery, and horse-racing, the so-called manly sports (although women now compete in the latter two). Robert Peck, "Chagi's charge," *Natural History* 107, no. 5 (1998): 28.

61 As early as the thirteenth century, travellers like Chao Hung wrote about horse-human cultures. Bat-Ochir Bold, "The Quantity of Livestock Owned by the Mongols in the 13th Century," *Journal of the Royal Asiatic Society* 8, no. 2 (1998): 237–46.

62 A. Neville Whymant, "Mongolian Proverbs: A Study in the Kalmuck Colloquial," *The Journal of the Royal Asiatic Society of Great Britain and Ireland* 58, no. 2 (1926): 257–67.

63 Hangin et al., "Mongolian Folklore."

64 See, for example, L. Munkhtur, *Words that Illustrate Mongolian Horse Appearance, Its Meaning and Structure* (Ulaanbaatar, Mongolia: Mongolian State University of Education, 2007).

65 In epic poems, horses possess mystic powers and offer sound counsel to the heroes. Chao Gejin, "Mongolian Oral Epic Poetry: An Overview," *Oral Tradition* 12, no. 2 (1997): 322–36; Ágnes Birtalan, "Some Animal Representations in Mongolian Shaman Invocations and Folklore," *SHAMAN* 3, no. 1–2 (1995, 2009): 17–32.

66 For new research, see Melanie Kiechle, "Preserving the Unpleasant: Sources, Methods, and Conjectures for Odors at Historic Sites," *Future Anterior* 13, no. 2 (2016): 22–32.

67 It is a very large part of avoiding colic, a common cause of death in horses and concomitantly a major concern for horse owners.

68 Perhaps transmitting a social message to the mare (or another stallion in the territory) such as "She's mine."

69 Hui-Yuan Yeh et al., "Intestinal parasites in a mid-14th century latrine from Riga, Latvia: fish tapeworm and the consumption of uncooked fish in the medieval eastern Baltic region," *Journal of Archaeological Science* 49 (2014): 83–89.

70 Fittingly.

71 Martina Burnik Šturm et al., "Sequential stable isotope analysis reveals differences in dietary history of three sympatric equid species in the Mongolian Gobi," *Journal of Applied Ecology* 54, (2017): 1110–19; Petra Kaczensky et al., "Resource selection by sympatric wild equids in the Mongolian Gobi," *Journal of Applied Ecology* 45 (2008): 1762–69.

72 Local people call their horses "Mongol" as distinct from the takhi. See Natasha Fijn, "The domestic and the wild in the Mongolian horse and the takhi," in *Taxonomic Tapestries: The Threads of Evolutionary, Behavioural and Conservation Research*, ed. Alison Behie and Marc Oxenham (Canberra: Australian National University Press, 2015), 282. *Aduu* refers to a horse in general; *Mor'* to a gelded horse, which is normally ridden.

73 "Local knowledge" (sometimes called traditional or Indigenous knowledge) is knowledge that has dynamically developed over time and is tailored to local culture and environment.

74 Jo Guldi and David Armitage, *The History Manifesto* (Cambridge: Cambridge University Press, 2014).

75 Petra Kaczensky et al., "Stable isotopes reveal diet shift from pre-extinction to reintroduced Przewalski's horses," *Scientific Reports* 7 (2017), https://doi.org/10.1038/s41598-017-05329-6. This could be a particularly rich archive for ordinary Mongolian horses too, as many homes preserve tail hair as sacred, and the *moriin khuur* or horsehead fiddle has bow and strings traditionally made of horse hair.

76 This is a contested topic, with new research arguing that the damage to Botai horses' teeth is not from bits, but just from natural grazing. This study argues that it signals harvesting of takhi, and so perhaps horses were domesticated elsewhere. William Taylor and Christina Barrón-Ortiz, "Rethinking the evidence for early horse domestication at Botai," *Scientific Reports (Nature)* 11 (2021), https://doi.org/10.1038/s41598-021-86832-9.

77 Charleen Gaunitz et al., "Ancient genomes revisit the ancestry of domestic and Przewalski's horses," *Science* 360 (2018): 111–14.

78 Barbara Wallner et al., "Fixed nucleotide differences on the Y chromosome indicate clear divergence between *Equus przewalskii* and *Equus caballus*," *Animal Genetics* 34, no. 6, (2003): 453–56.

79 Some "strains" spoken of include the Galshar (in the east) or the Darkhad (in the high mountains of the north). See Gro Bjørnstad, N. Ø. Nilsen, and Knut Røedl, "Genetic relationship between Mongolian and Norwegian horses?," *Animal Genetics* 34, no. 1 (2003): 57.

80 Stallions can breed with mares from other herds if they can defeat the competition.

81 Fijn, "The domestic and the wild," 284–85.

82 Emphasis added. Sándor Bökönyi, *The Przevalsky Horse* (London: Souvenir Press, 1974), 85, 45.

83 There are so many overlapping ways to classify horses: by condition (a worn-out horse = *adasq-a mori*; a slow horse = *bolki mori*), by context (a horse of the steppes = *keger-e-yin mori*; a horse kept separately as a reserve = *ongquu mori*), by work (a horse trained to work with a pole lasso = *ury-a(n) mori*; a relay horse = *ulay-a(n) mori*), by state of education (a trained horse = *kölücin*; a horse that has not been ridden for at least one year = *qur [baiysan] mori*), by sex or reproductive state: hence, a gelding = *ayta mori*; a mare that produces a foal only once every three years = *esgel*; a sterile mare = *eremeg gegüü*. Horses can also be classified by gait (a racing horse = *aryamay* [may also designate a thoroughbred, or simply a good horse]) or spiritual classification (a horse used in a sacrifice to Chinggis = *morin ödke*). From Ruth Meserve, "The Expanded Role of Mongolian Domestic Livestock Classification," *Acta Orientalia Academiae Scientiarum Hungaricae* 53, no. 1/2 (2000): 23–45.

84 Gelding is an undeniable difference between wild and domesticated horses—castration is unlikely ever to happen to (even a very unlucky) "wild" horse. Castration means that males can continue to stay in their birth herds instead of being chased out by the stallion.

85 The stallion's job is to ensure mares are pregnant or nursing to create milk for *airag* (fermented milk beer). Mares require an engagement with human bodies despite not being ridden as they are milked. Foals are tied up near the *ger* while their mothers graze without restraint except for being milked several times a day. At night, foals and mares graze together. Fieldwork, July 2013.

86 Some horses have sheared off manes, but stallions' manes are not trimmed; like the biblical Samson, their hair is their strength.

87 Fieldwork, 23 July 2013.

88 The "taming" process (a necessary act even in domesticated horses) has a history that calls out for analysis—through oral history. The one act I witnessed closely was violent and involved hitting the horse with a long rope line and shouting *chu chu*; the aim was to tire him and frighten him into a kind of submission. A little girl watching this process wandered away and then eagerly copied him—with a calf.

89 For discussion of vernacular/local/traditional/Indigenous knowledge in animal history, see Sandra Swart, "Writing animals into African history," *Critical African Studies* 8, no. 2 (2016): 95–108.

90 Fieldwork, Khustain Nuruu, 21 July 2013.

2

Occupational Hazards: Honeybee Labour as an Interpretive Device in Animal History[1]

Jennifer Bonnell

In an influential 2003 article in *Labor History*, Jason Hribal argued that "animals are part of the working class." Like human labourers, horses, oxen, mules, and other working animals came to form a kind of proletariat in the context of industrializing nineteenth-century cities and farms. They registered instances of resistance, including violent outbursts and refusals to work, which prompted varying forms of negotiation by their human employers. Recognition of the interconnected exploitation of animals and workers, Hribal argues, led nineteenth-century reform organizations to initiate linked movements for worker and animal rights. Human and animal workers, he concludes, shared a "mutual struggle" against exploitation in industrializing economies.[2]

Questions of animal agency, however, have limited usefulness in interpreting historical records.[3] The extent to which working animals resisted their plight can tell us only so much. Ultimately, those instances of animal agency that we can interpret from our sources reinforce what we already know to be true: animals were, and are, sentient creatures with motivations of their own and forms of intelligence that, collectively, we have been unable or unwilling to comprehend.[4] As Joanna Dean and Jason Colby demonstrate in this volume, we might better comprehend the historical lives of animals by considering the work they performed—either for their human keepers or for reasons of their own—and the changing circumstances within which they worked.

This chapter modifies Hribal's challenge to consider animals—in this case, honeybees—not as a proletariat that resisted their oppression, but rather as workers whose changing work environments had repercussions for their health and the viability of their keepers' operations. If, in taking up Hribal's logic, we regard honeybees as workers (the familiar classification of the adult female majority as "worker bees" simplifies this leap), we can extend this logic to consider the environments they labour within as places of work with better or worse working conditions. To be clear, following Donna Haraway and Edmund Russell, I consider honeybees to be neither human slaves nor wage labourers but rather animal labourers "who produce surplus value by giving more than they get in a market-driven economic system." Beekeepers "enlist their cooperation" in the productive and reproductive jobs they perform in service of the colony as a superorganism. Bees work, in other words, but they do not (at least purposefully) work for us.[5] Regarding honeybees as animal workers allows historians to take their labour, and the changing conditions within which they worked, seriously. We can consider the risks and opportunities presented by a given environment from the perspective of the worker (the bee) and the beneficiary of that work (the beekeeper). Further, we can attend to the ways in which beekeepers responded to the experience of their bees and sought to direct, maximize, and protect their productivity.

Conceiving of animals like honeybees as "workers" rather than as "resources" has implications for our understanding of political economy more broadly, displacing an anthropocentric assessment of usefulness with a recognition of the ecological relationships that exist regardless of our presence.[6] Animals, from this perspective, are transformers of non-human nature in their own right: through their labour, honeybees transform nectar into honey, just as barn swallows transform mud pellets into cup-shaped nests and bison turn grass into insect-sustaining dung. Appreciating the intersecting roles of humans in this process, as beneficiaries and enablers, casualties and disruptors, is one of the central projects of environmental history.

Certainly, a large literature exists on the history of animal labour. While much of the scholarship on occupational hazards has focused on human work environments, historians of labouring animals have taken an ecological approach to examine the role of changing environments on labouring animal bodies. Clay McShane and Joel Tarr's classic study of working horses in nineteenth-century American cities, for example, explores the problem of limited access to drinking water on city streets and the hazards of fire and disease exposure in crowded city stables (on the latter, see Kheraj in this volume).[7] Explorations of animal labour and working conditions, however, have largely been confined to animals traditionally conceived of as "labourers": horses, mules, donkeys, oxen, and elephants. A more expansive view of human-animal working relationships—and the ways humans have profited from animals that labour *for themselves* and for their own societies—has featured in more recent scholarship.[8]

Scholarship that has taken up the topic of labour as a combination of human and non-human forces offers some useful direction. Among environmental histories, Richard White's *Organic Machine* was one of the first to examine the ways that human labour and engineering intersected with the non-human entity of the Columbia River in the production of work.[9] More recently, Thomas G. Andrews' *Killing for Coal* presents the concept of "workscapes," "places shaped by the interplay of human labor and natural processes." By conceiving of work as a "constellation of unruly and ever-unfolding relationships" between land, air, water, bodies, and organisms, Andrews suggests historians can treat people and, in this case, animals as "laboring beings who have changed and been changed in turn by a natural world that remains always under construction."[10] The relationality between humans, other animal species, and non-human entities, such as rivers, tides, and coal seams, in this conception of work offers space for thinking about the ways all participants are transformed in the process.

Beekeepers, like hydro-electric engineers and coal company managers, operated within complex and changing workscapes that blended human and animal labour with the work of natural processes. In my larger study of beekeeping and environmental change in the Great Lakes region in the late nineteenth and early twentieth centuries, I have reviewed decades of detailed beekeeper association records, such as those of the Ontario Beekeeping Association, published annually since 1881, and bee-keeping periodicals, such as the weekly *American Bee Journal* (distributed in the United States and in Canada). These records document beekeeper concerns as managers of honeybee labour and work environments. And they place into relief the considerable limits in control that beekeepers exercised over the semi-domesticated foraging insects that they kept.

Fundamentally, the work that honeybees do (and which their human keepers benefit from) involves gathering pollen and nectar from flowering trees and plants and transforming these floral essences into products (most notably honey) for human consumption. Beekeepers, in return, provide a suitable structure where honeybee colonies can live and work, where they can access floral landscapes and sources of water, and where they can have limited protection from other, non-human predators (such as bears, badgers, and predatory insects). In addition, beekeepers assist in maintaining the sanitary condition of the hive (honeybees do the bulk of this work themselves), and they monitor the health of their worker colonies. In this way, honeybees and beekeepers are, in Haraway's words, "mutually adapted partners" in the work of production and reproduction.[11]

Beekeeper management, however, is challenged by the unusual degree of liberty enjoyed by their workers. Honeybees, unlike most forms of livestock, cannot be fenced in. Neither fully domesticated nor fully wild, they possess a freedom to forage. Honeybees are not alone in occupying this liminal status between wild and domesticated: historically and in limited instances into the present, they have shared this status with other animals, such as cattle in the pre-barbed-wire American and Canadian West, reindeer herds in the Global North, and the feral horses that Swart explores in Chapter 1.[12] In each case, forage freedoms have been accompanied by varying burdens of risk for human keepers. What honeybees find, and fail to find, on their foraging flights has long been a source of concern for beekeepers. The costs of this freedom range from unpalatable honey due to unintended forage sources, exposure to parasites and infectious disease, and losses resulting from insecticide poisoning. This fundamental inability of beekeepers to control the movement of their bees led them to direct their energies instead to mitigating the risks presented by their working environments.

Working conditions for honeybees, furthermore, did not remain static over my period of study. My sources document a shift from the relatively untroubled years of beekeeping in the Great Lakes region in the mid-nineteenth century to the novel concerns that emerged in the 1880s and 1890s. As agriculturalists adopted increasingly industrial forms of production in this period, honeybees and their keepers became the unintended targets of responses to insect outbreaks and reductions in wildflowers and other forms of "bee forage." Honeybees also became subject to disease risks and pests of their own. As working animals within industrializing agricultural landscapes, honeybees not only suffered the consequences of industrial-scale food production (through disease, parasites, and insecticide poisoning), but also took on industrial functions themselves in this period as pollinators of expanding and increasingly monoculture orchard crops.[13] The records I examine describe the onset of these changes in the late nineteenth and early twentieth centuries and document the responses of beekeepers, entomologists, and government officials to these concerns. Through toxicity studies and observations of honeybee behaviour, entomologists and beekeepers "read" the bodies their bees to better understand honeybee working environments and the opportunities and threats they presented.

This chapter examines three significant episodes of change in the working environments of honeybees in the late nineteenth and early twentieth centuries, and the responses these changes generated among their keepers:

1. changes in the diversity and extent of bee forage in the context of industrializing agricultural production;

2. the advent and spread of American foulbrood (AFB), a highly contagious bacterial disease of honeybee larvae that devastated North American beekeepers in the late nineteenth and early twentieth centuries; and

3. rising incidents of honeybee poisoning due to growing insecticide use in the same period.

In the following pages, I read between the lines of beekeeper records to glimpse honeybees as historical creatures in their own right, whose relative freedom and changing ability to thrive prompted specific and vigorous responses by their keepers. An appreciation of honeybees as historical actors illuminates changes in honeybee behaviour and vitality over the course of my period of study, as they responded to new pathogens and poisons and declining or homogenizing forage sources. These changes can be discerned through the concerns, actions, and decisions of beekeepers, who learned about environmental risks in surrounding landscapes through the behaviours and bodies of their bees. Bees provided information to their keepers not only in life, through the direction of their flight and the flowering plants they chose to frequent, but also in death, as their bodies became data sources for toxicity studies and, less frequently, litigation. At the root of these threats to honeybee health, and beekeeper livelihoods, lay the nature of honeybees as semi-domesticated animals with a fundamental freedom to forage.

Changing Sources of Bee Forage

The work that honeybees[14] do (for themselves and for their human keepers) begins in the early spring, when adult female workers leave the hive to gather pollen and nectar from flowering trees and plants. Beekeepers have historically called these kind of plants "bee forage" or "bee pasture," drawing deliberate connections between the honeybees they tend and other forms of livestock as a way of asserting their legitimacy as agricultural producers. A female worker makes roughly a dozen foraging trips daily in fair weather, typically within a three-kilometre range of the hive. She uses her straw-like tongue, or proboscis, to reach inside the flower, sucking up the sugary nectar into her "honey stomach," a second stomach used only for nectar. Here, the nectar mixes with enzymes that transform its chemical composition and pH to make it more suitable for long-term storage. She then moistens the hairs on her front legs and uses them to brush and compress the flower pollen clinging to her body into the "pollen baskets" on her back legs. When her honey stomach is full, she returns to the hive and regurgitates the nectar to share with other female workers, who chew the nectar to break down the sugars and evaporate some of the water. The bees then store the nectar in honeycomb cells—like tiny jars made of wax—fanning it with their wings to dry it further before sealing the cell with a wax lid to keep it clean. They draw upon the resulting stores of honey to feed their brood and nourish the colony over winter.[15]

Beekeepers, then and now, take advantage of these accumulation and storage activities by harvesting the surplus honey that honeybees create. Standard commercial box hives, whose design has not changed markedly since the 1850s, comprise a series of stacked compartments or "supers," each with frames upon which bees build their honeycomb. As the bees fill up these "supers" with honey for the winter, the keepers harvest the surplus, taking care to leave enough for the bees (or, as is common in commercial operations, supplementing stored honey with sugared water in fall and winter). One colony of 40,000–50,000 bees typically produces about ten kilograms of "surplus" honey each year.

Beekeepers direct honeybee labour by locating hives adjacent to desirable forage sources and relocating hives as different plant sources come into bloom. Honey bears the flavour of the blossoms from which it is produced, and beekeepers deliberately select certain kinds of bloom to produce certain kinds of honey, from the delicate taste of wildflower or linden tree honey to the more acquired, earthy taste of buckwheat honey. This ability to produce single-source variations of honey is aided by the tendency of honeybees to forage on one kind of flower on any single trip (a co-evolutionary strategy that also allows for cross-pollination of blossoms among a single plant species). A forager travelling to blackberry blossoms, for example, will keep going to blackberries until there are no more blackberry flowers, and then she will switch to something else. Foraging, it should be noted, is very hard work: it is the last in a series of tasks a worker bee performs in her five-to-eight week lifetime, and it is the most taxing. An average worker typically forages only four to five days before she dies.[16]

By the late nineteenth century, deforestation, urban development, and agricultural modernization across the Great Lakes region brought changes to the diversity and extent of forage sources. The first cause for concern was the flowering linden (or basswood) tree, which had become increasingly scarce throughout the region by the 1890s. Known commonly as the "bee tree," its highly aromatic blossoms provided an important source of nectar for struggling honeybee colonies in the spring and produced a highly prized "water-white" honey.[17] But soft, light-weight basswood was

Fig. 2.1 Blossom and leaf of the basswood (linden) tree. Source: Frank C. Pellett, *American Honey Plants: Together with Those Which Are of Special Value to the Beekeeper as Sources of Pollen* (Hamilton, IL: American Bee Journal, 1920), 33.

also valued for its suitability for a wide range of other products, from musical instruments to fruit baskets to window blinds. Alarmed beekeepers pointed to rapid declines of linden trees in urban and rural areas at annual meetings of beekeeping associations and in the columns of apicultural journals, calling for collective efforts to protect them. Ontario beekeeper Allen Pringle warned the members of the Ontario Beekeeping Association (OBA) in 1893: "the Linden tree is rapidly disappearing down the open and capacious maws of the pulp machines, the sawmills and the fallow fires. It is disappearing much faster than the uprising sprouts and saplings (spontaneous and cultivated) are taking its place." Another from Cincinnati encouraged beekeepers to "take up the chorus of plant! plant! plant! . . . [P]lant lindens on your roadsides, the division lines of your farms and unproductive hillsides."[18]

The growing scarcity of the linden tree was just the first of a series of changes that would significantly reduce wild sources of bee forage and dampen the viability of beekeeping in the region by mid-century. From the 1930s on, the expansion of commodity crops resulted in the steady disappearance of nectar-producing wildflowers, shrubs, and trees. New agricultural technologies and practices associated with the shift to monoculture production had unintended consequences for apiculture in the region. As Gordon Townsend, provincial apiarist for Ontario in the 1940s, recalled, the introduction of balers and forage harvesters in the 1930s and 1940s removed clover from fields before it came into bloom, and efforts to accommodate such large equipment resulted in the removal of hedgerows, another source of bee forage. Following World War II, crop scientists promoted continuous plantings of corn (which does not secrete nectar) on the same fields. Together with the routine spraying of roadside vegetation, according to Townsend, widespread continuous corn production "struck the final blow" to honey production from wild plant sources. These changes together led to dramatic declines in the diversity and abundance of bee forage in southern Ontario. Sweet clover, for example, an abundant source of bee forage in the 1920s and 1930s, declined by over seventy-five per cent from a peak of 400,000 acres in 1928 to less than 100,000 acres by 1947. "From that time on," Townsend concludes, "the decrease was so rapid that no statistical records were kept." Alsike clover, another major honey producer, declined by more than eighty-five per cent in the same period, and buckwheat, which covered 300,000 acres in 1929, "was almost nonexistent" by 1961.[19]

Reductions in bee forage had repercussions for the health of honeybee workers and the economic viability of their keepers. As experienced beekeepers know, fewer sources of forage reduce the longevity of individual workers by requiring them to fly longer distances on each foraging flight.[20] Knowledge from more recent studies of honeybee health tells us, too, that reductions in the diversity of forage sources had negative ramifications for honeybee nutrition. Honeybees harvesting nectar and pollen from a narrower range of floral sources contributed to reduced resilience in the face of other stressors, including disease, parasites, extreme weather conditions, and insecticide exposure.[21] These factors, combined with competition from western honey producers, contributed to a steady decline in the number of beekeepers and the viability of commercial operations from the 1930s on in Ontario and neighbouring US states.[22] Less nectar to gather and fewer operating beekeepers ultimately resulted in declining honeybee populations. In Ontario, for example, data from agricultural censuses shows that the number of honeybee colonies declined steadily from a peak of about 260,000 in the mid-1940s to less than 100,000 by 1973 and an average of 74,000 by the early 2000s.[23]

Exposure to Disease

If declining forage opportunities represented one change in honeybee working conditions, exposure to disease was another. For honeybees, susceptibility to disease transmission is exacerbated by their freedom to forage and by behavioural responses to nectar shortages. Foraging worker bees will collect sugary substances from any source they can find, including jars of honey or sugar syrup, honey collecting equipment, and in some circumstances, other honeybee colonies. In the late summer or early fall, when flowers are past their prime, nectar sources are scarce, and bees are hungry, foraging workers will seek out colonies that are smaller, weaker, or otherwise vulnerable to rob their honey stores. In just a few hours, a hungry forager can recruit a supporting crew of robbers from her own hive and overwhelm a weaker colony. Together they will fight resident bees to access and plunder their honey stores, and many bees die in the process.[24]

When an outbreak of American foulbrood (AFB), a deadly bacterial disease of honeybee brood, or larvae, struck Great Lakes apiaries in the late 1870s, beekeepers struggled to protect their worker colonies from infection. Long a scourge of beekeepers in Europe, and in North America from at least the 1670s, AFB is caused by spore-forming bacteria (another non-human actor in this story). Honeybee larvae eat the spores, which then grows like a mold and consumes the larvae. In cleaning the hive of dead larvae, adult worker bees spread the bacteria further.[25] Outside the hive, the disease can be spread through infected honeycomb and equipment, and by harvesting honey and pollen from infected hives.

Robber bees also spread AFB spores when they periodically rob the honey from infected hives. Colonies weakened by AFB are especially susceptible to attack, and in these attacks, disease is spread. Spores travel in plundered honey and on the bodies of robber bees returning from diseased hives. Once contracted, AFB will destroy a colony: while it does not affect adult bees, the destruction of the brood eliminates the possibility of replacement when adult workers reach the end of their short, five-to-eight week life spans.[26] Because AFB is indiscriminate, affecting strong and weak colonies equally, it carries the potential to destroy apiaries within a three- to eight-kilometre range (the flight range of foraging workers) of infected hives.

Honeybee colonies struggling with an AFB infection produce less honey. As worker numbers dwindle and more of the colony's energy is devoted to removing dead brood, fewer workers are available to gather and process floral nectar. Weakened colonies also struggle to fend off apiary pests like wax moths, which feed on honeycomb. Beekeeper sources for Ontario show, for example, that honey production declined by over forty per cent between 1891 and 1901. These changes were the product not only of honeybee mortality (the number of colonies in the province dropped by twenty per cent in this period), but also of reduced productivity in surviving colonies.[27]

Early responses to the disease by beekeepers often had the unwanted effect of exacerbating its spread. In the 1880s, deficits of knowledge about the nature of the disease and the absence of coordination between beekeeping organizations meant beekeepers were too often unsupported in their efforts. For many, detection came too late to remedy the problem. Others attempted to rid their colonies of disease by physically shaking adult bees onto new, uncontaminated hive frames. The "shaking" method, however, like other "sanitary" responses advocated in this period before germ theory was widely understood, sometimes did more harm than good. While some experienced beekeepers publicized their success, others struggled to replicate their methods and ran the risk of further spreading the disease.[28] Like Hodgins' livestock farmers (Chapter 5), beekeepers struggled to respond to a novel problem with often ill-suited or outdated practices. The hardiness of AFB spores, furthermore—they can survive for more than forty years in honey and beekeeping equipment—meant it wasn't long before bee colonies became reinfected.[29] By the early 1900s, entomologists and state beekeeping associations agreed that the best solution was to burn infected colonies, contaminated hives, and equipment—a devastating and expensive proposition for beekeepers.

Another response to the disease involved controlling the movement of honeybee workers. As Olmstead and Rhode have shown for crop science in this period, close study of the habits of insects and the nature of disease allowed farmers and scientists to achieve some "remarkable successes" in controlling biological hazards in the decades before the emergence of chemical controls. In an effort to prevent robbing of infected hives, beekeepers devised ways to close hive entrances with wire mesh or to deter intruders by stuffing entrances with grass. A wet blanket draped over the hive was another method used to discourage robbing while allowing the passage of resident bees. Producer associations and state and federal regulatory institutions developed important supports. To control honeybee movement over longer distances, beekeeping associations pressed for quarantines of infected apiaries and legislation prohibiting the import and sale of bees on honeycomb, wherein AFB spores could lie dormant. Ontario required permits for local honeybee sales from 1906 on; in 1923, it passed legislation prohibiting the import of bees and beekeeping equipment, with the exception of honeybee queens. By 1925, five US states, including Michigan and Illinois, had passed similar legislation for interstate and international imports and a further twenty-five required health certificates before bees on comb could enter the state.[30]

Responses by beekeepers to the threat of AFB infection in the 1880s and 1890s had the effect of re-articulating beekeeping organization and practice throughout the Great Lakes region and beyond. The need for a coordinated response to AFB and other honeybee diseases resulted in the establishment of provincial- and state-level beekeeping associations to support local and regional organizations. AFB dominated the agenda, for example, of the OBA's second annual meeting in 1882.[31] Reflecting similar developments in plant disease control and livestock inspection in the same period, state and provincial beekeeping associations appointed foulbrood inspectors to inspect and destroy infected hives.[32] In the OBA annual reports and weekly issues of the *American Bee Journal* in this period, foulbrood inspectors detailed the number of infected colonies identified and destroyed. They also documented their encounters with obstreperous apiarists who resisted the reach of state inspectors on their property and the economic losses that accompanied burned hives and equipment. Concern about disease transmission ultimately led to the passage of state and provincial legislation obligating beekeepers to immediately report cases of diseased hives and to cooperate with state or beekeeper association inspectors in eradicating the disease.[33]

By the 1910s, responses by beekeepers and state agricultural authorities had begun to make some headway. Changes in Ontario's foulbrood legislation in 1906 expanded government-sponsored inspection services six-fold, replacing a lone foulbrood inspector with six area-based inspectors. The introduction of mandatory burn requirements for infected hives in this period also bore out in modest signs of recovery. The 1911 agricultural census showed a six per cent increase in honeybee colonies from 1901, and, significantly, a forty-four per cent increase in worker productivity (honey production) over the same period. By 1925, Ontario, Michigan, and Illinois led the way in adopting "area clean-up" methods, which combined the destruction of all diseased colonies in a designated area with a three-year period of quarantine and regular inspection. Ontario destroyed fifty-eight per cent of inspected colonies when the program began in 1926; by 1929, only two per cent of inspected colonies were infected. By 1940, these combined practices of thorough inspection, burning, and quarantine reduced disease rates to less than three per cent across the Great Lakes region. The introduction of sodium sulfathiazole, an antibiotic that slowed the growth of foulbrood bacteria, gave a further boost to AFB control efforts by allowing individual beekeepers to treat diseased colonies at the first sign of infection, with less reliance on the inspection system.[34]

The virulence of AFB in the Great Lakes region in the late nineteenth and early twentieth centuries created disease environments that threatened the health of honeybee workers and the economic viability of the apiaries within which they laboured. Honeybees' freedom to forage, and their tendency to rob weakened or infected hives of honey stores, made disease control especially challenging for beekeepers. The coordinated responses that beekeeping associations and state agricultural authorities developed at the provincial and state level reconfigured beekeeping practice, introducing legislation and inspection that laid the foundation for state apicultural authorities in the post-war period. Inspection services not only brought the disease under control, but also educated individual beekeepers on effective disease diagnostics and early responses. By the 1930s, these changes significantly reduced the risk of disease contraction and spread for foraging honeybees.

Exposure to Insecticides

Perhaps the most pernicious of risks that honeybees faced on their foraging flights was exposure to insecticides. The danger was especially high

Fig. 2.2 Spraying fruit trees with a horse-powered spray jig near Ayr in southwestern Ontario, ca. 1910. Source: Robinson Studio Photographs Fonds F4592-7, H-1015, Archives of Ontario.

in the industrializing orchards of the region, where mounting challenges with insect pests had prompted fruit growers to experiment, beginning in the 1870s, with the application of arsenic-based insecticides.[35] The effectiveness of these insecticides in improving yields of marketable fruit, coupled with advocacy for their use by influential entomologists and state horticultural officials, led growers across the region to apply ever-increasing quantities of insecticidal sprays to apples and other orchard crops.

Foraging honeybees began encountering orchard blossoms sprayed with Paris Green (aceto-arsenite, a highly toxic copper-arsenite) with greater frequency beginning in the late 1880s; by the early 1900s, they were more likely to encounter the sticky and even more lethal residues of lead arsenate. Foragers that ingested the poison through contaminated nectar or water sources were likely to die in the field, before reaching the hive. For those that carried contaminated pollen back to the hive, the damage was much more extensive. Pollen contaminated with arsenical insecticide remains toxic for months, killing both the nurse bees that ingest the pollen to feed it to the brood, and the brood bees as well. Poisoned bees experience distended abdomens, diarrhea, and an inability to fly. Poisoned nurse bees, for example, will often attempt to leave the hive, fly a short distance, and end up hopping or crawling on the ground in front of the hive.[36]

One of the earliest reported incidents of insecticide poisoning was related by beekeeper John G. Smith of New Canton, Illinois, in the 25 May 1889 issue of the *American Bee Journal*. The apple bloom that year, he reported, proved a "'death-warrant' to millions of bees in [his] immediate neighbourhood" when the owner of a neighbouring orchard sprayed his trees with a solution of Paris Green when the trees were in full bloom.[37] Smith lost sixty of his own honeybee colonies, and by his estimate "ten or twelve bee-keepers" in the area surrounding the orchard were "totally ruined, as far as getting a spring crop of honey [was] concerned."[38]

Faced with the impossibility of containing their bees, beekeepers on both sides of the border made collective efforts to mitigate the risks within honeybee working environments. Early investigations established the toxicity of arsenate insecticides to honeybees[39] and confined the problem to the timing of the spray: honeybees visited fruit-tree orchards to forage for nectar and pollen only when the trees were in bloom. Their exposure to risk was limited to a brief, two-week window when the blossoms still clung to the branches, before the fruit began to form. State entomologists and prominent beekeepers proposed a simple solution: refrain from spraying during the bloom.

Doubts persisted, however, among growers reluctant to circumscribe their activities, and scientists enamoured with the results of insecticide use. Despite efforts to educate neighbouring growers about the risks of insecticide use and the value of honeybee pollination to their operations, poisoning incidents continued. With limited avenues to recoup their losses, beekeepers turned increasingly to legislative tools for protection.

Ontario was the first to pass protective spraying legislation. In the spring of 1892, a month before the publication of Cook's first toxicity study, a delegation from the OBA to the Ontario Ministry of Agriculture resulted in the passage of *An Act for the Further Protection of Bees*. The

Act—the first of its kind in North America—stipulated that fruit trees could be sprayed only *after* the bloom had fallen, thereby protecting bees from harm.[40] Several US states followed, passing legislation similar to Ontario's, including Michigan and Vermont (1896), Colorado (1897), and New York and Washington State (1898). Others, including Ohio, Illinois, and California, had spraying bills rejected in response to counter-lobbying by fruit-growing interests.[41]

Growers expressing their opposition to spraying legislation sometimes made direct comparisons to protective legislation for human workers in the same period. In 1890, editors of *American Garden* railed against beekeeper advocacy for a spraying law in Michigan: "Surely, fruit is of more importance than honey! If those busy workers must have [l]egislation, let us advocate a training school for bees, in which they may be taught to keep out of the orchards at the dangerous period."[42] Like Chris Sellers' conclusions for human exposure to workplace toxins in the same period, modifying worker behaviour or access to toxic environments was seen as preferable to ensuring safe working conditions.[43] If trespass laws applied to cows and other domesticated animals, the editors concluded sardonically, why should they not be applied to bees? Their commentary pointed to two central challenges at the heart of the spraying debates: the fundamental "uncontainability" of bees as semi-domesticated foraging insects; and the limited and variable knowledge of growers about the value of honeybee pollination to the orchard. At a time when the role of bees in fruit pollination was not widely understood, bees were often viewed more as an enemy than an aid to the orchard.[44] Honeybee labour, freely offered, was often under-appreciated by growers.

In the end, legislation, however promising, proved difficult to enforce.[45] Beekeepers made greater headway in demonstrating the value of honeybee labour to crop production in neighbouring orchards than they did in advocating for legislation. A series of pollination studies conducted by supportive entomologists in the 1890s demonstrated conclusively that trees in full bud exposed to honeybee pollination produced exponentially more fruit than unexposed trees.[46] In 1894, for example, USDA entomologist Merton B. Waite proved that for pears "the common honey-bee is the most regular, important and abundant visitor, and probably does more good than any other species."[47]

The dissemination of expert opinion by horticultural scientists such as Waite in respected horticultural magazines, such as *Better Fruit* and *Green's Fruit Grower*, helped to raise awareness about the role of honeybees in pollination. Coupled with advocacy efforts by beekeeping associations, it also reduced the frequency and severity of poisoning incidents. By the turn of the century, beekeepers could feel more confident that their bees could forage in neighbouring orchards without risk of poisoning. Commentators at a Beekeepers' Convention in Chicago in April 1898, for example, praised "the horticultural societies and newspapers" for "[taking] up the subject so thoroughly that almost all who do spray now will spray at the proper time."[48] Ignorant or malicious activities continued, but as the exception rather than the norm.

As orchardists intensified production in the early twentieth century, however, increases in the frequency and quantity of insecticide applications, coupled with the introduction of new compounds (lead arsenate replaced Paris Green by the 1900s, and a host of synthetic insecticides became available in the 1940s), forced beekeepers to engage in what would become cyclical debates about the timing of the spray and the toxicity of ever-new insecticidal compounds to honeybee workers.

Conclusion

In each of these instances—declining forage sources, exposure to disease, and insecticide poisoning—beekeepers learned about environmental risks in surrounding landscapes through the behaviours and bodies of their bees. The concerns they reported, and the evidence they produced, allow me to interpret changes not only in their own ability to thrive as marginal agricultural producers, but also in the behaviour and vitality of the animals they kept. As working animals who formed a nexus between industrializing environments and human producers and consumers, honeybees provide useful indicators of environmental change. Unlike the thousands of native bee species that occupy the North American continent, whose history is largely obscure to us, honeybees were and are animals whose health and numbers were monitored and recorded. Through the surviving records of beekeeper associations, entomologists, and state agricultural agencies, we can document the mounting environmental stresses on these animals, and the resulting economic vulnerability of their keepers.

As Linda Nash has shown for the industrializing landscapes of central California, the bodies of human workers changed environments, and environments, in turn, changed workers' bodies, compromising their health.[49] My sources demonstrate that this was also the case for animal workers. The modernization of agriculture in the Great Lakes region between 1880 and 1940 brought what historians Alan Olmstead and Paul Rhode have described as an inevitable acceleration of pests and diseases as time passed and plantings intensified.[50] Honeybees were not only the unintended targets of responses to insect outbreaks by neighbouring farmers, they also became increasingly subject to disease risks and pests of their own, in the form of mites and other parasites. Changing environmental circumstances, such as reductions in the use of clover as a fallow crop and the loss of lindens and other flowering trees from roadsides and hedgerows, reduced honeybee resilience and made honeybees and their keepers more susceptible to other risk factors and to seasonal variations such as drought, late frost, or heavy rainfall.

The extent to which I can read the experience of honeybees in the records of their keepers relies in large part on the specialized environmental knowledge and sharpened powers of observation common to apiarists. Nineteenth- and early twentieth-century beekeepers provided such useful sources for my study, in other words, because they were themselves attentive to their bees as sources in their own right. In life, and in death, honeybees provided valuable information. In life, the landscapes they navigated and the types of nectar they harvested influenced the taste and quality of the honey they produced, and beekeepers paid attention to these pathways. As much as bees communicated with each other, performing the "waggle dance," for example, to describe the location of forage sources, they also provided information to their keepers through the direction of their flight. Observant beekeepers like John Smith could determine from the flight paths of their bees not only the location of forage sources, but also the origins of insecticide poisonings. In death, the bodies of bees confirmed or refuted suspicions in toxicity studies and served in rare instances as the basis for litigation and compensation claims.[51]

By concentrating on the labour and working conditions of honeybees, I have attempted to get closer to a honeybee's experience of environmental changes in this period. But recent advancements in scientific understanding of honeybee behaviour highlight the limits of this conceit. Studies have shown that female foragers not only communicate their findings to other workers, but also respond to the communication devices of the floral landscapes they forage within. Flowers attract bees with colourful petals, welcoming "landing platforms," and distinctive patterns called "nectar guides" that are often invisible to humans. Sunflowers, primroses, and pansies, for example, produce nectar guides that are only visible in ultra-violet light: unseen by humans but extremely attractive to pollinators.[52] Other flowers signal to bees by refracting light to cast an attractive "blue halo" over their blooms.[53] Just as beekeepers "read" the bodies and behaviours of their bees, bees themselves read flowers as texts to understand their working environments. Scent is another factor: a foraging worker may avoid a particular flower because she can smell the odour of the previous foraging bee.[54] Thus, while honeybee labour is certainly part of the story—fewer foraging sources, for example, mean longer flight distances and reduced longevity for individual workers—history from the honeybee's perspective might best be written in stories of odours familiar and strange, and of diminishing reflections of welcome blue light.

NOTES

1   Thanks to the two anonymous reviewers and Dolly Jørgensen, Sean Kheraj, Claire Campbell, Melanie Kiechle, and Andy Robichaud for their thoughtful comments on earlier versions of this paper. Research for this chapter was made possible with support from Canada's Social Sciences and Humanities Research Council.

2   Jason Hribal, "'Animals Are Part of the Working Class': A Challenge to Labor History," *Labor History* 44, no. 4 (November 2003): 435–53.

3   Joshua Specht joins others in recommending that agency "should always be the start of the analysis, rather than the conclusion of the argument" in "Animal History after Its Triumph: Unexpected Animals, Evolutionary Approaches, and the Animal Lens," *History Compass* 14, no. 7 (2016): 332.

4   Scholars in animal behaviour sciences have made some headway on studies of animal intelligence in recent decades. See, for example, Edward A. Wasserman and Thomas R. Zentall, eds., *Comparative Cognition: Experimental Explorations of Animal Intelligence* (London: Oxford University Press, 2009).

5   Donna J. Haraway, *When Species Meet* (Minneapolis: University of Minnesota Press, 2008), 55; Edmund Russell, "Can Organisms Be Technology?" in *The Illusory Boundary: Environment and Technology in History*, ed. Martin Reuss and Stephen H. Cutcliffe (Charlottesville: University of Virginia Press, 2010), 249–62. As Haraway reasons,

positioning working animals as labourers within a capitalist system is "more than an analogy, but it is not an identity." Working dogs, for example, are "paws, not hands." Following Russell, she argues that "organisms shaped for functional performance in human worlds" might best be understood as "biotechnologies," biological tools "shaped by humans to serve human ends." Honeybees differ from dogs, however, in the extent to which their genetics have been shaped by humans. Unlike dogs and other domestic animals, which have been selectively bred by humans for thousands of years, honeybee breeding was not successfully controlled by humans until the advent of instrumental insemination techniques in the 1940s. Furthermore, selective breeding does not "stick" for honeybees in the same way it does for dogs. Despite the ability to produce gentler, more productive or more resilient stock through controlled breeding of queens, the benefits of breeding quickly dissipate when the daughters of these queens mate freely with "open stock." As Rusty Burlew observed in a 2018 article in the *American Bee Journal*, "within a generation or two, the descendants of these super bees are right back to square one." As a result, honeybee "races" (including Caucasians, Carniolans, and Italians) have much greater genetic variability than other breeds of domestic animals. Rusty Burlew, "Honey Bee Genetics: Why Breeding is So Difficult," *American Bee Journal* (August 2018), https://americanbeejournal.com/honey-bee-genetics-why-breeding-is-so-difficult; John R. Harbo and Thomas E. Rinderer, "Breeding and Genetics of Honey Bees," *Beekeeping in the United States,* Agricultural Handbook No. 335 (US Department of Agriculture: October 1980), 49–57, https://beesource.com/resources/usda/breeding-and-genetics-of-honey-bees/.

6   In both Canada and the United States, honeybee colonies are enumerated as economic units of production, or resources, in agricultural censuses.

7   Clay McShane and Joel A. Tarr, *The Horse in the City: Living Machines in the Nineteenth Century* (Baltimore: Johns Hopkins University Press, 2007). See also Ann Norton Greene, *Horses at Work: Harnessing Power in Industrial America* (Cambridge, MA: Harvard University Press, 2008). For ecologically inflected analyses of risk in human working environments, see Christopher C. Sellers, *Hazards of the Job: From Industrial Disease to Environmental Health Science* (Chapel Hill: University of North Carolina Press, 1997) and Linda Nash, *Inescapable Ecologies: A History of Environment, Disease, and Knowledge* (Berkeley: University of California Press, 2007).

8   See, for example, Timothy J. LeCain's discussion of silkworms in *The Matter of History: How Things Create the Past* (Cambridge, MA: Cambridge University Press, 2017). Virginia Anderson, Ted Steinberg, Catherine McNeur, and Andrew A. Robichaud have explored the ways that free-ranging pigs in rural colonial and later urban environments performed a kind of labour that humans profited from, converting household and urban waste into meat for human consumption. Anderson, *Creatures of Empire: How Domestic Animals Transformed Early America* (New York: Oxford University Press, 2004); Steinberg, *Down to Earth: Nature's Role in American History* (New York: Oxford University Press, 2002); McNeur, *Taming Manhattan: Environmental Battles in the Antebellum City* (Cambridge, MA: Harvard University Press, 2014); Robichaud, *Animal City: The Domestication of America* (Cambridge, MA: Harvard University Press, 2019).

9   Richard White, *The Organic Machine: The Remaking of the Columbia River* (New York: Hill and Wang, 1995). Recent work on the Anthropocene employs White's approach to consider the blend of human labour and capital with non-human fossil

fuel energy sources. See, for example, Andreas Malm, *Fossil Capital: The Rise of Steam Power and the Roots of Global Warming* (London: Verso, 2016); and Jason W. Moore, ed., *Anthropocene or Capitalocene? Nature, History, and the Crisis of Capitalism* (San Francisco: PM Press, 2016).

10 Thomas G. Andrews, *Killing for Coal: America's Deadliest Labor War* (Cambridge, MA: Harvard University Press, 2008), 125.

11 Haraway, *When Species Meet*, 55. Sean Kheraj has described relationships between humans and domestic animals as a form of "asymmetrical symbiosis" in his "Animals and Urban Environments: Managing Domestic Animals in Nineteenth-Century Winnipeg," in *Eco-Cultural Networks and the British Empire: New Views on Environmental History*, ed. James Beattie, Edward Melillo, and Emily O'Gorman (London: Bloomsbury, 2015): 263–88.

12 On Texas longhorn cattle, see Richard White, "Animals and Enterprise," in *The Oxford History of the American West*, ed. Clyde A. Milner II, Carol A. O'Connor, and Martha A. Sandweiss (New York: Oxford University Press, 1994), 237–73; and Joshua Specht, "The Rise, Fall, and Rebirth of the Texas Longhorn: An Evolutionary History," *Environmental History* 21, no. 2 (April 2016): 343–63.

13 For a more detailed discussion of industrializing organisms, see Philip Scranton and Susan R. Schrepfer, eds., *Industrializing Organisms: Introducing Evolutionary History* (New York: Routledge, 2004).

14 The Western honeybee (*Apis mellifera*) is just one of the over 4,000 species of bees in North America. Unlike its wild counterparts, *Apis mellifera* was introduced from Europe, following (and according to some accounts by Indigenous peoples, often preceding) frontiers of European colonization. It is one of only two species of bees (the other, the Indian honeybee, *Apis cerana indica*) that has been domesticated for human agricultural production.

15 Mark Winston, Chapter 10: "The Collection of Food," in *The Biology of the Honey Bee* (Cambridge, MA: Harvard University Press, 1991).

16 Worker lifespans depend on seasonal factors, food availability, and the intensity of work they perform: while highly active summer brood typically live fifteen to thirty-eight days, those born in spring and fall live as long as thirty to sixty days, and those that remain mostly inactive over winter survive as long as 140 days. Winston, *The Biology of the Honey Bee*, 55, 101.

17 T. R. Crow, "*Tilia Americana L.*, American Basswood," in *Silvics of North America*, vol. 2, *Hardwoods*, ed. Russell M. Burns, and Barbara H. Honkala (Washington, DC: United States Forest Service, 1990), https://srs.fs.usda.gov/pubs/misc/ag_654/volume_2/tilia/americana.htm; Frank C. Pellett, *American Honey Plants: Together with Those Which Are of Special Value to the Beekeeper as Sources of Pollen* (Hamilton, IL: American Bee Journal, 1920): 32–33.

18 Allen Pringle, "Apiculture at the World's Fair," *OBA Annual Report* 1893, 29–30; Henry K. Staley, "Forestry and Apiculture," *American Bee Journal* 28, no. 25 (December 1891), 781–82.

19 Gordon F. Townsend and Henry Theo T. Hiemstra, *History of Beekeeping in Ontario* (Milton: Ontario Beekeepers' Association, 2006), iii–iv.

20 Winston, *The Biology of the Honey Bee*, 101.

21 Dhruba Naug, "Nutritional Stress Due to Habitat Loss May Explain Recent Honeybee Colony Collapses," *Biological Conservation* 142, no. 10 (October 2009): 2369–72; Winston, *The Biology of the Honey Bee*, 55.

22 Like Ontario, which saw its dominance in apiculture eclipsed by western provinces from the 1930s on, New York, Ohio, Illinois, and other Great Lakes states saw their production overshadowed by California, Colorado, and other western states by mid-century. Stoll, *The Fruits of Natural Advantage*, 52–54; United States Department of Agriculture, Census of Agriculture 1920, 686–89; Townsend and Hiemstra, "History," 85; M. B. Holmes, "Progress of Beekeeping in Canada," *American Bee Journal* 37, no. 51 (December 1897): 802.

23 Statistics Canada, Table 32-10-0353-01: "Production and value of honey," annual, https://www150.statcan.gc.ca/t1/tbl1/en/tv.action?pid=3210035301, accessed May 1, 2020. Similar declines in colony numbers are apparent in New York State beginning in the mid-1950s (USDA, National Agricultural Statistics Service, "Honey Production and Value, 1939–2007.") See also Dennis van Engelsdorp, and Marina Doris Meixner, "A Historical Review of Managed Honey Bee Populations in Europe and the United States and the Factors That May Affect Them," *Journal of Invertebrate Pathology* 103 (January 2010): S80–95.

24 Ryan Willingham and Jeanette Klopchin, "Robbing Behavior in Honey Bees," *Entomology and Nematology* (August 2018), https://edis.ifas.ufl.edu/in1064; Winston, *The Biology of the Honey Bee*, 115.

25 Tammy Horn, *Bees in America: How the Honey Bee Shaped a Nation* (Lexington, KY: University Press of Kentucky, 2006): 37, 66.

26 Francis L. W. Ratnieks, "American Foulbrood: The Spread and Control of an Important Disease of the Honey Bee," *Bee World* 73, no. 4 (1992): 177–91; Willingham and Klopchin, "Robbing Behaviour."

27 Townsend and Hiemstra, "History," 93.

28 Townsend and Hiemstra, 119–20, 123.

29 Horn, *Bees in America*, 37.

30 M. G. Dadant, "Distribution of American Foul Brood," *American Bee Journal* 66, no. 9 (September 1926): 429; Townsend and Hiemstra, "History," 120–22.

31 Townsend and Hiemstra, "History," 117; Dadant, "Distribution of AFB," 429–31.

32 For comparable developments in plant and livestock disease control, see Lise Wilkinson, *Animals and Disease: An Introduction to the History of Comparative Medicine* (London and New York: Cambridge University Press, 1992); and Alan L. Olmstead and Paul W. Rhode, *Creating Abundance: Biological Innovation and American Agricultural Development* (New York: Cambridge University Press, 2008).

33 Michigan was the first to pass disease control legislation in 1881. Ontario was next with the passage of its *Act for the Suppression of Foulbrood among Bees* in 1889. Other Great Lakes states followed: New York in 1893, Wisconsin in 1897, and Ohio in 1904. By the 1920s, all but a handful of US states had passed legislation to prevent the spread of AFB. See Townsend and Hiemstra, "History," 120; *Recent Laws Against Insects in North America: Together with the Laws Relative to Foul Brood*, US Department of Agriculture,

Division of Entomology, 1898; *The Laws in Force Against Injurious Insects and Foul Brood in the United States*, US Department of Agriculture, Bureau of Entomology, 1906.

34 Dadant, "Distribution of AFB," 430; Townsend and Hiemstra, "History," 126. Sodium sulfathiazole prevents the growth of AFB bacteria but does not destroy the spores that cause its spread. While it gave beekeepers an important tool in AFB control, the development of resistant strains of AFB bacteria ultimately reduced the effectiveness of sulfa drugs and other antibiotics. Today, burning diseased colonies and equipment is still considered the most effective remedy.

35 I examine the relationship between orchardists and beekeepers in greater detail in "Early Insecticide Controversies and Beekeeper Advocacy in the Great Lakes Region," *Environmental History* 26, no.1 (January 2021): 79-101, https://doi.org/10.1093/envhis/emaa059. See also James Whorton, *Before Silent Spring: Pesticides and Public Health in Pre-DDT America* (Princeton, NJ: Princeton University Press, 1974); and George M. Cook, "'Spray, Spray, Spray!' Insecticides and the Making of Applied Entomology in Canada, 1871–1914," *Scientia Canadensis* 22, no. 51 (January 1998): 7–50.

36 Laura K. Fujii, "Oral Dose Toxicity vs. Tissue Residue Levels of Arsenic in the Honey Bee (Apis Mellifera L.)," M.Sc. Thesis, University of Montana, 1980, 10.

37 John Smith, "Ruined by Paris Green," *American Bee Journal* 25, no. 21 (May 1889): 331.

38 *American Bee Journal* 25, no. 21 (May 1889): 331; *American Bee Journal* 27, no. 16 (April 1891): 505.

39 A. J. Cook, "Spraying Fruit-Trees While in Bloom," *Gleanings in Bee Culture* 20 (May 1892): 322–23.

40 Legislative Assembly of Ontario, *An Act for the Further Protection of Bees*, April 8, 1892, reprinted in *OBA Annual Report*, 1891, 29.

41 R. F. Holtermann, "Spraying Fruit-Trees—The Ontario Law," *American Bee Journal* 40, no. 18 (May 1900): 277.

42 S. I. Freeborn, "Spraying Trees: Some Foolish Advice Given by Editors," *American Bee Journal* 26, no. 4 (January 1890): 53–54.

43 Sellers, *Hazards of the Job*.

44 Whorton, *Before Silent Spring*, 27.

45 Holtermann, "Spraying Fruit-Trees," 277.

46 See, for example, Prof. V. H. Lowe's studies at the Geneva Experiment Station in 1899 (referenced in E. R. Root, *The Bee-Keeper and the Fruit-Grower*, 1920 edition, 7).

47 Merton B. Waite, "Pollination of Pear Flowers," Bulletin No. 5, USDA, 1894, cited in A. J. Cook, "Bees and Pollination of Blossoms," delivered to S. CA Pomological Society at Pasadena. *American Bee Journal* 33, no. 22 (May 1894): 694–96.

48 *American Bee Journal* 38, no. 14 (April 1898): 213.

49 Nash, *Inescapable Ecologies*.

50 Olmstead and Rhode, *Creating Abundance*.

51 Bonnell, "Early Insecticide Controversies."

52 Sharla Riddle, "How Bees See and Why it Matters," *Bee Culture*, May 20, 2016, https://www.beeculture.com/bees-see-matters/.

53 Nicola Davis, "Flowers use 'blue halo' optical trick to attract bees, say researchers," *The Guardian*, October 18, 2017, https://www.theguardian.com/science/2017/oct/18/flower-nanostructures-optical-trick-attract-bees-pollinators-blue-halo.

54 ScienceDaily, "Honey Bee Chemoreceptors Found For Smell And Taste," accessed May 1, 2020, https://www.sciencedaily.com/releases/2006/10/061025181706.htm.

Hearing History through Hoofbeats: Exploring Equine Volition and Voice in the Archive[1]

Lindsay Stallones Marshall

When asked about the relationship between the Lakota people and horses, Lakota language teacher Albert White Hat replied, "we don't have any word for 'animal' in our language. Animal as I understand means a second-class citizen that doesn't have a mind.... We call them 'oyate'—nations."[2] Oyate is the same word used to describe human groups within the Oceti Sakowin, such as the Oglala Lakota Oyate. This is not the language of metaphor or poetry. Lakota teaching does not encourage adherents to think of non-human animals as if they are nations; it teaches that they are nations. In stark contrast to the modern Euro-American sharp division between humans and non-human animals, Lakota teaching instead presents more-than-human animals in a relationship of mutual dependency beyond mere material need with humans. Most historical writing about Lakota Nation, however, presents horses the way most Euro-American writing does, as expendable resources without volition of their own.

Animal history too often fails to consider the Indigenous point of view of human-animal relations. In large part, this is because in animal history scholars must wrestle with a foundational question: Is it possible for humans to see the past through the eyes of another species? Reporting the past from the points of view of different humans is fraught enough with potential to misunderstand, misinterpret, and obscure voices from the past without considering the interpretive barriers that an inter-species study presents. If we were to write without considering this question, animal history would be nothing more than a form of speculative fiction rooted more in the historian's imagination than in historical animals' experiences.

However, there is equal danger in assuming that humans cannot investigate animal points of view. This risks what Robin Wall Kimmerer calls another form of anthropomorphism by treating animals as alien beings who can only be understood as a collection of stimuli and responses driven by instinct for physical survival.[3] In fact, the assumption that humans are so fundamentally different than non-human animals that interpreting any thought or emotion from them is mere human projection is itself deeply anthropocentric. More importantly, such a view denies the validity of ways of knowing beyond the modern Euro-American epistemological framework. To say that Albert White Hat's teachings about Horse Nation are simply metaphorical, or to dismiss Indigenous knowledge as unscientific and therefore non-academic, is not simply too narrow a methodology for animal history; it is also an approach deeply rooted in intellectual traditions of white supremacy.

As Sandra Swart notes in her chapter in this volume, archives are constructed by humans and reflect a human story that includes the biases, weaknesses, and prejudices of the humans who constructed them. Conventional historical methods reproduce white supremacist frameworks for studying animal history because white supremacist epistemologies that exclude Indigenous knowledge permeate the archive. Therefore, scholars cannot simply apply conventional historical methods to the study of animal history in the archive, especially as recent developments in ethology help Euro-American science catch up with Indigenous knowledge. Indigenous knowledge does not, of course, need ethologists to confirm its findings; it is, however, useful for addressing skepticism from settler scholars to note the fact that Euro-American knowledge systems that have long dismissed Indigenous knowledge seem to be finding their way to similar conclusions. Most archival sources for animal history were constructed by people who dismissed Indigenous knowledge. In order to ask new questions about old sources, animal historians need a new lens of analysis. Given their near-constant presence in North American history, and therefore their ubiquity in the archive, horses provide an excellent model for developing and testing this lens. By using a multi-disciplinary approach that draws from environmental history, animal behaviour science, Indigenous knowledge, and horsemanship traditions from multiple cultures' histories, historians can use archival documents to recover how horses exerted their volition on historical events.[4]

Using a horse-centred lens raises new questions about settled (and settler) narratives. To push against analytical frameworks that have historically ignored Indigenous knowledge, I chose to prioritize Indigenous knowledge in the construction of a horse-centred lens of analysis, focusing specifically on teachings from two Indigenous nations known especially for their horsemanship: Comanche Nation and the Oceti Sakowin.[5] Centring the horse as a historical actor challenges settler epistemologies that sharply divide human and animal experiences, and expands historical methodologies that prioritize Euro-American archives and interpretations. To demonstrate this horse-centred analysis, I focus on two examples of culturally specific interactions between horses and people in the nineteenth-century US West: a Comanche wild horse capture in the 1840s and the Battle of the Greasy Grass in 1876.

Constructing a Horse-Centred Lens of Inquiry

Scholarship that effectively analyzes the complex narratives surrounding horses and the military, political, social, and economic human systems they inhabited already exists. Both the New Indian History and the New Western History turns inspired scholars of the US West to consider the environmental histories of older narratives. Scholars like Dan Flores, James Sherow, Andrew Isenberg, and Pekka Hämäläinen incorporated horses and their social and ecological impact in writing Indigenous histories. My suggestion is not to discard their body of work, but rather to move beyond the human-centred framework that their work employs, a framework that offers rich analysis of equestrian histories in the US West but that employs Euro-American epistemologies, which can obscure or misrepresent historical horse-human interaction.[6] What is lacking in human-centred analysis is a lens to examine horses' experiences beyond strict Eurocentric categories of experience, to capture a between-the-ears shot of the horse in the archive, especially when the humans recording them were looking elsewhere. This horse-centred analysis is not meant to be an interpretation on its own, but rather a corrective lens for probing settled narratives. When we neglect to take the central role of the horse seriously, historians leave valuable questions unexamined and entire methodologies untapped.

Understanding the role of historical animals through archival documents is an act of recovery that requires scholars to interrogate the points of view of the humans who constructed those documents and those who preserved them. Scholars must contextualize the animal subject in time and space as completely as possible before we can pursue questions about the role of these subjects in historical events. This requires constant evaluation of the processes and ideologies that shaped how humans created and catalogued archival animals. When these human sources assumed horses were incapable of exercising volition, for instance, their archival reproductions of those horses reflected that assumption. The archives therefore assume those logics, take them up, and reproduce them. It is the job of animal historians to question that foundation, and we must challenge conventional historical methodologies to do so.

In order to design a horse-centred lens of analysis, I examined principles from Indigenous knowledge, the European classical equitation tradition, "natural horsemanship," recent developments in animal behaviour science, and my own experiences as an equestrian.[7] Just like human-historical action, horse-historical action is deeply rooted in the specificity of time and place. Analyzing historical sources with horses as the subject requires careful attention to those variations in specificity, and it would be unwise to assume that horses interact with humans in the same way regardless of time and place. However, comparing records across multiple human cultures and times, I have identified two guiding principles that tend to influence horses' interactions with humans: horses are fundamentally relational and they are expert communicators.

As herd animals, horses are fundamentally relational beings; every interaction they have centres on their relation to the other members of the herd. They have long offered that bond to humans. Comanche and Oceti

Sakowin teachings already focus on the relational interaction of all beings, enabling members of those nations to form close relationships with their horses. Sitting Bull descendant Moses Brings Plenty describes his Nokota gelding, a descendant of Sitting Bull's herd, as a brother. Their shared ancestral bond forms a unique, profound relationship.[8] Peter Lengkeek, organizer of the Dakota 38+2 Memorial Ride to address historical trauma experienced by members of Dakota Nation caused by the mass execution of Dakota men after the 1862 Minnesota War, tells the story of when Dakota horses, poised for slaughter by the US military, broke free and rather than escaping ran to their human companions, each horse carrying their own rider to safety before collapsing of exhaustion themselves.[9] The closeness of that relationship and the horsemanship feats it produced often struck Euro-American observers as mystical. But if Euro-Americans thought mysticism was the only explanation for Plains peoples' prowess as equestrians, it was because they had forgotten their own horsemanship traditions.

European and American horse trainers have written extensively about the centrality of relationship. Some of the earliest surviving writing on the subject comes from Xenophon's *The Art of Horsemanship* (fourth-century BCE). Describing the best way to train a horse, Xenophon writes, "See to it that the colt be kind, used to the hand, and fond of men when he is put out to the horse-breaker. . . . [C]olts must not only love men, but even long for them."[10] That ethos is foundational to the European classical tradition, repeated across the centuries in writings by masters like Guériniére, Pluvinel, and Podhajsky. These relationship-focused practices have become especially popular in recent decades, reintroduced in the teachings of Ray Hunt, Bill and Tom Dorrance, and Buck Brannaman. As ethology continues to uncover the mechanics of the horse-human bond, Euro-American science and experience reinforce the long-held belief that horses offer relationship to human companions.[11]

The second guiding principle for analyzing historical horse-human interaction is communication. Humans and horses forge such strong relational bonds in part because horses seek relationship and humans respond, but it is our ability to communicate that allows the relationship to flourish. That communication is intensely physical, especially in the case of horseback riding. Lynne Ferguson, who runs an equine-assisted therapy program rooted in Comanche horsemanship, urges her students to work with minimal tack, removing as many barriers between horse and human body as possible. Doing so, she says, horse and human can learn to communicate so closely that a horse will respond to changes in the rider's breathing patterns.[12] Xenophon would agree, having written that a rider could temper a high-mettled horse by controlling his own body when in contact with the horse.[13] Inter-species communication between humans and horses relies on what equestrians often call "feel," either direct or indirect contact between horse and human in which both beings respond to each other's energy through movement. Explaining feel, Bill Dorrance writes that a horse "will respond to a person's indirect feel, which means that he will either react to or ignore a person's presence—and how a horse responds depends entirely on the person."[14] As Sandra Swart reported from her experience riding in Mongolia, establishing feel with one horse does not necessarily transfer to another. Humans and horses, as individuals, negotiate this communication together through direct and indirect contact. Feel is a profoundly physical and emotional communicative connection made possible by the evolutionary development of the modern horse and meticulous study and practice on the part of the human.

In recent decades, ethological studies have deepened their exploration of the extent of horses' role in engaging in this communication. By examining horses' sensory laterality and signalling to humans in controlled experiments, animal behaviourists and sociologists have analyzed horses' volition in engagement with humans. A 2010 study of equine visual laterality found that horses prioritize human activity above other stimuli, and a 2018 study indicated that the sensory laterality horses displayed suggests their responsiveness to human activity not as stress, but as attention and a desire to respond quickly.[15] Beyond simply waiting for commands, other researchers found that horses prompt humans for assistance and even make judgements about whether a human is able to assist with a problem.[16] In the past few years, studies have highlighted horses' abilities to read and exhibit complex facial expressions, and even to request to be blanketed on a cold day.[17] These studies demonstrate what people who work with horses have long reported: horses are not merely expert communicators; they appear to have a special aptitude for communicating with humans and a desire to do so.

Both Comanche and Oceti Sakowin horse teaching and historical practice emphasize the importance of being in good relation with individual horses and entering their communicative world in order to partner with them. Horsemanship traditions from Europe and North America reflect the same principles, dating as far back as the fourth century BCE, and ethological advances have increased scholarly focus on the horse's ability to intentionally participate in these relationships. Using these principles as analytical guides, centring horses in archival documents raises new questions about horse volition in historical events.

Centring Horses in Comanche Wild Horse Capture

Some of the most foundational documentation about the history of the US West in the nineteenth century comes from Europeans and Euro-Americans, like Balduin Möllhausen and George Catlin. More recent scholarship on horses in the US West moves beyond the romanticized claims of these travel writers, but it does not yet question their fundamental characterization of the horse-human interactions they observed. That has left recent environmental histories of equestrian cultures in the US West grounded not in Indigenous histories, but rather Euro-American impressions of them.[18]

Both Catlin and Möllhausen, impressed as many outsiders were by Comanche equestrian expertise, wrote specifically about Comanches capturing and "taming" wild horses. In 1844, Catlin reported observing Comanches on horseback capture wild horses with ropes, writing "the Indian dismounts from his own horse, and holding to the end of the laso, choaks [sic] the animal down, and afterwards tames and converts him to his own use."[19] Möllhausen's 1858 *Diary of the Mississippi* describes the same practice but elaborates further: "the mustang falls half-suffocated; a leathern thong is quickly passed round his forelegs, and then the lasso round his throat so far relaxed as to avoid quite choking him. The Indian then fastens a rein to the lower jaw of his prisoner, breathes several times into his open nostrils, takes the fetters from his neck and feet, and jumps upon his back."[20] Centring the horse reveals how observers' assumptions about both horses and Comanche people led them to misunderstand what they were observing.

Both Catlin's and Möllhausen's descriptions of the practice made practical sense from the perspective of people who view interaction with animals as primarily an exercise in authority. These accounts do not, however, make sense within the context of Comanche horsemanship. For example, Möllhausen presents a distinctly European description of horse-human interaction defined by dominance when he describes the horse as a prisoner, but in the same sentence reports a practice that refutes that characterization. When horses meet for the first time, they often breathe into each other's nostrils. The Comanche man Möllhausen describes was entering the communicative world of the horse and presenting himself as a companion, not a master. This technique was common and continues in practice today. Comanche educator, poet, and artist Juanita Pahdopony reports that Comanche Tribal Chairman Wallace Coffey used this method to calm a nervous wild horse during a commemoration event in Texas in 1995. Trainer Chris James demonstrated the method to Comanche children at the 2001 Comanche Youth Horse Program.[21]

Catlin's and Möllhausen's misunderstandings begin with relationship. In the mid-nineteenth century Euro-Americans considered domestication to be a necessary foundation for horse-human relationships. However, domestication itself is a concept rooted in Euro-American notions of hierarchy, power, and a division between humans and animals. Making a relationship with a horse contingent upon the ability to control and benefit materially from that horse both prioritizes Euro-American cosmology and denies the horse as a full participant in that relationship. Given wild horses' familiarity with the people who shared their home, Comanches' reliance on wild horses for their livelihoods, and Comanches' superior horsemanship on the hunt and in battle, it is unlikely that choking out a horse could have been the foundational practice of Comanche wild horse catchers.

Horses have long memories, especially when those memories are connected to pain. As far back as the fourth century BCE, Xenophon cautioned against using violent force against a horse, especially a frightened horse, because "when horses are at all hurt at such a time, they think that what they shied at is the cause of the hurt."[22] Trainers across the spectrum of equestrian arts caution against approaching a horse in anger or administering correction with physical violence. In 2018, a team of researchers reported that horses even remember facial expressions they've seen from specific human individuals and responded negatively to humans who exhibited angry facial expressions in the past even if they wore neutral ones at the moment.[23]

The skepticism inspired by a horse-centred examination of Catlin's and Möllhausen's reports also provides support for views expressed in Comanche sources. According to Comanche author Weyodi, elders report that Comanches used ropes to capture wild horses but did not choke horses into submission because that would make it impossible to earn the horses' trust.[24] Clinton Smith, a former Comanche captive, even reported that as he and his brother were taken back to camp upon their capture in 1871, their captors roped a wild horse and tied the captured boys onto it. By the time they returned to camp, the horse had stopped bucking and stayed with the Comanches.[25] While no human of any culture is incapable of animal cruelty, to attack a wild horse in the way Catlin and Möllhausen describe is inconsistent with Comanche horsemanship history. Möllhausen is careful to end his account by saying "wildly and cruelly as the Indian appears to go to work on such occasions, he is extremely cautious not to break the spirit of the mustang in taming him, for in that case the flesh would be all he would get by his dangerous and exhausting labour."[26] Such a statement makes no sense from the horse's point of view. A first impression of pain and violence would make a horse reluctant to connect with humans, and people whose entire culture relied on close relation with horses would certainly understand that.

Reading Catlin and Möllhausen with horse behaviour at the centre strips away the colonial structures that cloud both the authors' and contemporary historians' understandings of historical Comanche horsemanship. Most powerfully, reading against the colonial structures embedded in these narratives suggests that, at some level, horses chose to partner with the Comanche Nation. Catlin's and Möllhausen's observations make sense in the context of a European-influenced horsemanship tradition that was already beginning to give way to an era of mechanization in which horses were primarily valued for the material labour they could produce and, outside the haute école (High School of equestrian arts) and precision of cavalry training, brute force through rough handling and harsh equipment was a means of coercing horses into offering their labour.[27] But centuries of horse experience insist on the horse's volition in relationships with humans.

Centring Horses at the Battle of the Greasy Grass

A horse-centred approach can also probe calcified narratives about historical events whose historiographies are well-trodden ground. In the post–Civil War history of the US West, few incidents have attracted more historical attention from professionals and amateurs than the Battle of the Greasy Grass. A curious footnote to that fateful day, however, indicates an unexplored lens of analysis of the battle and its outcome that has implications for all cavalry-driven military history.

On the day when George Armstrong Custer tried to repeat his genocidal action at the Washita and ordered his famously catastrophic attack on the Lakota, Cheyenne, and Arapahoe summer camps along the Greasy Grass River, a young private in Marcus Reno's command suffered an unusual fate. Reno ordered a charge into the valley that he was forced to abruptly halt as the size of the gathered Indigenous nations became clear. Company M came to a halt except for one horse and rider. The horse carrying Private James Turley refused to halt and carried his rider straight into enemy lines. In an interview with the *Hardin Tribune* in 1923, Company M officer John M. Ryan reported that Turley "could not control his horse which carried him toward the Indian camp."[28] Turley was found in the aftermath of the Seventh Cavalry's defeat, his own knife hilt-deep in his right eye, his horse missing.

For the US press, Custer's shocking demise overshadowed Turley and his horse. Historians, too, have long overlooked his story. Despite intense scouring of the battle's history conducted by veterans, professional historians, and fanatical amateurs, Turley's misfortune is only mentioned a handful of times, most notably as an aside in the letters of veteran Frank L. Anders and Custer researcher R. G. Cartwright. They report the incident inaccurately without even naming the unfortunate private, saying merely in an account of the soldiers lost in Reno's unit "I am not counting the two men who were carried into the Indian camp due to unruly horses."[29] And in the course of the battle, one private losing control of his horse at its fringes is hardly the turn of the tide.

Scholars and battle enthusiasts have long speculated about the role of horses in the Seventh Cavalry's defeat at the Greasy Grass. Jody Hodgins' chapter highlights the value of examining popular animal health manuals to better understand the historical reality of animal histories, and cavalry history is no exception. Veterinarian Elwood Nye posited that Custer's unusual cruelty on the march contributed to poor horse condition, which explained their defeat. Not only does that argument seek to discredit the considerable military prowess of the combined Indigenous forces who resoundingly prevented Custer's attempt at a second genocidal attack, but it flies in the face of clear evidence. As John S. Gray argues in his veterinary history of the battle, Custer's horses, while likely deprived of adequate water and forage on the day of battle, were otherwise well-tended under the care of Dr. Charles A. Stein.[30] Furthermore, other commanders of the US cavalry, such as Alfred Terry and George Crook, were notorious for mistreating cavalry horses yet did not suffer a defeat on the scale of Custer's.

Surprisingly, especially in light of the long history of European cavalry traditions, to which the US cavalry aspired, as well as Steven Kearny's *The Cavalry Manual* (1840), which stipulated gentle treatment of cavalry horses, Gray neglects to examine the possibility that horses could be a determining factor in the battle's outcome. Frederick Benteen's relief force was late to arrive, Gray argues, even after noting that Benteen's tardiness was due to a delay caused by mishandling of the pack train. Horse condition was irrelevant to the battle because Custer's men mostly fought on foot that day, Gray argues, without asking why trained cavalry men would so readily abandon their hungry and thirsty mounts.[31] Turley's experience that day suggests that turning attention to the horses themselves might reveal a more complicated narrative.

Private Turley was a twenty-five-year-old recruit who joined the Seventh Cavalry in October 1872. His entry in the Register of Enlistments records him as a labourer from Troy, New York. Census records from 1860 identify Turley's father as a local tavern keeper in Troy, born in New York, and do not indicate that the children attended school. Like so many members of the cavalry who came from the working class back East, James Turley appears to have been too young for the Civil War draft; after taking on manual labour in the industrializing town, he joined the army to head west after the war. It is unclear whether Turley's work or early life involved horses, but he was assigned to Company M of the Seventh Cavalry.[32]

In addition to the horses' hunger, thirst, and weariness that day, sources indicate other factors that could explain Turley's inability to control his horse. First, many privates in the Seventh Cavalry had little training with horses. In April 1876, Seventh Cavalry Lieutenant John M. Ryan was court-martialled for mistreating a private who cut a harness off a horse rather than properly removing it, indicating that the men in his unit might not all have been experienced horsemen.[33] Second, and to the chagrin of several of the Seventh's officers, Custer reshuffled the mounts in each company right before the column left Fort Abraham Lincoln in May 1876. Custer assigned the same colour horse to each member of the company to allow commanders to clearly see the location of different companies on the battlefield. This practice presupposed that horse and rider pairings were interchangeable. A trained cavalry mount could easily work with a responsive rider but given the reported advantages of a strong relationship between horse and rider, especially when facing the superior horsemanship of the Plains nations, which was based on that relationship, the practice could easily have put Custer's troops at a disadvantage, especially for the greenest privates.

Sources do not record why Turley's horse bolted, whether out of fear, defiance, or even thirst. Company M was the "mixed" company to which leftover horses from the other colour-coordinated units were assigned; even if Turley was riding the horse he had ridden since his recruitment four years earlier, it is possible that the reshuffle caused conflict among the horses that distracted Turley's mount as they were in full charge. Regardless of why the horse bolted, seeking to understand his motivation could illuminate other horse-human interactions on the battlefields of the US West. If cavalrymen believed that coercion was effective communication, historians could analyze battlefield failures in an entirely different interpretive context. If cavalrymen did understand the concept of relation, the slaughter of Indigenous nations' horses at places like Tule Canyon was much more nefarious than simply depriving their enemies of means of resistance and subsistence. These questions can only be answered by leading historical horses from the margins of the narrative into the centres of their texts.

Conclusion

Turley's horse did not turn the tide of battle at the Greasy Grass but acknowledging his volition as a full participant in the battle can dramatically change our understanding of it. Centring horses as relational beings and sophisticated communicators who materially influence historical events rightly reorients methodologies and epistemologies that have long considered the value of their bodies and labour but not their minds, wills, and partnerships. This reorientation also challenges narrative frameworks that characterize horses, and by extension their Indigenous human companions, as interlopers on the land with which they remain in relation. Such an approach pushes against Euro-American historical practices that cast skepticism upon Indigenous histories, as well as scientific knowledge that fails to account for Indigenous knowledge in its theories. Therefore, centring horses and their experiences in historical narratives is a powerful tool for decolonizing historical research.

As it is in so many other areas, Euro-American science is catching up to Indigenous knowledge in its understanding of the horse-human relationship. Historical methodology can follow the same path to develop interpretations of historical events that account for the full participation of horses in relationship with their human partners. A horse-centred analysis is one of many species-specific animal history methods that offer historians greater opportunity to complicate our narratives and weave seemingly disparate pieces of narrative together, a necessary step to understanding the interactions of the past as they happened to the best of our ability. In addition, as J. Keri Cronin reminds us, the animal images we study have real-world consequences for how humans treat animal bodies. Centring horses as historical actors makes us better historians in the archive and better relatives to our horse companions beyond its walls.

NOTES

1. This work exists because of teaching, support, and encouragement from the late Juanita Pahdopony, Kathleen Brosnan, Sandra Swart, and Elizabeth Hameeteman; the generosity of Lynn Schonchin, Jr., Moses Brings Plenty, Lynne Ferguson, and Patrick Allori who shared horse knowledge with me; the generosity of Dianne Stewart, the late Noel Powers, Marie Elgenberg, Susan Patten, and Carrie Hare who shared their teaching and horses with me; my husband Nate who makes both my time in the saddle and writing about it possible; and the many horses who with infinite patience have taught me better ways to be human. I was able to write this chapter because I was employed by a land-grant university on land forcibly taken from Peoria, Kaskaskia, Piankashaw, Wea, Miami, Mascoutin, Odawa, Sauk, Mesquaki, Kickapoo, Potawatomi, Ojibwe, and Chickasaw Nations. My hope is that this work contributes to efforts to disrupt the narratives that perpetuate that dispossession.

2. *We Are a Horse Nation*, directed by Keith Brave Heart (2014; Mission, SD: Sinte Gleska University Media), film.

3. Robin Wall Kimmerer, *Braiding Sweetgrass: Indigenous Wisdom, Scientific Knowledge, and the Teachings of Plants* (Minneapolis: Milkweed Editions, 2013), 57–58.

4. I use the word volition rather than agency to capture the cognitive process implying horses' intent.

5. The seven nations of the Oceti Sakowin should not be conflated as historians have long done under the word "Sioux." However, in recent years, members of Lakota, Dakota, and Nakota Nations have come together to share horse teachings common among them through the documentary *We Are a Horse Nation*, Horse Nation of the Oceti Sakowin exhibit, and the upcoming documentary *Inspired*. I approached their collective teachings as they presented them.

6. Scholarship about Indigenous horse economies developed entirely new ways to think about the interrelated fields of Indigenous, environmental, and military histories in the US West, including works like James Sherow's "Workings of the Geodialectic: High Plains Indians and Their Horses in the Region of the Arkansas River Valley, 1800–1870," *Environmental History Review* 16, no. 2 (Summer 1992), 78–79; and Dan Flores' "Bringing Home All The Pretty Horses: The Horse Trade and the Early American West, 1775–1825," *Montana: The Magazine of Western History* 58, no. 2 (Summer 2008): 3–21, 94–95. However, much of the literature about horse pastoralism in North America relies on data from settler colonial institutions, like the Bureau of Land Management. As ecologist Patrick Duncan reports in *Horses and Grasses: The Nutritional Ecology of Equids and Their Impact on the Carmague* (New York: Springer-Verlag, 1992), most equine nutrition studies rely on data from domestic equids. Indigenous sources that contradict Euro-American reports of horses' failing health or overgrazing are not yet central to this body of literature.

7. The movement came to be collectively referred to by the name "natural horsemanship," though its modern founding practitioners and many current instructors reject the term.

8. Moses Brings Plenty. Image and text posted to Facebook by CANA Foundation, 29 March 2019. Personal interview at Natsu Puuku Tribal Horsemanship Camp, 17 May 2019.

9. *We Are a Horse Nation*, 2014. The Dakota 38+2 Memorial Ride is a healing ceremony held each December in which participants ride over 330 miles from the Lower Brule

Reservation in South Dakota to Mankato, Minnesota to memorialize the forty Dakota men hanged at the end of the Minnesota War (sometimes called the US-Dakota War) in 1862.

10   Xenophon, *The Art of Horsemanship*, trans. by Morris H. Morgan (Mineola, NY: Dover Publications, Inc., 2006), 21.

11   Multiple studies on horse cognition have demonstrated that horses are capable of distinguishing between familiar and unfamiliar humans visually, olfactorily, and auditorily, and that they can do so through cross-modal recognition, allowing them to identify familiar humans through a range of multi-sensory cues even if one sense occurs in isolation from the others. Jessica Frances Lampe and Jeffre Andre, "Cross-modal Recognition of Human Individuals in Domestic Horses (Equus caballus)," *Animal Cognition* 15 (2012): 623–30. These studies support true recognition on behalf of the horses, nullifying any concerns about the Clever Hans effect in which a horse might respond favourably to a human as a means of friendly communication rather than recognition.

12   Lynne Ferguson, personal interview, 16 March 2017.

13   Xenophon, 52.

14   Dorrance, 1.

15   Kate Farmer, Konstanze Krueger, Richard W. Byrne, "Visual Laterality in the Domestic Horse (Equus caballus) Interacting with Humans," *Animal Cognition* 13 (2010): 229–38; Kate Farmer et al., "Sensory laterality in Affiliative Interactions in Domestic Horses and Ponies (Equus caballus)," *Animal Cognition* 21 (2018): 631–37.

16   Monamie Ringhofer and Shinya Yamamoto, "Domestic Horses Send Signals to Humans When They Face with an Unsolveable Task," *Animal Cognition* 20 (2017): 397–405. The study tested horses' signalling to humans in order to find hidden food. Researchers found that horses altered their communication with humans based on whether or not the horse saw where the human hid the food.

17   Leanne Proops et al., "Animals Remember Previous Facial Expressions that Specific Humans have Exhibited," *Current Biology* 28 (2018): 1428–32; Cecilie M. Mejdell et al., "Horses Can Learn to Use Symbols to Communicate Their Preferences," *Applied Animal Behavior Science* 184 (2016): 66–73.

18   For example, studies of the ecological impact of horse pastoralism in Plains environmental history prioritize Euro-American data and often rely on conjecture. In "Workings of the Geodialectic," for instance, James Sherow argues that US Army horses were "better conditioned" than Indigenous horses because they were fed on grain and hay rather than prairie grass and cottonwood. But Sherow's argument is built on the assumption that "if Army horses suffered from the heat, then surely Plains Indian horses endured similar distress." Though he cites Army sources that detail the struggle Army horses had when forced to adapt from grain to grass, it does not follow that Indigenous horses were similarly undernourished simply because they fed on available forage, especially when Indigenous sources report otherwise. See Sherow, "Workings of the Geodialectic," 78–79. Likewise, Pekka Hämäläinen argues that horse "nomadism" (a problematic characterization in itself) caused ecological catastrophe on grasslands ecologies and bases the claim in similarly settler colonial studies. "The Rise and Fall of

Plains Indian Horse Cultures," *The Journal of American History* 90, no. 3 (December 2003), 833–62.

19 George Catlin, *Letters and notes on the manners, customs, and condition of the North American Indians* (London: David Brogue, 1844), 142.

20 Balduin Möllhausen, *Diary of a Journey from the Mississippi to the Coasts of the Pacific* (London: Longman, Brown, Green, Longmans, and Roberts, 1858), 186.

21 Personal interview, 24 February 2017; "Comanche Youth Horse Program," home video recorded by Lynn Ferguson in the summer of 2001. This DVD copy is in the author's possession.

22 Xenophon, 38.

23 Proops et al., 2018.

24 Weyodi Squid, personal email, September 11, 2019. Pahdopony referred me to Weyodi for details about historical practices of horsemanship among Comanche people.

25 Clinton L. Smith and Jefferson D. Smith, *The Boy Captives* (Bandera, TX: Frontier Times, 1927).

26 Möllhausen, 187.

27 Pooley-Ebert's chapter comparing Chicago and rural Illinois workhorses contains a sobering examination of the cruelty and disposability of horses in Chicago. Andria Pooley-Ebert, "Species Agency: A Comparative Study of Horse-Human Relationships in Chicago and Rural Illinois," in *The Historical Animal*, ed. Susan Nance (Syracuse: Syracuse University Press, 2015), 148–65.

28 *Hardin Tribune*, June 22, 1923.

29 Frank L. Anders to R. G. Cartwright, June 13, 1954. John M. Carroll, ed. *The Frank L. Anders and R. G. Cartwright Correspondence: Volume 3* (Bryan, TX: John M. Carroll, 1982), 51. From available sources, it is unclear why Anders suggests this happened to two men instead of one, but he may be referring to Second Lieutenant Benjamin Hubert Hodgson who was killed near Turley in the Valley Fight. Sources indicate Hodgson was killed crossing the ford, but do not mention him losing control of his horse.

30 John S. Davis, "Veterinary Service on Custer's Campaign," *Kansas Historical Quarterly* 43, no. 3 (Autumn 1977): 249–63.

31 Dismounting to fight on foot was a common cavalry strategy during the wars for westward expansion, but the fact that Custer's men killed their mounts in order to use them as cover suggests that this was an act of desperation.

32 "United States Census, 1860," database with images, *FamilySearch* (https://familysearch.org/ark:/61903/1:1:MCW7-FKC : February 18, 2021), James Turley in entry for James Turley, 1860; "United States register of Enlistments of the US Army, 1798–1914," database with images, *FamilySearch* (https://familysearch.org/ark:/61903/1:1:QJDR-3777: 3 March 2021), Henry Turley, 29 October 1872; citing page 17 of volume 76, Troy, New York, United States, NARA microfilm publication M233 (Washington D.C.: National Archives and Records Administration, n.d.), roll 40; FHL microfilm 350, 346. James Henry Turley goes by both names in different records, but testimony from members of Company M confirm it is the same person.

33 John M. Ryan, *Ten Years with Custer: A 7th Cavalryman's Memoir*, ed. Sandy Barnard (Terre Haute, IN: AST Press, 2001).

PART II:

Traces

4

Who is a Greyhound? Reflections on the Non-Human Digital Archive

Susan Nance

Here is a puzzle: As a historian of animals, how can I write historically about the *recent* past of a specific group of non-human animals? In this case, my group consists of dogs caught up in greyhound breeding, racing, and adoption in the United States and Canada since 1990. I seek to document their stories since they are among only a few dogs custom bred for commercial use (as racers) and, when they are no longer profitable, they are asked to transition into private households to serve as companions.[1] Beyond documenting these dogs' lives and labour simply because they lived, which is a political choice grounded in an animal rights advocacy perspective, I seek to tell their stories since greyhounds have been largely unique among dogs in straddling the commercial sporting and consumer petkeeping worlds. (Beagles adopted from scientific research facilities and pit bulls removed from wagered fighting operations are similar but less numerous examples.) As animals purpose-bred to perform at a commercial dog track, where they are group-housed and tended by a series of trainers and kennel staff, then later adopted into private homes, they must adapt to two very different settings. The contrast between the institutional and private settings has become increasingly obvious to the public in the era of "multi-species families." That is, since the late-twentieth century, consumers, veterinarians, and pet product manufacturers have deemed companion animals as beings who should and do shape domestic life since human owners believe dogs' needs are equal, or nearly so, to those of human members of the household.[2] The historical experiences of greyhounds can tell us how an industrially produced animal came to shape human life in a non-monetized role in that larger context.

The difficulty in finding primary sources that document the lives of dogs in the recent past is two pronged. Firstly, dog racing is a topic essentially ignored by the kinds of archives that one might suspect would document it. For instance, the National Sporting Library, focused on elite horse racing, and the Library of Congress, with its vast international mandate, so far exclude this topic. Even in states that have hosted dog tracks or dog breeding farms, institutions like the Kansas State Archives or the Florida Historical Society have very little: a promotional postcard or two online, or a few holdings of state committee proceedings and legislation related to parimutuel wagering, or perhaps in a folder in their vertical files some old newspaper clippings or a few odd brochures from a long-defunct local dog track. Such materials remain, not to document dogs or people who built the sport, but as a record of state regulatory activity and efforts to promote that economic sector. Certainly, it is a truism in the work of animal history that people design, fund, and build public archives to create a record of human agency, telling the story of material donors or the entity funding the archive. Government records of wagering legislation or dog track promotional items are in typical form—where in those documents will we learn what it was like to be one of the dogs who made that industry possible but was later asked to adapt to a private household?

Secondly, the materials that do exist may be difficult or impossible to access since they are held by private individuals or groups, such as the National Greyhound Hall of Fame in Abilene, Kansas. That section of the Great Plains has been the geographical heart of greyhound breeding and racing in the US for a century. I have visited the materials in the basement storeroom at the Hall of Fame four times to find a collection, as Harriet Ritvo puts it, "not necessarily in a setting that is recognizably archival."[3] Each time I was aided by the helpful and knowledgeable staff there whose memories house all the institutional knowledge needed to interpret their holdings—who donated which item, what dogs they owned, where their farm was. Yet the Hall of Fame may be an endangered industry institution and its collections have an uncertain future. The community of dog breeders, trainers, track operators, and racing fans that the Hall of Fame has served since the early 1960s is dwindling (along with the facility's sources of funding) as the industry contracts, with tracks continuing to shut down, state by state. Equally, pro-racing advocates can be suspicious of outsiders. Only at their convenience do I visit their filing cabinets of photos and racetrack programs, shelves sagging under the weight of old studbooks, back issues of *Greyhound Racing Record*, and dozens of dust-coated trophies donated by industry families over the decades. Moreover, although their storeroom holds many important sources for the period before large-scale ex-racer adoption began in 1990, critical documentation from more recent decades is sequestered in the private files of the racing greyhound registry organization, the National Greyhound Association, at their offices on the other side of that Kansas town.

Thus, perhaps I need to build my own archive? Research by Lynda Birke on lab rodents actually helps us understand this archival conundrum and its importance to historians of animals. In dog racing's institutional settings at greyhound breeding farms and dog tracks, like in laboratories with rats and mice, people work to turn greyhounds into data, namely race finish statistics and stud tables, and if possible producers of puppies to feed the system.[4] It is no accident that the industry website charting race results and lineages resides at www.greyhound-data.com. People involved with the industry take greyhound lineages as records of the work of their human engineers. No less than the horses Sandra Swart and Lindsay Stallones Marshall discuss in this volume, these dogs' very bodies are archives of that human labour, an analysis of which would require deep study of graphic records of how dogs looked and moved in league with the studbooks and industry accounts of the human work of matching sires with dams, different tools than I employ here. At the same time, I see those greyhound bodies as evidence, not simply of countless hours of labour and ingenuity by breeders and trainers, but also as evidence of decades of short-sightedness in mass breeding dogs for a gaming industry chronically operating in the red, with no intention of breeding them for their own genetic health and, until comparatively recently, no plan for allowing them to grow old.[5] Yet, unlike what Birke terms the "many millions of rats and mice . . . used annually in the service of science, [of whom] we know remarkably little about their characteristics as species," we actually know quite a lot about the behaviour and needs of greyhounds from various scientific discourses and, not least, the thousands of self-reporting greyhound trainers, adoption groups (pro- and anti-racing), veterinarians, and adopters who work and live with dogs from the industry.[6]

What was it like to be a dog raised in the greyhound breeding and racing business, then released at age two or five or eight years into life as a household companion? What might the history of those greyhound lives and transitions tell us about the decline of dog racing in the United States or about the history and development of animal advocacy movements in the digital age? These are some of the questions we must hurry to investigate before the seemingly limitless sources that might elucidate them disappear. This is a paradox of what Ian Milligan has called "the age of information abundance." It is, he says, a "revolutionary shift we are witnessing as historians," wherein traces of people's lives that throughout human history before the 1990s were seldom or never recorded are now a flood of "born-digital text . . . [a] constellation of text that we can now preserve, alongside increasing numbers of images, videos, sounds, and beyond."[7]

Digital sources can supply a counterpoint or confirmation to the kinds of reporting codified in industry-defences of dog management or proscriptive books of adoption advice by both pro-racing and anti-racing veterinarians and adoption advocates. They also provide a diversity of graphic and video evidence of dogs and their behaviours, plus countless detailed, first-hand accounts of these dogs in different settings—crowdsourced on the Web and social media sites—the likes of which are simply not to be found in documents created before the digital age. (It is overwhelming to me to even imagine having such detailed sources focused on animal behaviour and bodies from the nineteenth century or earlier periods!) To those ready to point out the problems and questions with these ephemeral sources, those who question the motives of the people who initiated them, or those who say that we should halt the analysis because there is too much risk of misunderstanding historical animals and their people, or that we will be tempted to impose subjective attitudes on historical animals who are ultimately unknowable, I ask: What is the risk if we do not try? These seemingly trivial or subjective sources abound in the digital age: for these greyhounds, they may be the only sources documenting their lives.

Digital Primary Sources and Dogs

To find evidence of greyhound lives and transitions, since 2007, I have been building an archive of materials, gathered from Google alerts and news, Facebook pages, email lists, industry and advocacy blogs and websites, as well as personal correspondence with greyhound people. It has required that at times I become an anthropologist or quasi-participant in order to be in the room, so to speak. One must be immersed in such digital sources for a long time in order to wade through such information and decide how to use it, understand why people are posting it, and know who else probably saw it.

One might employ scripts and bots to scrape large amounts of data from websites and other digital places as quantitative historians do to learn things that numerical or statistical data can show. In a manner similar to Sean Kheraj's analysis of the movement of the 1871 equine epizootic, I can imagine using the records of races and online studbooks before and after the advent of adoption programs for ex-racing greyhounds to chart the rise and fall of numbers of dogs registered by the NGA (National Greyhound Association) and map out the circulation of dogs on the continent as a commercial population.[8] Yet, in such an approach, the individual stories of dogs and people would be obscured, or one might inadvertently collect information that would be unethical to employ because its original authors created it with an expectation of limited or complete privacy.[9] Instead, I have captured hundreds of examples manually, one at a time, downloading PDFs and MP4 files, or cutting out screenshots with Apple's Preview software to create PNG and JPG files of webpages. By not employing software to harvest massive amounts of data, I can collect and cite only sources that are ethical to show and analyze. These items are "surrogates" for the originals and capture what users saw at a precise moment in time, such as social media posts or news items with comments sections that change over time.[10] I intend for these screenshots, PDFs, and other items to ultimately reside in an online archive so that users can interact with them in ways similar to paper-based collections. Historians often rely on original collectors and donors of materials to assemble related items together and in doing so make clear how individual items help explain other items in the same collection, forming a network of evidence and information.

In a way, as a collector of digital ephemera, my work is like that of the old scrapbook keepers of the nineteenth and twentieth centuries, who put newspaper clippings, photos, keepsakes, and souvenirs into inexpensive paper scrapbooks, which were organized according to their own interests and logic. Likewise, the trade-off is that readers and fellow scholars must trust my judgement in presenting typical sources and case studies that illustrate broader patterns that I have seen in the sources (and not "cherry picking" evidence) simply because I have been immersed in them for over a decade. "Sources don't speak for themselves," Trevor Owens and Thomas Padilla remind us in exploring how digital sources require an understanding of historical technological context—who created them, how, why, and in what ways algorithms, screen resolutions, and other hardware and software issues shaped what people could create and how it was displayed or stored.[11] As they note, the fragility of digital sources comes not simply from the complacency that their current abundance may inspire in us, or from neglect or forgetfulness as sites go untended over time, passwords are forgotten, digital hosting companies go out of business. The fragility is also a political fragility. Some things are taken down or deleted later because they are deemed no longer appropriate or relevant, or they are perceived to be detrimental to an industry that imagines itself under attack by outsiders who will misconstrue any bit of bad news, no matter how factual. Likewise, online content may be censored in a way if it is protected by passwords or other barriers that limit who can see what posts and that give for-profit companies the final say over access and retention of materials.[12]

At the same time, in contrast to the interviews collected by oral historians, these digital sources allow us to listen in without disturbing the conversation and to see people candidly discussing what is important to them, or posturing for one another, such as it may be. This is not to say that we discover "the truth" (no historian takes any primary source that way). However, today the American dog track industry is collapsing due to broad public distaste for the sport and decades of declining revenues, with only two tracks expected to be in operation for the 2023 season from a network that at its peak featured over fifty tracks nationwide. Industry insiders feel utterly under siege, many believing that false information spread by critics destroyed the industry, not competition from casinos and other economic factors. Many informants are thus wary of divulging information to strangers. In some cases, as Jason Colby shows elsewhere in this volume, oral history and animal history are incompatible if informants in controversial fields of animal use worry the researcher may not write about them in anything but the most glowing and selective ways.[13] There are some ethical issues to consider when seeking access to sources, material or oral, if they are not housed in a conventional, non-partisan archive where one can ask for things and not be questioned about why or what one's main argument will ultimately be.

Born-digital sources and their surrogates offer problems but also crucial opportunities. These powerful but fragile digital sources tell us about greyhounds, their behaviour, and their lives in ways that proscriptive literature, pro- or anti-industry sources, and journalism about the industry conceal or ignore when generalizing about NGA greyhounds. They tell us about day-to-day living and realities, about people's actual experience and practice with greyhounds rather than just their intentions, and behaviour and experience among dogs who made the transition into a multi-species family and shaped the nature of those relationships.

Greyhounds and Dog Tracks: Historical Context from Traditional Sources, Mostly

Sighthounds looking and behaving similarly to NGA greyhounds have existed for millennia. Greyhounds are among a whole range of lithe dogs with elongated muzzles, a group that includes the Saluki, Whippet, Borzoi, Scottish Deerhound, Italian greyhound (the toy breed), Galgo Español, and others with varying coats but always the distinctive deep chest, flaring thighs, powerful shoulders, long neck, flexible spine, and superior eyesight. For centuries, men employed these dogs in competitive coursing trials in which rabbits or other game were set loose in a field with two or more dogs while men wagered which dog would catch the creature. In North America, initially dogmen and bettors gathered in informal colonial-era competitions that congealed into organized coursing clubs during the nineteenth century.[14]

By 1906, breeders formed the NGA (known as the National Coursing Association until 1973) to register dogs and keep studbooks.[15] In the 1920s, greyhound history intersected with the histories of wagering and mass consumption in Oklahoma to produce the first commercial dog track employing a mechanical lure, a furry dummy whisked around the track surface on an electrified track. The lure was a humane innovation that meant no rabbits would be killed before spectators during races, although training young racers on remote properties with live lures persisted. That format soon spread across the US, and later to Britain, Ireland, Australia, Macau, and New Zealand.[16] Early dog tracks were controversial for various reasons related to the morality and regulation of gambling and the industry's ties to organized crime. At the time, there was little public concern about the mental and physical well-being of racing greyhounds. Gradually, a nationwide track network proliferated and, especially in mid-twentieth-century Florida, the working and middle classes flocked to dog tracks to gamble, drink, see and be seen in an entertainment context many took to be glamorous and exciting.[17]

As the tracks spread and an electronic national market for betting on dogs through simulcasting developed, a speculative market for greyhounds that had simmered along for over a century began to boom. Investors and breeders sought out winning dogs by systematic breeding programs, wherein industry insiders bred, employed, and destroyed greyhounds (generally by the age of five, at the most) in an industrial-agriculture-style system where each dog was first and foremost an investment that needed to pay for itself.[18] Unlike pet breeds mass produced for the consumer market, people bred greyhounds primarily for performance, not appearance. Still they were vulnerable to practices that left too many dogs with nowhere to go when they could no longer race. If they were adopted, they faced life potentially coping with ailments caused by old injuries, neglect, or genetic manipulation that resulted in dental problems, arthritis, toe corns, and a great likelihood of developing bone cancer.

After the glamour of the 1950s and 1960s faded, revenue and patronage at dog tracks began to decline, which correlated with the industry's inability to get a lucrative contract for television broadcasts just as customers began turning to other forms of sports betting, state lotteries, and casinos packed with slot machines. The industry responded with uncoordinated lobbying for the opening of new tracks to create the appearance of growth. The rush to fill the kennels at those new tracks drove a speculative mass breeding of greyhounds, some of them churned out at Florida or Kansas "mega-farms," holding many hundreds of dogs each. Soon there was a flood of unproven dogs. Only about thirty per cent made it to the track, with some spending only a short time there before being graded out and killed at the age of one to five.[19]

Before the 1990s, there was no greyhound adoption community to speak of, and already-burdened city dog shelters and humane societies would have been unable to take in the thousands of ex-racers, even if industry people had sought their help. Each year, kennel operators killed or sold many tens of thousands of NGA dogs that were too slow or injured to earn their keep. Some dogs went to class B dog brokers, whose business it was to collect and sell dogs for scientific experimentation.[20] The level of routinized destruction of racers by greyhound breeders and trainers drew criticism, not least from some ambivalent family members. In Australia, where similar practices and tracks proliferated, the step-daughter of one greyhound breeder recalled,

> As a young child I was told to keep my mouth shut when I asked where some of my stepfather's greyhounds had gone. . . . He had taken them out to the bush and shot them in the head. It was awful enough to see them locked in a tiny cage all day every day, only walked twice a day and taken out when it was time for a run . . . but to learn that they had been shot in the head, well, I didn't understand. These dogs were the most placid, friendly dogs . . . killed to focus money on a faster runner.[21]

To those who supported the status quo in the industry, cultivating breed and racing community cohesion was more important than any individual dog's life or experience. For, although members did compete with one another to produce winning dogs or to book lucrative contracts at top tracks, in other ways they were united as a community connected by the work of breeding and monetizing elite dogs. NGA greyhounds were a vehicle for membership in that close-knit community.[22] However, by the early 1990s, the escalating scale of breeding and killing clashed with a growing pet culture that challenged the commodification of pet stock and extended consideration to greyhounds as dogs like any other—that is, as potential family members with intrinsic value.

Two decades of damaging media coverage followed documenting the fate of the overwhelming majority of greyhounds in the industry who were killed because they were unprofitable, which in the US was estimated at between 30,000 and 50,000 per year in the 1970s–1990s. Greyhound adoption and anti-racing groups proliferated and, in league with investigative journalists, publicized a number of horrifically graphic but not uncommon cases of greyhounds killed by gunshots discovered in piles and pits in remote properties in Arizona, Florida, Alabama, and New Hampshire. There, some kennel operators had employed the least expensive and low-profile means of disposing of healthy NGA greyhounds, although some veterinarians did euthanize dogs at the track.[23] The most assertive anti-racing groups demanded outright abolition and confronted the public with slogans like "They die? You bet. They die" to additionally implicate gamblers in the "wastage" within the industry.[24]

Regulated at the state level with only a patchwork of unevenly enforced regulations, the industry as a whole displayed resentment toward public oversight, even though dog tracks had long been subsidized by state-funded racing commissions and generous tax breaks.[25] For instance, there was long-term resistance to the issuing of public injury and death reports for dogs at any given track. During races, dogs may sprain or break their legs or, if they fall while running at top speed, their necks and backs. Greyhounds at breeding farms also fell under an agricultural exemption for livestock such that anti-cruelty statutes for dogs did not (and still do not) apply to greyhounds—unless they are in an adoptive home. Still, beginning in about 1979, some of the earliest adoption efforts came from within the industry. Dozens of volunteers founded adoption organizations and fundraising schemes to pay the expense of collecting "retired racers" from tracks and farms, housing them until they could be adopted by members of the public.[26]

The industry continued its slow decline in the 1990s and 2000s nonetheless. The rise of competing entertainment, especially online gaming and Native American-run casinos, offered bettors slot machines or other electronic games that provided instant gratification without the delays between races that were common at the track. Well-maintained, glittering casinos only made the now sparsely attended and often rundown local dog track appear more incongruous and depressing as greyhounds raced before rows of empty bleachers in venues devoid of spectators.[27]

This is the contentious recent history that many people have in mind when they disagree about whether the fate of the greyhound is tied to, on the one hand, commercial dog tracks, the National Greyhound Association, and the rural breeders and dog traders who supply them, or, on the other hand, the pet keeping community that seeks to maintain greyhounds as a breed outside the gaming industry.

Discovering Greyhounds in Small Spaces, Using Digital Sources

Over the last thirty years, greyhounds have struggled to overcome assumptions about how breed membership, lineage, and early life experience shaped them and their needs, and thus who had the authority to speak for them, provide them an opportunity to express their inborn desires, and be "happy." Indeed, as much as animal welfare, human identities were at stake when this group of animals transitioned to the role of pet in the care of an "adopter," who in turn existed within a larger social community of like-minded people who believed dogs should live at leisure. Following Birke, Hockenhull, and Creighton's research on the ways horse people define themselves by reference to the horses for whom they care,[28] in private adoptive homes, no less than at the dog track or puppy farm, people imagine these greyhounds as "abstractions" representing their work with the dogs. In the industry context, the labour consists of turning greyhounds into data and vehicles for community cohesion; in private adoptive homes, the work consists of rehabilitating formerly institutionalized greyhounds to adapt to life outside the track or farm, while incorporating the dogs into family structures and routines in ways that often flatter human adopters as "rescuers."[29]

What was it like to be one of the dogs who lived first in institutional settings then in a consumer household, transitioning from group-housed investment to family member and from expression of a breed registry to individual? Here, digital sources are crucial since members of the industry and the adoption community talked constantly about these issues online in often-contentious debates and discussions undergirded by support from or opposition to the industry. The history that follows is drawn from printed and online proscriptive literature from adoption groups and veterinarians, pro-industry narratives about greyhounds on YouTube and public blogs, as well as the well-known online public discussion board GreyTalk.com. In all cases, I chose these sources for their explicit discussion of the typical settings, events, and talk about greyhounds' transition from track to home, most of which discussions are still viewable online.

Most NGA greyhounds were born on rural farms dedicated to breeding dogs for the race track. Bitches were impregnated using straws of semen purchased from other owners. Brood bitches and puppies spent their first days together in a whelping box—often a kiddie pool—that offered a clean, enclosed space that prevented puppies from wiggling away. The vast majority of pet-bred dogs in those years (and still today) were taken from their mothers as early as seven weeks, while still nursing and physiologically and emotionally vulnerable. By contrast, greyhound pups routinely spent many months with their mother, then moved to group housing with other young hounds, often their siblings. Indeed, until adoption, these dogs spent their whole lives surrounded by other greyhounds, learning to be articulate in canine communication skills and etiquette.

At breeding farms, adult dogs were housed in long, rectangular fenced runs that included a shelter or house, an outdoor space, and (at more highly capitalized operations) mowed grass, which is more sanitary than sand or dirt. There, dogs could sprint, play, and relieve themselves far away from their bedding of hay or shredded paper. Young greyhounds were taught to chase a mechanical lure on a sandy track in an enclosed training pen through various techniques that drew on an inborn prey drive and the ability to run at high speed.[30] Those who were too slow were either shot and disposed of in a pit on site or euthanized by a local veterinarian.[31] At about eighteen months of age, those who survived were either leased or sold to a kennel operator with a contract to a particular track venue. They travelled in a dog hauler, a vehicle outfitted with small compartments that prevent jostling, to a commercial track. There they usually raced twice per week, earning points and corresponding money for their owners, who shared the earnings with track kennel operators and any partner investors.

At the track venue, housing was substantially different from the farm. A 1990s-era video commissioned by Gulf Greyhound Park in La Marque, Texas, euphemistically explained, "there's a more businesslike manner expected" from young racers.[32] That is, greyhounds' freedom of movement was restricted and routinized almost entirely in the service of race performance and the staffing levels of a given kennel. At any track, there were multiple cinder-block kennel buildings, collectively housing hundreds of dogs. From the relatively spacious dog run of the farm, greyhounds moved into 31 × 32 × 42–inch or 35 × 36 × 49–inch (depending upon the dog and kennel) stacked metal crates, lined with shredded paper or a removable rectangle of wall-to-wall carpet.[33] In these spaces, greyhounds spent up to twenty-two hours per day. Critics argued that the largest dogs were unable to fully stand up in these enclosures and that, if they were suffering diarrhea or other troubles, it was common for dogs to sit in their crates in contact with their mess for hours at a time.[34]

To many in the industry, there was no other safe way for one or two people to manage fifty or more dogs than by compartmentalizing them in such efficiently arranged containers. Yet, one noted advocate for the industry, Dennis McKeon, explained this practice, not as one of human convenience or financial efficiency, but as one that catered to greyhounds rather than their human managers,

> All canines are "denners." This means that left to their own devices, they will seek out places to sleep and rest that provide close cover and protection, not only from the elements, but from their enemies. . . . Each pack member in the racing kennel has his/her own "den," which we (and those companies who sell them commercially) refer to as crates, and anti-racing propagandists prefer to call "cages," for maximum negative connotation.[35]

The idea of a dog crate or hauler slot as a "den" is an old one but leaves out one critical element: wild canines may choose when to enter a den and how long to remain there. Greyhounds were locked inside their crates until a person released them, so their movement was limited by trainers' needs or abilities to cope with kennel workload. Still, the idea of the crate as den showed how supporters of racing defined greyhounds' needs in ways that normalized industry practices.

Beyond the crate, dogs spent a minority of their time in a turn-out pen (while wearing a basket muzzle to prevent injuries from nips and bites), in a long, rectangular training run, or in the jinny pit. This last space is a marshalling area where dogs are dressed in racing silks (numbered jackets), weighed, examined by the track veterinarian, have urine collected for drug testing, and stored in crates near the starting box for up to five hours before race time in order to restrict access by people who might seek to drug the dogs to enhance or impair their performance. Dogs occasionally tested positive for cocaine and other substances designed to enhance or bog down a dog's performance, nonetheless. Overall, this kind of captivity may have been comparable to many animal shelters, such as those at university or private research institutions that housed dogs for experimental purposes, but it was far better than many commercial breeding facilities ("puppy mills").

One classic breeder's account said of the greyhound, "He has been bred for one purpose, and one purpose only—speed, sheer speed."[36] Indeed this has been true, in large part. And yet somehow the range of mental skills and temperament traits selectively bred over the centuries in order to produce dogs who were (most of them) not only capable of high speed but also eager to use that speed to chase and catch game additionally produced a gentle, emotionally expressive, quiet, patient, and resilient breed. Generalizing somewhat, the breed has long been made up of, as the truism goes, "forty mile an hour couch potatoes," who demanded only limited exercise and bonded mightily with human housemates. This has been the janus-faced nature of the breed—speed machine and sensitive companion. It confused debates over greyhound confinement since many people who believed they understood these dogs perhaps knew or chose to emphasize one element or another of their natures as inborn and normative.

As grassroots volunteer adoption groups appeared all around the US and Canada in the 1990s, soon the balance of ex-racers were being adopted out. By 2002, the industry claimed that up to ninety per cent of the 22,000 dogs then in the track system would end their days as house-pets.[37] Many adoption groups were either staffed with volunteers, who were also investors (who owned racing dogs) and pro-racing adopters, or groups that maintained friendly relations with track kennel operators and investors by refraining from publicly supporting or condemning the industry so as to protect their access to dogs. Plenty of investors, kennel operators, and farm operators made it known that they would boycott anti-racing adoption groups, thus those groups tended to link up with neutral adoption groups and humane societies who quietly passed dogs along to anti-racing groups for homing.[38]

As greyhounds began proliferating around the continent as household companions, adoption organizations and adopters reported that dogs coming out of the tracks exhibited many psychological and physical conditions that outsiders found unacceptable. Many adopters critical of the industry took them as evidence of neglect or abuse. Advice for new owners of retired NGA racers included information about how to recognize and manage dogs who displayed strange behaviours. "At first your new greyhound may stare ahead and seem unresponsive. This is typical greyhound stress behaviour. Remember it is undergoing stress adjusting to its new environment. Quiet and calm is the way to go," advised one group in Massachusetts.[39] Other colloquial advice warned that some dogs might arrive underweight, with teeth that "look dreadful," perhaps ground down from chewing crate bars due to frustration or boredom. They might also display scars on their skin and coat, or so-called baboon butt baldness on the thighs.[40]

On Facebook and various pro-industry blogs, former dog trainer Dennis McKeon addressed adopters regarding a greyhound's transition to household living, arguing that those outside the industry might not know greyhounds as well as they think:

> There are many challenges ahead for both the Greyhound and his new adoptive owners. Your Greyhound is about to embark on a voyage to an entirely new and alien universe. He has left behind his littermates and pack members, some of whom he has been with since birth. . . . He has bid fond farewell to his human familiars and caretakers, their voices and their touch, to the regimented, predictable routines and the security of his racing environs, and he is now faced with novelty at every turn. The Greyhound

> no longer has the outlet of training and racing—"hunting" with the pack, to expend his excess energies, and to express himself in the fashion that forged his very being. . . . Greyhounds thrive on punctuality and routine. They prefer the known to the unknown. Novelty can be their undoing. Novelty is what they face with beginning their lives as house pets.[41]

For industry insiders like McKeon, adoption was a worry in some ways since greyhound investors gave away their dogs when they stopped racing knowing that not every adoptive owner would understand his or her greyhound's past experience, and that—as with trainers and kennel operators—some adopters would be lazy or selfish caregivers to their dogs. So, by their interpretation, track captivity was normative, household life potentially lonely and traumatizing.

Ex-racers' uncertainty in new environments and their ostensible love of routine may be produced in part by breeding dogs who thrive in the quasi-industrial system of production, training, and racing. Equally, it may be a sign of captive animals who have adapted to a stressful or boring situation by focusing on routine as a way to cope, but emerging from the experience always more reticent than dogs with more diverse life experiences.[42] Or perhaps it was a combination of the two: breeding and management that made the NGA greyhound novelty-averse, at least when they first left the track or farm? Thinking again of Birke, Hockenhull, and Creighton's research, indicating that people often create a particular animal and life story for themselves that flatters their self-image, it is no doubt the case that kennel operators limited greyhounds' experiences, forcing them into carefully timed routines that created the ostensible reticence of racing greyhound as much as catering to it.[43] That is, the track kennel context produced the very novelty-averse NGA greyhounds that industry people argued were bred to be crated and confined the majority of the time so they would not be upset by "the unknown."

Turning now to the question of a greyhound's life after the track, digital sources can supply a counterpoint or confirmation to the kinds of reporting codified in industry-defences of dog management or proscriptive books of adoption advice by veterinarians and adoption advocates. First, as an example, take the non-profit Detroit group Michigan

Retired Greyhounds as Pets (MI ReGAP), one of a number of state-based "ReGAP" groups in the nation. For the twenty years they were active in adoption, the non-profit group employed a system for retraining and finding permanent homes—"forever homes," as the adoption groups phrase it—for greyhounds and claimed that 1,800 dogs passed through their hands.[44] Many of their greyhounds came from Mobile Greyhound Park in Theodore, Alabama, although others made their way to the group from farms and tracks in Florida, West Virginia, and occasionally elsewhere.

For ReGAP greyhounds, exiting track captivity and entering household captivity began with a trip to a local veterinarian for "vetting" as the colloquialism goes, then a van haul north where ReGAP volunteers would meet at a half-way point. Arriving in Detroit thereafter, the first stop was the Dapper Dog Wash, where a crew of volunteers washed the greyhounds and took initial photographs for the ReGAP adoption website.[45] ReGAP owned no kennel and philosophically supported housing dogs in a foster home where they would most quickly adjust to non-institutional housing. Not all groups agree about how to house ex-racers. By contrast, the non-profit Greyhound Pets, Inc. adoption group in Woodinville, Washington, for instance, house their greyhounds at a recently-constructed kennel, which relieves the group of finding foster homes but requires owning and running the facility. At the facility, dogs live in indoor runs of approximately fifty square feet.[46] An anonymous source said to me of this method, "Yeah, it's a nice kennel, but it is still *a kennel*," meaning that, although leash trained and socialized extensively, the dogs kept there are delayed in learning the life skills necessary for house dog living.[47]

Once in a foster home, members of a given household observed new ReGAP dogs and reported to volunteers on their progress. It is true that, just off the track, NGA greyhounds still need to learn life skills that most dogs absorb as young puppies, including house training, how to travel up and down staircases, not to attempt to walk through windows or wall mirrors, not to eat off the table or kitchen counters (known as "counter surfing"), for some, how to answer to a name or interact with cats, small dogs or children, and finally, how to respond to the word "no." Some proved frightened of new things: a woman walking in high heels, the sight of rolling suitcases or kids on skateboards, the sound of holiday fireworks, or a flight of stairs. Most greyhounds learned all these things quickly, proving themselves adaptable within the confines of a household. With their deep rib cages and bony bodies, ex-racers became especially famous for their ability to find a soft spot to lie down, especially beds and couches. Nonetheless, ReGAP recommended crating greyhounds in the house when they could not be immediately supervised, demanding that foster homes promise to honour their "responsibilities," including: "To use a crate of recommended size whenever the dog is unattended. This includes while at work, etc. The crate must be placed in a main room in the house NOT in an isolated area. The crate must be used throughout the foster period unless specific authority is obtained from the foster coordinator. If you do not have a crate, MI REGAP will provide one free of charge."[48]

Meanwhile, many adopters reported abandoning crating as soon as feasible. Some said they opposed "cages" or found them unsightly or inconvenient to have in the house. Others discovered that, for a breed of supposed "denners," as industry advocates would have it, many greyhounds resisted crating by injuring themselves, defecating or urinating, or vocalizing while inside.[49] Here, seemingly ephemeral or trivial digital sources provide detail that conventional textual sources cannot. "Help! New Greyhound Pooped All Over His Crate When We Left Him," said the subject line on a 2012 post by a new adopter, fluteplayer67, on the discussion site GreyTalk.com. This site and its parallel Facebook page have for about twenty years been a place where those living with greyhounds could discuss their behaviour as they transitioned from institutional living to household living. The post continued:

> We are brand new owners of the sweetest two-year-old greyhound. We read several books, etc., but lavished him with attention when he arrived. He stayed in the crate while we went to church last Sunday with no problem. That night I left him in our bedroom alone for about 15 minutes while I was getting my son to bed. He pooped on the bedroom floor while I was away. Then he kept rearing up when I tried to crate him during the week. I am a stay at home mom so I am around a lot. When we crated him to go the grocery store a few days later he had diarrhea all over the crate and himself and had some blood on his paws from trying to get out. He is an angel in all other ways, great with the kids, fine with

the cat, just a joy. I am wondering what to do now.... He loves his little area with blankets and I would leave him out of the crate there but am afraid something will happen. Thanks for any suggestions, we love our Jett!!!![50]

Considering how many adopters reported that in the household context their greyhounds appeared to "hate" being in a dog crate by refusing to go inside on command, or barking, whining, chewing their paws or kennel bars, or shivering while inside, it appears that, once they were given another option, many NGA greyhounds rejected being enclosed in a small space. Indeed, it was an extraordinary irony that a breed designed for speed, that "loves to run" as wisdom goes, should ever be confined much of the day in a crate in order to be seen to live up to his or her potential or protected from injury.

Sixteen readers of the post replied with advice and their own stories of dogs' resistance to being in confined spaces, especially if crated in secluded areas of the household. "Luna was a disaster with her crate when I first got her, and would chew the bars until her gums bled," said the site user schultzic. "He may really be telling you he doesn't want to be 'locked in'—fine to leave the door open for him to enter at his choosing.... My guess is that it's anxiety driven," said Trihounds. Of his own dogs, he explained, "Bumper—first dog... crated for about a month.... No issues. I'll tell you though, he was a crate chewer at the track and I was told he messed his crate more than normal. Guess he didn't like it. Squirt—crated 2 days. Waste of time, she hated it, let everyone know it, and never needed it thereafter." Guest Gillybear agreed, "We tried crating our first grey but she had diarrhea and had actually bent the metal wire with her nose! She was allowed to roam after that."[51]

GeorgeofNE had similar experiences, but explained things in ways that demonstrated how in a household adopters believed they have a responsibility to adapt animal management routines to an individual dog (not vice versa, as would have been the case at the track where things were supposed to be more "businesslike."[52]) This adopter explained:

> Turns out the Greyhound I adopted considered being crated like being sent to *his own private hell*. He was beyond miserable. I

know because I videotaped him after I had neighbor after neighbor (I live in a condo) complain that he was "howling for hours." I didn't believe them. When I watched the tape, I cried.

Before my door was even all the way shut, he tipped back his head and howled until the 2 hour tape ran out. Oh sure, in between howls he might have licked his Kong [dog toy filled with peanut butter] for a second or two. But that was all. He never relaxed.... George was nearly 5, and had been in a kennel environment his entire life.... Why wouldn't he be OK in the crate? Well, cause in a kennel, there are dogs above you, next to you, across from you. Very, very different than being locked in a wire box all alone in a condo while the person you just met disappears. (emphasis in original)[53]

Here, people discussed greyhounds as individuals who changed over time and exposed their own belief that, as adopters (or "rescuers," often) they had a responsibility to ask for advice or use trial and error to create a feasible context for their greyhounds by working within each dog's limitations. This ethos was a challenge to industry marketing or proscriptive adoptive literature that dominated most textual understandings of these dogs as beings native to the crate and would have explained self-injury or vocalization by crated greyhounds as simply a failure of the dog's training.

Within the confines of a household, a greyhound's welfare is arguably better than at a dog track, although pro-industry people would argue against that forcefully. Beyond the group housing and mass management at the track kennel, former racers have freedom to move—to look out a window, to find a new sleeping spot, to travel across the room to drink water and stretch their legs, to interact with people, dogs, cats of the household, or not—and to negotiate with human cohabitants about how they will live. In private households, greyhounds are more able to practice species-typical behaviours of social interaction and explore their surroundings, while enjoying a larger variety of mental stimulation and thus improved welfare.[54] The Internet abounds with photographs and artwork depicting ex-racers lolling on couches, dog beds, or human beds in these homes, indicating that many do indeed believe that they "have died and gone to Heaven," as one advice manual for adopters put it.[55]

Foster home and adopters' discussions of specific behaviours suggests that some of these dogs found the transition to a new context difficult, but also a kind of opportunity perhaps. Suddenly offered a choice and a new context, they devised ways of intervening to change household routines. These kinds of digital sources, of which there are many, show that some of these dogs appeared to have forgotten or were uninterested in the older routines or limitations they experienced out of necessity living at a dog track.[56]

Conclusion

The digital record of greyhound and adopter behaviour is abundant but also fragile. Historians need to take these sources seriously as historical documents before they are gone. The digital record gives us great insight into the communities of people who have supported and opposed dog racing since the 1990s, and it gives us a ring-side seat to the often uncivil arguments that go on between the industry and its critics. At the same time, if we take historical animal experience and behaviour to be historically relevant—either for a record of these dogs and their intrinsic value, or for what it tells us about the experiences of the people around them—we have a way of documenting the efforts of dogs and people to figure out how greyhounds would transition from a life as an institutionally housed investment to a life as a family member. For greyhounds and their adopters, this transition could be a confusing process. Yet, those difficulties help us understand the nature of petkeeping and animal advocacy in the digital age, when communities became capable of finding and supporting one another in ways that might have been impossible in earlier historical periods, before discussion boards, email, and Facebook. These stories of a continental community of adopters constitutes a history of NGA greyhounds in the late twentieth and early twenty-first centuries. We should see those dogs' history in the context of expanding public efforts to redefine pet ownership with the responsibility to tackle and solve new animal welfare and behaviour issues in conversation with dogs, who arrived a little older and carrying the baggage of often-difficult individual pasts and experiences.[57]

My digital archive on greyhounds, greyhound breeding, and racing, and the advocacy and adoption communities consists of fragile historical sources that can be surprisingly ephemeral; many of these posts and pages will be gone in hours, days, weeks, months or (certainly) years. These sources need to be captured—the Internet Archive's Wayback Machine will not suffice since it can only reproduce webpages if users already possess a historical webpage URL or unique keywords to sift out relevant pages from the billions stored.[58] The blunt nature of the Wayback Machine repository compounds the problem that, as is a truism in our field, archives are designed to save a record of human agency, capturing records of animals only by accident. So, historians of animals interested in the recent past are obligated to build their own archives and to take these sources seriously *as* archival material. The question that remains is how such self-made archives might be more formally preserved beyond the computer of any individual researcher.

NOTES

1 Raymond Madden, "Imagining the Greyhound: 'Racing' and 'rescue' narratives in a human dog relationship," *Continuum: Journal of Media & Culture Studies* 24, no. 4 (August 2010): 504–05.

2 Eben Kirksey, "Multispecies Families," in *Emergent Ecologies*, ed. Eben Kirksey (Durham, NC: Duke University Press, 2015), 134–35.

3 Harriet Ritvo, "Combinations and Conjunction," in *Traces of the Animal Past*, ed. Sean Kheraj and Jennifer Bonnell (Calgary: University of Calgary Press, 2022).

4 Lynda Birke, "Who—or What—are the Rats (and Mice) in the Laboratory," *Society and Animals* 11, no. 3 (2003): 216–18.

5 Sandra Swart, "Kicking Over the Traces? Freeing the Animal from the Archive," and Lindsay Stallones Marshall, "Hearing History through Hoofbeats: Exploring Equine Volition and Voice in the Archive," in *Traces of the Animal Past*, ed. Jennifer Bonnell and Sean Kheraj (Calgary: University of Calgary Press, 2022).

6 Birke, "Who—or What," 217. In this research, I rely upon animal welfare science research on domestic dogs to get some sense of why greyhounds behave as they do in various settings.

7 Ian Milligan, *History in the Age of Abundance? How the Web is Transforming Historical Research* (Montreal/Kingston: McGill-Queens University Press, 2019), 9, 15.

8 Sean Kheraj, "Spacial Analysis and Digital Urban Animal History," in *Traces of the Animal Past*, ed. Jennifer Bonnell and Sean Kheraj (Calgary: University of Calgary Press, 2022).

9 Facebook can be a controversial digital source for some researchers. Ian Milligan argues that the entire platform is off limits due to ethical concerns. Milligan, *History*

in the Age of Abundance?, 16. In consulting with the Office of Research Ethics experts at my own university, I was advised that any public Facebook page open to search engines can be quoted and cited freely (say, pages run by adoption groups or industry organizations that routinely seek public attention and speak to journalists about their activities). However, any Facebook content that was accessed by becoming Facebook "friends" with the author or through the permission of a closed-group administrator can be cited or quoted only with the written permission of all authors concerned. Gaining permission to reproduce images found on those sites is even more complex, requiring permission of the original poster of the image as well as the social media platform company. With respect to publicly available but older websites, discussion boards, and social media posts effectively hidden by being buried in pages of search results or otherwise difficult to navigate to in chronologically displayed posts, Milligan argues that original authors have an expectation of privacy. Similarly, deleted online sources archived in a digital repository should be excluded or anonymized to protect the privacy of its original authors. This is problematic dilemma for professional historians who employ extensive notes and bibliographies of sources so that others may visit primary sources to examine them themselves. In this study, I cite digital sources in which the authors had no expectation of privacy either because they intentionally posted on public Facebook pages (viewable without a Facebook account) or other public websites specifically designed to reach a public audience, or they employed usernames that obscured their true names.

10 Trevor Owens and Thomas Padilla, "Digital Sources and Digital Archives: Historical Evidence in the Digital Age," *International Journal of Digital Humanities* (2020), https://doi.org/10.1007/s42803-020-00028-7.

11 Owens and Padilla, "Digital Sources and Digital Archives."

12 Glenn D. Tiffert, "Peering Down the Memory Hole: Censorship, Digitization, and the Fragility of Our Knowledge Base," *American Historical Review* 124, no. 2 (April 2019): 550–52.

13 Jason Colby, "Tuffy's Cold War: Science, Dolphins, and the US Navy," in *Traces of the Animal Past*, ed. Jennifer Bonnell and Sean Kheraj (Calgary: University of Calgary Press, 2022).

14 Cynthia A. Branigan, *The Reign of the Greyhound*, 2nd ed. (Hoboken, NJ: Howell Book House, 2004), 152–72; C. G. E. Wilmshurst, *The Book of the Greyhound* (London: Frederick Muller Limited, 1961).

15 Ryan H. Reed, *Born to Run: The Racing Greyhound From Competitor to Companion* (Lexington, KY: Bowtie Press, 2010), 94.

16 Laura Thompson, *The Dogs: A Personal History of Greyhound Racing* (London: Chatto & Windus, 1994), 50–72.

17 Branigan, *Reign of the Greyhound*, 199–200; Robert Temple, *The History of Greyhound Racing in New England* (n.p.: Robert Temple, 2011), 12–13; Gwyneth Anne Thayer, *Going to the Dogs. Greyhound Racing, Animal Activism, and American Popular Culture* (Lawrence, KS: University Press of Kansas, 2013), 6–7, 95–129.

18 Thayer, *Going to the Dogs*, 130.

19 Thayer, *Going to the Dogs*, 134–48.

20   Addie Patricia Asay, "Greyhounds: Racing to their Deaths," *Stetson Law Review* 32, no. 2 (2003): 449; Branigan, *Reign of the Greyhound*, 201.

21   Brenda Hume, comment, November 10, 2012, to *The Quick and the Dead, Transcript*. Radio National, Australian Broadcasting Company, http://www.abc.net.au/radionational/programs/backgroundbriefing/2012-11-11/4355398#transcript.

22   Justine Groizard, "Greyhounds and Racing Industry Participants: A Look at the New South Wales Greyhound Racing Community," *Animal Studies Journal* 8, no. 1 (2019): 138–42.

23   David M. Halbfinger, "Dismal End for Race Dogs, Alabama Authorities Say," *New York Times*, May 23, 2002, http://www.nytimes.com/2002/05/23/us/dismal-end-for-race-dogs-alabama-authorities-say.html; David Harkin, "Speaker: Dr. David Harkin, DMV," Heart of America Greyhound Gathering 2017, Abilene, Kansas, June 24, 2017; Thayer, *Going to the Dogs*, 150.

24   The term "wastage" is one commonly used in the regulation of dog racing in Australia and indicates all the dogs who are killed before old age. Some are culled as puppies when early training shows them to be lacklustre performers, others after injury sustained during a race, and other still due to some other calculation by an owner that they are no longer financially viable. Alexandra McEwan and Krishna Skandakmar, "The Welfare of Greyhounds in Australian Racing: Has the Industry Run Its Course?," *Australian Animal Protection Law Journal* 6 (December 2011): 64; Anna L. Palmer et al., "Patterns of Racing and Career Duration of Racing Greyhounds in New Zealand," *Animals* 10, no. 796 (2020), https://doi.org/10.3390/ani10050796.

25   Asay, "Greyhounds"; Grey2K USA Worldwide, *Fact Sheet: Greyhound Injury Reporting 2011*, www.grey2kusa.org/pdf/Fact_Sheet_on_Greyhound_Injury_Reporting.pdf; Darren Morris, *Training the Racing the Greyhound* (Ramsbury, UK: Crowwood Press, 2009), 77–116. On early adoption programs, see, for instance, Dennis McKeon, "The Roots of Anti-Racing Activism," *All About Greyhounds*, https://www.greyhoundinfo.org/?page_id=885.

26   One recent estimate is that 5,000 adoptions per year cost up to $1.25 million to the industry, which is drawn out of purse money. Or, put another way, others estimate that to transport and provide initial medical care for one retired racer amounts to $600 per dog, with housing and feed costs beyond that. In the 1980s and 1990s, many breeders and kennel operators would have gone out of business had they been required to shoulder a portion of those costs. Many in the industry also found it outrageous that they should thus be held morally or financially accountable to critics who would never visit a dog track in any event. Moira Corrigan, "Letter from the President," *The Bark. Official Newsletter of Greyhound Pets, Inc.*, no. 1 (Spring 2014): 1; Dennis McKeon, "Below is a Response to a Very Well-Thought Out Anti-Racing Post," Dennis McKeon's Facebook Page, April 7, http://www.facebook.com/dennis.mckeon.33/posts/10152166763176829; Thayer, *Going to the Dogs*, 14.

27   Thayer, *Going to the Dogs*, 101; Branigan, *Reign of the Greyhound*, 209.

28   Lynda Birke, Joanna Hockenhull, and Emma Creighton, "The Horse's Tale: Narratives of Caring for/about Horses," *Society and Animals* 18, no. 4 (2010): 331–47.

29   Madden, "Imagining the Greyhound," 510; Thayer, *Going to the Dogs*, 16.

30. Morris, *Training the Racing the Greyhound*, 38–45; Dennis McKeon, "For the New Adopter—A Simple Primer to Help You Understand Your New Greyhound," *All About Greyhounds*, May 4, 2011, http://www.greyhoundinfo.org/?page_id=1078.
31. See, for example, Roy Brindley, *Life's a Gamble* (London Transworld/Penguin, 2009), 113–19.
32. Gulf Greyhound Park, "The Greyhound - From Racing to Your Home," YouTube video, accessed December 1, 2017, http://youtu.be/Pwn9lLg5IeI.
33. Grey2K USA Worldwide, *Fact Sheet: Greyhound Racing in the United States, 2014*, http://www.grey2kusa.org/pdf/GREY2KUSANationalFactSheet.pdf; Penny Wick, "Crating for Safety and Wellbeing," http://www.ngagreyhounds.com/Debunking-Lies?h155=33, accessed December 1, 2017. See also, Frankstach, "Feeding Racing Greyhounds," YouTube video, November 16, 2009, https://www.youtube.com/watch?v=weUl_QeEgWw; Tucsongreyhound85713, "Tucson Greyhound Park, Mary Gray Kennel," YouTube video, January 27, 2012, https://www.youtube.com/watch?v=HPkjLtyTfo4.
34. Grey2KUSA Worldwide, "Confinement in Greyhound Racing," https://www.grey2kusa.org/about/confinement.php, accessed December 12, 2017.
35. This text appeared on Dennis McKeon's Facebook page, where I first encountered it, but also on various blogs and websites, and I cite the public sources of his writing. Dennis McKeon, "Couch Potato, Meet Crate Potato," *Awesome Paws & Camp Greyhound blog*, September 22, 2013, http://awesomepaws.proboards.com/thread/100/couch-potato-crate-dennis-mckeon#ixzz3Kzryh7hB.
36. Wilmshurst, *Book of the Greyhound*, 2.
37. Mark Derr, *A Dog's History of America* (New York: North Point Press, 2004), 334.
38. These observations come from hundreds of hours of reading discussions and arguments among greyhound adopters and adoption group volunteers on Facebook groups pages, many of them closed pages requiring an administrator to grant admission. I have yet to determine a feasible way to cite that kind of research such that readers could visit the sources to vet them and my analysis themselves.
39. The Greyhound Project, Inc., "The First Few Days in a New Home," http://www.adopt-a-greyhound.org/advice/the_first_few_days_in_a_new_home.shtml, accessed December 12, 2017.
40. Livingood, *Retired Racing Greyhounds*, 163. The phenomenon of thigh baldness was "just another one of the many things no one agrees upon," explained Lee Livingood. Some falsely believed it to be related to improper thyroid function, which some believed was common to the breed in any setting. Others chalked it up to kennel conditions like flea and tick infestations, or intensive confinement in which a greyhound's delicate fur was easily lost to stress or abrasion against crate or dog hauler compartment walls. Grassmere Animal Hospital, "Bald Thighs, Comedones, Happy Tail," accessed May 15, 2010, http://www.grassmere-animal-hospital.com; Carolyn Raeke, *The Best Finish: Adopting a Retired Racing Greyhound* (Neptune City, NJ: T. F. H. Publishers, 2004), 66; "Greyhound Glossary: Baboon Butt (Bald Butt)," *Houndlife Blog*, accessed March 2, 2008, http://houndlife.blogspot.ca/2008/03/greyhound-glossary.html.
41. McKeon, "For the New Adopter."

42   Sue Savage-Rumbaugh et al., "Welfare of Apes in Captive Environments: Comments On, and By, a Specific Group of Apes," *Journal of Applied Animal Welfare Science* 10, no. 1 (2007): 16.

43   Birke, Hockenhull, and Creighton, "Horse's Tale."

44   *Michigan Retired Greyhounds as Pets*, accessed January 7, 2014, http://rescuedgreyhounds.org/.

45   *Michigan Retired Greyhounds as Pets*, accessed January 7, 2014, http://rescuedgreyhounds.org/.

46   Greyhound Pets, Inc., accessed January 14, 2017, https://www.greyhoundpetsinc.org/.

47   Anonymous kennel volunteer, Greyhound Pets, Inc., Woodinville, Washington, personal interview, 15 December 2012.

48   Michigan ReGAP, "Your New Greyhound," adoption packet pamphlet, n.d.; Michigan ReGap, "Foster Home Agreement," 2009.

49   As with the digital sources discussed in note 38 of this chapter, this information is aggregated from many dozens of Facebook posts over a decade. How are historians to cite that?

50   Guest Gillybear, schultzic, Trihounds comments in "Help! New Greyhound Pooped All Over His Crate When We Left Him," July 11, 2012, www.greytalk.com, https://forum.greytalk.com/topic/288191-help-new-greyhound-pooped-all-over-his-crate-when-we-left-him/.

51   fluteplayer67 comment in "Help! New Greyhound Pooped All Over His Crate When We Left Him," July 11, 2012, www.greytalk.com, https://forum.greytalk.com/topic/288191-help-new-greyhound-pooped-all-over-his-crate-when-we-left-him/.

52   Gulf Greyhound Park, "The Greyhound - From Racing to Your Home," YouTube video, accessed December 1, 2017, http://youtu.be/Pwn9lLg5IeI.

53   GeorgeofNE comment in "Help! New Greyhound Pooped All Over His Crate When We Left Him," July 11, 2012, www.greytalk.com, https://forum.greytalk.com/topic/288191-help-new-greyhound-pooped-all-over-his-crate-when-we-left-him/.

54   Nicola Rooney and Kevin Stafford, "Dogs (*Canis familiaris*)," in *Companion Animal Care and Welfare: The UFAW Companion Animal Handbook*, ed. James Yeates (Hoboken, NJ: John Wiley & Sons, Ltd., 2019), 85–89.

55   Greyhound Pets, Inc., *The Greyhound Adopter's Guide* (Woodinville, WA: Greyhound Pets, Inc., 2008), 1.

56   Greyhound Pets, Inc., *Greyhound Adopter's Guide*, 1.

57   On advocacy and grassroots organizing since the advent of email, see Clay Shirky, *Here Comes Everybody: The Power of Organizing without Organizations* (New York: Penguin, 2009), 143–60.

58   The Wayback Machine is the rudimentary but growing archive of the Internet at the Internet Archive, https://archive.org/web/.

5

Accessing Animal Health Knowledge: Popular Educators and Veterinary Science in Rural Ontario[1]

Jody Hodgins

Before veterinarians were commonplace in rural Ontario, people purchased popular animal health manuals to learn more about the animals in their care. The manuals met a demand for a cost-effective way to access veterinary science and provide better health care to animals around the world.[2] However, veterinary professionals argued that the information in these manuals was "moth-eaten by its age."[3] In 1920, a majority of students enrolled at the Ontario Veterinary College (OVC) petitioned the provincial government to recognize institutional standards of veterinary care.[4] OVC's students argued that they were placed in an "illogical position" where it made "little sense" to continue investing their time and money into receiving a four-year institutional degree, when they could receive a diploma or certificate from The London Correspondence School's manuals in only eleven months.[5] As veterinary science developed, licensing standards were contested and institutional education became standard for veterinary experts to receive accreditation. However, this transition did not happen overnight. In the late nineteenth century, veterinarians were few and far between, often travelling long distances to treat an animal. At the time, this was both impractical and costly for many farmers. In this chapter, I argue that the knowledge presented in popular animal health manuals offered insight into common animal health concerns and animal histories before veterinarians were widely accessible in rural Ontario.

In actuality, animal health care was not practiced at veterinary institutions. Yet researchers rely on institutional sources to write histories of animal health. Before advancements in the 1920s made rural areas more accessible, rural Ontarians relied on oxen, and later horses, for work and transportation. To maintain the health of the animals they relied on, they gathered animal health knowledge through experience and conversations with their neighbours.[6] Some farmers also gained understanding from animal health manuals purchased by subscription. This chapter focuses on the latter. Animal health manuals facilitated knowledge transmission over longer distances, communicating how other farmers had resolved the health problems that animals commonly faced. Together with distance education or "quack" veterinary schools, popular animal health manuals met a demand for animal health knowledge before veterinarians were readily available outside institutional centres.[7] For example, farmers used equipment they had on hand and learned to isolate and shelter ill animals in clean, well-ventilated stables before germ theory was widely accepted and before blood tests and veterinary visits were accessible.

The Ontario Veterinary Association and OVC's push to standardize veterinary training at institutions and legally regulate who was qualified to administer veterinary medicine affected how those in rural areas could treat their animals. Historian Charlotte Borst shows how this contentious divide was also evident in the human medical profession, which saw specialized, urban, laboratory science valued over localized observations.[8] Facing critiques of unscientific practices, farmers likely appreciated the localized knowledge promoted by authors of animal health manuals, many of which prioritized observation and quick recognition of symptoms in addition to the basics of veterinary science. For example, anatomical drawings presented scientific names, locations, and descriptions of healthy body parts to aid farmers in quickly recognizing problematic changes. However, distributing this empirical knowledge in animal health manuals directly to farmers "irritat[ed]" members of the veterinary profession "inside and outside the province" and sowed the seeds for larger debates about who had the right to access and practice veterinary science.[9] Ultimately, by 1920, after fifty years of debate, the veterinary profession's push for standardization saw licensing authorities prioritize institutional training in their review of rural practitioners' credentials, denying licensing to those who held empirical knowledge or qualifications from distance education or correspondence schools.[10]

The demand for knowledge of veterinary science in rural areas without veterinarians created what some scholars have described as a "book farming" market. Generally associated with a series of popular eighteenth-century publications employed by "gentlemen landowners [in] exerting control over their servants or tenants in the management of their own farms," book farming is nevertheless relevant to the farmer-landowners of nineteenth-century Ontario.[11] Historian James Fisher argues that book farming was "a symptom of social struggles generated by the shift to capitalist relations of agricultural production."[12] However, as I argue in this chapter, it also addressed a need for what one farmer described as an "interchange" of "intuitive knowledge" about animal health. Sold globally by subscription, the manuals examined in this chapter pooled collective wisdom and enabled the exchange of experiential animal health knowledge over long distances.[13]

Historical studies often overlook the realities of animal health in favour of the human perspective and "celebratory narratives of scientific progress."[14] Lisa Cox notes that "animals are unique historical actors, as they are everywhere and nowhere in history," which is also true in professional histories of veterinary medicine.[15] In *Valuing Animals: Veterinarians and their Patients in Modern America*, Susan Jones argues that changes in veterinary medicine and the socio-cultural role of animals cannot be understood as "processes isolated from each other."[16] In a similar vein, Abigail Woods maintains that studying medical history in isolation from the veterinary profession and the animal experience "grant[s] a timeless universality to scientific interpretations that are in fact products of specific historical circumstances."[17] Like Jones and Woods, I argue that animal health and veterinary medicine should not be studied in the absence of animals themselves. Etienne Benson argued that "traces" of the animal past found in human sources provide rich insight into "historical changes" in the animal-human relationship.[18] As historical traces of this changing relationship, popular animal health manuals offer a lens into common animal health realities in rural environments.

To access animal history as it occurred on the ground and without records from animals themselves, historians necessarily rely on anthropocentric interpretations of animals' lived experiences and what people felt was important to record. The animal health manuals included in this chapter do not focus on the life journey of specific animals or their feelings. Rather, these manuals focus on species as a whole and observed behaviours or physical evidence that provided readers with an understanding of how animals generally reacted or changed as an injury or illness progressed. Farmers reading these manuals found generalized examples of good health and what specific changes or behaviours might mean based on what others had experienced and what treatments they found successful, a dialogue that was also common in the correspondence sections of agricultural journals at the time. The animals in these manuals exist theoretically as a central object of concern. However, the anatomical drawings and descriptions of animal behaviour in each manual act, as Sandra Swart outlines in Chapter 1 of this volume, as a guide to animals' bodies that aid the reader in diagnosing animals and administering treatments. By conveying typical animal experiences and instructing readers on how to recognize and interpret changes in animal behaviour and physicality, animal health manuals offer an important corrective to the anthropocentric narratives of professional and institutional histories.

In this chapter, I will examine different editions of several popular animal health publications: *The Domestic Encyclopedia of Facts or Farmers, Mechanics, and Household Manual* (1879), *The Stockman Guide and Manual to Husbandry* (1903), the London Correspondence School's *The Veterinary Science* (1907), and Dr. George Bell's pamphlets advertising his "Veterinary Medical Wonder." These popular animal health manuals were discovered on the back shelves of rural public archives or in private family collections located within 300 km of Toronto (the original site of OVC), Guelph (the current location of OVC, established in 1920), and the London Veterinary Correspondence School. Farmers purchased these manuals by subscription, possibly after reading an advertisement in a local newspaper or agricultural journal. The prevalence of these manuals in rural archival collections signals their historical significance. Not only were they a significant aid to farmers in this period, but they were also a rich source of animal health solutions. Popular animal health manuals provide evidence of commonly observed animal behaviour and physical wellness, animal health practices in rural areas, and how these practices changed with the development of veterinary science and the professionalization of veterinary medicine.

Evidence of common animal behaviour and animal health practices can be found in the oldest animal health manual in this study, *The Domestic Encyclopedia of Facts or Farmers, Mechanics, and Household Manual*, by J. Gurnley Thompson. A. M. Schuyley Smith and Co. published this manual in 1879 during a period of increasing demand for animal health lectures at OVC. Thompson covered an extensive range of general topics that affected rural families and their household economies. He included specific chapters on horses, mules, cattle, sheep, swine, domestic animals, poultry, dogs, bees, and insects that contrasted with more thematic chapters on accidents and injuries, family physicians, recipes, and "How to be your own lawyer."[19] Thompson included illustrations and empirical descriptions to provide clear instructions for what he considered to be important animal health knowledge for farmers with varying levels of experience. This 746-page manual was "sold only by subscription" from Odebolt, Iowa, to a reader whose copy was donated to the Simcoe County archives, 200 km from Toronto and Guelph's OVC campuses.[20]

Thompson's drawings of prize-winning animals were added to the beginning of each section to illustrate breeding standards and to depict the "rapid and valuable improvements that have been made in stock-raising." He argued that this "should stimulate our farmers to active effort, [and] continued improvement in their Domestic Animals."[21] Thompson explained that desirable traits varied based on a farmer's needs. "Big hocks and knees, flat legs with large sinews, open jaws, and full nostrils" were desirable traits for all breeds of horses. However, Thompson noted that a horse with an "oblique shoulder-blade [was] an imperative necessity" for "speed and activity," although this trait was less desirable for workhorses because a "heavy harness" caused "pressure [on] the collar."[22] Experienced farmers likely already emphasized these values in their breeding practices.[23] At the very least, Thompson's descriptions provide researchers with an overall picture of how farmers with varying levels of experience understood breeding standards, and what was considered common practice or an advancement at the time.

Thompson recognized that people who worked with horses knew how to assess equine dental health because it was at the root of many health concerns, providing information about the age and health of the animal for sales and insurance purposes. A blacksmith with generational experience breeding horses in Simcoe County, where the manual was found, would have been aware of these dental assessment methods. But Thompson wanted others to appreciate the possible costs associated with not recognizing equine dental problems.[24] Thompson also used illustrations of equine dentistry to show animal owners how "dishonest dealers may attempt to disguise age, by reproducing the mark in the corner teeth by means of a hot iron or caustic" (Figure 5.1).[25] He considered this knowledge essential for new farmers but was quick to note that this type of fraud was "easily detected by a horseman" because the mark was "usually overdone."[26] This cautionary note illustrates the cruel treatment that some livestock animals were exposed to for financial gain. As Susan Nance argues in Chapter 4 of this volume, these animal histories are often overlooked or remain on the "periphery" of a human history about fraudulence, farm economies, and settler life.

Thompson continued by outlining other ways that fraudulent horse dealers may seek to mislead a buyer, like stimulating a horse to mask lameness, pain, injury, or disease.[27] He encouraged rural people to consult veterinarians, reasoning that the costs associated with a veterinarian's services would be less in the long term than purchasing an animal in ill health. Thompson recommended isolating animals on the first sign of disease.[28] His emphasis on isolating diseased animals, combined with his descriptions and illustrations of animal health, indicates how limited farmers' access to veterinary care was in this period. These descriptions also provide scholars with an understanding of the considerable knowledge about animal health and practical skills that livestock farmers possessed at the time of the book's publication in 1879.

Popular animal health manuals from the turn of the twentieth century included more veterinary science than earlier manuals. *The Stockman Guide and Manual to Husbandry* was not an exception. An edition

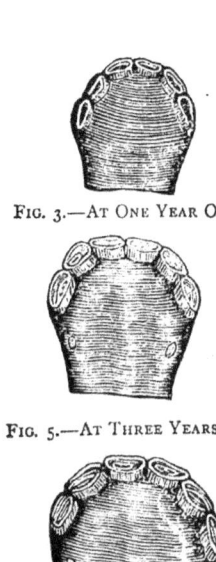

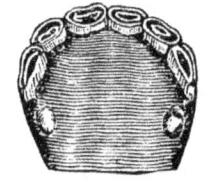

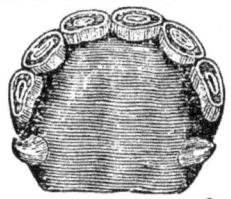

FIG. 3.—AT ONE YEAR OLD.
FIG. 4.—AT TWO YEARS OLD.
FIG. 5.—AT THREE YEARS OLD.
FIG. 6.—AT FOUR YEARS OLD.
FIG. 7.—AT FIVE YEARS OLD.
FIG. 8.—AT SIX YEARS OLD.
FIG. 9. AT SEVEN YEARS OLD.
FIG. 10—AT EIGHT YEARS OLD.
AGE OF THE HORSE, AS INDICATED BY THE TEETH.

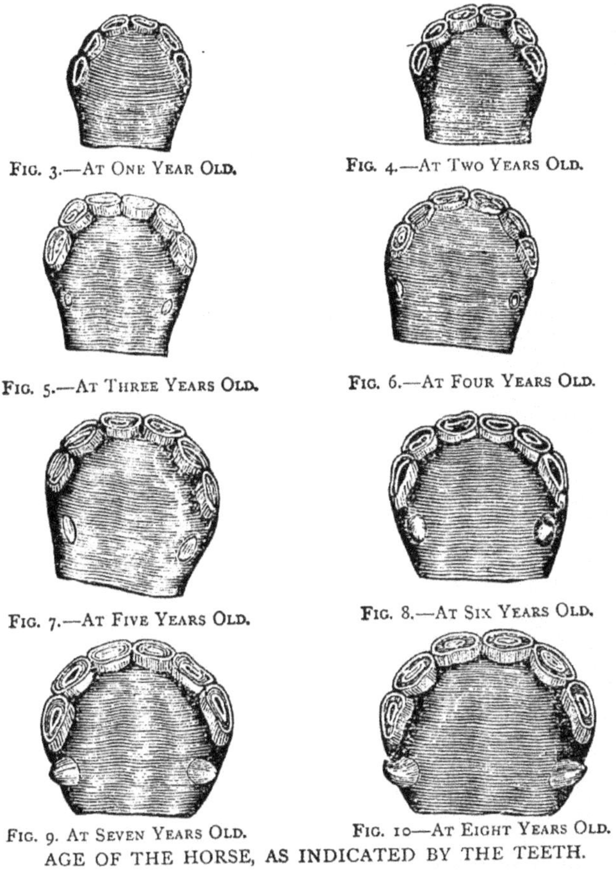

Fig. 5.1 An illustrative description of how to determine a horse's age based on their teeth. Source: Thompson, *The Domestic Encyclopedia*, 19.

published in 1903 offers 686 pages of illustrations, empirical evidence, and basic explanations of veterinary science that instructed livestock owners on how to care for their animals when faced with well-known injuries or disease. Different editions of *The Stockman Guide* are preserved in rural county archives. For this chapter, I focus on an edition from the private collection of a family with an extensive history of breeding workhorses and, later, racehorses.[29] This edition was distributed by the King-Richardson Company. As one of the largest subscription firms in the United States in 1891, the King-Richardson Company took advantage of a new tariff law that allowed subscription books to be sold in Canada as an educational book at a lower rate of duty.[30]

The Stockman Guide and Manual to Husbandry included chapters on horses (the first 250 pages), cattle, sheep, poultry, swine, "enemies of the potato," household remedies for humans and animals, fruit culture and insects, legal issues, and a glossary explaining scientific terms. The authors took the time to describe scientific terms for the "humblest reader" because they believed that knowing scientific terms were not necessary to provide animals with effective health care.[31] Rather, they valued observational and localized knowledge. The authors instructed farmers to become familiar with their animals' health so that they could recognize any changes quickly. Farmers' acquired knowledge, and the observations farmers made, would enable them to reach an animal in time to prevent or treat potentially fatal injuries, illness, or disease. Editor-in-chief Andrew A. Gardenier stated that the manual drew on the expertise of well-respected veterinary doctors to provide the public with an "accurate knowledge of the construction, location, and uses of the various parts of the body" for the first time.[32] The drawings are still valued: the owner of this manual, for example, took the time to first show me the flip-up anatomical drawings or "manikins" of a horse's circulatory system, muscles, skeleton, organs, and reproductive system (Figure 5.2).[33] Gardenier's goal was to provide farmers with quick and efficient access to an animal's anatomy. Today, the same drawings shed light on how some farmers understood animal anatomy at the turn of the twentieth century.

Gardenier's expertise in physiology provided rural animal owners with scientific knowledge of their animal's anatomy, instead of relying on experiential knowledge gained from an autopsy or through slaughter. The authors periodically referenced the book's anatomical manikins to convey the size and location of an animal's organs and encouraged the reader to become familiar with their animal's pulse, respiration, skin consistency, and behaviour. Observing changes in their animals' health ensured that farmers would quickly recognize and isolate outbreaks of disease to accurately diagnose and treat their animals.[34] For example, farmers knew that animals were most susceptible to pneumonia in the spring and fall, or after suffering from influenza. So the authors provided a brief description of recent pneumonia outbreaks, environments that may carry the contagion, and the animals that are most susceptible, before instructing the farmer on how to distinguish between pneumonia and fibrinous pneumonia.[35]

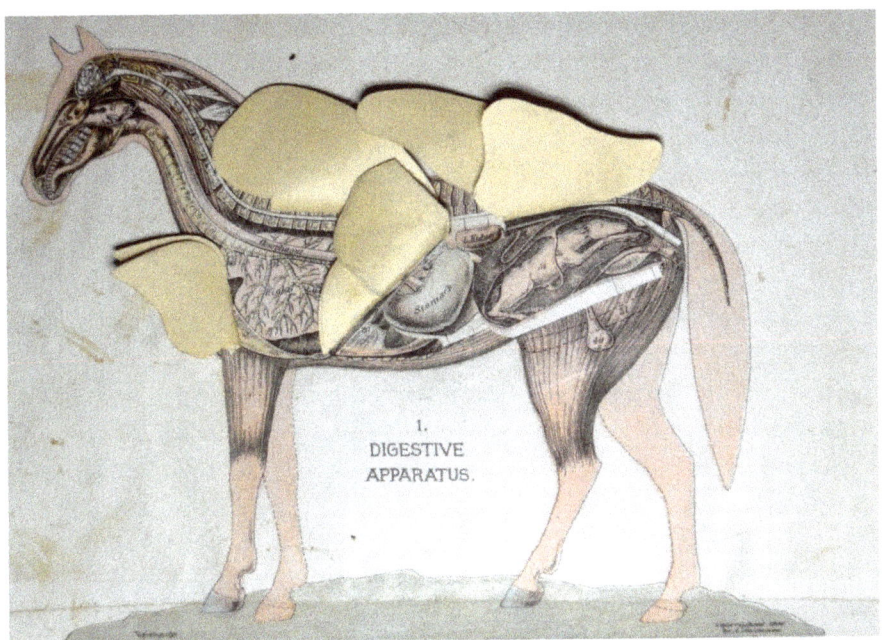

Fig. 5.2 An anatomical flip-up diagram of a horse in *The Stockman Guide and Manual to Husbandry*. Source: Gardenier, *The Successful Stockman and Manual of Husbandry*, 1.

Gardenier explained how farmers could make these distinctions by examining the progression of symptoms, considering environmental conditions, and listening to changes in an animal's cough, lung congestion, and pulse.[36] This approach saw authors of popular animal health manuals explain basic scientific advancements to aid farmers' localized observations. Animal health experts' emphasis on becoming familiar with animal health changes offers a lens into rural settlers' understanding of animal anatomy and the common experiences of domesticated animals in early twentieth-century Ontario.

The authors of *The Stockman Guide and Manual to Husbandry* were confident that their instructions would prove successful. However, they admit that farmers' "impatience" and their demands for immediate results were reoccurring problems that could hinder a farmer's ability to observe an animal's reaction, and consequently, their ability to provide proper care.[37] This insight demonstrates the authors' understanding of how their instructions were received and the significant gaps that could exist between animals who experienced farmers' care and the knowledge of veterinarians who were trained to deal with injuries and illnesses that farmers may not have previously experienced.

The transition to institutional veterinary training did not occur immediately after the Ontario Veterinary Medical Association was established in 1874. Veterinary historians argue that the London Correspondence Veterinary School, established in 1896, was a "notorious nuisance" in Canada, the United States, and countries as far away as New Zealand for some time.[38] Before 1920, people who made a one-time payment of $25 or several instalments amounting to $40 to the London Veterinary Correspondence School could become licensed veterinarians.[39] C. A. V. Barker, a veterinarian and founder of the C. A. V. Barker Museum of Canadian Veterinary History, and historian Margaret Evans argue that it was "absurd" for people to believe that a correspondence school could "turn 'all and sundry' into competent practitioners."[40] Yet hundreds of people continued to "naively" offer their veterinary credentials to state licensing boards "in the form of [a] very handsome but worthless diploma" after the Veterinary Science Practice Act was passed in 1920. The popularity of animal health manuals offers evidence not only of how farmers may have practiced animal health, but also of how loosely accredited animal health experts (who offered their services to others) practiced.

The London Correspondence School published many editions of *The Veterinary Science* that made their way into rural county archives. The 663-page text became very popular, with 107 editions published by 1907, and eighteen editions in its first year, with copyright in at least seven countries.[41] Given its popularity, it is clear that it met a demand for knowledge of veterinary science through correspondence or distance education delivered in the mail. The authors, J. E. Hodgins V.S. V.D., President of the Veterinary Science Company that ran the London Veterinary Correspondence School, and T. H. Haskett, D.V.D., the school's Secretary Treasurer, marketed their popular animal health manual as less costly and less time-consuming than institutionalized forms of education. They claimed that *The Veterinary Science* was "equivalent to a thorough practical course in a Veterinary College."[42] However, Barker and Evans argue that "gullible persons" were convinced to enrol in the correspondence course that was at a "level about that of a first-aid manual" where "science was a misnomer."[43] Nevertheless, it is clear that Hodgins and Haskett were meeting a demand for access to animal health knowledge. Their manual provides researchers with evidence of animal health care treatments that were likely experienced by the animals in the care of its readership.

Hodgins and Haskett simplified scientific descriptions, provided illustrative examples, and included an index of symptoms to bridge a gap in the "social organisation [and accessibility] of agricultural knowledge" and to set them apart from other animal health manuals.[44] The authors claimed that this made it "very easy to find out from what an animal [was] suffering" and quickly provide treatment.[45] They recognized a growing need to include scientific interpretations of animal anatomy and focus on disease and injuries that affected domestic livestock.[46] In revised editions, they added illustrations and plates, a chapter on domestic animals, and a greater focus on disease to "remain comprehensive, concise and abreast of the times in the latest and most approved methods of treatment."[47] For example, Hodgins and Haskett's illustration of a common technique for castrating a horse, called "Belt Tackling," shows landscaped environments and three farmers moving the horse using belts and pulleys to secure the horse (Figure 5.3).[48] The authors argued that this more technical approach was better than older methods, like *The Domestic Encyclopedia*'s reference to using chloroform and *The Stockman's Guide and Manual to Husbandry*'s written description of using a "web halter" to confine and "expose" the horse.[49] All of these approaches assumed the need to confine and limit an animals' movement rather than work with or distract the animal. The belt and pulley system was used to limit the animal's reaction to this treatment and, like Rothfels notes in Chapter 10 of this volume, shows "one layer covering a history of earlier stories" of what actually happened or what some experts imagined might happen. Hodgins and Haskett believed that their illustrative instructions would meet a demand for knowledge and improve animal health practices in rural areas, despite the implications this had for the confined horse. Their use of illustrations to disseminate knowledge of veterinary science provides evidence of the practical realities of animal health care in the early twentieth century.

A slow acceptance of germ theory meant that many farmers relied on folk remedies and "vernacular veterinary medicine" to treat animals

Fig. 5.3. An illustration of "The Belt Tackling" method for castrating a horse, which was regularly used by the authors and other Canadians. Source: Hodgins and Haskett, *The Veterinary Science*, 201.

into the early twentieth century.[50] Barker and Evans commend Hodgins and Haskett for using "common-sense" to recommend "send[ing] for a veterinary inspector if glanders was suspected."[51] However, they contend that "hog cholera was confused with anthrax, paralysis was listed among diseases, and rabies was described as originating spontaneously in hot weather." "Crude instructions were given for castration and spaying, the bleeding of a horse with fleams, the enucleation of a dog's eye without anesthesia, [and] the sewing of wounds with the small carriage trimmers' twine."[52] These treatments are clearly unacceptable compared to today's standards, but they reveal how farmers may have practiced animal health care at the time and what animals may have experienced. *The Farmer's Advocate* argued that these instructions allowed rural people "fired with ambition to obtain knowledge" to be "diverted from the right path into devious ways."[53] Yet by overlooking the procedures in support of a more linear narrative of the progress of modern veterinary medicine, researchers have ignored what the sources tell us about the everyday practices of farmers in caring for their livestock. Combining this information with evidence from other social and cultural sources offers insight into the health of animals and the common practices they may have experienced at the time, regardless of the efficacy.

Appeals to the Government of Ontario to resolve issues with accreditation and to close the London Correspondence School persisted until 1920. OVC graduates petitioned the provincial government to comply with OVC's standards "of entrance and study."[54] However, a clause in the Veterinary Practice Act indicated that "non-graduates who had been practicing in Ontario for a number of years [could] continue as before" without granting them "the title of Veterinary Surgeon or the privileges accompanying a college degree."[55] Ontario's Veterinary Practice Board questioned Hodgins about the integrity and ethical standards of his instruction before exempting his accreditation and making him an "Honorary Graduate of [OVC]."[56] He was listed as a Veterinary Surgeon in the City of London directory for five more years, two years longer than his book's publication lasted. However, Haskett, a self-styled veterinary dentist, and Secretary of the Veterinary Science Association, was denied certification and left the veterinary publication business.[57] Despite its faults, the Veterinary Science Practice Act in Ontario brought an end to almost fifty years of competition for certification between popular and institutional methods of disseminating veterinary knowledge.

Issues with popular alternatives to institutional veterinary medicine continued after the new law was passed and the London Correspondence School had dissolved. Dr. George Bell, developer of "Veterinary Medical Wonder," and "one of Canada's leading Veterinarians" for over forty years (as he claimed in his pamphlets from 1933) indicated that his popular cure-all medicine would treat a number of ailments for different animals.[58] He provided illustrative descriptions of animal suffering, specific diagnostic information, and precise dosages to quickly treat animals for a number of common ailments. Many of these pamphlets and advertisements are commonly found in rural county archives and online databases.

Formal institutional veterinary training and so-called "quack" medicine were not as distinct from one another as one may have thought. Bell graduated from OVC in 1880 and practiced in the United States for fifteen years before returning to Kingston, Ontario, to open and act as Principal of the Kingston College of Veterinarians. In only two years, however,

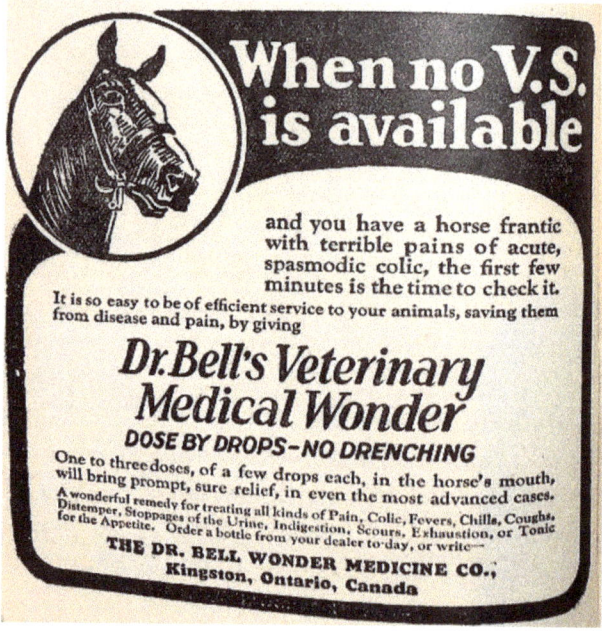

Fig. 5.4. This advertisement is from Dr. George Bell's animal health pamphlet. Source: Bell, "First Aid for Sick Animal, Sixth Edition" (Grey County), 18.

Bell's "entrepreneurial spirit" had conflicted with more "conservative and academic medical science faculty."[59] In 1897, Bell offered to resign in exchange for a negotiated offer of $125 and the ability to appoint his successor (who lasted three days before being replaced by Bell's adversary, Dr. A. P. Knight).[60] Regardless of Bell's institutional success, his entrepreneurial talent spoke for itself.

By 1933, the popularity of Dr. Bell's cure-all medicine and animal health pamphlets demonstrates farmers' desire for a quick, inexpensive alternative to veterinary care. To quickly treat white scours, a "dreaded" disease that affected cattle, Dr. Bell wrote that animal owners could "be of efficient service to [their] animals, saving them from disease and pain" by administering "one to three doses, of a few drops each." Dr. Bell argued that his medicine would bring "prompt, sure relief, in even the most advanced cases" (Figure 5.4).[61] This supposed cure-all exposed animals to belladonna (from a highly poisonous herb, deadly nightshade) and alcohol, among other ingredients that were regularly used in animal and human medicine at the time.[62] By indicating that animal owners did not have to wait for a veterinarian, Dr. Bell appealed to people who wanted to "sav[e] [animals] from disease and pain" without the expense associated with a veterinary visit. Animal owners could purchase the cure-all medicine directly from a dealer or through the mail for "$1.00 per bottle."[63] An online forum shows that Dr. Bell's medicine remained popular with people looking for replacement bottles as late as 2005.[64] Many bottles of Veterinary Medical Wonder are also preserved in Ontario museum collections.[65]

Dr. Bell's illustrated pamphlets provide evidence of animals suffering from common ailments. To treat pneumonia, Dr. Bell first provided illustrative evidence of a horse's suffering to show how a horse would remain standing through immense pain (shown in the horse's expression) due to the pressure on its lungs (Figure 5.5).[66] After ensuring that an animal had the opportunity to recover in a healthy environment, free from drafts and changes in temperature that occurred in the spring and fall, Dr. Bell instructed farmers to wrap a horse in a blanket with bandaged legs for warmth, and to feed "tempting foods" like carrots and apples rather than grains until after the fever had passed.[67] Then, Dr. Bell instructed farmers to give three dosages of his Veterinary Medical Wonder every hour; twenty to thirty drops for horses weighing 900–1,200 lbs, or thirty to forty drops for horses weighing 1,300 to 1,500 lbs.[68] Dr. Bell claimed that farmers could accurately diagnose ailments among all of their animals by using his descriptive and illustrative examples of animal suffering. While there is little evidence of the effectiveness of these treatments, aside from testimonies included in Dr. Bell's marketing, the popularity of his products shows that farmers placed some faith in them and continued to purchase them for several decades. Examining Dr. Bell's approach to animal health care provides insight into how animal owners prioritized access to quick and cost-efficient treatments as an alternative to costly veterinary care in the early twentieth century.

Students at OVC challenged the dissemination of veterinary science through animal health manuals because the popularity of these manuals meant that many people were treating animals using empirical knowledge rather than seeking the expertise of institutionally trained veterinarians. By providing glimpses into common animal health-care practices, popular animal health manuals yield valuable insight into the history of animal health. These sources expand historical knowledge of animal health practices beyond the bounds of formal institutional care. While they do not

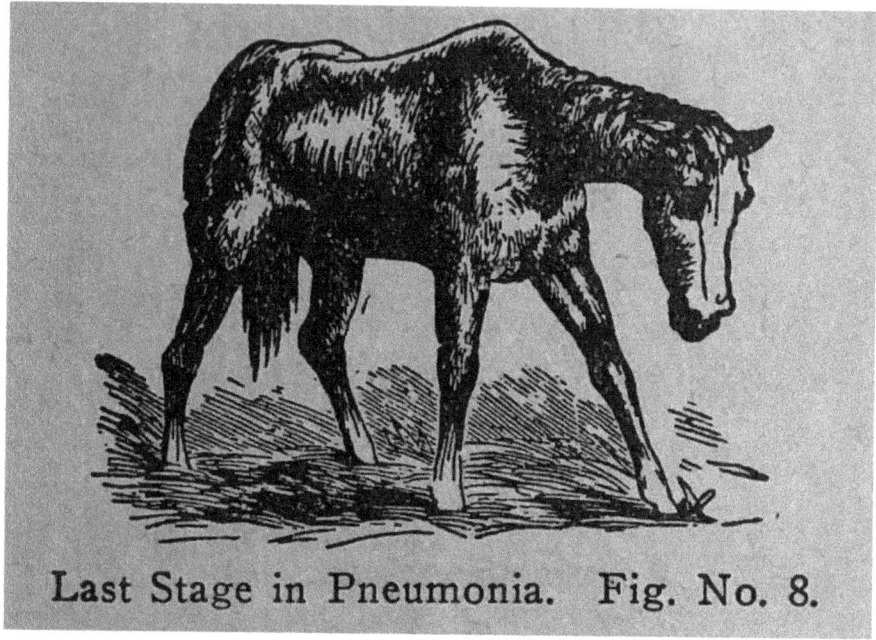

Fig. 5.5. This image depicts a horse suffering from pressure on its lungs in the late stages of pneumonia. Source: Bell, "First Aid for Sick Animal, Sixth Edition," 18.

provide specific examples of how farmers practiced animal health, their popularity shows a rural demand for this larger exchange of knowledge. Using these sources in combination with rural diaries, agricultural journals, newspapers, and advertising pamphlets grants historians access to the realities of animal health in rural environments.

Canada's institutionalization of veterinary medicine in 1862 did not instantly transform how rural people practiced animal health care or accessed knowledge of veterinary science. The animal health manuals examined in this chapter expose common issues that animals faced and popular strategies that rural owners may have used to care for their animals. These sources offer a window into animals' health and the common illnesses, diseases, or injuries that humans sought to heal in rural environments.

NOTES

1. The author is thankful to the organizers of the "Traces of the Animal Past" conference for inviting her to participate in such an inspiring conference, and to Jennifer Bonnell, Sean Kheraj, and other participants for their thoughtful comments. For their enthusiasm and commitment to finding these documents on their back shelves and the permission to use the images found in this chapter, the author would also like to thank the archivists and staff at Dufferin County Archives, Grey Bruce County Archives, and Simcoe County Archives. The author is also grateful to Helen (Bellwood) Hanna for taking the time to share her family's animal health manual.

2. J. E. Hodgins and T. H. Haskett, *The Veterinary Science* (HH-0009, Museum of Dufferin Archives, Dufferin County, 1907), preface.

3. "The Veterinary Correspondence School—A Fake," *The Farmer's Advocate and Home Magazine* XLV, no. 896 (November 24, 1909): 1571.

4. OVC was established to meet demands for innovative veterinary medicine in 1862 when Ontario's Board of Health enlisted the efforts of Andrew Smith in 1862, a veterinary surgeon educated in Scotland and a Fellow of the Royal Veterinary Society, to develop a formal veterinary curriculum. By 1920, seventy-two students submitted this petition to Premier Drury. C. A. V. Barker and A. Margaret Evans, *Century One: A History of the Ontario Veterinary Association, 1874–1974* (Guelph: Distributed by the Authors, 1976), 128–29.

5. OVC, located in Toronto, then Guelph, Ontario, was the first institution for veterinary medicine in Canada and sought to provide a curriculum equivalent to doctors of human medicine. The London Correspondence School offices were located in London, Ontario. Barker and Evans, *Century One*, 128.

6. Knowledge and labour exchanges between farmers were often intertwined. In *Tenants in Time* (Montreal: McGill-Queen's University Press, 2009), Cathy Wilson shows how farmers relied on labour exchanges with their neighbours to improve land, the raising of livestock, and overall farm economies. Rural diaries also show that farmers sought to limit their exposure to animal health risks, death, and the financial costs associated with this.

7. The term "quack" refers to practices in human and veterinary medicine that were unproven or did not meet professional and institutional standards. Alexander Bowman refers to farmers' empirical knowledge, noting that empirical knowledge has roots in anthropological and ethnographic research. It refers to knowledge exchanges and "reveals how this knowledge was developed through experience and informed by observation, local environments, peer learning, and lessons passed down." Alexander Bowman, "Dipping, Dosing, Drenching: Managing Unhealthy Beasts on British Farms," (PhD diss., King's College London, 2019), 2, 13.

8. Charlotte G. Borst, "'The Noblest Roman of Them All?' Professional versus Popular Views of America's Country Doctors," *Journal of the History of Medicine and Allied Sciences* 76, no. 1 (January 2021): 88, 100.

9. Barker and Evans, *Century One*, 127.

10. For examples of these type of cases, see Barker and Evans, *Century One*, 128–37.

11 James Fisher, "The Master Should Know More: Book-farming and the Conflict Over Agricultural Knowledge," *Cultural and Social History* 15, no. 3 (2018): 327.

12 Fisher, "The Master Should Know More," 327.

13 J. E. S. "Farm Intelligently," *Ohio Farmer* 52, no. 2 (July 1877): 19.

14 Abigail Woods et al., *Animals and the Shaping of Modern Medicine: One Health and Its Histories* (Cham, Switzerland: Springer, 2017), 11–12; Susan Jones, *Valuing Animals: Veterinarians and Their Patients in Modern America* (Baltimore: The Johns Hopkins University Press, 2002), 4.

15 Lisa Cox, "Finding Animals in History: Veterinary Artifacts and the Use of Material History," in *The Historical Animal*, ed. Susan Nance (Syracuse: Syracuse University Press, 2015), 99.

16 Jones, *Valuing Animals*, 4.

17 Woods et al., *Animals and the Shaping of Modern Medicine*, 13.

18 Etienne Benson, "Animal Writes: Historiography, Disciplinarily, and the Animal Trace," in *Making Animal Meaning*, ed. Linda Kalof and Georgina Montgomery (East Lansing: Michigan State University Press, 2011), 5–6.

19 J. Gurnley Thompson, *The Domestic Encyclopedia* (971.36, Simcoe County Archives, 1879), table of contents.

20 Other publications list London, Ontario, as the location of Schuyley Smith and Company's main office. Thompson, *The Domestic Encyclopedia*, front cover.

21 Thompson, *The Domestic Encyclopedia*, vii.

22 Thompson, 10.

23 Margaret Derry, *Art and Science in Breeding: Creating Better Chickens* (Toronto: University of Toronto Press, 2012).

24 William Standen, Diary Entries from 26 March 1879 and 2 March 1880 (Peterborough: Trent University Archives).

25 Thompson, *The Domestic Encyclopedia*, 19.

26 Thompson, 20.

27 Thompson, 21–25.

28 In 1879, before germ theory was widely understood, Thompson recommended isolating outbreaks of disease immediately. For examples of isolation recommended for cattle, see *The Domestic Encyclopedia*, 198, 701; for potatoes, see 432.

29 Provenance of Andrew A. Gardenier's, *The Successful Stockman and Manual of Husbandry* (Springfield, Mass: The King-Richardson Co, 1903), ix. From the private collection of Helen (Bellwood) Hanna, a resident of Stayner and later, Alliston, Ontario (Simcoe County). This edition includes a blank subscription form for *The Farmer's Advocate*.

30 The King-Richardson Co headquarters were in Springfield, Massachusetts, with branch offices spanning "all of the United States and Canada, with a few in such far-off places as Australia, Alaska and Bermuda." John Tebbel, *A History of Book Publishing in the United States*, vol. 2: *The Expansion of an Industry* (New York: R. R. Bowker Co., 1972), 459–61.

31 Gardenier, *The Successful Stockman and Manual of Husbandry*, xi.

32 Gardenier, xii. Gardenier received a PhD in physiology and also arranged anatomical manikins for the *Lancet's* first volume in 1890.
33 Gardenier, 1.
34 Gardenier, 1. For example, in reference to the size and location of a horse's organs, symptoms, and treatments, see pages 38, 68, 114, 119, 124, 161, and 170. For the author's plea to readers to become familiar with their horse's anatomy, see page 79. The author refers to the anatomy of horses, cattle, sheep, swine, and poultry.
35 Gardenier, 133.
36 Gardenier, 134. Hodgins and Haskett also used this method regularly in their manual describing cold skin and extremities as a "death-like feeling," the size of pupils, heavy moaning or becoming delirious, nasal discharge, swelling joints as "full of oil" and "out too far," or changes to a cow's milk. Hodgins and Haskett, *The Veterinary Science*, 151, 250, 303, 305, 386.
37 Gardenier, 134. Hodgins and Haskett's *The Veterinary Science* was published by The Veterinary Science Association, whose head office was in London, Ontario, and branch office in Detroit, Michigan. An edition published in 1896 is available through *Canadiana Online*.
38 C. A. V. Barker "History of Veterinary Medicine," *The Canadian Encyclopedia*, 7 February 2006, updated on December 16, 2013, https://thecanadianencyclopedia.ca/en/article/history-of-veterinary-medicine; Barker and Evans, *Century One*, 105.
39 "Veterinarians in Ontario," *Farmer's Advocate and Home Magazine*, 1003; Barker and Evans, *Century One*, 129.
40 "Veterinarians in Ontario," *Farmer's Advocate and Home Magazine* LIII, no. 1342 (June 13, 1918): 1003; Barker and Evans, *Century One*, 112, n. 31.
41 Barker and Evans, *Century One*, 127.
42 Barker and Evans, 127.
43 Barker and Evans, 127.
44 Fisher, *The Master Should Know More*, 317.
45 Hodgins and Haskett, *The Veterinary Science*, preface.
46 Hodgins and Haskett, 128.
47 Hodgins and Haskett, *The Veterinary Science* (HH-0009, Museum of Dufferin Archives, Dufferin County, 107th Edition, 1907), "Revised and Enlarged" Preface.
48 Hodgins and Haskett, *The Veterinary Science*, 200–1.
49 See Castration of a horse in *The Domestic Encyclopedia*, 124–25, *The Stockman's Guide and Manual to Husbandry*, 125, and *The Veterinary Science*, 200–4. These manuals also offer descriptions for castrating other animals.
50 For an account of how people used vernacular veterinary medicine, see Anthony P. Cavender and Donald B. Ball "Home Cures for Ailing Horses: A Case Study of Nineteenth-Century Vernacular Veterinary Medicine in Tennessee," *Agricultural History* 90, no. 3 (Summer 2016): 311–37.
51 Glanders is a fatal and incurable bacteriological disease that spreads quickly between horses in close quarters. Barker and Evans, *Century One*, 128.
52 Barker and Evans, 128.

53 The Veterinary Correspondence School-a Fake," *Farmer's Advocate and Home Journal*, XLV no. 896, (November 24, 1909): 1571.

54 Barker and Evans, *Century One*, 128.

55 O. P. A. Ferguson Papers, Agriculture Department, 1926. As found in Barker and Evans, *Century One*, 132.

56 Hodgins and Haskett, *The Veterinary Science*, 1897 and 1907, title page.

57 Hodgins and Haskett, title page; Barker and Evans, *Century One*, 129.

58 Dr. George Bell, "Prevention, Diagnosis and Treatment of Common Disease of Livestock" (A2019.017 PF2157F1I2, Grey Roots County Archives, Grey County, 1933).

59 Similar differences and division arose between Andrew Smith and Duncan MacEachern at OVC. Thomas W. Dukes, "On the Middle Road: Queen's University's foray into veterinary and comparative medicine," *The Canadian Veterinary Journal* 48, no. 9 (2007).

60 Dukes, "On the Middle Road," 31–34.

61 Dr. George Bell, "First Aid for Sick Animal, Sixth Edition" (A2012.084, Box 1, Collection of Sydney Jackson, Grey Roots County Archives, Grey County), 18.

62 Dr. Lisa Cox, Curator of the C. A. V. Barker Museum at OVC, personal communication, June 25, 2021. Cure-all medicines were commonly promoted as a way to self-heal for humans and a means for humans to treat their animals without access to doctors or veterinarians in rural areas. For a historical account of patent medicine development see Ross D. Petty, "Pain-Killer: A 19th Century Global Patent Medicine and the Beginnings of Modern Brand Marketing," *Journal of Macromarketing* 39, no. 3 (2019): 287–303; Denise Maines, "Why the Appeal? A study of almanacs advertising Dr. Chase's patent medicines, 1904–1959," *Pharmacy History* 145, no. 4 (2012): 180–85.

63 Bell, "First Aid for Sick Animal," 18, 44; Advertisements for Dr. Bell's Veterinary Medical Wonder appeared in many popular journals.

64 Online agricultural forums show how popular this drug was. One example shows people from Ontario, Texas, California, and Colorado commenting on its effectiveness. Some people were also still looking to buy replacements as late as 2005. "Dr. Bell's Veterinary Medical Wonder - Bull Session," https://ranchers.net/forum/viewtopic.php?t=2313.

65 The preservation of Dr. Bell's bottles would also be an insightful study that would speak to its popularity. C. A. V. Barker Museum of Canadian Veterinary History, Guelph, Ontario. Museum of Health Care at Kingston, Ontario.

66 Bell, "First Aid for Sick Animal, Sixth Edition," 18.

67 Bell, 17–18.

68 Bell, 18.

6

Animal Cruelty, Metaphoric Narrative, and the Hudson's Bay Company, 1919–1939[1]

George Colpitts

For the first time in its centuries-old history, the Hudson's Bay Company (HBC) had to confront the issue of cruelty to animals in the fur trade. In 1929, B. J. Davis, a shareholder, wrote a short letter to the HBC's executive secretary, attaching an article clipped from the *Daily Telegram*. The London newspaper had printed a report of fur-bearing animals suffering horrid deaths in steel leghold traps in Canada's north and seals being skinned alive by Newfoundland sealers. Deeply concerned, Davis asked, "whether the Hudson's Bay Company inflicts great pain on animals."[2]

HBC managers were aware of an anti-fur movement developing in the first decades of the twentieth century. As early as 1911, the *New York Times* reported that HBC and other traders in Canada's north were defending themselves from "'don't trap' propaganda ... from certain sources in this country."[3] Protest gained more momentum just after World War I, when British and American animal protectors organized fur boycotts and high profile demonstrations, and joined anti-steel trap leagues to put an end to cruelty in the fur trade.[4]

But how do we reply to Davis' seemingly simple question? As a fur buyer in North America, the HBC had little say over the activities and methods of independent trappers. At the same time, the HBC delivered trappers' furs to London wholesalers, and they in turn supplied dressers, furriers, and finally consumers. Surely all parties involved in fur trade and fashion shared some responsibility for the ways animals suffered in traps. In this modern dilemma, both the fur industry and its critics turned to metaphoric language to speak on behalf of animals. They did what humans do best: tell stories. Their animal stories served a clear purpose in the modern age when, as John Berger argues, urban life and industrialization obscured an understanding of the fundamental duality and interconnection between human and non-human animals. A tradition of anthropomorphic animal storytelling that had been "integral to the relation between man and animal and was an expression of their proximity" declined too.[5] Such storytelling has continued in the present era, but for "most modern, 'educated' readers," the moral qualities, intentionality, and individual personalities attributed to animals are read skeptically and make readers "uneasy."[6]

Both animal humanitarians and fur industry promoters nevertheless used metaphoric language very effectively to tell stories in the 1920s. They presented two different understandings of fur-bearers in nature to build an "oppositional argument," which Kathryn Olson and Thomas Goodnight have pointed out at play in the later anti-fur campaigns of the 1990s. Already in the 1920s, anti-cruelty advocates spoke "on behalf of beings" that were voiceless by "inventing and deploying oppositional arguments to block accepted opinions" about the fur industry.[7] In turn, the fur industry, including the HBC, advanced its own oppositional discourse, one offering quite a different understanding of animals.

If industry promoters and protesters shared common ground, it was in their audience. Both used modern communications media to present animals to consumers making purchasing decisions.[8] It is worth examining, then, as Joanna Dean suggests in this volume, just how much animals really figure in the record, the ways their realities were made invisible in archives, and, in this case, what form they ended up taking as story subjects. As Nigel Rothfels has suggested of "captured animals" in zoos, taxidermy collections, and picture books in the modern era, these wild animals communicated "very *un*natural histories" specifically to consumers.[9] In the oppositional discourse developing in the context of the anti-cruelty movement in the 1920s, fur industry protesters and promoters dramatized animals in nature and ascribed temperaments and morality to them that, in the end, resonated in the "quotidian terrain" of the commercialized city.[10]

The historian readily perceives modernist consumerism, grounded in the urban marketplace, significantly influencing views of wild animals in the twentieth century. As buying behaviours expanded up and down social classes with mail-order catalogue or department store purchases, Bettina Liverant argues that a new "consumer consciousness" emerged in twentieth-century urban, industrialized economies.[11] Fashion marketers and advertisers targeted women especially to shape their expectations and aspirations in a widening marketplace.[12] That animal protectors raised fur in consumer consciousness is not surprising. Conditions in cities had inspired new sensibilities toward work and animals, domesticated and wild.[13] As legislation in the nineteenth century began protecting animals as both common property and "sentient beings with a right to protection from suffering and neglect," urban animal protectors extended the "gospel of kindness" to animals in colonial settings, the countryside, and "wilderness" itself.[14]

Animal protectors took up the cause of wild fur-bearers in the spectacular take-off of fur fashion. From the 1890s onwards, consumers around the globe overtly and lavishly wore fur garments, hats, scarves, and boas. With a glut of industrially mass-dressed pelts to work with and new chemical dyes available, furriers produced goods for broad segments of the population, with cheaper furs within reach of mail-order catalogue shoppers.[15] Currents in fashion raised fur-bearing animals to spectacular visibility in urban spaces. Furriers offering the "Empire Figure" coat in the first decade of the century draped recognizable furs from a woman's shoulders.[16] More garishly, they wrapped the popular "animal style" stole, tippet, or scarf around a woman's neck with its animal head, paws, and tail intact. Consumers also wore furs year-round. By the end of World War I, designers used lighter furs to introduce the summer fur coat and accessory. Ironically, the modernist city, otherwise seen as separate from nature, was visually overrun by wild fur-bearers in coats, muffs, and stoles, both in winter and summer. In 1919, the American animal protector Alice Jean Cleator had seen enough. Women wore wild animals on "drab city street" and "on jostling, automobile-lined avenue." Fur appeared at the opera, social clubs, theatres, and churches. As Cleator pointed out, almost all these furs came from animals that suffered cruel deaths in steel leghold traps.[17]

But animal protectors had difficulty describing the natures and behaviours of animals in their welfare work. They joined a movement largely borne in the modernist city and, from a distance, could only imagine the emotion, psychology, and sensations of animals killed in traplines. As David Matlass has observed in post–World War II Britain, sport hunters, fishers, and agriculturalists might still have shared something of a "visceral" perception of animals in their use for "pleasure, profit or food." Visitors to natural areas influenced by "new naturalism," meanwhile, perceived animals from afar, worked to preserve them in nature without human interference and interaction, and came to know them in abstract ways, often in home science reading, bird watching, or naturalist observation during day hikes.[18]

It was across such geographic and imaginative distances that one of the first urban newspaper stories criticizing trappers and fur consumers appeared in 1899. The story ran in the *Chicago Tribune* to be carried in wire services to other papers. The writer felt that women now preferring to wear a seal, marten, or beaver pelt "to that of the sheep" were responsible for a rapid global disappearance of animals. It was "not highly unlikely" that a new form of the Audubon Society would organize to publicize "the agonizing cruelty which attended the capture of many of the wild mammals in order that woman may be warmly clad."[19] Most of the writer's criticisms fell on Canadian trappers, especially northern Indigenous hunters "scattered all over the immense British-American territory." These hunters earned a pittance by killing all manner of animals and selling pelts to the HBC so "that some far-off woman may wrap herself in furs when she does her Christmas shopping." Animals suffered accordingly. The writer recounted the story of "an old trapper named Noyes" who for thirty-seven years had not been south of the "town of Edmonton." Noyes estimated that every tenth pelt he had trapped "had but three feet," the animal having had to chew off a leg previously to escape from another trap.[20]

In 1904, a British newspaper reprinted a report denouncing the "Cruelties of Fashion," describing the fate of fur seals used in fashion coats: "Gangs of men on the beach entice the seals from the water, and drive them inland, panting and helpless. Then when the end of their journey is reached, the poor creatures are formed into long columns, three or four abreast, and made to pass between men armed with heavy clubs." Seal hunters as "inconceivable savages" and "the scum of the earth" did their work ultimately for the fur market: "Such is the price of vanity."[21] Such stories prompted leading women in Manchester in 1907 to convene an anti-fur fashion show "to demonstrate that without using fur, feathers, or leather women can dress smartly and economically."[22] Lady Clare Annesley, an organizer, admitted that urging women "to wear humane clothing" instead of fur was difficult "because the suffering caused seemed so removed."[23] In the same decade, a woman's fashion compendium referred readers to the efforts of E. Alexander Powell, of the Royal Geographical Society. An "intercessor" working on behalf of fur-bearing animals, Powell protested the use of leghold traps, telling his audiences at public talks: "If only those furs which you wear so becomingly and so carelessly could talk, dear lady, what tales they would unfold."[24]

When the American SPCA (ASPCA) printed its "Cruelties of Fashion" pamphlet at the turn of the twentieth century, excerpts of its most sensational claims ran in both American and British newspapers. In 1912, a *New York Times* article reprinted the ASPCA's descriptions of seal hunters tormenting animals. It reported hunters killing weasels not with traps but with large pieces of iron coated with grease. In cold winter temperatures, these animals "lick the grease, and then this intense cold of the iron causes the tongue to freeze fast to it. From this there is no escape except by pulling out the tongue by the roots." Marten hunters were using dogs to tree animals and beat them down "with long poles into nets beneath."[25] The reports made a terrific impact. "Winifred," a fashion authority, even included the information in one of her 1913 "Fashion Fancies" columns in an English weekly newspaper. After discussing straw hats in fashion that year, she reprinted the ASPCA's information in stark bullet points, adding that "many members of the most exclusive circles of American Society are wearing no furs this winter, on account of the recent disclosures regarding the cruel practices on the animals that yield the valuable pelts."[26]

Protesters focused most of their concerns on the leghold trap. The leghold, or gin trap, was already criticized in the English countryside where it was used for rabbit hunting. In the fur trade, hunters could use relatively cheap legholds to kill animals more efficiently to produce far more pelts, which were rising in price in the last decades of the century. By the 1920s, about fifteen manufacturers mass-produced some eight to nine million leghold traps annually for the fur trade.[27] In their pamphlets, news reports, and other publications, activists used text and images, often photographs, to graphically present the leghold and develop key ideas about wild animals, their environments, and humans in nature. Many of their depictions capitalized on a contemporary idealized understanding of nature as wilderness.[28] Protectors drew inspiration from a narrative technique already developed at the turn of the century in animal stories written by Ernest Thompson Seton, G. D. Roberts, and William J. Long. Adopting a wild animal's perspective, these stories individualized the animal subject and attributed human emotions and intentionality to it. Immensely popular among the urban middle classes, these stories helped urbanites understand "wilderness" as a curative space to redress the problems of modernity.[29]

Fur protestors wrote animal stories in the flagship monthly of the Massachusetts SPCA, *Our Dumb Animals*, just after WWI. By then, fur fashion rebounded to new heights and year-round use. In 1919, the *New York Times* reported that the American Blue Cross Society and the New York Women's League for Animals were campaigning against the leghold trap and "the summer fur craze."[30] American actor Minnie Fiske, a prominent animal protector, mounted boycotts against fur purchases.[31] Major Edward Breck began speaking tours to urge legislation to ban steel traps across North America. He asked all like-minded societies to join his "Anti-Steel Trap League."[32]

After 1919, almost every issue of *Our Dumb Animals* drew attention to the leghold. Alongside photographs of a trapped bear, fox, or other animal, contributors typically wrote poetry to recount from an animal's perspective its life and death in a trap. Ellen Master's "Trapped," for instance, told the story of an animal as "he trod the pathless forest wild, with easy stealth and grace, nor dreamed there lurked a deadly foe in such familiar place."[33] Henry Flury's poem "Lady in Furs" gave a voice to the fox that made up a woman's garment: "You look fine in your furs, my lady; if you only knew what they cost. . . . All night long, freezing in the snow with my right paw in a cruel trap." The fox tells the woman that it was the "father" of six cubs, "the cutest babies you ever saw, but you envied my hide so now, they will starve."[34] Similarly, a 1919 issue of *Our Dumb Animals* ran an illustration showing a woman, in sweltering summer temperatures, wearing a wolf stole in animal style. The woman finds the wolf's ghost trapped in a leghold at her feet, imploring her not to wear summer furs. A poem accompanying the image, "The Kind Lady's Furs," tells the story of a weasel (or ermine) living in nature, away from humans. After successfully evading a pack of wolves, the weasel steps into a trapper's leghold. "A white man came ere the wolves might come, and he carried that ermine's peltry home. Milady she wears it with joy and pride, not caring a whit how the ermine died!"[35]

Another very different counter-narrative developed to support the fur industry as it grew in scale in the late nineteenth century. Naturalists, hunters, and conservationists had taken umbrage with the sentimental portrayal of animal stories. In the "nature faker" controversy of the early twentieth century, John Burroughs and later Teddy Roosevelt publicly denounced animal sentimentalists and argued that "ruthless competition, survival of the fittest and instinct" dominated "Nature."[36] Burroughs, taking exception to "natural history romancers" who ascribed "almost the entire human psychology" to animals reminded his readers that animal intelligence, or "wit," was largely unknowable and likely attributed to primal emotions, "fear, love and hunger," which, in some animals, prompted subtle, bloodthirsty, and even cruel behaviours.[37]

Fur industry supporters capitalized on this understanding of nature as a competitive and violent place to create their own moralized stories. These stories, written in a more objective voice, were often framed in scientific observations of animals. For instance, author Mabel Osgood Wright in 1898 wrote a children's book about a family spending a season on a farm where the children learn about animal life, the differences between domesticated and wild animals, and how animals in their classification divide between their kingdoms, classes, families, and species. But Wright took license to ascribe morality to the animals she depicted. When the children visit a trapper's cabin in the woods, they learn about the animals that provide furs for urban fashion. The trapper teaches them that weasels "are the most malicious, blood-thirsty, and wasteful of all our fourfoots," adding that they killed "merely for the pleasure of it . . . only taking a suck of blood here and a bite of flesh there" among its victims. In nature, the mink nearly equalled the weasel in its "steady-goin' mischief." The children are surprised by what they learn: "It seems very queer that mother's [mink] muff once went sneaking and tramping all over the country," one exclaims. If their mother knew "how savage they are, I'm sure she would be afraid of her little tippet with the head and claws."[38] The trapper also describes the cruel nature of pine martens: "If those martins ain't got tempers!" the trapper explains, "And don't they just fight fierce when once they start! I saw one kill a Rabbit; it wasn't satisfied with killin' it, but went on and tore and clawed it all to bits."[39]

That animals were themselves cruel with one another could justify their use in fashion, a point underlined by Agnes C. Laut. In 1921, the Canadian-born journalist and popular writer of numerous fur trade histories, wrote a book about the modern fur industry. She included chapters on the wonders of industrialized fur dressing, and others providing women with information to make informed choices when they purchased furs from stores. The first sentence of her book *The Fur Trade of America* asks, "Is fur trading founded on cruelty?"[40] She pointed out that, "For the past few years, there has been a campaign waged in the United States, which almost charges any one wearing a piece of fur with murder." Laut provided the rejoinder: "And I answer unhesitatingly—it is not."[41]

Laut pointed out the economic reasons why trappers killed animals quickly and without suffering since a trapped animal's trauma and struggle devalued its fur when sold.[42] But she defended fur consumerism more explicitly on the basis of how fur-bearers acted with one another: "However cruel trapping may seem to the tender-hearted city dweller, who knows wild life only from books and not from direct contact, trapping is kindness itself compared to the sufferings and deaths of fur animals in wild life."[43] Laut stressed that "you have to go to the wilds and go only once to realize natural life is crueler by far than the most careless, thoughtless fur hunter." In a world where there "is no such thing as a natural death in the wilds," a rabbit fell prey to the weasel, the weasel to the wolf or bear. "Each creature in the animal world preys on the creature one degree smaller or weaker than itself. That failing they eat their own young like rats, or disembowel their mates as the wolves and minks do." Laut drew from the works of contemporary scientific authorities to describe animals and their temperaments this way. For instance, William T. Hornaday described the mink as a "wanton murderer" and the weasel as a "courageous and aggressive" animal that sometimes killed "purely to gratify its murderous disposition."[44] Laut characterized weasels as "blood-suckers and blood-drunkards," the mink as a "murderer" hunting "for the sheer deviltry of killing."[45] In respect to the latter, "my sympathies don't run out to the mink," she wrote, "when he is transformed into fur."[46] As for protests against the seal hunt, Laut used the naturalist observations of Henry Wood Elliott to describe how cruel Pacific hair seals were one with another: males fought other males for rights to "harems" of females in "the cruelest thing in all the cruelties of fur life." She wished that "sentimentalists who rail against fur" would see that male seals would "kill thousands of mothers and thousands of pups" if many of them were not themselves killed fighting each other.[47]

Separated through commodity chains from animals in nature, metropolitan fur buyers, like the HBC, London wholesalers and furriers initially remained aloof from the protest. The HBC's new Development Department, which formed in 1925, only briefly inquired into the possibility of developing a new trap for the industry. Animal protectors in the US had already started sponsoring annual contests among inventors of box or instant kill "humane" traps that might replace legholds in the trade, none proving successful in that regard.[48] The HBC's development department was well-positioned to take up the same research, having been formed to apply science and technology to improve and market HBC-branded products.[49] Its new director, Charles Townsend, who had run a similar department at the global soap giant, Lever Soap company, wrote a memo to the HBC's governor in 1926 to point out that, "as you probably know, there is often a good deal of agitation regarding the method by which furs are obtained." Animals caught in the "iron jaws" of leghold traps "die very slowly and in great anguish with hunger and cold."[50] Townsend believed it would be "comparatively easy" to devise a trap with an explosive charge to kill an animal instantly. He admitted that such a device had to be "foolproof" since any explosive mechanism might pose threats to children "in the native tent or hut."[51] Townsend then wondered "whether it would be possible to contrive a trap which on being sprung would release some kind of anaesthetic? Probably a wild idea."[52] There is no archival evidence that the HBC's governor, Charles Sale, bothered replying to Townsend's far-fetched ideas. British humanitarians did send the company several alternative trap prototypes in the hopes that the Canadian fur trade would adopt them for use. The London office, in turn, sent some for examination by its Winnipeg-based Canadian Committee. Given that many were designed in the English countryside, they were deemed unsuitable and impractical for the climate, habitat, and animals of Northern Canada.[53]

In the meanwhile, the HBC avoided engaging with the protest even when urged to do so, such as in 1929 when one of its city wholesalers, concerned by anti-trapping pamphlets (singling out the cruelty of the fur trade in Canada), implored the company's governor to issue a "reassuring statement" to the newspapers. The company's secretary thought it would be unwise to do so, "as we think such a reply could not put to rest the exaggerated accounts which appear from time to time."[54] Like the London Fur Trade Association in 1930, the HBC resisted going to newspapers with its own damage control when a British Labour MP proposed, unsuccessfully, a ban on fur imports "on the grounds that their procuring involves cruelty and the fact that cheaper warm fabrics, known as artificial furs, can now be obtained."[55]

But in 1929 the company did need to respond to shareholders writing letters to the governor after they grew concerned by assertions made by a London anti-cruelty campaigner. Major Charles C. Van Der Byl had been circulating his own pamphlets against fur fashions by the mid-1920s and publishing letters in prominent London dailies. He even visited the HBC's London offices to ask pointed questions about trapping in Canada. When the company received B. J. Davis' letter in 1929, himself troubled by Van Der Byl's report in the *Daily Telegram*, J. Chadwick Brooks arranged a meeting with the shareholder. Brooks believed that Van Der Byl's reports were "obviously highly coloured and incorrect as to facts in several instances," having gone over Van Der Byl's published pamphlets to highlight hearsay "sensational" reports made in them. These included the claim that hunters were using frozen iron bars to trap martens by their tongues, and the "popular fallacy" being reported that sealers were killing mothers for their fetuses.[56] In their meeting, Brooks explained to Davis the reality of Canadian trapping as he understood it. In a follow-up letter, he reiterated the same assertions Laut had made in her book: a trapper had every economic incentive to visit his traps regularly and kill animals quickly before they suffered; Indigenous people depended on trapping income and they would become a burden on the state without it; and, finally, that it was "doubtful" that a trapper "is more cruel than nature itself." Davis pointed out "the pain which must follow to an animal seized by another as its prey, and to the practice of certain animals of playing with a wounded victim before killing it."[57]

Throughout the 1930s, the HBC responded in the same manner to a growing number of letters from shareholders and then the British public. These included a writer who had "worked with animals all [his] life and love[d] them" expressing his wonder that such cruelties existed in the fur trade. "What use are our churches, I ask?"[58] Another challenged, "your own women folk or your shareholders to be present at your inevitable holocausts [on the trapline] and not come away revolted and sworn not to use wraps or adornment so bloodily procured."[59] Yet another had been shown "photographs of the methods employed by Canadian trappers" and demanded assurance that HBC furs "were not taken in such a manner."[60] Others wanted the company to sell only farmed furs, and to sew labels in them certifying that they were "humane."[61] By the end of the 1930s, the HBC was contending with Canadian animal humanitarians in Toronto, Ottawa, and Halifax who joined the protest against leghold traps, promoted the purchase of "humane" furs from farms, and encouraged humane trap development. In 1939, the Toronto Humane Society announced that the Duchess of Hamilton and Brandon was sending her coronation robes made of fake fur to crown that year's humane fur display at the Canadian National Exhibition.[62]

Few letters appear in the company archives dated during and after World War II, coinciding with a general decline in anti-trapping literature and attempted legislative action to ban legholds across North America.[63] Animal protectors nevertheless continued to sponsor humane trap designs. Though alternative traps were invented and marketed, it was really the work sponsored by Victoria, BC, animal protectors that led Canadian trapper Frank Conibear to perfect a practical and relatively cheap device that could replace the leghold. His collapsing "body-grip" box design killed rather than held an animal. The "conibear" proving successful in field tests in the early 1950s, the industry now had its "humane" trap.[64] Though it took decades for the conibear to replace legholds in traplines, the HBC could point to its existence to respond to a revived anti-cruelty protest and letter campaign in the 1960s.[65]

But as early as the 1950s and certainly by the 1970s, anti-fur discourse began changing from a moral to an ethical campaign.[66] John Gentile suggests that this later anti-trapping campaign, coinciding with a return to fashion of visually bulky, long-haired fur-bearers (fox, coyote, and racoon), was marked by more sophisticated professional lobbying, less sentimentalism, and more scientific research and evidence on both sides of the protest. More fundamentally, anti-trapping campaigns were now informed by animal rights as a philosophy.[67] Protesters reasoned that wild animals should not be killed for fashion at all, a position advanced in 1970s anti-seal hunt campaigns and more broadly in 1980s anti-fur campaigns.[68] The expanded North American urban base, with populations moving into secondary and tertiary economic sectors, proved receptive to this campaigning. As one study of the growing support for anti-trapping in the 1980s suggested, "most Americans know relatively little about animals. Most see wild animals only on television or in zoos, and most interactions with animals are with pets."[69] At present, many urbanites gain understandings of wild animals through the Internet, films, mall nature stores, and the discourse of animal rights organizations still problematizing consumer purchases with evocative images and metaphoric descriptions of animals. Animal rights groups count as a major triumph a recent fur ban occurring in California and major US retail chains now choosing not to carry fur products. In these successes, the anti-fur campaign has removed choice, at least in fur products, from modern consumer consciousness altogether.[70]

In the 1920s, as the fur industry grew in scale, both its protesters and promoters developed discursive oppositional arguments about wild animals, nature, and humans in nature. On one side of the debate, protesters anthropomorphized trapped animals suffering torment in the wilderness. Industry promoters developed their own narratives to portray animals as competitive, violent, and willfully cruel toward one another in nature. These storytellers ascribed human attributes to animals and made assumptions about animal nature, psychology, and intentionality. But rather than seeing either side of the protest as presenting animals in "right" and "wrong" ways, historians might further explore how metaphoric language for and against fur fashion served to shift the gaze of urban consumers toward wild animals. Storytellers interrogated buying behaviours in a widening consumer marketplace and forced its various consumers and suppliers, the HBC included, to conscientiously consider animal life far removed from everyday experience. Metaphoric language, then, had its merits. For this reason, David Copland Morris does not dismiss, as many literary scholars have, John Muir's 1909 anthropomorphic dog story, *Stickeen*. Muir used the story to counter a prevailing mindset of modernity, that "there is an unbridgeable chasm of difference between human and animal consciousness." Muir deftly crafted his anthropomorphic story in order to describe "the dog in a manner which tries neither to explain away human-like emotions, nor to attribute human emotions when there was no evidence for doing so."[71] In the past, anthropomorphic animal stories served as a means for humans to make sense of themselves in a changing world. Americans used such stories in the debate over whether or not to welcome the recently introduced eastern grey squirrel, which was proliferating in major urban centres by the end of the nineteenth century.[72] Metaphoric language can certainly affirm the dualism that exists between humans and their non-human counterparts and remind audiences of their significant interrelationship. Literary scholars studying children's stories have recently seen the value of anthropomorphic animal stories that were easily understood and remembered by young readers, but did not necessarily "lead children to hold unrealistic beliefs about the psychological properties of real animals and did not hinder recall of factual properties."[73] Chengcheng You suggests that anthropomorphic, rather than anthropocentric, animal stories can "contest species boundaries, revisit the animal in us humans, and encourage a nature-friendly perspective worthy of attention."[74] Such stories can serve as a "contact zone" between human and non-human animals in the reality of the Anthropocene.[75]

Historians, too, might consider the merits of anthropomorphic animal stories. Drawing on the wide variety of sources highlighted in this volume, they might, as John Muir did, use this story form to recapture the dualism and interrelationships that exist between humanity and these non-human "others." Stories are always an invention of human imagination. Historical narratives, whatever sources they draw from, ultimately reflect in some manner human ontology and epistemology. Historians run risks in attempting to bridge legal, linguistic, religious, and cultural divides to speak on behalf of historical "others" far removed in time and place. They should take risks to tell more, not less, stories of animals in the past. The animal stories that contributed to debates over fur fashion forced modernist consumers to consciously consider the ways that buying behaviours manifestly impacted the real world, perceptions, and experiences of wild fur-bearers, however they might be understood by humans. Historians might consider more carefully the ways anthropomorphic animal stories played a role in modernity, consumerism, and urban life, and how this story form might continue to enliven our own narratives that attempt to centre animals within history, rather than on its peripheries.

NOTES

1   The author was grateful to present this paper as the Avie Bennett-Historica Public Lecture in Canadian History in the context of the "Traces of the Animal Past Conference" in 2019. He thanks editors Jennifer Bonnell and Sean Kheraj for their encouragement and suggestions for revisions and improvements, as well as the anthology's readers in peer review. Research for this paper was made possible through a fellowship from the McGill Institute for the Study of Canada and funding by the Social Sciences and Humanities Research Council of Canada. The author is also thankful for the research support of the Hudson's Bay Company Archives in Winnipeg, and especially the help of archivist Chris Kotecki.
2   Letter from B. J. Davis, June 6, 1929, A.402/557, Hudson's Bay Company Archives [hereafter HBCA].
3   "Against 'Don't Trap' Movement," *New York Times*, January 11, 1911.
4   Thomas Dunlap, *Saving America's Wildlife: Ecology and the American Mind, 1850–1990* (Princeton: Princeton University Press, 1988), 93.
5   John Berger, "Why Look at Animals?," in *About Looking* (New York: Vintage Books, 1991), 11.
6   Berger, "Why Look at Animals?," 11.
7   "Entanglements of Consumption," *The Quarterly Journal of Speech* 80, no. 3 (August 1994): 253.
8   Kristoffer Archibald, "Presenting the Polar Bear: Mass Media Images, the Arctic, and the Creation of a Charismatic Species in Postwar North America" (master's thesis, Trent University, 2010), 22–23, 138–39.
9   Nigel Rothfels, *Savages and Beasts: The Birth of the Modern Zoo* (Baltimore: Johns Hopkins University Press, 2002), 6.

10 On American consumer culture and ideas of nature that are generated in the "quotidian terrain" of the city, see Jennifer Jaye Price, "Flight Maps: Encounters with Nature in Modern American Culture" (PhD diss., Yale University, 1998), 2–5, 60, 209–17.

11 Battina Liverant, *Buying Happiness: the Emergence of Consumer Consciousness in English Canada* (Vancouver: UBC Press, 2018), 15–43.

12 Donica Belisle, *Retail Nation: Department Stores and the Making of Modern Canada* (Vancouver: UBC Press, 2011); Cheryl Krasnick Warsh and Dan Malleck, eds., *Consuming Modernity: Gendered Behaviour and Consumerism before the Baby Boom* (Vancouver: UBC Press, 2013), 1–8; Jane Nicholas, "Beauty Advice for the Canadian Modern Girl in the 1920s," in *Consuming Modernity*, ed. Warsh and Malleck, 181–99.

13 Hilda Kean, *Animal Rights: Political and Social Change in Britain since 1800* (London: Reaktion Books, 1998), 31; J. Keri Cronan, *Art for Animals: Visual Culture and Animal Advocacy, 1870–1914* (University Park, PA: Penn State University Press, 2018), 7; Darcy Ingram, "Beastly Measures: Animal Welfare, Civil Society, and State Policy in Victorian Canada," *Journal of Canadian Studies* 47, no. 1 (Winter 2013): 221–52; Kathleeen Kete, The Beast in the Boudoir: Petkeeping in Nineteenth-Century Paris (Berkeley: University of California Press, 1994), 6–21.

14 Janet M. Davis, *The Gospel of Kindness: Animal Welfare and the Making of Modern America* (Oxford: Oxford University Press, 2016), 16, 28.

15 Harold Innis, *The Fur-Trade of Canada* (Toronto: University of Toronto Press, 1926), 14–17, 75–100; Arthur J. Ray, *The Canadian Fur Trade in the Industrial Age* (Toronto: University of Toronto Press, 1990), 50–95.

16 George Colpitts, "The Domesticated Body and the Industrialized Imitation Fur Coat in Canada, 1919–1939," in *Contests and Contestations: The Body in Canadian History*, ed. Patrizia Gentile and Jane Nicolas (Toronto: University of Toronto Press, 2013), 135–36.

17 Alice Jean Cleator, "Fur and the Steel Trap," *Our Dumb Animals* 52 (1919): 119.

18 David Matless, "Versions of animal-human: Broadland, c. 1945–1970," in *Animal Spaces, Beastly Places: New Geographies of Human-Animal Relations*, ed. Chris Philo and Chris Wilbert (London: Routledge, 2000), 115–40.

19 "Fur to be more expensive," *Chicago Tribune* article, appearing in the *Daily Picayune*, September 4, 1899.

20 "Fur to be more expensive."

21 *Good Health*, September 1904, reprinted from "A. M. in *The News*."

22 "Animals' Welfare Week," *Manchester Courier and Lancashire General Advisor*, November 13, 1907.

23 "Animals' Welfare Week."

24 Quoted in *The Woman's Athenaeum for the Intellectual, Industrial and Social Advancement of Women*, vol. 2 (New York: The Woman's Athenaeum, 1912), 295.

25 "Says furs are unhealthy," *New York Times*, December 1, 1912.

26 "Fashion Fancies," *Cheltenham Looker-On*, February 8, 1913.

27 Innis, *The Fur-Trade of Canada*, 93.

28 Matt Cartmill, *A View to a Death in the Morning: Hunting and Nature Through History* (Harvard University Press, 1996), 162–65

29   Mitman, *Reel Nature*, 9–11.
30   "Women to Save Fur Animals," *New York Times*, May 27, 1919;
31   "Prayer of a Trapped Animal," *Our Dumb Animals* 53, no. 1 (June 1920): 21; "Actress Addresses Washington Women," *New York Times*, March 20, 1925.
32   "20,000,000 Animals Tortured in Traps," *New York Times*, October 24, 1923.
33   "Trapped," *Our Dumb Animals*, 53, no. 5 (October 1920), 80
34   "Lady in Furs," *Our Dumb Animals*, 52, no. 8 (January 1920), 118
35   "The Kind Lady's Furs," *Our Dumb Animals*, 52, no. 1 (June 1919), 6.
36   Mitman, *Reel Nature*, 12.
37   John Burroughs, *Ways of Nature* (Boston: Houghton Mifflin Company, 1905), 14–19.
38   Wright, *Four-Footed Americans*, 185–86.
39   Wright, 187.
40   Agnes C. Laut, *The Fur Trade in America* (New York: The Macmillan Company, 1921), v.
41   Laut, *The Fur Trade in America*, v.
42   Laut, vii.
43   Laut, 51.
44   William T. Hornaday, *The American Natural History* (New York: Charles Scribner's Sons, 1904), 29; see also Hornaday's *The Minds and Manners of Wild Animals: A Book of Personal Observations* (New York: Charles Scribner's Sons, [1922] 1927).
45   Laut, *The Fur Trade in America*, 98–99.
46   Laut, 99.
47   Laut, xi., 127–29; see Henry Wood Elliott, *A Monograph of the Seal-Islands of Alaska* (Special Bulletin 176, Washington: US Commission of Fish and Fisheries, 1882), 32.
48   "Prize for Humane Trap," *Our Dumb Animals* 53, no. 11 (April 1921): 174; "New Humane Trapping," *Daily Mail Atlantic*, July 24, 1928; "Eighth Annual Humane Trap Contest," *American Humane Society* pamphlet, 1935. On early alternative traps, see John R. Gentile, "The evolution and geographic aspects of the anti-trapping movement: a classic resource conflict" (PhD diss., Oregon State University, 1983), 67–69.
49   Robrecht Declercq, "Natural Born Merchants: The Hudson Bay Company, Science and Canada's Final Fur Frontiers (1925–1931)," *Business History* (2019), 1–15.
50   Townsend Memorandum, February 24, 1926, Development Department Files, A.95/50, HBCA.
51   Townsend Memorandum, February 24, 1926.
52   Townsend Memorandum, February 25, 1926.
53   See Correspondence and designs of the "Gilpa," "Millow Humane Snare," and Van Der Byl's "Gripper Simplex" traps in A.402/557, HBCA.
54   Letter from W. L. Gower, July 8, 1929, A.402/557, HBCA.
55   Letter from B. G. Arthur, February 10, 1930, A.402/557, HBCA.
56   Secretary's copy, "The Horrors of Fur Trapping," A.402/557, HBCA.
57   Letter to B. J. Davis, June 18, 1929, A.402/557, HBCA
58   Falkiner W. Harding to Secretary, December 10, 1929, A.402/557, HBCA.

59   Letter from J. W. Rattray, April 23, 1933, A.402/557, HBCA.
60   Letter from G. M. West, November 1, 1934, A.402/557, HBCA.
61   Letter from Alma E. Barbour, November 28, 1935, and Dorothy E. Currie to Secretary, February 9, 1936, A.402/557, HBCA.
62   "Ducal Robe Used Against Steel Traps," *Globe and Mail,* June 24, 1938; "Steel Traps," *The Times,* November 22, 1938.
63   Samuel B. Linhart, "Furbearer Management and the Steel Leghold Trap," *Great Plains Wildlife Damage Control Workshop Proceedings,* 156 (December 1985), 56.
64   Eric Collier, "Revolutionary New Trap," *Outdoor Life,* (September/October 1957) 38–41, 68–73, 80–82. On earlier alternative traps, see Gentile, "The evolution and geographic aspects of the anti-trapping movement, 67–69.
65   The slow adoption of the conibear concerned Senator F. A. McGrand writing to the HBC, 30 March 1962 and J. de N. Kennedy, 19 February 1968. Still, the company felt confident that the conibear was being widely used as of 1970 and that "steel-toothed traps . . . are discouraged and are, I am glad to say not popular," Letter to Gary Boyart, 24 February 1970; all letters in A.402/557, HBCA.
66   Ethically-based anti-fur is found in EC Comics, "*What Fur?!*" 5 (October/November 1952); and Dodie Smith, *The Hundred and One Dalmatians* (Heinemann, 1956).
67   Peter Singer articulated the ethical basis to protest in *Animal Liberation: A New Ethics for Our Treatment of Animals* (Harper Collins, 1975).
68   Julia Emberley, *Venus and Furs: The Cultural Politics of Fur* (I.B. Tauris, 1998), 170–203; Olson and Goodnight, "Entanglements of Consumption," 249–76; Catherine Harper, "I Found Myself inside Her Fur. . . ." *Textile* 6, no. 3 (2008): 300–13
69   Linhart, "Furbearer Management and the Steel Leghold Trap," 54.
70   Sapna Maheshwari, "Macy's Home to $8,000 Mink Jackets, Will Stop Selling Fur Products by 2021," *New York Times,* October 21, 2019; Leticia Miranda, "Macy's, Bloomingdale's to Stop Selling Fur," *NBC News,* October 2, 2019; "California becomes the first state to ban animal fur products," *The Guardian,* October 13, 2019.
71   David Copland Morris, "A Dog's Life: Anthropomorphism, Sentimentality, and Ideology in John Muir's *Stickeen, Western American Literature,* 31, no. 2 (Summer 1996): 139–57.
72   Etienne Benson, "The Urbanization of the Eastern Gray Squirrel in the United States," *Journal of American History* 100, no. 3 (December 2013): 691–710.
73   Megan S. Geerdts, Gretchen A. Van de Walle, and Vanessa LoBue, "Learning about Real Animals from Anthropomorphic Media," *Imagination, Cognition and Personality* 36, no. 1 (2016): 19.
74   Chengcheng You, "The Necessity of an Anthropomorphic Approach to Children's Literature," *Children's Literature in Education* 52 (2021): 188.
75   You, "The Necessity of an Anthropomorphic Approach," 184.

PART III:
The Unknowable Animal

7

Vanishing Flies and the Lady Entomologist

Catherine McNeur

The flies began emerging from the wheat around dusk, giving Margaretta Hare Morris little more than half an hour to observe the tiny, delicate creatures as they flitted from stalk to stalk. Requiring a magnifying glass to see them in any detail, Morris had first observed the flies as flaxseed-like pupa sleepily clinging to the young wheat plants in her neighbour's field a few days prior, but now that they had fully transformed, there were too many and they were too quick to count. The swarms hovered over the wheat field, laying their eggs in the grain to secure a good food source for the next generation.[1]

That summer in 1836, months before what would become known as the Panic of 1837, farmers had discovered something ominous. Wheat fields that showed promise in May had withered by July, producing paltry harvests if any.[2] As this plight spread from field to field and state to state, the price of wheat doubled in most cities, impacting everything from flour to whiskey. Consumers, already shaken by other constrictions on their personal finances, felt this price hike in their growling stomachs.[3]

At the heart of this wheat crisis were the flies, and the most notorious wheat fly was the Hessian fly, named for the mercenary soldiers who fought alongside the British in the American Revolution at the same moment farmers first spotted the tiny, seemingly fragile fly and its devastating

Fig. 7.1 Margaretta Hare Morris, entomologist.
Source: Littell Family Papers, University of Delaware Special Collections.

effects. For more than a century, naturalists and then entomologists would debate whether the Hessian fly was truly Hessian.[4] Regardless of their origin, from the 1780s onwards, Hessian fly larvae would occasionally devastate wheat fields, consuming much of the young plants.

The wheat fields near Philadelphia were not immune, and the entomologist Margaretta Hare Morris was eager to study what to her was an "object of peculiar interest."[5] She was so singularly devoted to observing them that she filled countless conversations with excited details about everything she was learning. One friend remarked that "Margaretta's heart is as full of Hessian flies, as ever was a wheat field." After making her own initial set of observations about the fly in June 1836, Morris wanted to compare what she was finding with what the famed American entomologist Thomas Say had published about Hessian flies decades earlier in 1817 in the first volume of the *Journal of the Academy of Natural Sciences*. This was the first article to officially describe the fly and its life cycle. Say even gave the species its official name: "*Cecidomyia destructor* Say." Say's friend

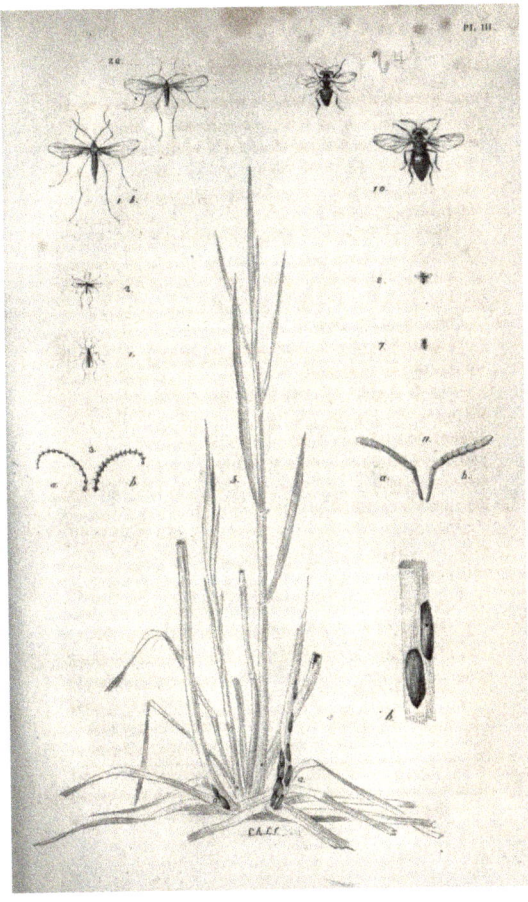

Fig. 7.2 The Hessian fly and its parasite, by Charles Alexandre LeSueur (1817). While there is no known extant image of the *Cecidomyia culmicola* (Morris), it so closely resembled the Hessian fly depicted by LeSueur as to be indistinguishable.

Charles Alexandre LeSueur provided illustrations a few months later in another issue of the journal (Figure 7.2).[6]

Morris was familiar with both Say and LeSueur as they had been her tutors when she was just a teenager. They taught her not only entomology but also drawing, and as she would later recount, they "made a pet" of her because of her scientific promise. Like many entomologists of the early nineteenth century, Morris was mostly self-taught, inspired by early curiosity, though she benefited from the lessons she received from the leading American scientists living in Philadelphia.[7]

Morris had not gone into the fly-infested field looking to prove her teachers wrong. She was there for the "love of the study." Still, as Morris read Say's article, she could not help feeling that something was off. Say's staccato description of the creatures seemed to ring true enough: "Head and thorax black; wings black, fulvous at base; feet pale, covered with black hair." His language was imprecise but that was also standard for the era, relating the length of one body part to another rather than providing precise measurements, and describing colours as "brownish" or "whitish."[8]

Morris' puzzle, though, came with his vague description of the fly's behaviour. Say began his narrative of their life cycle with a statement that seemed to lack confidence: "The history of the changes of this insect, is probably briefly this—." Appearing to make assumptions based on a limited study, Say went on to describe how the female fly deposited its eggs "between the vagina of the inner leaf and the culm nearest to the root of the plant."[9] This is where Morris had an issue, and it was not with the way female anatomy was being mapped onto botanical physiology. She believed she had witnessed the fly laying its eggs in the head of the wheat, amid the seeds—not in the groove between the leaf and the stem. Had Say been wrong? Or had Morris discovered a completely new fly?

* * *

As someone researching the work of a long-forgotten female scientist, I would love to determine what the fly was that Morris discovered, at the very least for the sake of setting the record straight. She was not the only one to witness a fly that appeared to be the Hessian fly but behaved differently; farmers had also reported similar observations in agricultural journals that summer and during the summers that followed as infestations returned.[10] And while her life's work included far more discoveries and insects than just this wheat fly, the fly was Morris' first step into the public scientific world of presentations and publications, as well as her first vetting. The controversy that ensued ultimately played a role in her erasure from historical memory.

Many of the chapters in this volume look to uncover how we can know more about the lives and histories of animals, despite their being hidden within archival collections. This task becomes even more difficult if the scientist devoted to learning about the creatures has been largely forgotten and is similarly hidden in the archives, which is the case for Margaretta Hare Morris. Despite being well known during her lifetime, her legacy has mostly been forgotten and her scientific records are, for the most part, hidden in the papers of entomologists she corresponded with. These erasures—of both the fly and the entomologist—in turn reflect not only power structures but also lost opportunities.

That a nineteenth-century woman of science has been forgotten or even deliberately erased is not terribly surprising. There are many hidden figures in the long history of science. Less discussed, however, is how much is lost from the exclusion of talented people because of their race, gender, or class. In this case, opportunities were lost to better understand a fly. If Morris had discovered a previously unknown and unnamed relative of the Hessian fly, the implications were significant. The price of wheat, a major staple crop, fluctuated wildly during infestation years, which resulted in political and economic fallout. Farmers were looking for methods to avoid ruin, and knowing what they were battling was an important first step. Whether they should plant the wheat early or late, plant an entirely new variety, apply some sort of pesticide, or burn the chaff at the end of the season—these were all decisions that required knowing much more about the behaviour of the wheat flies.[11]

There are many barriers that keep us from truly knowing this fly even today. Determining what a fly from the 1830s was in terms of twenty-first-century entomological nomenclature is a difficult feat, partly because the descriptions of the flies and their behaviour were vague at best, and images imprecise or nonexistent. Though Morris herself was a respected scientific artist, invited to illustrate scientific articles, any sketches or paintings of the insect she made do not seem to have made it into the archives.

It is all the more difficult to know this fly specifically because few contemporaries trusted Morris. Wary of making a public statement about her findings, Morris waited several years to present and publish her work—repeating her observations of the flies as the infestations continued. Finally, in 1840, she succumbed to the pleas of her cousin, the chemist Robert Hare, and allowed him to present her report to the American Philosophical Society (APS), the country's leading scientific association. Women rarely sent reports to the APS, but when they did it was typical to have a male member of the society read the paper on their behalf. By the time Morris was ready to share her work, the Panic of 1837 was long over, but it was clear that any entomological knowledge might help farmers avoid a similar economic and agricultural crisis in the future.[12]

After Robert Hare read Morris' report to the fraternity of male scholars, a committee reviewed her findings and deemed them plausible and significant enough to publish her report in the society's journal.[13] Knowing, however, that it would be another few years before the volume would be printed, they decided to immediately reach out to farmers, given how pressing the issue was. Benjamin Coates, one of the committee members, took the lead and wrote an article on Morris' behalf for *The Farmers' Cabinet*, introducing Morris and her findings to the world, with the APS' endorsement.[14]

The reactions from readers were swift, unkind, and mostly anonymous. One of the most vicious came from a writer who repeatedly referred to Morris as "*Miss Morris*," italicizing her name perhaps to emphasize her gender or at least marital status. Accusing Morris of reviving a long-settled debate, he called into question her scientific skills, claiming that her findings were "opposed by the every-day experience of thousands of observant farmers." What he found most upsetting, however, was that her study had the endorsement of "imposing names" from the APS.[15] In an article for the *Southern Planter*, based in Richmond, Virginia, an author reported on Morris' findings but mostly focused on her gender: "notwithstanding [the Hessian fly's] cunning, he has been unable to elude the feminine curiosity of the lady." Mocking Morris and her scientific skills throughout, he made a plea to readers: "As we know that some of our male friends ... entertain different views on the subject, we invite them, if their gallantry will permit, to entertain the lists with the lady."[16] By implying that it might not be worth the damage to their honour to even engage Morris in a debate, the author further excluded her as an outsider.

The fact that Morris herself was not a farmer was certainly one issue. Agricultural entomology, as a field, was in its infancy in 1840, and it is clear from the agricultural journals of the time that there was a general distrust of the urban scientists who instructed readers on how best to manage their farms. "Book farming," as it were, received some pushback. The fact that Morris was a woman only compounded this outsider status. These journals, however, were an important space for vetting and spreading agricultural information through the reprinting of articles in geographically diverse journals, and if the information she provided about the fly's behaviour and appearance was swatted down before it ever spread, that information would fail to reach many readers.

Farmers may not have trusted Morris for not being a farmer herself, but entomologists hardly trusted her either. In the mid-nineteenth century, entomologists—like other scientists—were forced to depend on the observations of others to make sense of species that were not available for them to see with their own eyes. Careful drawing and painting skills, as well as specialized jargon and descriptions of anatomy, were integral for communicating with other naturalists if specimens could not be sent. Peer review and the support of institutions like the American Philosophical Society were even more vital. But even if the observer's drawings were perfect and the description precise, even if he or she used a microscope to amplify observational skills, trust remained central. And most entomologists did not trust Morris.[17]

The entomologists most interested in and critical of Morris' findings were Thaddeus William Harris and Edward Claudius Herrick, university librarians who fit insect studies in after their workdays. At the time that Morris had sent her report to the APS in Philadelphia, Harris was busy writing a book on the insects of Massachusetts. Herrick was the closest thing to an expert on wheat pests since Thomas Say's death several years prior. Performing experiments in his backyard in Connecticut, Herrick helped Harris verify a lot of what was going into the book and the two exchanged letters regularly.[18]

When Harris read the *Proceedings of the American Philosophical Society*, the brief mention of Morris' report caught his eye. Immediately recognizing the threat that it would pose to the accuracy of a large section of his book, Harris breathlessly penned a letter to Herrick to alert him to the controversy. He urged Herrick to publish something quickly that he might then be able to cite in his book, thus putting to rest the egg-laying controversy.[19]

Following Harris' advice, Herrick did just that and published an article in the *American Journal of Science and Arts*. The puzzle was how to publish something that would dismiss Morris without insulting the men at the American Philosophical Society who had endorsed her observations. Herrick did this by arguing that Hessian flies never laid their eggs in the seed, without ever directly referencing Morris or the APS. Knowledgeable readers would understand what he was doing. By not mentioning Morris' name and refusing to engage with her directly, he avoided elevating her fame or notoriety, while simultaneously excluding her from the fraternity of entomologists. This also erased her from the historical record.[20]

Meanwhile, Thaddeus William Harris finished writing his *Report on the Insects of Massachusetts* in the summer of 1841, feeling all the more confident about his section on Hessian flies now that Herrick's research had been published.[21] Harris, throughout his entire volume, was fastidious in giving credit to the entomologists whose discoveries he relied on. It is in that way that it becomes possible to pick up his subtle tone of disrespect toward Morris, as he suddenly refrained from his more typical offerings of praise and gratitude when discussing her work. Harris described Morris as reviving an "old discussion," implying that it had long ago been settled and discredited. After describing her intervention briefly, he shot it down, writing "The fact that the Hessian fly does ordinarily lay her eggs on the young leaves of wheat, barley, and rye, both in the spring and in the autumn, is too well authenticated to admit of any doubt." He later explained to Herrick that he had only even mentioned Morris' "pretended discoveries" in his book because she had been so warmly defended by the men at the Philosophical Society. His tone and emphasis in the book, though, successfully worked to support Herrick's claims and dismiss Morris', disregarding the possibility that Morris had discovered something that needed addressing in the wheat fields of Pennsylvania.[22]

* * *

One of the ways we might be able to make heads or tails of this debate would be to see the specimens that Morris collected. Modern-day entomologists might then be able to help determine what the fly is known as today. Even in 1841, Morris understood how important obtaining a full set of specimens was for her being trusted. Perhaps her critics would never believe her when she told them what she had seen, but they would have to believe it if they saw it for themselves.

After all of the controversy she had stirred up that winter, Morris was worried that she might lose the support of her local endorsers. Her greatest discovery, therefore, came right in the nick of time. In July 1841, she caught sight of a female wheat fly laying its eggs among the grains of wheat. The fly, interrupted in the process, began laying those eggs on Morris' finger. Excitedly, she wrote: "I have seen a Tipulous fly in the act of placing her eggs on or in a grain of wheat. This fly and these eggs I have in good preservation." Comparing the fly to the one drawn by LeSueur in 1817, Morris found only minor differences. The male version of the insect looked precisely like those described by Say and illustrated by LeSueur, according to Morris. The female, however, did not. Her body was entirely black or blackish-brown and her wings "destitute of the hair fringe so conspicuous in the male." With the new evidence in hand, she could now confidently assert: "These important facts and specimens may prove my theory correct or that there are two species of this distinctive pest." The next month, Morris submitted an extensive letter documenting her observations to Philadelphia's Academy of Natural Science, another leading if young scientific organization. She also triumphantly submitted the indisputable evidence she had collected. After several summers of gathering infested sheaths of wheat and putting them under bell jars in her library only to find that the flies had died or failed to mature, she finally had a complete set.[23] Unfortunately, this would not be enough.

The specimens that Morris hoped would finally silence her critics were so disregarded and neglected by the scientists at the Academy of Natural Sciences that the flies and eggs were destroyed. The Academy's members did not study them in any way that might officially corroborate Morris' findings. When Morris learned of the fate of her prized collection years later, not only was she disappointed, she was distressed. Finding a full set of the flies required summers of infestation that were not as regular as they had been a decade earlier. Determined to replace what had been destroyed, she had the great fortune of finding and collecting new pupa in 1847 that she happily deposited with the Academy of Natural Sciences. The set, however, was incomplete, and it, too, no longer exists. When I reached out to the entomological curators of the Academy of Natural Sciences, now a part of Drexel University, they reported that they no longer have specimens from that era. Any chance of seeing or testing the creatures that Morris so painstakingly hunted for have vanished.[24]

Still, despite not finding a full replacement set of the fly that she studied for years, in 1849 Morris, with encouragement from the entomologist

Samuel Stehman Haldeman, gave the fly its name: "*Cecidomyia culmicola* Morris." Haldeman suggested using *culmicola* as the fly moved into the culm or stalk of the wheat plant to mature, something that distinguished it from other *Cecidomyia* flies.[25] Morris sent a letter to the corresponding secretary of the Academy of Natural Sciences, officially announcing the name and giving a brief description of its defining characteristics with the promise to donate a full set of specimens as soon as she was able to obtain them.[26]

Morris was never able to get that full set again though. The fly rarely returned with the frequency it once had.[27] Still, in 1852, she was able to send pupa of the *Cecidomyia culmicola* to Thaddeus William Harris to satisfy his request, and his response was likely very satisfying: "you have sent to me the puparia of your *Cecidomyia culmicola*. Any person familiar with the puparium of the Hessian fly cannot fail to perceive that these are totally different."[28] Despite this late verification, despite the fact that Morris gave her fly a name, it still managed to vanish. Part of the reason has to do with the endless published critiques Morris received.

* * *

When Morris had initially submitted her report about the wheat fly, she had been reluctant to make a public statement at all. Years later, after receiving a relentless stream of critiques, something in her had changed. Asa Fitch, an entomologist more than two hundred miles away in New York State, sought to make a name for himself in 1845 by publishing a series of articles about wheat flies in the *American Journal of Agriculture and Science*. Morris was disgusted to find what he had written about her. In these articles that were republished together as a pamphlet in 1847, Fitch catalogued not only the habits of the fly but also the various ways American scientists had described the fly over the previous half century. He included some of Morris' publications in the list, but toward the end he made space to dismiss her account completely, saying "it appears manifest that the lady was widely misled at the very outset of her observations" and claimed, erroneously, that she must have known she was wrong because she stopped publishing on the topic.[29] She had not stopped publishing. Morris fumed over the fact that Fitch had found "every other publication on the subject" but conveniently missed hers.[30]

Initially, Morris decided to ignore Fitch's insult, or, in her words "to pass him by in silence as I had my other opposers," but she was overruled by her friends who encouraged her to stand up for herself. In a polite but fierce letter published in the April 1847 issue of the *American Journal of Agriculture and Science*, Morris wrote that she craved Fitch's indulgence to "point out a slight error in his statement, which has arisen from misinformation." After defending her research and publication record, she put the onus on Fitch to determine what the species of fly actually was, if she was mistaken. Well aware that Fitch and other entomologists like Harris and Herrick questioned her observational skills, Morris pushed back. She emphasized her close inspection of her subjects, writing: "If Dr. Fitch will prove that the flies I so carefully watched for so many years, whose larva feeds in the centre of the straw, as seen by hundreds in this neighborhood, is 'the fly he suspects it to be,' I will acknowledge my error as frankly as I now maintain my difference of opinion." Morris not only emphasized how carefully she observed the specimens, later bringing up her use of a microscope to augment her sight, but she also asserted that her observations were corroborated by "hundreds in the neighborhood" who saw it themselves. Fitch had not only challenged Morris and her scientific authority, in other words, but also local environmental knowledge more generally.[31]

Morris recognized the inequities inherent in why people did not trust her observations. Even with the support of the most elite scientific societies in the country, her research was still being dismissed. She made a plea for the trust given so freely to other entomologists:

> I do not, nor have I ever doubted the statements of gentlemen so learned in the science of Entomology . . . their assurance that they had seen the insect in its different states of egg, larva, pupa, and perfect fly, was sufficient to satisfy me that it was so; I therefore, in all fairness, claim the same indulgence from them and others, when I state that I saw, captured, and glued to a piece of paper, a fly, while in the act of depositing her eggs on a grain of wheat, so like the drawing made by LeSueur, of Say's *Cecidomyia destructor*, that it not only deceived me, but all to whom I showed it.

Morris, called on her critics to push aside any issue with her gender and treat her as an equal. What was at stake was not just whether farmers and scientists would take Morris and her research seriously, but also whether her critics' inability to do so might mean that a tiny, powerful pest would continue to gorge itself in American wheat fields without farmers being able to muster an educated defence.[32]

Morris' defences of her methodology and skills, valuable as they were, ultimately did little to shape the future discussion of her work. The damage done by those who dismissed Morris in print echoed in the entomological literature over the next century and beyond, as they became invaluable references for those making sense of the flies threatening wheat. Morris' discovery of the *Cecidomyia culmicola* was occasionally mentioned in the entomological literature, starting with the second edition of Thaddeus William Harris' *A Treatise on Some of the Insects of New England* (1852). Even Asa Fitch came around, in 1851, and essentially apologized to Morris for dismissing her work, accepting that she likely discovered another species of *Cecidomyia*, though he buried this *mea culpa* in an article directed at a different topic entirely. In addition, Ebeneezer Emmons' *Agriculture of New-York* (1854) includes extensive coverage of Morris' fly. Other entomologists continued to include Morris' discoveries in their bibliographies and announcements of new wheat fly species, both in the United States and abroad.[33]

However, in 1897, something changed. In an extensive article about *Cecidomyia* flies, the French entomologist Paul Marchal dismissed Morris' diagnosis as unsatisfactory and the discussion of its life cycle as problematic, without going into further detail. Perhaps Marchal, relying heavily of Asa Fitch's extensive essay on the fly, was swayed by his initial dismissal of Morris' work fifty years earlier. Whatever the case, after Marchal's denouncement, other entomologists followed suit. In 1900, J. J. Kiefer, another French entomologist, decided that the *culmicola* was likely just a misidentified Hessian fly, and eleven years after that the American entomologist Ephraim Porter Felt followed suit.[34] So in 1954, when H. F. Barnes, a British entomologist who specialized in *Cecidomyia*, wrote in a reference book for agricultural entomologists that continues to be cited that Morris must have been confused, observing several different kinds of flies and conflating them as one species, he had more than a century's worth of doubters to reference. By 1989, when Raymond J. Gagne wrote *The Plant-Feeding Gall Midges of North America*, he made the decision not to mention Morris or the *culmicola* at all.[35]

Whether Morris was mistaken, or whether her critics' words outlasted her rebuttals, the *Cecidomyia culmicola* has in many ways vanished. As Barnes wrote at the end of his description of the fly: "the name *Cecidomyia culmicola* Morris can only be of historical interest."[36] Without specimens for modern entomologists to reference, any solution to the mystery remains elusive. A 2016 study of Canadian insects estimates that in Canada alone there are 16,000 species of *Cecidomyia*, and over 1.8 million worldwide, with only a tiny fraction of those named. It is likely that the *Cecidomyia culmicola* is now part of the unknown, anonymous masses.[37]

The story of Margaretta Morris and the vanishing *Cecidomyia culmicola* underscores the dangers of not trusting scientists because of their sex (as was the case for Morris), race, or class. Thanks to such social inequities, knowledge was lost and opportunities missed, further revealing the social contingencies in scientific taxonomy and the historical archive.[38] We may never know the *Cecidomyia culmicola* that Morris studied year after year in her neighbour's field, the one that lived under the bell glass on her desk and that she pinned and sent to a number of entomologists around the country. Any attempts to understand this creature—its behaviour, its appearance, its life cycle—continue to be lost because in the 1840s a number of people refused to believe that a "lady entomologist" knew what she saw. The authority they held and hold and the ways their critiques have rippled outward in entomological literature means that the fly and Margaretta Morris have been lost to history, or at least human history. The flies, after all, no matter their name, might still be enjoying the fields of wheat, flitting from stalk to stalk.

NOTES

1. Margaretta Hare Morris, "On the Cecidomyia Destructor, or Hessian Fly," *Transactions of the American Philosophical Society of Philadelphia* Series 8 (1843): 49–51; M. H. Morris to Thaddeus William Harris, September 12, 1847, Thaddeus William Harris Papers (hereafter TWHP), Museum of Comparative Zoology, Harvard University.

2. Henry Green, "The Wheat-Worm," *The Cultivator* (June 1836): 53; "The Harvest Prospect," *The Cultivator* (July 1836): 59; "A Preventive of the Wheat Fly," *The Farmer's Cabinet* 1, no. 5 (September 1836): 73; William Penn Kinzer, "The Cut Worm and Hessian Fly," *The Cultivator* (October 1836): 109; "The Crops," *The Cultivator* (September 1836): 87; J. Hathaway, "Italian Spring Wheat," *The Cultivator* (September 1836): 94; "Enemies of the Wheat Crop," *The Cultivator* (September 1836): 93; "Lime as a Manure for Wheat," *The Farmers' Cabinet* 1, no. 6 (October 1836): 85–85; "Hessian Fly," *The Farmers' Cabinet* 1, no. 12 (January 1837): 185–86; "The Observer—No. 5," *The Farmers' Cabinet* 1, no. 19 (April 1837): 290; "The Observer—No. 6," *The Farmers' Cabinet* 1, no. 20 (May 1837): 306–7; "Wheat—Important Discovery," *The Farmers' Cabinet* 1, no. 23 (June 1837): 359–61.

3. "Price of Flour—Comparative Table," *The Farmers' Cabinet* 1, no. 19 (April 1837): 303; "High Price of Provisions," *Connecticut* Courant, October 15, 1835; Jessica M. Lepler, *The Many Panics of 1837: People, Politics, and the Creation of a Transatlantic Financial Crisis* (New York: Cambridge University Press, 2013), 67–70; Sean Wilentz, *The Rise of American Democracy: Jefferson to Lincoln* (New York: Norton, 2005), 456–57.

4. Philip Pauly, *Fruits and Plains: The Horticultural Transformation of America* (Cambridge, MA: Harvard University Press, 2007), 33–50.

5. M. H. Morris to T. W. Harris, September 12, 1847, TWHP; M. H. Morris to T. W. Harris, 31 August 1843, TWHP; W. Edmunds Claussen, *Wyck: The Story of an Historic House, 1690-1970* (Philadelphia: Printed for Mary T. Haines, 1970), 108.

6. Mary Donaldson to Ann Haines, October 13, 1841, Series II Box 267, Folder 418, Wyck Association Papers, American Philosophical Society; Thomas Say, "Some account of the Insect known by the name of Hessian Fly, and of a parasitic Insect that feeds on it," *Journal of the Academy of Natural Sciences* 1, no. 3 (July 1817): 45–48; Charles Alexandre LeSueur, "Plate III," *Journal of the Academy of Natural Sciences* 1, no. 4 (August 1817): 64–65.

7. M. H. Morris to T. W. Harris, November 6, 1850, TWHP; M. H. Morris to T. W. Harris, September 12, 1847, TWHP; Deborah Jean Warner, "Science Education for Women in Antebellum America," *Isis* 69 (1978): 58–67; Margaret Rossiter, *Women Scientists in America: Struggles and Strategies to 1940* (Baltimore, MD: Johns Hopkins University Press, 1982), 1–28; Kimberley F. Tolley, *The Science Education of American Girls: An American Pursuit* (New York: Routledge Falmer, 2003).

8. M. H. Morris to T. W. Harris, September 12, 1847, TWHP; Thomas Say, "Some account of the Insect known by the name of Hessian Fly;" Charles Alexandre LeSueur, "Plate III."

9. Say, "Some account of the Insect known by the name of Hessian Fly," 47.

10. "A Preventive of the Wheat Fly," *The Farmer's Cabinet* 1, no. 5 (Sept 1836): 73; "Lime as a Manure for Wheat," *The Farmers' Cabinet* 1, no. 6 (Oct 1836): 85–85; "Hessian Fly,"

The Farmers' Cabinet 1, no. 12 (Jan 1837): 185–86; "The Observer—No. 5," *The Farmers' Cabinet* 1, no. 19 (April 1837): 290; "The Observer—No. 6," *The Farmers' Cabinet* 1, no. 20 (May 1837): 306–7; "Wheat—Important Discovery," *The Farmers' Cabinet* 1, no. 23 (June 1837): 359–61.

11 For more on nineteenth-century American women in science, see, for instance: Rossiter, *Women Scientists in America;* Tolley, *The Science Education of American Girls*; Sally Gregory Kohlstedt, "In from the Periphery: American Women in Science, 1830–1880," *Signs* 4, no. 1 (Autumn 1978): 81–96; Margaret W. Rossiter, "The Matthew Matilda Effect in Science," *Social Studies of Science* 23, no. 2 (May 1993): 325–41; Vera Norwood, "The Illustrators: Women's Drawings of Nature's Artifacts," in *Made from This Earth* (Chapel Hill: UNC, 1993), 55–97; Debra Lindsay, "Intimate Inmates: Wives, Households, and Science in Nineteenth-Century America," *Isis* 89, no. 4 (Dec 1998): 631–52; Tina Gianquitto,*"Good Observers of Nature": American Women and the Scientific Study of the Natural World, 1820–1885* (University of Georgia Press, 2007); Renee Bergland, *Maria Mitchell and the Sexing of Science: An Astronomer among the American Romantics* (Boston: Beacon Press, 2008); Renee Bergland, "Urania's Inversion: Emily Dickinson, Herman Melville, and the Strange history of Women Scientists in Nineteenth-Century America," *Signs* 34, no. 1 (October 2008): 75–99; Tina Gianquitto, "Botanical Smuts and Hermaphrodites: Lydia Becker, Darwin's Botany, and Education Reform," *Isis* 104, no. 2 (June 2013): 250–77; Jenna Tonn, "Extralaboratory Life: Gender Politics and Experimental Biology at Radcliffe College, 1894–1910," *Gender & History* 29, no. 2 (August 2017): 329–58; Kara Swanson, "Rubbing Elbows and Blowing Smoke: Gender, Class, and Science in the Nineteenth-Century Patent Office," *Isis* 108, no. 1 (March 2017): 40–61; Britt Rusert, "Sarah's Cabinet: Fugitive Science in and Beyond the Parlor," in *Fugitive Science: Empiricism and Freedom in Early African American Culture* (New York: NYU Press, 2017), 181–218.

12 M. H. Morris to T. W. Harris, September 12, 1847, TWHP; "Stated Meeting, October 2," *Proceedings of the American Philosophical Society* 1, no. 13 (1838–1840): 282; "Stated Meeting, December 18," *Proceedings of the American Philosophical Society* 1, no. 14 (Nov-Dec 1840): 318–19; Morris, "On the Cecidomyia Destructor, or Hessian Fly." On women having men present their findings, see Kohlstedt, "In from the Periphery," 90.

13 Morris, "On the Cecidomyia Destructor, or Hessian Fly."

14 Benjamin H. Coates, "Hessian Fly," *The Farmers Cabinet* 5.6 (January 1841): 201–05. On the role of agricultural journals as spaces for public science, see James E. McWilliams, *American Pests: The Losing War on Insects from Colonial Times to DDT* (New York: Columbia University Press, 2008), 16–24.

15 "Observer—No. 24: 'Who Shall Decide, When Doctors Disagree?'" *The Farmers' Cabinet* 5, no. 7 (February 1841): 237–39.

16 "Hessian Fly," *Southern Planter* 1, no. 1 (January 1841): 14.

17 On the early professionalization of American entomology and the limitations of the field, see W. Connor Sorensen, *Brethren of the Net: American Entomology, 1840–1880* (Tuscaloosa, AL: University of Alabama Press, 1995); James E. McWilliams, *American Pests: The Losing War on Insects from Colonial Times to DDT* (New York: Columbia University Press, 2008), 26–55.

18 Clark A. Elliott, *Thaddeus William Harris (1795–1856): Nature, Science, and Society in the Life of an American Naturalist* (Bethlehem, PA: Lehigh University Press, 2008), 33, 48–50, 62–65; Thomas Anthony Thacher, *Sketch of the Life of Edward C. Herrick* (New Haven: Printed by Thomas J. Stafford, 1862); "Death of Edward C. Herrick, Treasurer of Yale College," *New York Times*, June 22, 1862. A selection of the letters between Herrick and Harris are excerpted in *The Entomological Correspondence of Thaddeus William Harris*, ed. Samuel H. Scudder (Boston: Boston Society of Natural History, 1869), 181–207. Many of the originals as well as additional letters are in the TWHP and the Edward Claudius Herrick Papers, Yale University Manuscripts & Archives. For more on the role of correspondence in nineteenth-century science, see Janet Browne, "Corresponding Naturalists," in *The Age of Scientific Naturalism*, ed. Bernard Lightman and Michael S. Reidy (London: Pickering & Chatto, 2014), 157–70.

19 "Stated Meeting, December 18," *Proceedings of the American Philosophical Society* 1, no. 14 (Nov-Dec 1840): 318–19; T. W. Harris to Edward Claudius Herrick, March 6, 1841, TWHP.

20 Edward C. Herrick, "Art. XV.—A Brief, Preliminary Account of the Hessian Fly and its Parasites," *The American Journal of Science and Arts* 41 (1841): 155.

21 T. W. Harris, *A Report on the Insects of Massachusetts, Injurious to Vegetation* (Cambridge, MA: Folsom, Wells, and Thurston, 1841), 423–24, 426–27, 431–32, 440–41.

22 Harris, *A Report on the Insects of Massachusetts, Injurious to Vegetation*, 429–32; T. W. Harris to E. C. Herrick, Esq., copy, November 24, 1841, Series 1, Box 2, Folder 19, Edward Claudius Herrick Papers, Yale University Manuscripts & Archives.

23 M. H. Morris to Benjamin Hornor Coates, June 9, 1841, Asa Gray Papers, Library of Congress, Box 1, Folder 11; M. H. Morris to Dr. B. Coates, July 14, 1841, Special Collections, Pennsylvania State University Library, 104 Paterno, Vault, 1986-0104R VF Lit; "Verbal Communications," *Proceedings of the Academy of Natural Sciences in Philadelphia* 1 (June 1841): 44–45, 54–56; "Written Communications," *Proceedings of the Academy of Natural Sciences in Philadelphia* 1 (June 1841): 57; (August 1841): 66–68.

24 M. H. Morris to T. W. Harris, September 12, 1847, TWHP; M. H. Morris to W. R. Johnson, July 20, [1847,] ANSP Correspondence, Coll. 567, Folder 276, Academy of Natural Sciences Philadelphia, Drexel University, Philadelphia, PA; W. H. Morris [sic], "Hessian Fly," *American Journal of Agriculture and Science* 6, no. 16 (August 1847): 105–6; Email from Jon Gelhaus, Academy of Natural Sciences to author, May 16, 2018.

25 Samuel Stehman Haldeman to M. H. Morris, May 21, 1849, Asa Gray Papers, Box 1, Folder 8, Library of Congress, Washington, DC.

26 M. H. Morris to W. R. Johnson, July 21, 1849, Academy of Natural Sciences; *Proceedings of the Academy of Natural Sciences in Philadelphia* 4 (1849): 194.

27 M. H. Morris to Dr. Leidy, September 10, 1852, Joseph Leidy Correspondence, Collection 1, Box 4, Folder 112, Academy of Natural Sciences Archives; Thaddeus William Harris to Margaretta Hare Morris, March 17, 1852, Asa Gray Papers, Library of Congress, Box 1, Folder 9, Library of Congress, Washington, DC.

28 T. W. Harris to M. H. Morris, December 1852, TWHP.

29 Asa Fitch, *The Hessian Fly: Its History, Character, Transformations, and Habits* (Albany, NY: C. Van Benthuysen and Co., 1847): 23, 42–43.

30 "Stated Meeting, 10 August 1841," *Proceedings of the Academy of Natural Sciences in Philadelphia* 1, no. 5 (August 1841): 65–68; M. H. Morris to T. W. Harris, September 12, 1847, TWHP.

31 M. H. Morris to T. W. Harris, September 12, 1847, TWHP; Morris, "Controversy Respecting the Hessian Fly," *American Journal of Agriculture and Science* 5, no. 12 (April 1847): 206–8.

32 Morris, "Controversy Respecting the Hessian Fly," 207.

33 T. W. Harris, *A Treatise on Some of the Insects of New England Which Are Injurious to Vegetation*, 2nd ed. (Boston: White & Potter, 1852), 464–66; Asa Fitch, "Wheat Insects—Joint-Worm," *The Cultivator* 8, no. 10 (Oct. 1851): 321; E. Emmons, *Agriculture of New-York* (Albany: Printed by C. Van Benthuysen, 1854) 5: 179–80; Benedict Jaeger and Henry C. Preston, *The Life of North American Insects* (New York: Harper & Brothers, 1859), 306; Entomologischer Verein in Stettin, *Linnaea Entomologica: Zeitschrift Herausgegeben von dem Entomologischen Vereine in Stettin* (Berlin: Ernst Siegfried Mittler, 1860) 14: 263; Entomologischer Verein zu Stettin, *Entomologische Zeitung* 22 (1861): 420; United States Bureau of Entomology, *Bibliography of the More Important Contributions to American Economic Entomology* (Washington, DC: Government print office, 1889), 66–68; Lawrence Bruner, *The Insect Enemies of Small Grains* (Lincoln, NB: Nebraska State Board of Agriculture, 1893), 361, 367; Lawrence Bruner, *A Preliminary Introduction to the Study of Entomology* (Lincoln, NB: J. North & Co., 1894), 205.

34 Paul Marchal, "Les Cécidomyies des Céréales et Leurs Parasites," *Annales de la Société Entomologique de France* 66 (Paris: Au Siege de Société, 1897): 64; J. J. Kieffer, *Monographie des Cécidomyides d'Europe et d'Algérie* (France: Société Entomologique de France, 1900), 413–14; E. P. Felt, "Hosts and Galls of American Gall Midges," *Journal of Economic Entomology* 4, no. 10 (October 1911): 473.

35 H. F. Barnes, *Gall Midges of Economic Importance*, vol. 7: *Gall Midges of Cereal Crops* (London: Crosby Lockwood & Son, 1956), 84; Marion Harris, email to author, 4 August 2017; Raymond J. Gagné, *The Plant-Feeding Gall Midges of North America* (Ithaca, NY: Cornell University Press, 1989), 30–32.

36 Barnes, *Gall Midges of Cereal Crops*, 84.

37 Paul D. N. Hebert et al., "Counting Animal Species with DNA Barcodes: Canadian Insects," *Philosophical Transactions of the Royal Society* 371, no. 1702 (September 2016), https://doi.org/10.1098/rstb.2015.0333; Gagné also talks about the vast number of *Cecidomyia* that remain unnamed and unstudied in *The Gall Midges of the Neotropical Region*, ed. Raymond J. Gagné (Ithaca, NY: Comstock Publishing Associates, Cornell University Press, 1994), 2.

38 For more on taxonomies and their fallibility, see Harriet Ritvo, "Species," in *Critical Terms for Animal Studies*, ed. Laurie Gruen (Chicago: University of Chicago Press, 2018), 383–94.

8

Guinea Pig Agnotology[1]

Joanna Dean

> Into your veins we inject all the ills and poisons of our higher civilization: anthrax, and diphtheria, cancer, smallpox and tuberculosis, leprosy, meningitis, pneumonia, typhus and typhoid, and all the infections of the eye and ear, of nose and throat, of bone and muscle and cartilage and nerve and gland, which humanity has accumulated in its march upward. All these bitter questions we put to you with the hypodermic needle and the scalpel and you react positively or you react negatively, but always to the full measure of your ability, and most often at the cost of your life....
> Yes, you do your best, silent brother.
>
> Simon Strunk, *Professor Latimer's Progress* (1918)[2]

In the laboratory, animals are made invisible: their invisibility continues in the archives and extends into the stories told. As the authors of the *Oxford Handbook on the History of Medicine* observe, "In no body of scholarship is it more obvious, puzzling and true to say that 'animals disappear.'"[3] Even the guinea pig, the animal whose name has come to stand for the hapless victims of experimental medicine, has largely disappeared from the records. This chapter explores how this happened. It draws upon agnotology, a concept developed by historians Robert N. Proctor and Londa Schiebinger, who argue that "a great deal of attention has been given to epistemology (the study of how we know) when 'how or why we don't know' is often just as important, usually far more scandalous, and remarkably undertheorized."[4] The chapter will track the disappearance of the guinea pig in the records of the Connaught Laboratories in Toronto and consider the cognitive dissonance created by the gulf between the guinea pig's role as a laboratory animal and its role as a much-loved pet. I will suggest that in the early twentieth century an emerging antivivisection movement shaped actions within and without the laboratory and altered the nature of the records kept and stories told. Even today, in order to access the archives of the Connaught Laboratories on the sprawling modern Sanofi Pasteur Canada campus, the researcher must be accompanied by the archivist, approved by staff, and, like all visitors to the facility, must pass through a security gate, overseen by security personnel. Animal research is ongoing at the laboratory and so security is tight.

The story of the University of Toronto's Connaught Laboratories begins in 1913, when John G. Fitzgerald constructed a stable in his obliging assistant's yard on Barton Avenue in downtown Toronto. In 1917, the laboratories moved to their current location north of the city where an elegant stucco stable was built. The original Barton Avenue stable was relocated to the site in 1935 and restored as a museum in 2004.[5] It now stands incongruously on the Sanofi Pasteur campus, where it serves as a material reminder of the laboratory's humble origins, memorialized as "The Miracle Factory that began in a Stable."[6]

The Barton Avenue stable housed two species: horses and guinea pigs.[7] Horses were the living factories from whose blood antitoxins were extracted. Guinea pigs were the living meters. The little animals were injected with a fatal dose of diphtheria or tetanus toxin and then given varying amounts of horse serum to counter the toxin. Their fate calibrated the serum's potency. Horses became the heroes of laboratory medicine, trotted out time and again as the photogenic saviours of countless small children.[8] They continue to be memorialized in the stable museum, in online exhibits and in Connaught publications (Figure 8.1). The guinea pigs, by contrast, were and are invisible. Their unpleasant fate could not be glossed over as any kind of heroic service to mankind, and they rarely

Fig. 8.1 The horses used for the production of antitoxin were celebrated as equine heroes. This lantern slide is one of a series produced by Connaught Laboratories to make the public comfortable with the new biomedical products. Source: Lantern Slide Ags020, Sanofi Pasteur Canada (Connaught Campus) Archives, Toronto.

figure in laboratory publicity. There is no reference to their existence in the stable museum. They appear only occasionally in the archives.

Guinea pigs (*Cavia porcellus*) are native to the Andes, where they have served as an important source of protein since at least 2,500 BCE and possibly as early as 5,000 BCE (which makes their relationship with humans as long standing as that of their stable mates on Barton Avenue).[9] They were imported to Europe in the sixteenth century, where they became pets, first among the aristocracy, then more widely.[10] By the nineteenth century, they were so familiar in Britain that their round little bodies were used to describe the morphology of such North American species as the beaver, the woodchuck, and the chipmunk.[11] In Canada, a guinea pig was used to illustrate the letter G in the *Canada Spelling Primer* (1850), evidence of both the exoticism of the little animal and its growing familiarity.[12]

Guinea pigs were, and are, docile and endearing pocket pets.[13] They do not carry associations with filth or disease, like mice and rats. They communicate with each other, and their handlers, with whistles (if excited), purring (when petted), squealing, rumbling and chirping. A series of letters in the children's section of the Toronto newspaper *The Globe* and the *Ottawa Journal* attest to their charm, especially it seems for little boys.[14] Roland Ellard of Pickanock, Quebec, wrote in 1898 that he had forty guinea pigs: "they will stand on their hind legs and 'squeak, squeak' when they hear my footsteps near their door. After I talk to them and pet them, they lie down quite contented, but I must let them know first that I have noticed them and must pet each one."[15] Thirteen-year-old Evelyn Wade of Renfrew, Ontario, described his guinea pigs as "very stupid" animals prone to fighting: "They have teeth about three quarters of an inch long," he observed, "Sometimes if you take one up when it is angry, it will bite you, and it hurts, because the teeth are so sharp."[16] It is only at the end of his letter that young Wade remembers that he hopes to win a prize, and notes that guinea pigs are nice pets for children because they are fun to play with and do not carry disease like cats and dogs.

The children's letters stand in odd contrast to contemporaneous articles describing the use of guinea pigs as test subjects. On the pages of the newspapers, guinea pigs are inoculated, time and again, with noxious substances to test their toxicity. Their use as test subjects was such common knowledge that guinea pig trials featured in a long running series of advertisements for a dandruff treatment. As a 1907 ad boasted in large font, "The Guinea Pig Proved It."[17] This curious pairing of the pet and the laboratory test subject is repeated in a photograph taken in the 1920s of a young boy playing with the Connaught guinea pigs (Figure 8.2).

Guinea pigs were known for their innocence. As early as 1811, a natural history text noted: "These animals are, of all others, the most helpless and inoffensive."[18] This innocence could at times be understood as a kind of purity: when a distraught child asks whether animals go to heaven in the evangelical classic *The Gates Ajar* (1869), she chooses the guinea pig as her most compelling example: "O mamma mamma, Don't little CLEAN –*white* – *guinea-pigs* have souls?"[19] Her mother allows that the gates of

Fig 8.2 Boy playing with guinea pigs at the Connaught Laboratories Farm, ca. 1920s. Source: Photograph Acc1741, Sanofi Pasteur Canada (Connaught Campus) Archives, Toronto.

heaven might open for the guinea pig. But such sweet innocence could also be cast as stupidity: Wade described his pets as "very stupid." The author of *Three Hundred Things a Bright Boy Might Do* (1910) noted: "Some who ought to know better have said that cavies are very dull, stupid little animals."[20] Like young Wade, he was quick to make a disclaimer, noting "I entirely disagree with this." In 1915, a breeder described the guinea pig as a "singularly inoffensive and defenceless creature," noting that they lack "that intelligence which usually characterises domestic pets."[21] There seems to have been a wide consensus that the guinea pig was a much loved and responsive little pet but that it had none of the answering intelligence of a dog.

At the end of the nineteenth century, a guinea pig fancy developed. Hobbyists bred what they called cavies in a wide range of exotic colours, coat patterns, and coat types. In 1888, a correspondent in Canada's *Pigeons and Pets* described the cavies at Britain's Crystal Palace Show and urged Canadians to pursue the hobby: "They should be worth taking up, as they are very little trouble, and present many opportunities for scientific breeding." Poultry and farm exhibitions began to include entries for different kinds of cavies: Peruvians (with long silky hair), Abyssinians (with rosettes), and English short hairs. In 1892, the publisher of *Pigeons and*

Pets, H. B. Donovan, imported three Peruvians, three Abyssinians, and eight English short-hair cavies from England. By 1892, he was advertising offspring "bred direct from my English stock" for three to five dollars a pair in his *Canadian Poultry Review.* Guinea pigs reproduce quickly, and two years later Donovan was offering free stock in a subscription drive: an Abyssinian he claimed was worth three dollars and a smooth coated guinea pig worth two dollars.

It was likely a breeder like Donovan who supplied Fitzgerald with the Connaught's first colony of guinea pigs. Fitzgerald had famously purchased his first five horses from the "glue factory" (presumably the slaughter house) for three dollars apiece, and it is likely he was equally parsimonious in acquiring his guinea pigs. Certainly, the animals described in the 1913–15 Connaught laboratory books were a motley lot: #76 was black and white and tan on neck; #77 was black and white and tan on the rump; #78 was simply brown; and #87 was white and tan with a brown spot on the head. None are described as having long hair, or rosettes, though #104 is described as "curly, brown and white."

Fitzgerald's methods were modelled upon those used at the laboratories he had visited: the Pasteur Laboratories in France, the Lister Institute in London, and public health laboratories in New York City. By 1914, enormous numbers of small animals were used in the routine testing and calibration of biomedical products. Most laboratories bought their guinea pigs from small scale breeders, and over time "cavy ranching" became a lucrative industry.[22] Prices increased during the First World War in the face of a "guinea pig famine," reaching two dollars in Canada.[23] The American author of *Cavy Culture: A Book of Practical Instructions on the Raising and Marketing of Guinea Pigs* (1920) observed optimistically that a three-month-old pig could be raised to market for ten to fifteen cents, and a breeding female could produce twelve to fifteen young a year. A colony of five to six females could be lucrative: "Thus at a very conservative estimate one may reasonably expect about one hundred offsprings [sic] at the end of the first year, which should be worth from $75.00 to $125.00 according to their size."[24] In 1924, in "Making More Money. . . . With Guinea Pigs," the *Windsor Star* quoted a Boston-area breeder: "In spite of the fact that the guinea pigs increase with great rapidity, says the owner of the 'cavy ranch,' the supply always falls short of the demand and it is because of this that the raising of the pets is lucrative, as well as a most interesting business." He claimed they could be sold at "excellent prices" to "laboratories, hospitals, and experimental stations."[25] At Toronto's 1925 Royal Winter Fair, testimonials from laboratories in Ontario and Alberta were on display. An article in *The Globe*, titled "The Humble Guinea Pig," noted that the Toronto General Hospital alone used thousands of guinea pigs in a year; a "lady exhibitor" was quoted as saying: "The guinea pig is absolutely indispensable."

Prices, however, had declined by 1925 to one dollar for a large animal, and sixty-five cents for the smaller ones.[26] After the Second World War, small holders were squeezed out of the market as more centralized breeding facilities were developed, in Britain taking what Robert G. W. Kirk has described as a socialist form with the Laboratory Animals Bureau, and in the United States, a more privatized form with such facilities as the Wistar Institute.[27] A series of booklets from the US Department of Agriculture chart the shifting market: the author of the 1949 brochure was cautious about the potential for sales. By 1962, they made the following recommendation: "*Do not expect to make large profits immediately by raising laboratory animals*"[28] (italics in original).

Scientists at the Connaught Laboratories chose to breed much of their own stock, following the practice of elite British laboratories. It was not easy. They experimented with housing and diet until an outbreak of streptococcal infection wiped out the original colony, which was replaced by 125 white pedigreed guinea pigs purchased from the Lister Institute in London in 1930 (Figure 8.3). Even these struggled. A report in the archives provides a rare glimpse of the difficulties faced by the laboratory (and, of course, the guinea pigs): the laboratory attributed the deaths of the first generation of Lister animals to the rigours of travel, and the deaths of the Connaught-born animals to premature breeding. (This is not entirely surprising. The animals were bred early: of the 93 of 205 pregnant females that died, 39 of them were bred before they were 60 days old, and another 31 before they were 30 days old.[29]) The diet may also have been deficient, as the Connaught Laboratories experimented with various formulations of prepared food. A 1947 article on the care and feeding of guinea pigs observed that "the aim of evolving a dry pelleted stable diet completely adequate for guinea-pigs has not yet been realized," and

Fig 8.3 Connaught guinea pig colony, August 1929. The laboratory struggled to maintain the colony, and the following year these animals were replaced by white pedigreed guinea pigs from the Lister Institute. Source: Photograph Acc0048, Sanofi Pasteur Canada (Connaught Campus) Archives, Toronto.

noted that a pelleted diet must be supplemented with "fresh greenstuff, dried cabbage or ascorbic acid."[30] The Connaught report makes no reference to supplements. British scientists were disparaging of the breeders who supplied guinea pigs to laboratories, describing them as "largely undereducated, working-class, 'every-day sorts'" who "cannot spell their name in block letters."[31] But books by breeders emphasized the need for greens; even the boys writing to *The Globe* described the need for a variety of vegetables.[32] Eventually, mice came to be preferred to guinea pigs at Connaught Laboratories. A 1969 article on the animal colonies in their internal publication, *The Contax*, attributed the shrinking size of the guinea pig colony to difficulties breeding: guinea pigs are much more difficult to breed than mice. Females cannot be mated until they are fourteen weeks old, the gestation period is sixty-three days, and, on average, only three young are produced per litter. The production life of a female guinea pig is 16–18 months."[33] Also, as Karen Rader has noted, mice carried little of the affective value of such pets as dogs, and, we might argue, guinea pigs.[34]

Even when they were breeding and using thousands of the little animals, the guinea pigs were largely invisible in the public relations campaigns of the Connaught Laboratories. Their absence is most apparent in comparison to the extraordinary visibility of the horse. The archives are replete with heroic horses: the researcher is introduced to Crestfallen, the diphtheria horse; Brick Top, the tetanus horse; and Molly, the meningitis horse. Collages include photographs of horses running free through bucolic fields. The newspaper article that introduced the laboratory to Toronto in 1916 set the tone: the laboratory supplied carefully posed photographs of calm horses being bled and offered reassurances about the horses' well-being: "Now most people think that the bleeding causes the horse to suffer. As a matter of fact, the horse hardly seems to notice it but stands quietly and patiently while the blood is being taken." The reference to the guinea pigs contains no such reassurance: "These guinea pigs are used to standardise the doses of anti-toxin. A little guinea pig is given a fatal dose, say one unit of diphtheria toxin, then the anti-toxin is injected. In this way it is found how much anti-toxin is needed to neutralize the diphtheria toxin, so that it can be reckoned how much anti-toxin should be injected into a patient suffering from diphtheria to counteract the disease." There are no photographs, no textual description of the guinea pigs, and no discussion of the degree of suffering.

Although the horses are initially identified by name in Fitzgerald's lab books (Crestfallen, for example, appears repeatedly as a donor of serum), the individual guinea pigs remain anonymous. As Figure 8.3 shows, the guinea pigs are identified by appearance and number in the lab books before they either succumb to diphtheria or are "discarded." The first guinea pig, for example, was white, weighed 252 grams, and lived less than forty-eight hours after being injected subcutaneously with 0.1 cc of prepared serum in 0.9 cc NaCl (salt solution) on 27 October 1913. The second, a white and black guinea pig weighing 275 grams, was injected on October 31 and succumbed two days later. Their deaths were marked with a cross. These first two were assigned numbers after the fact, and all subsequent guinea pigs are in neat sequential order: #3, a fawn weighing 280 grams, died at three days; #4, another white and black fawn was discarded; and #5 is missing. On November 7, a second toxin was tested on #6, black with fawn at 315 grams, who died after 3–4 days. On November 17, a third toxin was tested on #7, white at 280 grams, and #8, black with a brown collar at 250 grams, both of whom were "alive and well" on December 8, and both discarded. As time went on, Fitzgerald noted the weights on survival before discarding them.[35]

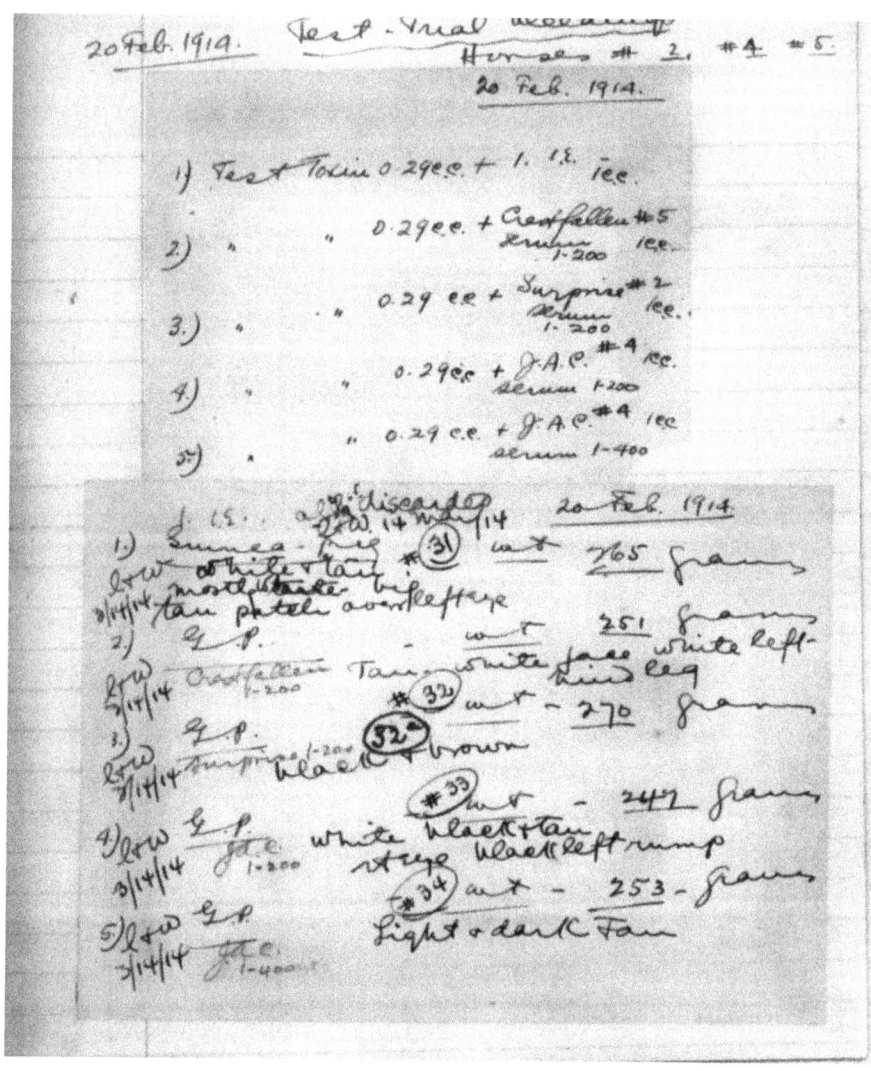

Fig. 8.4a and 8.4b In James G. Fitzgerald's laboratory book (4a) horses are identified by name as well as number, and guinea pigs by weight and coat colour. Numbers appear to have been inserted later. On the other page (4b) the escape of the guinea pigs is noted. Source: James G. Fitzgerald, "Record of Diphtheria Toxins. 1913–1914–1915," Department of Hygiene, University of Toronto. Sanofi Pasteur Canada (Connaught Campus) Archives, Toronto.

Determination L+ dose.

12 March 1919.

I)   12 Mar. 1919

Test Toxin + Immunity unit.

1.) ~~guinea-pig~~ #㊴ – white-black left eye – wt 202 grams
2.) ~~guinea-pig~~ #㊵ – black + tan – wt 209 grams
3.) ~~guinea-pig~~ #㊶ – white-black ears + black rt hind leg. wt 226 grams
4.) ~~guinea-pig~~ #㊷ – white-tan eyes – wt 250 grams

repeated – guinea-pig disappeared from pen. found + 25 March 1919

II)   12 March 1919.

~~Test Toxin~~ + Immunity unit.

1.) Toxin 0.30 cc. + 1 immunity unit
2.) Toxin 0.31 cc. +   "   "
3.) Toxin 0.32 cc. +   "   "
4.) Toxin 0.33 cc. +   "   "

The "discarding" of tested animals was a precaution: the author of *Cavy Culture* noted that "used" guinea pigs—those that had been used for testing antitoxins—were sometimes resold by "small and unreliable institutions."[36] Such animals dangerously altered results if they were used a second time. The Connaught Laboratories did not record their methods of disposal, but *Cavy Culture* noted that "used guinea pigs" were suffocated in large gas machines.

The descriptions in the Connaught laboratory books are just adequate to distinguish one guinea pig from his or her companions. Most descriptions are simple: #45 was simply black; #47 was dark brown; #46 was white with a "tan left ear, tan left hind leg, and on back"; and #48 was an elaborate patchwork ("black, white and tan, black left eye, tan right, black saddle, brown right hind leg"). In these early years, their weights varied between 240 to 280 grams with occasional outliers at 215 grams (#28), 300 grams (#30), and even 370 grams for an unidentified specimen on 25 September 1914. These were young guinea pigs; the standard size of an adult guinea pig in 1947 was 800–900 grams.

There is little evidence of agency on the part of the animals. On 12 March 1914, four guinea pigs (#39, #40, #41, and #42) disappeared from their pen. They were found dead on March 25. Multi-coloured guinea pig #48 may have squirmed: Fitzgerald noted (using an awkward third person construction that may reflect some embarrassment at his clumsiness) that, "in injecting some of the mixture escaped." Toxin was a deadly poison, for human scientists as well as laboratory subjects, so slips were dangerous. Devices like the Voges holder (Figure 8.5) were often used to restrain the animals. As their use became routine, the guinea pigs disappear completely from the second laboratory book. On December 15 [1914?], a note directs readers: "for potency and sterility tests see files." The files have not been archived, and even this note disappears on subsequent pages. Over time, guinea pigs were made increasingly invisible until they disappeared entirely from internal laboratory reports, of no more note than the other tools of laboratory medicine.

Was their invisibility simply due to the routine nature of the guinea pig's role in the antitoxin laboratory? Or could it be related to rising antivivisection sentiments? Antivivisection movements were vocal by this time in the United States and Britain, and although there was as yet no

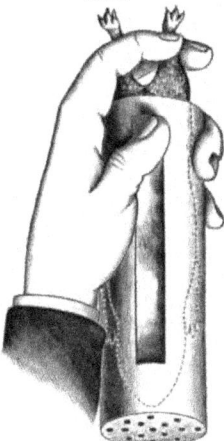

Fig. 8.5 The Voges holder made guinea pig handling more efficient. Source: A. C. Abbott, M.D., *The Principles of Bacteriology: A Practical Matter for Students and Physicians* 8th ed. (1909). Accessible via Internet Archive: https://archive.org/.

organized movement in this country, well-read Canadians were aware of the issue. Darcy Ingram has argued that the more radical wings of animal advocacy were deliberately suppressed in Victorian Canada, and, as I have argued elsewhere, Canadian apprehensions about the growing power of laboratory medicine appear to have been channelled through the antivaccination movement in the first two decades of the twentieth century. Public relations of another Toronto laboratory suggest that scientists were feeling defensive in 1912. A newspaper story, titled "Toronto's New Laboratory is Best on the Continent," featured a photograph of a bank of guinea pig cages, but the animals are out of sight and the visual emphasis is on the modern technology of metal cages, with glass above and plumbing below. The text reassured readers that the guinea pigs were not kept for vivisection. The distinction drawn is revealing: "They are not kept for purposes of vivisection, but as a medium to receive inoculations of certain germs when human life is at stake." Guinea pigs were simply a "medium." They were diagnostic tools whose aliveness was irrelevant, and whose deaths did not fit the narrow definition of vivisection.[37]

In 1921, the Canadian Anti-Vivisection Society took form in Toronto, and similar groups subsequently appeared in other major centres, such as Montreal, Ottawa, Calgary, and Victoria.[38] The membership of Canadian groups, like those in Britain and the United States, was largely made up of women. They were linked to the suffrage movement. Flora Macdonald Denison, a theosophist and suffrage writer, had been influential in the formation of the Toronto group. Her sister, Agnes Stanley, and her son, Denison, were among the forty members at the first 1921 meeting, where Stanley, who took on a leading role, noted that she took up the work on her sister's account.[39] Toronto's medical officer of health Dr. Hastings had already dismissed the concerns of antivivisectors on gendered grounds in 1918, saying that "only a small proportion of the population—the feather brain portion—will object to the experimental inoculation of animals." (One letter writer took issue and responded, "As one of the 'feather brained.'"[40]) In 1922, facing an organized antivivisection society, Hastings was blunt. He is quoted as saying (in a newspaper article positioned directly below an item about an antivivisectionist speaker from Britain and probably solicited for the purpose), "the foes of vivisection put themselves in the strange position of preferring the lives of guinea pigs and rabbits to those of human beings. 'They put pigs before babies,' says the Medical Officer of Health."[41] The direct linkage of guinea pig suffering to the protection of infants was a line of argument well honed by defenders of laboratory medicine.[42]

A second line of argument was that the guinea pigs did not suffer. Representatives of the Montreal General Hospital had made this distinction in 1895: when the president remarked on whether vivisection was practiced, the secretary said that "no pain was inflicted upon the animals; they were simply pricked with a hypodermic needle. There was no cutting at all. The guinea pigs were only poked with a needle."[43] (This emphasis on "cutting" is preserved in the definition of vivisection in the *Oxford English Dictionary*: "The action of cutting or dissecting some part of a living organism; *spec.* the action or practice of performing dissection, or other painful experiment, upon living animals as a method of physiological or pathological study.") In 1923, a Montreal serologist, Dr. F. A. Bert, gave a talk on serums in which he described the benefits of diphtheria antitoxins, and reassured his listeners that the horses are better treated in the lab than on farms. Without going into detail, he also reassured his listeners that no maltreatment of guinea pigs is tolerated and "ether is administered to avoid suffering."[44]

A very different line of argument emerged four years later in the melodramatic *Microbe Hunters* (1926) by American microbiologist Paul de Kruif. The book is credited with inspiring a generation of microbiologists. Chapter Three, "Massacre the Guinea Pigs," briefly deploys the first argument about the protection of infants, but dwells on the horrors of early work on antitoxins: "It was to save babies that Roux and Behring launched into the most relentless massacre of guinea pigs that the scientific world had heard of."[45] De Kruif describes in excruciating detail the "vast butcheries of guinea pigs and rabbits," explaining how the scientist Emile Roux "became a murderer in his heart" as he looked for "ruffled hair, the dragging hind legs, the cold shivering bodies" of his victims and watched the toxin "do dreadful things to his animals" in the "vast slaughterhouse of dead and dying guinea pigs his laboratory was." "The guinea pigs which survived probably wished they were dead, for, while the trichloride was curing them it was burning nasty holes in their hides too—they squeaked pitifully when they bumped these gaping sores. It was an appalling business." The pain is dwelt upon, almost pornographically, and it is described as a necessary prelude to the cure: "those maimings and holocausts and mistakes, always the necessary prelude to his triumphs." This chapter, which was reprinted in newspapers, represents an interesting shift: the pain inflicted by the scientist is glorified as a burden he (and it was almost always he) must carry in order to develop a cure.

It was not an easy burden to carry. John G. Fitzgerald, the brilliant scientist behind the Connaught Laboratories, suffered a mental breakdown at the age of fifty-six in 1938 and died by suicide in 1940. We will never know the cause of his distress. Could the "maimings and holocausts and mistakes" inherent in this form of work have exacted a toll on the researcher in the form of a post-traumatic stress disorder? In a series of letters written from a sanatorium in 1939, Fitzgerald repeatedly referred to having committed "the unpardonable sin," for which, "the penalty is death."[46] The idea that cruelty to animals is an unpardonable sin is common in antivisection literature.[47] James Fitzgerald explored his grandfather's difficulties in a melodramatic book about the family history of mental illness; he attributed John G. Fitzgerald's distress to overwork, and although he describes the deaths of thousands of guinea pigs, their squirming during treatment, and the necessity for cruelty in laboratory science, he does not consider the emotional toll of his grandfather's work with laboratory animals.[48] Is the failure to consider this possibility a further expression of agnotology? Robert G. W. Kirk argues that scientists, and their historians, have shied away from considering the emotional impact of the lived experience of working with and caring for experimental animals: "Where emotion appears in existing historiography on animal research it tends to be framed in such a way as to conform closely to the sciences' own terms; emotions are problematic and they are recognised only insofar as they have to be controlled and removed from the experimental encounter."[49]

The docile guinea pig was peculiarly vulnerable to the hardening of the heart. The contrast with the dog is revealing. In 1923, the Connaught media campaign slipped badly in what was their greatest success, the discovery of insulin. Connaught scientist Frederick Banting was impolitic enough to describe his work in detail in the *Toronto Daily Star*. On reading his account, Agnes Stanley (founding member of the Canadian Anti-Vivisection Society in Toronto, as noted above) wrote a sarcastic letter commending Banting for his honesty: "Even Dr. Banting, in a very touching report of his Detroit speech, told of his distress at the suffering of the little dog who had assisted him so valiantly in his experiments. Dr. Banting seems to have no illusions concerning the cruelty of his experiments."[50] The difficulty was compounded by Banting's candour about the source of his dogs. As the reporter put it, the scientist resorted to "slinking in the midnight shadows on the trail of homeless canines."[51] Pet owners in Toronto were understandably alarmed, and the new Anti-Vivisection Society claimed to have collected 8,000 signatures asking the provincial government to ban the use of dogs in vivisection.[52] The British *Abolitionist*, drawing on information provided by the Ottawa Anti-Vivisection Society, published an article titled "Dr. Banting as a Dog Stealer," with a cartoon of Banting in a white lab coat, knife in hand, threatening to cut the pancreas from a sweet puppy dangling from his other hand.[53] (The laboratories, for their part, re-invented Banting's dogs as a heroes on par with diphtheria horses: as Matthew Klingle has shown, "Marjorie" is now a poster child for insulin.[54])

Lessons were learned from Banting's mistake. Over time, as Susan Lederer has shown, the individual sensing animal was excised from medical journals and descriptions of experiments were edited to reduce their emotional impact. Significantly, these efforts focused on the dog: researchers were advised to refer to the "animal," rather than the "dog." The efforts to minimize the number of dogs in reports of medical experiments did not extend to guinea pigs, rats, and mice. These small animals were of less concern.[55] When he reflected on the uproar about his research a number of years later, Banting made the same distinction. He explained that the guinea pigs' physiology did not lend itself to experimentation on insulin. The implication was that he would have preferred to use the guinea pig, because, unlike the dog, the guinea pig was an expendable species. Antivivisection groups continued to emphasize the mistreatment of dogs, and largely overlooked the routine use of enormous numbers of guinea pigs in laboratories in diagnostic work and biomedical products.[56] The horse and the dog occupy a special place in human sympathies; science is showing that these two species are remarkably attuned to humans. Thousands of years of partnership have made them expert at reading and responding to human emotions; conversely, we are attuned to theirs. The little guinea pig does not participate in such a privileged relationship.

What conclusions can be drawn from the disappearing guinea pig? The first is that we need to be attentive to absences, especially in the archives, and ask what lies behind them. As Proctor and Schiebinger have pointed out, agnotology is rarely accidental. The simplest explanation for the absence of the guinea pig is that it was part of an orchestrated public relations strategy: horses were elevated as heroes, and guinea pigs, whose pain could not be explained away, disappeared. Medical historians have had little interest in digging further, as the story of the guinea pig only undermined the narrative of medical progress. But the absence exists prior to medical history and prior to public relations; it begins in the lab reports, which suggests that the full explanation lies within the scientist's mindset: a kind of cognitive dance by which the pain of the animal other could be hidden even from the self. What is most intriguing about the absence of the actual guinea pigs is the way in which this absence is paralleled by the remarkable presence of the metaphorical guinea pig. Invisibility is cloaked by visibility. The guinea pig has come to be the animal most identified with experimental medicine. Even today, when the guinea pig itself has been largely replaced by other species in the laboratory, we still use the term "guinea pig" as shorthand for our own sense of vulnerability before the forces of medicine and science. The power of the metaphorical guinea pig hides the absence of the material and historical one.

NOTES

1   I would like to thank the organizers of the "Traces of the Animal Past" conference for asking me to develop my original blog on the guinea pig, "Guinea Pig Mea Culpa," and the other participants for their comments. I would also like to thank Christopher Rutty, archivist at the Connaught Campus, Sanofi Pasteur Canada, Toronto, for his assistance. All errors are my own. Joanna Dean, "Guinea Pig Mea Culpa," February 24, 2017, available at http://activehistory.ca/2017/03/guinea-pig-mea-culpa/.

2   Simon Strunsky, *Professor Latimer's Progress; A Novel of Contemporaneous Adventure* (New York: H. Holt, 1918; Toronto: McClelland, Goodchild and Stewart, 1918), 39. A professor launches into this soliloquy after releasing a guinea pig caught on a fence.

3   Robert G. W. Kirk and Michael Worboys, *The Oxford Handbook on the History of Medicine* (Oxford: Oxford University Press, 2011), 561. I owe this reference to Abigail Woods et al.'s excellent *Animals and the Shaping of Modern Medicine. One Health and its Histories* (London: Palgrave Macmillan, 2018). See also Jed Mayer, "The Expression of the Emotions in Man and Laboratory Animals," *Victorian Studies* 50, no. 3 (2008): 399–417; and Paul White "The Experimental Animal in Victorian Britain," in *Thinking with Animals: New Perspectives on Anthropomorphism*, ed. Lorraine Daston and Gregg Mitman (Columbia University Press, 2005). Mayer argues that cross-species sympathy ultimately banished the experimental animal from the public gaze, as scenes from the laboratory were considered too disturbing for readerly sensitivity.

4   Robert N. Proctor and Londa Schiebinger, eds., *Agnotology: The Making and Unmaking of Ignorance* (Stanford, CA: Stanford University Press, 2008), unpaginated preface.

5   For these dates and photographs of the museum, see Christopher J. Rutty, "From Insulin to Heparin: Innovation at Connaught Labs During the 1930s," at *Connaught Fund*, accessed September 30, 2019, http://connaught.research.utoronto.ca/history/article5/. For an account of the heritage restoration, see "Barton Avenue Stables," *Stevens Burgess Architects*, accessed September 9, 2019, http://www.sba.on.ca/projects/barton-avenue-stables.

6   June Callwood, "The Miracle Factory that began in a Stable," *Macleans*, October 1, 1955.

7   *The Contract Record*, October 24, 1917, 882. These same two animals were also intended to have occupied the 1917 stable: diphtheria and tetanus horses were stabled downstairs (with the addition of calves used for the production of small pox vaccine) and the guinea pig colony was to be housed in the hayloft, directly opposite an apartment for the resident lab technician's family. It appears, however, that the guinea pigs were instead housed in an outbuilding

8   For a discussion of the Connaught's fashioning of the heroic horse, see Joanna Dean, "Species at Risk: C. Tetani, the Horse, and the Human," in *Animal Metropolis: Histories of Human-Animal Relations in Urban Canada*, ed. Joanna Dean, Darcy Ingram, and Christabelle Sethna (Calgary, AB: University of Calgary Press, 2016).

9   Edmundo Morales, *The Guinea Pig: Healing, Food, and Ritual in the Andes* (University of Arizona Press, 1995).

10 They were described as early as 1554 by Konrad Gessler in his *Historia Animalium*. See, for example, the multi-coloured guinea pigs in paintings by Jan Brueghel the Elder: "Garden of Eden" (1610–12) and the "Entry of the Animals into Noah's Ark" (1615) in the Stapleton Collection, South West London, UK. Archeological findings at Hill Hall, Essex, provide evidence that guinea pigs were pets in middle class, as well as aristocratic families. Fabienne Pigière, Wim Van Neer, Cécile Ansieau, and Marceline Denis, "New Archaeozoological Evidence for the Introduction of the Guinea Pig to Europe," *Journal of Archaeological Science* 39, no. 4 (April 2012): 1020–24.

11 For the woodchuck, see Charles G. D. Roberts, *Babes of the Wild* (Toronto: Cassell, 1912), 64; for the beaver, see Charles Eden, *The Home of the Wolverene and Beaver, or, Fur-Hunting in the Wilds of Canada* (London: Society for Promoting Christian Knowledge, 1876) and for the chipmunk, see George Henry, *The Emigrant's Guide, or, Canada as It Is* (Quebec: W. Gray, 1835), 167.

12 Alexander Davidson, *The Canada Spelling Book.* (Toronto: Brewer, McPhail and Co., 1850), 15. See also Davidson's 1845 edition published in Niagara. An 1892 news article suggested that the Abyssinians at least were still a novelty: "A Big Show of Feathers: The Annual Exhibition of the Poultry, Pigeon and Pet Stock Association," *The [Montreal] Gazette*, June 28, 1892, 8. "Among the queer things were Abyssinian cavys."

13 Two novels that use the guinea pig in a pocket as a device are Marshall Saunders, *Beautiful Joe* (London: Jarrold, 1895), 164–65, and Alfred Tresidder Sheppard, *The Rise of Ledgar Dunstan* (Toronto: W. Briggs, 1916).

14 See, for example, the letters published in "The Boys Exchange," by sixteen-year-old Joseph S. Bricker of Listowel, Ontario, "How to Care for Cavies," *The Globe*, February 3, 1906, 10; "Fred's Pets," a letter from nine-year-old Fred Hodgkins in *The Globe*, December 7, 1907, 10; "Our New Baby," by ten-year-old Kenneth F. McCuaig of Toronto in *The Globe*, March 28, 1908, 10; and "Anah in King," by Anah Baldwin, aged nine, in *The Globe* October 24, 1908, 10. Boys are repeatedly associated with the guinea pig. It is the first of the pets described in *Three Hundred Things a Bright Boy Can Do* (Toronto: Musson, 1910). Lorne Sully's guinea pigs were reported as drawing special attention from "the small boy portion of the crowd," at the Russell County Fair, in *The Ottawa Journal*, September 15, 1892. The guinea pig is recommended as a class pet in *The Nature Study Course with Suggestions for Teaching It* (Toronto: Copp Clark, 1905).

15 "Pet Guinea Pigs," *Ottawa Journal*, October 22, 1898, 9. His letter was one of several sent in the hopes of winning a prize.

16 Evelyn Wade, "Our Guinea Pigs," in "Playtime Monthly Prizes," *The Globe*, April 15, 1913.

17 The advertisements for Newbro's Herpicide ran in many Canadian and American newspapers for several years. For an early Canadian example, see the *Ottawa Citizen*, August 1, 1905, 2. The guinea pig is rubbed with a pomade made of dandruff scales, and promptly loses its hair. The title in large font was a variation on the theme and appears in the *Ottawa Citizen*, November 30, 1907, 10.

18 *The Natural History of Quadrupeds and Cetaceous Animals from the Works of the Best Authors, Antient and Modern, Embellished with Numerous Plates.* vol. 2 (Bungay [England]: Brightly and Co., 1811). The quote refers to the guinea pig as a pet.

19 Elizabeth Stuart Phelps, *The Gates Ajar* (Cambridge, MA: Harvard University Press, 1869; 1964), 124. Cited in Philip Howell, "A Place for the Animal Dead: Pets, Pet Cemeteries and Animal Ethics in Late Victorian Britain," *Ethics, Place & Environment* 5, no. 1 (March 2002): 5–22.

20 *Three Hundred Things a Bright Boy Can Do*, 228.

21 J. Henri Wagner, *The Cavy: Our Fancy Guinea Pig* (Pet Stock World Company, 1915). Charles Eden was similarly disparaging when he compared the beaver to the guinea pig: "In shape it resembles a magnified guinea pig, but only in shape, and I should not degrade the intelligent beaver by comparing it to such a useless little animal did I know any other at all familiar to English readers." Eden, *The Home of the Wolverene and Beaver*, 64.

22 For the guinea pig market in Britain, see Robert G. W. Kirk, "A Brave New Animal for a Brave New World," *Isis* 101, no. 1 (March 2010): 62–94; and "'Wanted—Standard Guinea Pigs': Standardisation and the Experimental Animal Market in Britain ca. 1919-1947," *Studies in History and Philosophy of Biol & Biomed Sci* 39, no. 3 (2008): 280–91. For the United States, see the advice offered by the US Department of Agriculture in Orson N. Eaton, *The Guinea Pig*, USDA Leaflet 252 (1949) and *Raising Guinea Pigs*, Leaflet 466 (1962).

23 "Humble Guinea Pig is a Valuable Aid: Display at Winter Fair Recalls Use in Medical Research," *The Toronto Globe*, November 21, 1925. The *Ottawa Daily Citizen* reported prices in Boston as high as $150 a pair in "Odd Occupations," September 12, 1895, 3.

24 E. Michaels, *Cavy Culture: A Book of Practical Instructions on the Raising and Marketing of Guinea Pigs* (Philadelphia: E. Michaels, 1920), 71.

25 "Making More Money: The Big Problem That Interests Everyone – With Guinea Pigs," *The Windsor Star*, January 19, 1924, 28.

26 "Humble Guinea Pig is a Valuable Aid: Display at Winter Fair Recalls Use in Medical Research," *The Globe*, November 21, 1925.

27 In Britain, a guinea pig glut between 1948 and 1950 resulted in a price collapse, and then a shortage in 1951. Kirk, "A Brave New Animal for a Brave New World," footnote 24.

28 By 1949, the USDA pamphlet, *The Guinea Pig*, cautioned breeders to find a buyer before raising stock, because so many institutions raised their own, or contracted with specific breeders.

29. "Analysis of 342 Death Records of Breeding Female Guinea-pigs Period December 1930 – March 1933," Sanofi Pasteur Canada (Connaught Campus) Archives, Toronto.

30. H. Bruce and A. Parkes, "Feeding and breeding of laboratory animals III. Observations on the feeding of guinea-pigs," *Journal of Hygiene* 45, no. 1 (1947): 70–87. "The general level of requirement indicated by these experiments is vastly in excess of that of the rabbit, and the problem of meeting it, without feeding greenstuff, by a diet which can be made in bulk and stored under ordinary conditions, does not seem to have been attacked" (70). The vitamin was destroyed in the pelleting process, which was not a problem with rabbits as they synthesize their own vitamin C. The 1930s had been a period of general experimentation with processed food for laboratory animals (as with other livestock). Between 1930 and 1933, the Connaught Laboratories experimented with the guinea pig diet; they first fed them a wet mash of oats, middlings, bran wheat germ, casein, salt, and bone meal for eleven months, then a prepared rabbit chow for fifteen months, and then another dry mash similar to the wet one.

31. Kirk, "A Brave New Animal for a Brave New World," 15. Kirk cites the 1945 "Conference on the Supply of Experimental Animals," which was organized by a coalition of scientific organizations.

32. For example, see C. Cumberland, *The guinea pig or domestic cavy for food, fur and fancy* (London: Upcot, 1896); William F. Roth, and Charles T. Cornman, *Rabbit and Cavy Culture; a Complete and Official Standard of All the Rabbits and Cavies* (Sellersville, PA: Poultry Item Press, 1916); J. Henri.Wagner, *The Cavy: Our Fancy Guinea Pig* (Baltimore: Pet Stock World Company, 1915), and Michaels, *Cavy Culture*.

33. "Of Mice and Men," *Contox*, no. 16 (April 1969). Sanofi Pasteur Canada (Connaught Campus) Archives, Toronto.

34. Karen Rader, *Making Mice: Standardizing Animals for American Biomedical Research, 1900-1955* (Princeton University Press, 2004).

35. The method applied here is that described by Dr. E. Roux in "The Serum Treatment of Diptheria," *Dominion Medical Monthly* 4, no. 1 (January 1895): 8.

36. Michaels, *Cavy Culture*, 8.

37. "Toronto's New Laboratory is Best on the Continent," *The Toronto Daily Star*, May 8, 1912, 2.

38. Darcy Ingram, "Beastly Measures: Animal Welfare, Civil Society, and State Policy in Victorian Canada," *Journal of Canadian Studies/Revue d'études Canadiennes* 47, no. 1 (Winter 2013): 221–52. See also J. T. H. Connor,"Cruel Knives? Vivisection and Biomedical Research in Victorian English Canada," *Canadian Bulletin of Medical History* 14, no. 1 (1997): 37–64.

39. Details of the Society's founding meeting on 4 July 1921 were published in *The Canadian Theosophist*, September 15, 1921, 106. Flora Macdonald Denison had recently died. For the emergence of the organized antivivisection movement in Canada out of an antivaccination movement, see Joanna Dean, "Animal Matter: The Making of 'Pure Bovine Vaccine at the Connaught Laboratories and Farm at the Turn of the Century," in *Landscapes of Science*, E-book, ed. Tina Adcock (Toronto: Network in Canadian History and Environment, 2019).

40. E. Tennyson Smith's letter was published under the title "Vivisection," *The Toronto Daily Star*, March 25, 1918, 19. She identified herself as a visitor from England.

41 "Facts Figures Show the Value of Vivisection," *Toronto Daily Star*, September 25, 1922. Hasting's comments were made in response to a public lecture given by British antivivisectionist Walter P. Hadwen on September 21 and were run by the *Star* directly above a story about Hadwen's lecture.

42 See, for example, Richard M. Pearce, *Animal Experimentation in the Diagnosis, Treatment, and Prevention of Diseases of Children*. Defense of Research Series, Pamphlet XXVII (Bureau on Protection of the Medical Research of the Council on Health and Public Instruction of the American Medical Association, 1915), 6.

43 "General Hospital: The Adjourned Quarterly Meeting Held Yesterday," *The [Montreal] Gazette*, November 21, 1895, 6.

44 "Discussion Took Unexpected Turn: Anti Vivisectionist Protested Against Arguments at Chemical Society," *The [Montreal] Gazette*, October 30, 1923, 4. See also the letter by J. J. Heagerty, MD in the *Ottawa Citizen*, March 27, 1925, 18, describing the benefits of vaccination and concluding: "Mr. Franklin will still continue to prate largely. He will continue to gather around him gentle kindly folk and send delicious shivers up and down their spines, by picturing to them the terrible sufferings of motherless cats caused by dour visage surgeons whose hands are dyed red in the blood of innocent guinea pigs."

45 These quotes are taken from a 19 September 1926 article in the *Minneapolis Sunday Tribune*, called "The Microbe Hunters: Roux and Behring Massacre Guinea Pigs to Save Babies from Diphtheria." The first line of Chapter Three reads: "It was to save the babies that they killed so many guinea pigs." For the vast influence of this book on a generation of young microbiologists, and millions of general readers, see William C. Summers, "*Microbe Hunters* Revisited," *International Microbiology* 1 (1998): 65–66. This line of argument was not new. See also A. W. H. Bates, "Vivisection, Virtue Ethics, and the Law in 19th-Century Britain," *Journal of Animal Ethics* 4, no. 2 (2014): 30–44. Curiously, at the end of the chapter, Roux abandons science for sentiment when he administers his cure to human babies. Faced with the scientific mandate to treat half the babies in order to create a control group, Roux gives all the human babies the cure, rather than scientifically selecting half.

46 James Fitzgerald, *What Disturbs Our Blood: A Son's Quest to Redeem the Past* (Random House, 2010), 147, 400–1. A psychiatric report dated October 22 stated, "He continues to have numerous ideas about an unpardonable sin that he has committed" (401). Chapter Eight is titled. "The Unpardonable Sin." In an otherwise positive review, eminent medical historian Michael Bliss criticizes the book for "contrived melodrama" in his review in the *Canadian Bulletin of Medical History* 28, no. 2 (2011): 404. J. T. H. Connor's review in the *Canadian Historical Review* is also critical of the "flamboyant and journalistic prose," *Canadian Historical Review* 92, no. 4 (December 2011) 732–33.

47 *Merriam-Webster.com Thesaurus* defines the adjective "unpardonable" with reference to animal cruelty, s.v. "unpardonable," accessed June 20, 2021, https://www.merriam-webster.com/thesaurus/unpardonable. American antivivisectionist Mary E. Lovell described vivisection as "the worst form of cruelty and cruelty as the deadliest sin" Craig Buettinger, "Women and Antivivisection in Late Nineteenth-Century America," *Journal of Social History* 30, 4 [1997]: 863. On the first page of the *Sunday New York Times*, November 29, 1908, the popular writer Mrs. Humphrey Ward referred to vivisection as "the intolerable and unpardonable torture." Only two years before Fitzgerald's death, a Nobel prize–winning author wrote: "To a man whose mind is

free there is something even more intolerable in the sufferings of animals than in the sufferings of man. For with the latter it is at least admitted that suffering is evil and that the man who causes it is a criminal. But thousands of animals are uselessly butchered every day without a shadow of remorse. If any man were to refer to it, he would be thought ridiculous. And that is the unpardonable crime." Romain Rolland, *Jean Christophe*, trans. Gilbert Cannan (New York: The Modern Library, 1938).

48   See pages 207–8 of Fitzgerald's *What Disturbs the Blood* for the "violent and fatal reactions of the guinea pigs to injections of horse serum," and page 237: "Gerry instructs his sister to hold down a squealing guinea pig as he injects the antitoxin to test its potency." Neither reference is footnoted. On page 251, he describes the casual cruelty of one of Fitzgerald's mentors, Simon Flexner, quoting Flexner as saying: "No one can run an institution, unless he has the capacity to be cruel."

49   Robert Kirk, "The Experimental Animal," in *The Routledge Companion to Animal-Human History*, ed. Hilda Kean and Philip Howell (Oxford: Routledge, 2020), 134. Kirk says there is an urgent need for historical enquiry into "the question of how affective, moral and ethical values have been enacted within, and thus transformed by, animal research," and calls for "a moral ecology of science." As he notes, Vinciane Despret makes a similar point in "The body we care for: figures of anthro-zoo-genesis, *Body & Society* 10, no. 2 (2004): 111–34.

50   "Antivivisection," *The Globe,* April 6, 1923, 4.

51   "Loyalty to Early Friends Distinguishes Dr. Banting," *Toronto Daily Star*, November 20, 1923, 10.

52   "Anti-Vivisection Society Holds Its Annual Meeting," *The Globe,* February 1, 1923.

53   For the role of the Ottawa Anti-Vivisection Society in raising international condemnation see "Dr. Banting as a Dog Stealer," in *The Abolitionist*, February 1, 1924, 17, https://insulin.library.utoronto.ca/islandora/object/insulin%3AC10119. Medical historian Michael Bliss notes in his review of the Fitzgerald biography that "a very large number of Fitzgerald relatives, friends, and professional associates, including such giants of Canadian medicine as Banting and Best, were also mentally ill, unstable, and/or addicted to alcohol or drugs." *Canadian Bulletin of Medical History* 28, 2 (2011), 404–5.

54   Matthew Klingle, "The Multiple Lives of Marjorie: The Dogs of Toronto and the Co-Discovery of Insulin," *Environmental History* 23, no. 2 (2018): 368–82.

55   Susan E. Lederer, "Political Animals: The Shaping of Biomedical Research Literature in Twentieth Century America," *Isis: Journal of the History of Science in Society* 83 (1992), 29.

56   See J. C. Russell and D. C. Secord. "Holy Dogs and the Laboratory: Some Canadian Experiences with Animal Research." *Perspectives in Biology and Medicine* 28, no. 3 (1985): 374–81. As one example, the Montreal antivivisection group made reference to the suffering of the animals in the productions of serums, but explicitly focused their work on dogs. "Anti-Vivisection League Started," *The [Montreal] Gazette,* April 22, 1922, 6.

9

Tuffy's Cold War: Science, Memory, and the US Navy's Dolphin

Jason M. Colby

The news reports appeared in August 1965. A US Navy–trained bottlenose dolphin named Tuffy would be assisting American aquanauts aboard Sealab II, an underwater habitat stationed off La Jolla, California. Navy spokesmen explained that the young animal would deliver messages to the station as well as possibly protect divers from shark attacks. Appearing amid the surging popularity of marine parks and the *Flipper* television series (1964–1967), the story captured broad public interest, and when the operation launched the following month, newspapers closely followed Tuffy's involvement. Yet it was just one part of the young dolphin's journey. Captured off Gulfport, Mississippi, in 1962, he had spent two years performing at a waterfront marine park in Santa Monica before being moved to the US Naval Missile Center at Point Mugu, California. There, he became one of the first non-human inductees into the US Navy Marine Mammal Program. Trained by his Navy handlers, he made cutting-edge research in diving physiology possible, helped the Navy develop a new deep-sea ordnance recovery program, and became the first cetacean in history to perform tasks on command in open water—leading to his assignment to Sealab II.

But what did Tuffy make of all this? Captured at a young age and torn from his environment and social connections, he found himself confined to small tanks with strange dolphins, swimming in unfamiliar waters, and placed in dangerous situations in order to fit the research and operational needs of the US Navy. He nearly drowned in his sea pen during a storm off the California coast, became the first cetacean to fly aboard a helicopter, and briefly escaped captivity only to return to his handlers. In the end, Tuffy died understanding neither the Cold War politics that had conscripted him nor the impact of his life on human science and culture. Yet in the memories of the people who knew him best, Tuffy was an eager and essential contributor to the early work of the Navy Marine Mammal Program, which continues to this day.

This chapter grapples with the challenge of finding Tuffy in the archive. The attempt to know any individual non-human animal—particularly a dead one—can seem like an exercise in scholarly hubris. Yet as Nigel Rothfels shows in his exploration of the captive elephant Tusko (Chapter 10), the biography of one celebrity animal, however contested the facts and interpretation, can tell us much about shifting human relations with a species or group of species. In Tuffy's case, sources are abundant, but the record is entirely human, consisting of veterinary notes, scientific papers, grainy videos, and hazy memories. This is a problem. Despite counterculturaldreams of inter-species communication, and the confident claims of his Navy handlers, we can't know what Tuffy thought and felt. To be sure, we can examine his recorded interactions with people and draw tentative conclusions, but here, too, perils present themselves. Both oral history and the written record contain vexing silences, particularly when dealing with a subject as politically charged as the military use of marine mammals. Interviewees have hidden motives and varied understandings of consent and captivity. And memory is a fickle thing. In the case of the Marine Mammal Program, the legacy of military science and secrecy competes with the very human reflections and emotions that captive encounters evoke. It is here, at the nexus of human culture, animal agency, and Cold War science, that we search for Tuffy.

Dreams of befriending dolphins have deep roots. Writing in the first century CE, the Roman naturalist Pliny the Elder asserted that the dolphin "does not dread man, as though a stranger to him, but comes to meet ships, leaps and bounds to and fro," and he cited stories of dolphins carrying drowning children to safety.[1] In later centuries, although many European and North American fishers viewed various species of dolphins as pests—"herring hogs"—some dreamed of using them to herd fish, and naturalists and casual observers alike were transfixed by the graceful movement of dolphins through water. In the early decades of the twentieth century, most marine mammal research dealt with dead specimens. This included animals killed in the Cape Hatteras bottlenose dolphin fishery, which extracted oil from their heads for use in precision timepieces. Beginning in the 1930s, however, scientists had the opportunity to observe dolphins alive in captivity, particularly at Marineland in St. Augustine, Florida.[2] In the process, some researchers began to suspect, like fishers before them, that dolphins use sound to navigate brackish coastal waters—an ability that might offer insight for human efforts to develop systems of "sound navigation and ranging"—or sonar—during World War II.

With the coming of the Cold War, these prospects became even more compelling. In response to the rapid expansion of the Soviet submarine fleet, the new Office of Naval Research channelled funds into oceanographic studies, some of which looked to marine mammals for innovation and inspiration.[3] One area of focus was hydrodynamics. Scientists had long noted that dolphins appeared to move through water with greater ease than their muscle mass should allow, and some theorized that the study of their bodies could lead to more efficient torpedoes and submarines. Among the earliest to explore this possibility was Max Kramer, a former Nazi engineer brought to the United States after World War II. Funded by the US Navy, he began studying dolphin anatomy in the late 1940s and later invented a synthetic material modelled on dolphin skin. Other researchers examined the shape of dolphin bodies to improve submarine design.[4]

The second area of emphasis was marine acoustics. With the growth of the Soviet fleet, the Navy was keen to develop its capacity for active sonar, and some officials believed dolphins held the key. In 1959, researchers at Marineland of the Pacific in California proved conclusively that bottlenose dolphins use biosonar to echolocate.[5] Meanwhile, a neuroscientist named John Lilly had received funding from the Navy and NASA to build an experimental laboratory for captive dolphins on Saint Thomas in the

US Virgin Islands. In 1961, he published his initial findings in *Man and Dolphin*, which predicted that communication between dolphins and humans would soon become possible. In doing so, he speculated on how cetaceans might view human politics. "If dolphins come to understand our cold war and similar quarrels between large segments of the human race, we don't know how they will proceed to operate," Lilly mused. "They may all be pacifists; on the other hand, they may be highly military types." At the very least, Lilly believed cetaceans "might help in rescuing survivors of plane crashes and shipwrecks. They might search for survivors, protect them from sharks, provide them with food." But he also suggested military applications for dolphins, including surveillance, deep sea retrieval, and even tactical Naval operations.[6]

Amid rising Cold War tensions, these suggestions piqued the interest of William B. McLean, head of the Naval Ordnance Test Station at China Lake, California. Having invented the heat-seeking Sidewinder missile in his garage, McLean embraced innovation, and he hoped dolphins might help Navy engineers design faster and quieter torpedoes. In 1960, his team acquired a female Pacific white-sided dolphin named Knotty and began studies of her locomotion at the Convair Laboratory in Southern California. Soon after, Bill Evans, an acoustic engineer at Lockheed, used the cadaver of a spinner dolphin to assess the directional capabilities of its biosonar.[7]

In the fall of 1962, just after the Cuban Missile Crisis, the Navy opened a cetacean research facility at the Naval Missile Center at Point Mugu, California. Among its first hires was Sam Ridgway, a twenty-six-year-old veterinarian from South Texas who had previously cared for dogs in the Air Force and had never before seen a dolphin. Inspired by the engineers and scientists he met, some of whom believed marine mammals could help Americans colonize the seafloor, Ridgway took charge of medical care for the Navy's growing assortment of marine mammals.[8] Initially, the program's cetaceans consisted only of Pacific white-sided dolphins, but Ridgway and his assistants struggled to keep the species alive in captivity, owing particularly to water quality problems at the Point Mugu facility. Taking their cue from the marine park industry, Navy officials soon turned to bottlenose dolphins, which seemed to thrive in captivity.[9] And as luck would have it, they were about to acquire a star.

Fig. 9.1 "Tuf Guy" arrives at Point Mugu, May 1964. Courtesy of the US National Archives.

In March 1964, Pacific Ocean Park on the Santa Monica pier closed, prompting two of the facility's trainers—Wally Ross and Morris Wintermantel—to accept jobs with the Navy Marine Mammal Program. They brought with them an adult male bottlenose dolphin whom park staffers had dubbed "Tuf Guy," owing to what they perceived as his belligerent attitude toward humans. At seven feet long and two hundred and seventy pounds, "Tuf Guy" was a bit of a runt, and his time in captivity had not been kind to him. As Ridgway observed, the "emaciated" dolphin had "lost so much weight that the transverse spines of vertebrae appeared as bumps protruding in a row on either side of his body." Equally troubling, his skin was crisscrossed with scratches and scars made by the teeth of his fellow dolphins in the marine park tank. Over the following weeks, Ridgway and other staffers nursed him back to health, but the young dolphin—increasingly referred to as "Tuffy"—didn't seem happy in his new home. Despite the presence of the familiar Ross and Wintermantel, he avoided human contact and chased away anyone who attempted to enter the water with him. "When he was not hungry," Ridgway noted, "the dolphin kept his distance, eyeing people suspiciously from the center of the pool."[10]

Speaking to me more than fifty years later, Ridgway reiterated this first impression of Tuffy's personality. "He was a very pugnacious animal," Ridgway recalled. "Unlike the average dolphin, which is very docile and quiet, this guy didn't take anything from people."

"Sort of an alpha male?" I asked.

"No, more of a feisty little guy," responded Ridgway. "He was very small. He just didn't want to be picked on."[11]

In fact, the young dolphin was almost surely traumatized by the experience of capture, transportation, captivity, and now an unfamiliar home with new schedules and demands. "Unlike most bottlenose dolphins, he was irascible and even downright dangerous," wrote program director Forrest Wood. "When upset about anything—and it didn't take much—he would bite or butt."[12] Soon trainers were refusing to work with him, and Wood feared the dolphin would be of little use to the Navy. Then Tuffy made a friend.

In the early summer of 1964, Ridgway hired a young biology student named Deborah Duffield as his research assistant. Although her primary task was assisting Ridgway in his laboratory, she repeatedly asked to spend time with Tuffy outside her work hours. The all-male crew of trainers was skeptical, warning Duffield to stay clear of Tuffy, but she was determined to make a connection. Over the next three weeks, she hand-fed the wary dolphin and patiently conditioned him to her presence in his pool, even coaxing him to accept her touch. There were hitches along the way. On one occasion, a zipper on her wetsuit caught Tuffy's fin. He immediately turned and bit Duffield's hand, leaving eleven puncture wounds. Nevertheless, the tenacious student continued to work with Tuffy, training him to retrieve objects at the bottom of his pool and even swim blindfolded through rings upon command. This critical interlude in Tuffy's life was captured in the short publicity film *The Dolphins That Joined the Navy* (1964), narrated by actor Glenn Ford. Among other things, the film shows Duffield running Tuffy through swimming drills in his pool. "Quick as a flash, he is off, and speeding through the hoops with unerring accuracy," intones Ford. "Tuf Guy is also trained to retrieve this weighted disk from the bottom of the pool. He pounces upon it and returns it with his usual self-assurance."[13]

Today, Dr. Deborah Duffield is a distinguished marine mammalogist. She runs the Marine Mammal Laboratory at Portland State University and is the director of the Marine Mammal Stranding Network for the National Oceanic and Atmospheric Administration for the Pacific Coast. Jars and instruments fill her massive lab, and when I visited in February 2018, she had just finished dissecting a sea lion in an adjoining abattoir. It had been more than half a century since she worked with Tuffy at Point Mugu, but the experience had clearly left an impression. Photographs and memorabilia of the feisty dolphin adorned the walls as she reflected on her connection to him.

"Tuffy came along so fast," she recalled.

"What explains that—his progress with you?" I asked.

"Well, the one thing that made a difference in my ability to train him versus what they were doing with the other animals was that . . . I really thought that you needed the training time, but then you'd have a free period when the animal decides what to do, not you just ordering the animal. I did that with Tuffy, and it made a huge difference."

"In your relationship with him?"

"Oh, totally," she explained. "There would be times when we had a schedule and other times when I would be standing in the pool. And if there was something he wanted to do, we'd do it. That really altered how we worked our way through what we were doing. Within a very short period of time, he was wearing a harness and working easily with us."

"So your work with him made him more cooperative for the program?"

"Well, not just that," she reflected. "He was a unique, individual animal. He was curious, and he didn't like to do that same thing over and over. He was engaged."[14]

When summer ended, Duffield returned to university. But her success with Tuffy convinced Ridgway that the spirited dolphin might be trained to perform dive work in open water. Late that autumn, trainers moved Tuffy from his tank to a small sea pen. He was still in the new enclosure weeks later when Duffield returned to Point Mugu for a visit during her winter break. Eager to see Tuffy, she pulled on her wetsuit and climbed into

Fig. 9.2 Tuffy takes fish from a Navy trainer, 1965. Courtesy of the US National Archives.

his old pool. To her disappointment, however, the dolphin in the murky water kept its distance. Meanwhile, she could see another dolphin in a floating pen out in the lagoon. "The dolphin in that pen was jumping and landing on its side, splashing water high into the air," recalled Ridgway. "She could hear the animal snort and slap its tail repeatedly against the surface of the water in its excitement." It was only after a trainer informed Duffield that the agitated animal in the distant pen was, in fact, Tuffy that she realized her error and rushed to see him. "It was hard to tell who was more excited," joked one of the trainers, "the girl or the porpoise."[15]

In February 1965, Tuffy began his open water work. At first, trainers rigged up a leash with Wally Ross holding one end from a skiff. Soon after, they began allowing him to swim freely alongside the boat. "We simply stopped using this last vestige of our physical power over the dolphin," Ridgway later wrote, speculating that "some less-tangible bonds held Tuffy."[16]

After moving the dolphin's pen into deeper water, about two hundred metres from shore, staffers began trials that attempted to assess his maximum diving depth. At the time, most researchers assumed dolphins dove no more than about seventy metres, but they hoped to push Tuffy deeper. The following month, the *San Diego Union* published a feature on the Navy program, emphasizing Tuffy's willingness to follow a boat and dive on command. When asked about the purpose of the research, base commander Captain Carl O. Homquist explained, "it is part of the Navy's business to know about anything that goes on in the ocean, and to make use of any possible means to achieve its military missions." As reporter Bryant Evans noted, this included plans to develop "a hand-held sonar that works on the porpoise system."[17] Just days later, the program had a scare when heavy seas hit Point Mugu. Unable to approach Tuffy's pen by boat, Ridgway convinced the base commander to allow him to use a helicopter to drop fish to the hungry dolphin. Although the manoeuvre worked, Ridgway fretted that the pen would break apart, entangling Tuffy in his containment net. Even if the pen remained intact, the high waves made it difficult for the dolphin to manoeuvre and surface to breathe. When the storm finally passed, Ridgway and several trainers sped out to the pen. To their relief, they found a hungry, but uninjured, Tuffy.

In the summer of 1965, Tuffy began training for Sealab II. Although his primary task consisted of carrying messages to and from the station, some handlers also envisioned him protecting the divers from sharks. As the *Los Angeles Times* informed readers, "a pugnacious porpoise named Tuffy will get a chance soon to play bodyguard, shark-fighter and rescuer for divers in the Navy's underwater hut, Sealab II." In the process, the paper offered a partly fictionalized biography of Tuffy. "Now about 10 years old, the shark-scarred Tuffy was captured in the Atlantic three years ago and spent two years in oceanariums. Brought here in April 1964, he frequently attacked trainers and earned the nickname Tuf Guy." For their part, Navy handlers were confident in Tuffy's ability to complete his tasks. "He's so well-trained he can come down, tap a lost diver on the shoulder, and hand him a life line," observed one Navy torpedoman.[18]

In late August 1965, Sealab II was lowered seventy metres to the seafloor off La Jolla. Its crew consisted of three teams of aquanauts, each of which would rotate there for twelve days. In command was former astronaut Scott Carpenter, who would remain in the habitat for the full forty-five days.[19] Tuffy's work began with the second team, which descended to Sealab II on 12 September 1965. On the following day, Tuffy flew from Point Mugu to Mission Bay in San Diego aboard a Navy helicopter. From there, a boat delivered him to his sea pen near Sealab II. In his first attempt, Tuffy descended only part of the way to Sealab II. In his second, he approached the facility but failed to deliver his package of mail. As one reporter noted, "aquanaut John Reaves, who was about 50 feet from the lab, clicked his photographic strobe light, and Tuffy swam to him, but wouldn't approach close enough for his load to be unhitched." Worried trainers struggled to explain the dolphin's reluctance. "Porpoises are afraid of being trapped under water because they'll drown if they don't surface within five minutes," noted a nervous Navy spokesman. "Apparently Tuffy thought the wires and cables were some kind of a net."[20]

The following day, things turned around. Tuffy made two successful deliveries in rapid succession and then consistently completed his tasks over the following nine days.[21] On the tenth day, however, the divers stopped rewarding him with fish, and he immediately balked at trainers' commands.[22] In all, Tuffy made seven successful trips to Sealab II. "Aquanauts crowded about the portholes of their 12-by-58-foot capsule home 205 feet below the surface to wave goodbye as Tuffy made his final dive," noted one reporter. "In recognition of his nearly flawless service, Tuffy was made an honorary member of the Sealab crew."[23]

Tuffy's exploits hardly passed unnoticed. The following month, Navy officials asked program director Forrest Wood if the dolphin could assist in the recovery of Regulus II missile cradles, which often splashed down in water too deep for Navy divers to reach. With each cradle worth $4,700, officials hoped Tuffy might be able to locate the items at open sea if acoustic buzzers were attached. Once again, he succeeded, gaining notice from the *Los Angeles Times*. Noting the "famed" animal's role in Sealab II the previous summer, the newspaper explained that "with unerring accuracy the dolphin led a squad of Navy frogmen to the buzzing cradle, resting in 50 feet of water." According to the newspaper, thrilled Navy officials were already making plans to train another dolphin—Buzz Buzz—"to assist Tuffy in future recoveries."[24] Soon after, Tuffy enabled the recovery of a rocket-launched depth charge off San Nicolas.[25] So useful had the dolphin

Fig. 9.3 Tuffy breaching in open water near Point Mugu, 1966. Courtesy of the US National Archives.

become that general panic ensued at Point Mugu in July 1966 when Tuffy and another Navy dolphin vanished from their sea pen, apparently released by recreational boaters. A day later, after an intensive search, trainers located Tuffy fifty kilometres up the coast, off Carpinteria.[26]

Over the following two years, Tuffy remained the centrepiece of the Navy Marine Mammal Program. In spring 1967, staffers began studies for the potential use of marine mammals for harbour defence, particularly in the interdiction of enemy divers. In May 1967, the Navy flew Tuffy to the Mine Defense Laboratory at Panama City, Florida, where he joined two other bottlenose dolphins, two sea lions, and a harbour seal. For six weeks, the animals ran harbour defence drills. Upon his return to Point Mugu, Tuffy was the main subject in a deep diving study. By 1968, trainers had conditioned him to descend to prescribed depths and exhale into an underwater funnel, enabling Ridgway and others to complete some of the first scientific analyses of cetacean diving physiology.[27] Such trials were especially important as the Navy hoped to use Tuffy for the upcoming Sealab III expedition, which would be placed three times deeper than its predecessor. In June 1968, he made his deepest recorded dive—more than two hundred metres—deep enough to reach Sealab III. Although funding shortages scuttled the project, his Navy handlers had big plans for Tuffy, and in their eyes, much of his usefulness stemmed from the pugnacity they had once considered an impediment. As Wood reflected:

> We had known that there is great individual variation in temperament and trainability, but it was now forcefully brought home to us that for future open-sea work some technique for selecting likely candidates was desirable. It was interesting that the 'feisty' animals, of which Tuffy was a prime example, seemed to be smarter and more reliable than the ones of placid temperament.[28]

But the program's time with their star subject was running out. In the spring of 1970, trainers noticed an oozing wound on Tuffy's underside. Ridgway immediately treated it and administered antibiotics, but the infection spread quickly, paralyzing the dolphin's lower half. "Tonight, as I watched Tuffy drift around his pool, I was heartsick," Ridgway later wrote. When the dolphin died shortly after, the young veterinarian was despondent. "All of us who had worked with him grieved for the loss of his marvelously complex life," he reflected. "For me it was not so much that I had lost a valuable research animal.... Far more important was that I had lost a beloved friend who had helped me to learn more about my world and his."[29]

Later that year, Ridgway took a temporary leave from the program, accepting a fellowship to pursue doctoral studies at Cambridge University. Meanwhile, Tuffy's legacy lived on. That same autumn of 1970, the Navy deployed trained dolphins to South Vietnam. Dubbed Project Short Time, their mission was to protect the military depot at Cam Ranh Bay from Vietnamese sappers who might approach by water and attempt to plant explosives.[30] By that time, the Marine Mammal Program had become classified, and few in the public seemed to remember the Navy dolphin who had once garnered headlines. And over the following decades, as the

Fig. 9.4 Tuffy assists Navy diver, 1969. Courtesy of the US National Archives.

politics surrounding marine mammal captivity shifted, those who knew him best revised their thoughts about his life and legacy.

In early 2016, forty-six years after Tuffy's death, I set out to convince Sam Ridgway to sit for an interview with me. It wasn't an easy task. The release of the documentary *Blackfish* (2013) had altered the political landscape, and those involved in marine mammal captivity were leery of public attention. Although SeaWorld had taken most of the heat, some activists had the Navy Marine Mammal Program in their sights. In May 2014, author Philip Hoare had published an op-ed in the *New York Times* calling for an end to the Marine Mammal Program. Ridgway had responded with a letter to the editor defending the program. "We do not take dolphins from the wild," he asserted, adding that "our animals seem happy to reproduce. They work with us in the open sea, where they could easily swim away. To me they seem happy and enthusiastic. They like their jobs."[31]

It was surprisingly unscientific language for the distinguished researcher—"to me," "happy," "enthusiastic." Clearly, the criticism had touched an emotional nerve in Ridgway's own understanding of the program—one which I hoped to explore, if I could find him. He was listed as director of the Marine Mammal Foundation—but what and where was that? When I tracked its location using Google Earth, I came to an empty office in an isolated San Diego marina staffed by a lone, suspicious secretary. It was likely only the presence of my young sons with me that convinced her to answer the door when I knocked.

"Hi there," I smiled. "Is this the Marine Mammal Foundation?"

"Who are you, and why do you want to know?" she asked, barely cracking the door. I explained that I was a historian looking for Dr. Ridgway, and passed my contact information to her on scrap paper. I assumed it would go directly into the bin. But much to my surprise, Ridgway phoned me a few weeks later, and soon after we sat down at a San Diego restaurant. I had a lot of questions.

"You dedicated your widely used 1972 textbook, *Mammals of the Sea*, to Tuffy, and I wanted to ask why. What did Tuffy mean to you?"

"He worked with us in the open ocean," responded Ridgway. "He allowed us to determine that they could dive to a thousand feet, which was a good demonstration for the Navy."

"Because nobody thought they could dive that deep?"

"That's right. And he would stay with us in the open ocean. He could swim with us and he would work on command in the open ocean."[32]

From where Ridgway sat, it was a logical, if subdued, response. It was just three years since *Blackfish*, and the Navy program was under heavy scrutiny. On the surface, it also seemed in character. In recent years, Ridgway had publicly scoffed at the sentimental assertions of animal rights activists and their demands for the release of captive cetaceans, implicitly contrasting such emotionalism with the presumed objectivity of science. Yet Ridgway's time with Tuffy had clearly affected him in profound ways, as his 1987 memoir, *Dolphin Doctor*, makes clear. "When Tuffy died, I grieved almost as much as if he had been a beloved family member," he had then written, describing the book itself as "an encomium—an unabashed story of praise—about one special dolphin whom I still regard as my friend from the sea."[33]

In our interview, Ridgway wasn't willing to explore such emotional depths. He reiterated that Tuffy had been useful to the Navy and his research, but he had little time for the anthropomorphizing that he believed drove his critics. Yet once again, his earlier memoir told a different story. "As time passed I began to realize that in my musings about Tuffy, I often assumed that some intellectual process akin to human thought churned inside his gray head," he had written:

> Of course, I may have been guilty of allowing my emotions about the animal to cloud my perception and credit the animal with humanlike characteristics. Yet this anthropomorphic attitude is difficult to avoid when we observe and work with animals that we come to know as friends. . . . Based on my scientific knowledge and my intuition about dolphins, I could not help believing that some form of silent thought ticked behind Tuffy's large, alert eyes as he stared back at me from his world.[34]

What accounts for this change? Had Ridgway's identity as a scientist prompted him to re-evaluate the dolphin's meaning to him since the writing of his memoir? Had the passage of time and debate over captivity caused him to repress his emotional response to Tuffy? Or was he simply unwilling to open himself up to a researcher whom he barely knew?

In the end, such questions are likely unanswerable. But they left me with a conundrum familiar to oral historians, and particularly vexing in animal history, when non-human experiences are invariably mediated through human perception and memory. "Remember," another interviewee had once cautioned me when describing his encounters with orcas, "I'm not remembering events and feelings as they happened. I'm remembering my memories."[35] That warning seemed particularly pertinent for my approach to Ridgway. How could I navigate the maze of human memory and emotion at the heart of Tuffy's story? What was my most reliable source: Ridgway's published research? His written account, crafted somewhat apart from his identity as a scientist? His responses to me now, mediated by time, controversy, and caution? Duffield's memories? And could any of them get me closer to Tuffy's lived experience as a Navy dolphin?

Perhaps not. But what was undeniable was the impact of this singular dolphin on the people he encountered as well as his larger impact on human science and culture. Pulled at random from the waters of Mississippi in 1962, at the height of the Cold War, Tuffy had survived travel across the country, captivity on the Santa Monica Pier, and acclimation to life on a US Naval base. Scarred and wary, he had resisted the demands of trainers until he found a tender connection with young Debbie Duffield, in the process helping to inspire her career as a marine mammalogist. His subsequent cooperation with Ridgway and other researchers broadened the horizons for marine mammal research while helping the fledgling Marine Mammal Program extract support and funding from the US Navy. And even if he hadn't understood the human politics that had conscripted him, his unique personality left its mark on history. The same feistiness that had once seemed a liability earned him a leading role in projects such as Sealab II, which helped reframe public views of human relations with dolphins and other marine mammals.

NOTES

1. *The Natural History of Pliny*, trans. John Bostock and H. T. Riley (London: Henry G. Bohn, 1855), vol. 2, chapter 8.
2. David S. Cecelski, "Of Time and the Sea: Nye's Clock Oil and the Bottlenose Dolphin Fishery at Hatteras Island, North Carolina, in the Early Twentieth Century," *North Carolina Historical Review* 92, no. 1 (2015): 49–79; D. Graeme Burnett, *The Sounding of the Whale: Science and Cetaceans in the Twentieth Century* (Chicago: University of Chicago Press, 2012), 192–96; Gregg Mitman, *Reel Nature: America's Romance with Wildlife on Film* (Seattle: University of Washington Press, 1999), chapter 7.
3. Jacob Darwin Hamblin, *Oceanographers and the Cold War: Disciplines of Marine Science* (Seattle: University of Washington Press, 2005).
4. Joshua Horwitz, *War of the Whales: A True Story* (New York: Simon and Schuster, 2014), 232–34.
5. Leslie Lieber, "Porpoise with a Purpose: Kathy's Teaching the Navy 'Second Sight'," *Science*, 13 March 1960, A28. See also Winthrop N. Kellogg, *Porpoises and Sonar* (Chicago: University of Chicago Press, 1961).
6. D. Graeme Burnett, "A Mind in the Water," *Orion*, April 20, 2010; John C. Lilly, *Man and Dolphin* (New York: Pyramid Books, 1961), 125–26.
7. Burnett, *Sounding of the Whale*, 547–52.
8. Sam Ridgway, *The Dolphin Doctor* (Dublin, NH: Yankee Books, 1987), 30–33. On Cold War schemes to colonize the ocean "frontier," see Helen M. Rozwadowski, *Vast Expanses: A History of the Oceans* (London: Reaktion Books, 2018), especially chapter 6.
9. Author interview with Ridgway, June 21, 2016.
10. Ridgway, *Dolphin Doctor*, 57–59.
11. Author interview with Ridgway, June 21, 2016.
12. Forrest G. Wood, *Marine Mammals and Man: The Navy's Porpoises and Sea Lions* (Washington, DC: Luce, 1973), 134.
13. *The Dolphins That Joined the Navy* (Periscope Films, 1964), https://www.youtube.com/watch?v=TIiMshOook4.
14. Author interview with Duffield, February 14, 2018.
15. Ridgway, *Dolphin Doctor*, 106–08.
16. Ridgway, 106–08.
17. Bryant Evans, "Porpoise Obeys Man's Words in New Language," *San Diego Union*, March 20, 1965.
18. "Make Rescues, Repel Sharks: Porpoise to Get Tryout as Guard for Navy Divers in Deep Sea Lab," *Los Angeles Times*, August 9, 1965.
19. On the objectives of Sealab II within the context of US oceanographical projects, see Rozwadowski, *Vast Expanses*, 178–80.
20. "Porpoise Fails Sealab Tryout as Postman," *Los Angeles Times*, September 17, 1965.
21. "Porpoise Makes Good, Delivers Sealab Mail," *Los Angeles Times*, September 18, 1965.
22. Wood, *Marine Mammals and Man*, 138–40.

23 "Tuffy Waggles Nose in Goodby to Aquanauts," *Los Angeles Times*, September 19, 1965.
24 "Porpoise Points the Way to Missile's Cradle," *Los Angeles Times*, November 16, 1965.
25 Wood, *Marine Mammals and Man*, 145–46.
26 "2 Navy Porpoises Go AWOL," *Los Angeles Times*, September 6, 1966; Wood, *Marine Mammals and Man,* 193–95.
27 Sam H. Ridgway, B. L. Scronce, and John Kanwisher, "Respiration and Deep Diving in the Bottlenose Porpoise," *Science* 166 (1969): 1651–54. For more on these experiments, see Wood, *Marine Mammals and Man*, 173–78.
28 Wood, *Marine Mammals and Man*, 154–56.
29 Ridgway, *Dolphin Doctor*, 155.
30 Harold W. Goforth, *Defender Dolphins: The Story of Project Short Time* (Jacksonville: Fortis, 2012).
31 Philip Hoare, "Let Slip the Dolphins of War," *New York Times*, May 5, 2014; Sam Ridgway, letter to the editor, *New York Times*, May 12, 2014.
32 Author interview with Ridgway, June 21, 2016.
33 Ridgway, *Dolphin Doctor*, 10.
34 Ridgway, 102.
35 Author interview with Don White, September 28, 2013.

10

The Elephant in the Archive[1]

Nigel Rothfels

In a warehouse belonging to Hogle Zoo in Salt Lake City is a carefully wrapped relief sculpture of an elephant who was known as Princess Alice. The work was unveiled in August 1931, fifteen years after the elephant herself came to Utah and just a couple of weeks after the zoo moved from a city park to its new grounds at the mouth of Emigration Canyon. For over eighty years, the sculpture adorned the front of the old elephant house, and when the building was finally razed in 2012, the relief was kept with the hope that it might be used again on a future elephant building. When Alice arrived in Salt Lake City as a purchase from the Sells Floto Circus in 1916, she was pregnant with her fourth calf, and Prince Utah was born at the end of April 1918.[2] The young elephant only lived for eleven months but Alice survived decades more and died in 1953. Knowing that the sculpture on the front of the elephant house was modelled on a real elephant who had once lived at the zoo was one of those facts that a kid knows because his school class got a special tour of the zoo. When I was growing up and visiting the zoo in the 1970s, I used to look up at the sculpture of Alice above the lion-mouth drinking fountain. The sculpture made me wonder about an elephant's life. Along with the building itself, the sculpture is part of a particular elephant's archival legacy.

Over the many years that I have been researching and writing about animals and history, I have been particularly interested in exploring the records of elephant pasts. I have looked for them in both more and less traditional places. On the more traditional front, I have read accounts of elephants reaching back to classical times, including some well-known accounts and other fairly obscure ones. Among the former are works by Pliny, Buffon, Brehm, Iain and Oria Douglas-Hamilton, and Cynthia Moss. Among more obscure accounts is a remarkable compendium of elephant knowledge published in Germany in 1715 called *Elephantographia curiosa* by Georg Christoph Petri von Hartenfels, a work purporting to contain everything then known about elephants. But I have also sought elephants in less traditional archives. I have photographed elephant bones in off-exhibit collections of natural history museums in Europe and the US, I have worked in the archives of zoos and circuses. I have researched sculptures of elephants, like Alice, on buildings, and I have spent time with elephant keepers *and* with elephants.[3]

It was in 2005 that I first heard of Ned. At the time, I had been regularly checking in on a blog authored by William "Buckles" Woodcock Jr., a retired elephant trainer whose family had been in the American circus business for over 150 years.[4] Buckles posted what to me seemed an amazing photograph (Figure 10.1).

The image was taken some time between 1915 and 1921 on the M. L. Clark and Son's Circus, a show led by Mack Loren Clark that had roots reaching back to the mid-1880s. In 1895, Clark owned a small medicine show that travelled from town to town in the American Southeast putting on minstrel shows and selling elixirs. In an effort to bring in more people, Clark purchased a Bactrian camel and a small female Asian elephant, allegedly from Carl Hagenbeck, a famed animal dealer in Germany. The animals were delivered by train to Mena, Arkansas, and Clark decided, so the story goes, to name the elephant Mena. The show was on the road every year from early spring to late fall and wintered in Alexandria, Louisiana. At the end of the 1903 season with audiences growing, Clark purchased some horses, equipment, and a second elephant, named Ned, from a certain William F. Smith, who had been proprietor of a circus that toured the Northeast from 1901 to 1903 under three different names—the Great Syndicate Shows, then the Great Eastern Shows, and then Howe's Great London Circus. The last was a name that had been and would continue to be used for a whole series of enterprises; name recognition has always been part of the circus business. This second elephant for the Clark circus

Fig. 10.1 Ned and Mena from Buckles Blog.

was a male of unclear age (as young as five and as old as fourteen), who had, it is claimed, originally come from Siam (Thailand) by way of the New York animal dealer Louis Ruhe in either 1901 or 1902. Preparing for the 1904 season, Clark purchased a larger tent that would accommodate two rings and much bigger audiences. The circus continued to grow, and by 1910, M. L. Clark and Son's travelled on more than sixty wagons. It had eighteen cages for animals, over two hundred horses, and a 120-foot round-top main tent.[5]

The two big elephants—Mena and Ned—would walk along with the wagons as the circus slowly moved about the South. Other circuses began to use trucks and trains; the Clarks ended up experimenting with both, but they kept coming back to the wagons. One of the advantages of the trains was that they allowed the larger circuses to skip the small towns and visit farther-flung, mostly larger cities where they might have multi-day stands. The Clark circus, though, moved from small town to small town on dirt and mud roads. Travelling in the evenings or overnight, the circus would be in a new town every day where it would put on one or two shows in the afternoon. The elephants would walk along with the wagons and work around the lots, raising the tent poles, pulling up the canvas, and moving wagons around the yard by pushing with their heads or pulling with harnesses.

In the photograph (Figure 10.1), Ned stands prominently and massively, chained to the older Mena. To the side of Ned, in front of Mena, and holding a whip in his right hand is one of the workers with his stock horse. Behind the group, we can see a wagon, hitches of horses, and a Bactrian camel. The image is the sort of staged marketing shot one finds in old circus route books and programs and seems to have been intended to show what life on the road looked like for the circus. The animals and people seem relaxed and the whole picture has a quiet quality. When I saw it, I wanted to know more about both of the elephants, but I was particularly drawn to Ned because there were just not that many large male elephants travelling with circuses in the early decades of the twentieth century. I wanted to know how he was able to cope with circus life—a challenge for any elephant but often a particular challenge for male elephants. To make a long story about elephant physiology and training techniques short, male elephants in the twentieth century often struggled with the physical, intellectual, emotional, and social constraints of living in circuses and zoos. Their basic physiology, their usual ways of living in the world, their huge size, and how they were generally acquired as very young animals, set most male elephants up for lives filled with conflict and difficulty. Of course, there were exceptions, and it is clearly not the case that every day these animals lived was one of torture and pain. Ned and elephants like him had good days, but it was still fairly easy for me to guess when I saw that first picture of him, that Ned was likely to have had many difficulties living in North America in the early twentieth century. From the chains alone, it was clear that he was becoming a handful and looking at the photograph I couldn't help but wonder about what happened to him.

But where does one start researching the life of an elephant like Ned? One thing I had going for me was simply his distinctiveness. While it is true that every elephant looks different from every other, it can often be difficult to tell them apart if you don't know them personally. A tusked male Asian elephant, however, tends to stand out, even in a crowd of elephants. And, as much as Ned stands out in historical photographs, he also stood out for people who saw him, so there is more of a written record of his travels in newspapers, memoirs, and other sources. Historians of the circus have paid attention to him, too. Of the thousands of modern elephants that have lived in North America, probably fewer than a hundred have received sustained attention in articles and books, and Ned is one of them.

But the existence of historical records presents other problems. In introducing Ned and Mena above, I used expressions like "allegedly," and "the story goes," and "it is claimed," because although the basic biographies of these elephants have been told many times, the details are always a little different, and it is difficult to fact-check any of them. For example, at some point along the line, someone said that Clark purchased Mena from Hagenbeck, that Hagenbeck shipped the elephant from Germany, and that she arrived in a box car in Mena, Arkansas, leading to her being named Mena. The Hagenbeck records are spotty, but the company does have some surviving account books that tracked transactions with institutions and individuals. Alas, there are no records of Hagenbeck ever selling anything to Clark, let alone an elephant. Similarly, a group of camels associated with Clark are also attributed to Hagenbeck. The claim is that Clark picked them up from Hagenbeck after the 1904 St. Louis World's Fair, where Hagenbeck had a large exhibit. Again, there are no records of such a purchase, but it seems that Hagenbeck lost control of all the animals he exhibited in St. Louis to apparently unscrupulous American partners.[6] Part of the problem in the cases of Mena and the Hagenbeck camels is that the name "Hagenbeck" meant something in the first decades of the twentieth century, even in an American context because of a travelling circus bearing the name and articles that appeared in the American press about the world-renowned German animal dealer. Wherever Clark got these animals, then, there would have been good reasons for him to say he bought them from Hagenbeck because saying so raised the credibility of his whole operation. He may in fact have purchased them from Hagenbeck or from one of Hagenbeck's agents, but he may not have, too. As for where Mena got her name; well, the story has appeal, but that's all I can really say.

The facts surrounding the importation of Ned present similar problems. Gus Knudson, director of the Woodland Park Zoo in Seattle from

1922 to 1947, wrote to Louis Ruhe and Sons in 1932 to confirm details about the elephant and received word that the company did not have any record of selling an elephant to someone named William F. Smith. But that did not mean they hadn't. A company representative could only write: "We remember selling Elephants to Howe's Great London Circus at various times, but we cannot trace any of these Elephants after so many years."[7] Given that the name "Howe's Great London Circus" was used by a variety of different operations over decades, the letter from Ruhe and Sons does not help much. In the end, Knudson decided to accept the story that Ned had been sold by Ruhe and that he had been imported from Siam in 1902 at about the age of twelve, but no actual evidence of this appears to exist. Knudson's decision was then accepted by others and so the story was passed down, again. But other histories are out there. The circus historian Homer Walton discussed Ned's background in the 1950s with Lee Clark, the "Son" of M. L. Clark and Son's Circus, and concluded that Ned was only five or six years old when the Clarks purchased him, not fourteen.[8] Faced with the question myself, I have ended up accepting the younger age for Ned's importation because it simply makes more sense from a logistical point of view. It was essentially always easier to ship a young elephant, and shipping a twelve-year-old male elephant from Asia to the US in 1900 would have been highly unusual.

In the end, it probably doesn't matter very much how old Ned was when he was brought to the US, and it probably doesn't matter either who managed to import him or Mena. But the uncertainties around their provenance point to larger problems with stories about circus elephants. The records are usually problematic in one way or another and often seem the result more of a desire for publicity than a commitment to getting the facts straight. This is certainly the case with Ned, about whom histories usually feel more like tall tales. A typical one, for example, is about the day in 1913 when he was put in a ring to fight bulls in Mexico. Completely contradictory versions of this story have been related over the years. There are accounts of Ned parrying the attacks of up to twenty bulls and others of him standing quietly while bull after bull tries desperately to escape the arena. So I went looking for contemporary accounts and eventually found similar versions of an article appearing in newspapers in the early summer of 1913 in towns around the Southeast. The papers included the

Tensas Gazette of Saint Joseph, Louisiana, the *Altoona Tribune* of Altoona, Kansas, the *Bucklin Banner* of Bucklin, Kansas, the *Madison Journal* of Tallulah, Louisiana, and the *Winston County Journal* of Louisville, Mississippi. The problem with the article is that the more times I read it, the more it began to feel like something that could have been written by anyone, whether they saw the event or not. The version of the article that appeared in the Kansas *Lyons Republican* on 3 June 1913 led with the headline: "Bull in a Fight with an Elephant: Queer Combat Is Described by an American."[9] The "American" in question is someone named "Mr. H. F. Lang of Philadelphia." There is no author attributed for this article—it is an anonymously written article by someone claiming to have heard a story about a spectacular fight between an elephant and a bull from someone else who claimed to have been there. If that is all one had, maybe one could be content. But forty-five years after the event, Lee Clark, who said he was there with Ned, shared quite a different version of the story. According to Clark, five bulls were successively brought out to fight Ned but none charged. Apparently, the circus was to get $2,500 and a print of a film of the fight, but because the audience was upset that there was no fight, Clark was arrested instead and fined $500. He was not put in jail, though, because no one else could handle the elephant, and in the middle of the night, he simply walked Ned back across the bridge to El Paso and never paid the fine.[10] Should we believe versions of an article that appeared months after the supposed event took place published in newspapers from the very towns that the Clark circus regularly visited, and thus towns in which the circus would have wanted press? Or should we believe the story told by Lee Clark, who would have had his own reasons for remembering and telling the story in ways that made him look like he was the only reasonable person around on the day the events supposedly took place? This one is a tough call.

Returning to Ned's story, as best as I can tell, he was owned by M. L. Clark for eighteen years, from the fall 1903 to July 1921. According to most accounts, the Clarks were increasingly struggling with the elephant, and another circus, which travelled on rail with a home in California, wanted the huge animal. Or maybe just the price was right? In any case, Ned was sold to the Al G. Barnes Circus for $6,000 and, we are told, he had to crawl on his knees to enter a train car in Seligman, Missouri, because he was simply too big to stand up in a standard car.[11] When Ned joined the Barnes circus in Minnesota (or perhaps in Wisconsin or elsewhere, because knowledgeable accounts vary), his name was changed to Tusko and a whole new (and, again, often shifting) biography was invented for the elephant advertised as "The Mightiest of Living Creatures." In one account, for example, Barnes claims that Tusko had been working in a lumber camp in Tibet when he was found by an animal dealer who sent the elephant's measurements to Barnes. Claiming that the measurements he received would have made Tusko the largest elephant ever captured and perhaps the largest elephant in the world, Barnes bought the elephant sight unseen and had him shipped to the US. (A reminder: this is an elephant who had already been walking around the US for decades.) After spending some time with the elephant, Barnes concluded that Tusko was "no ordinary elephant, but that he breeds back to the mastodon strain."[12]

Like the Clarks, Barnes, too, had ways of amplifying stories about his elephant, an elephant he constantly promoted to greater fame. When Tusko, therefore, got loose in the countryside near the town of Sedro-Woolley in the Skagit Valley of Washington state in 1922, there was no downside for Barnes in making sure that a maximum amount of violence and damage was reported in newspapers across the country—even in the *New York Times*. Over the following months, published accounts of the "rampage" provided ever more details and damage estimates rose from a couple of thousand dollars to as much as $75,000. As for Tusko, the exaggerations continued apace. Before long, newspapers reported that the circus had acquired the monster for the staggering cost of $100,000, that the elephant's age was "reckoned well along in the hundreds," and that he weighed over 20,000 lbs.[13] The stories of Tusko became so important to the circus that when the decision was finally reached that it was just too dangerous to take him on the road, Barnes decided he needed to buy another large male elephant, named Diamond, whom he quickly renamed Tusko. People came, saw a large, tusked elephant, and were satisfied that they had seen the real Tusko. It was—one should note—Diamond and not Tusko who would eventually kill a bystander.

In tracking the path of Ned/Tusko, I kept finding what appeared as objective, carefully researched records that somehow always boiled down to being just something someone said at some point. For example, the

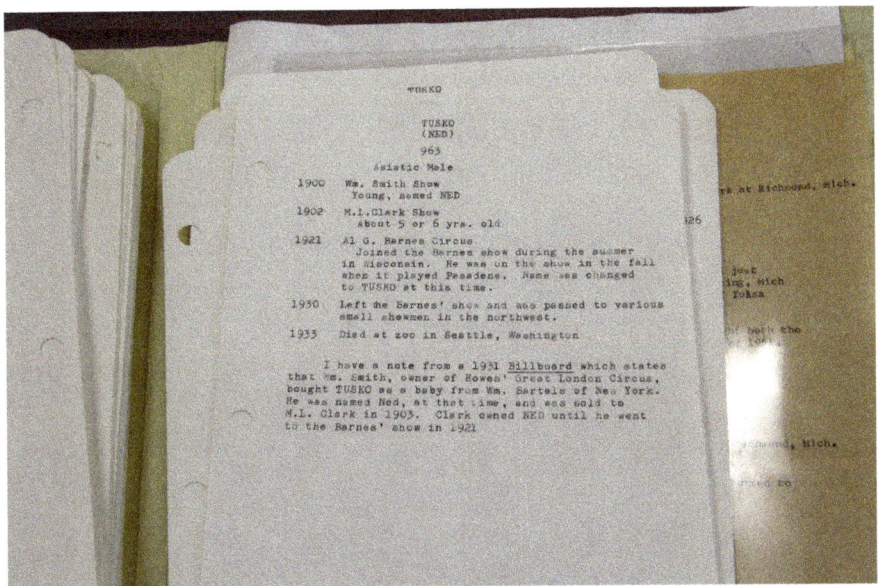

Fig. 10.2 Chang Reynolds Biography of Tusko (Ned) #963. Photograph by Nigel Rothfels. Courtesy of the Circus World Museum, Baraboo, Wisconsin.

Robert L. Parkinson Library and Research Center of the Circus World Museum in Baraboo, Wisconsin, holds a collection of elephant biographies compiled by Charles W. "Chang" Reynolds (1933–86). The card for "Tusko (Ned) #963" (Figure 10.2) is the sort of document that historians love. Even though it does not have that much information, its organization just feels credible. I took a photo and then dutifully entered the data into a spreadsheet with the expectation that I would expand upon it as I found out more. There was just something about the card that pulled me in. Maybe it was how the card for #963 rested in a stack with hundreds of other cards; maybe it was the typeface of the typewriter. Whatever the case, I was quickly convinced that the information must somehow be accurate and objective.

At another point in my research, this time in the Municipal Archives in Seattle, Washington, I found similarly compelling documents put together in 1932–33 by Gus Knudson, then director of the zoo. My guess is that the documents were the result of an effort to learn as much about

Tusko's past as possible, because the zoo and the city were facing a lawsuit over the animal. Knudson assembled a list of men who had handled Tusko over the years and wrote letters requesting any information people might have about Tusko's past. In the end, from information he gleaned from a variety of sources, he settled on a document with eleven numbered paragraphs outlining Tusko's life. He concluded: "Have spent considerable time and seen different people in tracing this history down, and I think I have secured a true story. Dr. Gus Knudson, Director Zoological Division, Seattle Park Department."[14] He expanded on this document with a two-and-a-quarter-page "History of Tusko, the Indian Elephant." The names and dates are echoed in other documents I have found and seem generally reasonable, but as more details entered the Knudson account, the less reliable it became. Knudson, for example, writes:

> Tusko was taken on the road in the spring of 1923 and 1924. In 1924, while showing in Sedro Woolley, Wash., Tusko ran amuck. It was at the beginning of the fourth performance, all the trappings had been placed on Tusko and a ladder leaned against his side to enable his rider to mount, for even Tusko knelt to the ground, a ladder was required with which to board him. When the rider, Mr. Peck, was almost half way up the ladder, Tusko suddenly rebelled. He jumped to his feet, throwing Mr. Peck and the ladder aside, and began backing up, swinging his head and trunk from side to side. His long tusks and huge size made him a frightful object, while his bellows of rage were terrifying. The people scattered in all directions in a panic.[15]

In the first sentence of this extract, Knudson tries to present some basic, albeit incorrect, facts—the events in Sedro Woolley occurred 1922 not 1924. But then the tone switches entirely as he relates an exciting account of what happened that night. This part of the text derives almost entirely from an interview conducted with Barnes nine years after the events, where much of what he says is preposterous, and from various newspaper articles that seem likely to have been at least partially written by Barnes' own people. Even the name "Peck" is a fiction. Although Knudson was clearly making a serious effort to record the facts about Ned/Tusko, the layers of stories upon stories make telling the actual life experiences of the elephant a serious challenge.

Still, concluding that Ned/Tusko's story is difficult to research should really not be that much of a surprise. Writing about any historical event or figure presents similar problems with the reliability of sources, the difficulty of being confident that events actually happened in the way they have been described, the task of deciding which moments in a life to highlight. These are the challenges that make writing history interesting and difficult, and why history is always an iterative process as later scholars learn more and challenge or refine earlier accounts. There are, of course, specific complexities in working with archival materials about animals. Indeed, as Jason Colby has made clear, even when "sources are abundant," they have been preserved, overlaid, and reinterpreted by the humans who have retained them. The biography of Ned/Tusko, like that of Colby's Tuffy or Emily Wakild's llama, Spook, will be built largely, but not always exclusively, from accounts, records, and materials preserved by humans.[16]

It isn't that animals are not in the archives. As Harriet Ritvo notes, "archives are full of animals, as have been the societies that they—however imperfectly—reflect and preserve."[17] Once we begin to look, we find remarkably rich records left by animals in the past, and many of those are records created by or made up of the animals themselves. Still, most of the remains of animals in most of the archives that we create are curated in one way or another. Alice on the front of a building in Salt Lake City is a representation by human hands; the skulls of the elephants that Theodore Roosevelt shot during his 1909 safari have been retained, conserved, and placed in a row of other skulls in a storage facility in Maryland to tell a particular human story, not the elephants' story; a collection of trilobites is organized to show overall taxonomic diversity over thousands of millennia rather than the immediate circumstances in which an individual creature died and left a record in Permian sands; an account of a gorilla attack will always be much more of an account of human thoughts than animal ones. Nevertheless, although the difficulties of recovering the presence of actual animals in the past are real, that does not mean the work is impossible or not worth trying to do. Historians interested in the lives of animals recognize that the records they use are essentially just like most other historical documents. Working hard with them to discover what happened in the past, and then trying to figure out what that past tells us about today, remain the tasks that all historians do, whether they focus on animal lives or not.

Consider a slightly different example. A few years ago I was contacted by a scientist studying the bones of an elephant sold to an American zoo by Hagenbeck at the beginning of the twentieth century. The scientist was interested in this particular elephant because there was documentation indicating where the elephant was originally captured, and that was an important piece of information for the research. The problem from my perspective *as a historian* is that while it is true that Hagenbeck told the director of the zoo that he had acquired the elephant in Assam, it is also true that Hagenbeck had good reason to say that regardless of the elephant's true origins. At the time, most Western zoo directors were convinced that the largest and so-called "highest caste" elephants in India came from Assam. By claiming, then, that this elephant came from that region, Hagenbeck could increase the potential value of his elephant knowing full well that it would be difficult to prove the animal's origins one way or the other. The elephant, of course, may well have come from Assam, but Hagenbeck was often accused of misrepresentation and there are good reasons to be skeptical of his account in this case. All I could really tell the scientist is that it is certainly possible that the elephant came from Assam, but it is far from certain that he did. That is a truer biography of this elephant than just saying, "we know this elephant came from Assam because that is what the documentation says."

In his final years as a circus elephant, and then as a stand-alone spectacle dragged from town-to-town in the Pacific Northwest affixed to a flatbed trailer, Ned/Tusko became perhaps most famous for the 1,000 lbs of chains that he often carried on his body. The chains prevented him from using his head, trunk, or legs to lash out, and when he was asked to walk, he could do so only slowly. Much of the time, each of his legs was chained to a stake driven deep in the ground. Ned/Tusko—an elephant who came to the US at the beginning of the twentieth century, who walked thousands of miles alongside Mena on the Clark show—became a chained monster, an exhibition of punishment. So many times, as I have looked at photographs of Ned/Tusko walking down a street in his chains, I could not help but feel he was on his way to his own execution. There were undoubtedly people who laughed when they saw him chained up, but it seems many were struck by what they saw as a spectacle of tragedy. Again, stories were put on top of older stories.

In an ending that could only happen in the context of American ideas about elephants from a century ago, Ned/Tusko's life did not actually end while being exhibited in a circus or in a rented barn on the outskirts of town. On 8 October 1932, Ned/Tusko was moved to the Woodland Park Zoo in Seattle where he became a major attraction. The story told at the time—and ever since—was that he was saved by the zoo. And in a way he was. At the height of the Depression and no longer part of a large circus, the elephant travelled with just one handler and was exhibited for a dime. At that rate, it was difficult to earn enough money to feed them both. Woodland Park offered a refuge as much for Ned/Tusko's handler as for the elephant. The zoo, claiming to have rescued Ned/Tusko, started a fund-drive to help pay for his food, but eight months after he arrived at the zoo, Ned/Tusko died at about thirty-five years old. People described him as an old elephant, but he was really quite young.

The expression "an elephant in the room" points to an issue that is clearly present but ignored because it is somehow too uncomfortable or too difficult to discuss. However difficult it might be to uncover the elephant in the archive, I believe that making the effort to do so can teach us a great deal about elephants and ourselves. Part of what distinguishes good historical writing is skepticism about sources and the realization that materials in any archive—in a book, a museum, an album of photographs, a stack of "elephant biographies," or a zoo-keeper's memory—can be both more and less than they appear. What one sees on the surface of the document, the story it appears to tell, is only one layer covering a history of earlier stories each told (or never told) for different reasons. At one point in researching the story of Ned/Tusko, for example, I found a cartoon in a newspaper showing the elephant reeling to face the charge of an infuriated bull in an arena in Mexico. The drawing was *not* a record of what happened; it was a record of what someone imagined might happen if an elephant ever fought a bull. I cannot be certain about what happened that Sunday in February 1913, when Ned crossed the border from El Paso to Ciudad Juárez. What I can know, though, is that the stories of what happened that day became part of the legend of Ned, part of what led him on his curious path through several decades of American history. The stories of Ned are *not* Ned, but they help explain much of what happened to him and help us better understand the history of how we have thought about elephants.

NOTES

1. My thanks to the organizers, sponsors, and participants in the "Traces of the Animal Past" conference for the opportunity to be part of the discussion that led to this essay.
2. See *Utah: A Guide to the State. Compiled by Workers of the Writers' Program of the Work Projects Administration for the State of Utah* (New York: Hastings, [1941] 1945), 254–55.
3. This essay presents some of the research problems I faced in one of the chapters for my book, *Elephant Trails: A History of Animals and Cultures* (Baltimore: Johns Hopkins University Press, 2021). For related work I have done about elephants, see Nigel Rothfels and Dick Blau, *Elephant House* (University Park: Penn State University Press, 2015); Rothfels, "Mammoths in the Landscape," in *Routledge Handbook of Human-Animal Studies*, ed. Susan McHugh and Garry Marvin (London: Routledge, 2014), 10–22; and Rothfels, "Elephants, Ethics, and History," *Elephants and Ethics: Toward a Morality of Coexistence*, ed. Chris Wemmer and Catherine A. Christen (Baltimore: Johns Hopkins University Press, 2008), 100–19.
4. I have written more about the Woodcock-Orton family history in Nigel Rothfels, "A Hero's Death," in *Animal Acts: Performing Species Now*, ed. Una Chaudhuri and Holly Hughes (Ann Arbor: University of Michigan Press, 2013), 182–88; and Rothfels, "Why Look at Elephants?," *Worldviews: Environment, Culture, Religion* 9, no. 2 (2005): 166–83.
5. See Homer C. Walton, "The M. L. Clark Wagon Show," *Bandwagon* 9, no. 2 (March-April 1965): 4–11; and Homer C. Walton, "Ned and Mena, Famous Elephants," *Bandwagon* 2, no. 6 (November-December, 1958): 7.
6. I discuss the exhibition in St. Louis and its legacies on the American circus business in Nigel Rothfels, *Savages and Beasts: The Birth of the Modern Zoo* (Baltimore: Johns Hopkins University Press, 2002).
7. "Louis Ruhe, Inc. to Dr. Gus Knudson, Director," November 28, 1932, Woodland Park Zoo History File, Record Series 8601-01, Tusko Misc. Correspondence, 1932–1934, Box 15, Folder 4, Seattle Municipal Archives.
8. Walton, "Ned and Mena, Famous Elephants."
9. "Bull in a Fight with an Elephant," *Lyons Republican*, June 3, 1913, 3.
10. See Walton, "The M. L. Clark Wagon Show."
11. Richard J. Reynolds, III, "Hold Your Horses, Here Come the Elephants!" presented at the Regional Workshop of the American Association of Zoological Parks and Aquariums, Knoxville, TN, 1979.

12 "What Happened When Tusko Went on a Rampage, As Told to Dave Roberson by Al G. Barnes," Typescript, Woodland Park Zoo History File, Record Series 8601-01, Tusko the Elephant Early Histories, Box 15, Folder 3, Seattle Municipal Archives.

13 See, for example, "What Happened When the Elephant 'Took a Notion,'" *Salt Lake Telegram*, June 25, 1922, 29.

14 Gus Knudson, "History of Tusko," Typescript, Woodland Park Zoo History File, Record Series 8601-01, Tusko the Elephant Early Histories, Box 15, Folder 3, Seattle Municipal Archives.

15 Gus Knudson, "History of Tusko: The Indian Elephant," Typescript, Woodland Park Zoo History File, Record Series 8601-01, Tusko the Elephant Early Histories, Box 15, Folder 3, Seattle Municipal Archives.

16 See articles in this volume by Jason M. Colby, "Tuffy's Cold War: Science, Memory and the US Navy's Dolphin"; and Emily Wakild, "What's a Guanaco? Tracing the Llama Diaspora through and beyond South America."

17 Harriet Ritvo, "Epilogue: Combinations and Conjunction," this volume.

PART IV:

Spatial Sources and Animal Movement

11

Making Tracks: A Grizzly and Entangled History[1]

Colleen Campbell and Tina Loo

What are historians really doing when they study animals? In 2002, Erica Fudge argued they were analyzing "the history of human attitudes toward animals," and suggested, provocatively, that there was no such thing as animal history; that is, there were no histories of animals themselves, ones that captured how they experienced the world over time.[2] In large part, as she and others in this collection have noted, this was because the traces of the non-human animal past we have are ones created by *Homo sapiens*. As Ann Laura Stoler contends, the archives scholars use are not just places to find facts; they are institutions that produce them. As a result, the knowledge that comes from the archives can work to uphold the perspectives, beliefs, and interests of the powerful.[3]

In that sense, animal history is "impossible" in both ways that anthropologist Michel-Rolph Trouillot used the word.[4] Trouillot was writing about the history of the Haitian Revolution, but there are parallels to be drawn with animal history. Like the Haitian Revolution, animal history is impossible because of the nature of the archive, a place where non-human animals are silent, present largely as property, commodities, and specimens. More fundamentally, animal history, like the history of the Haitian Revolution, was, and perhaps still is, impossible to *imagine*: for a long time, it was literally "unthinkable" because of our biases, which precluded considering certain groups as historical actors, whether enslaved people launching a successful revolution, as it was for Trouillot, or non-human animals who made their worlds and ours.

In the twenty or so years since Erica Fudge wrote her piece, animal history has changed: it is much more than a history of ideas and representations—as important as the insights from that work are and continue to be. There is a growing number of works that decentre humans, highlight their interdependence with other animals, and take the prospect of other-than-human intelligence and emotions seriously. They rely on a careful and creative use of conventional historical sources, as Jason Colby does with oral history (Chapter 9), but they also draw on new evidence, particularly scientific research on animal behaviour and cognition. Susan Nance's history of circus elephants uses this literature to understand animal agency and resistance, and Brett Walker draws on it to underscore how wolves in Japan adapted to their changing circumstances.[5] Sandra Swart (Chapter 1) uses this literature as well, but moves well beyond it. Focusing on the takhi, Mongolia's "wild horse," she makes a compelling case for examining what animal bodies—the hair, blood, bone, and feces—might tell us about their past and their experiences.

Our animal history also relies on a different kind of source and a different tool to analyze it. Specifically, we look at locational data tracking the movements of a population of grizzly bears (*Ursus arctos*) living on the eastern slopes of the Canadian Rockies from 1994 to 2004 and use GIS (Geographic Information Systems) software to analyze the data. In both these ways, our chapter complements the work of Sean Kheraj, who shows how GIS can be used to tell urban animal history (Chapter 12) and Emily Wakild (Chapter 14), who also uses the movement of animals as an entry point to telling stories about them. Grizzlies are brown bears or a kind of brown bear, the most widely distributed of the eight bear species. They are effective hunters, with large teeth, formidable foreclaws, and an acute sense of smell and hearing. Once occupying much of North America, these animals, like the wolf, were revered, then feared and hunted to near extinction by settlers in many parts of the continent. The remaining populations are found from Alaska to the Yukon, Northwest Territories, and south into western Canada and the northwestern United States. In all the places they currently exist, grizzly bears have been classified as threatened, endangered, or vulnerable species, sparking scientific research to inform better conservation and management policies.[6]

The locational data we use comes from one such research effort, which we describe in greater detail below. We use it to do two things: in the first and longest part of our chapter, we explore the possibilities of this data for telling a more animal-centred history, one that helps us understand how these grizzlies experienced the world. We then use the process of collecting and analyzing this data as a springboard to explore the idea of "entanglement," a concept central to animal studies that calls attention to how human lives are enmeshed with those of non-human animals.[7] Because people are so often oblivious to their entanglements with non-domesticated creatures—something that speaks to our power—animal studies scholars focus on moments of encounter, when what is invisible is revealed and can produce new insights about what it means to be human in an entangled world.

While we write in one voice in the first part of our chapter, we depart from this stylistically in the second part: there, we each discuss our encounters with the grizzlies of the eastern slopes, encounters that differ from the conventional stories about what happens when humans meet apex predators. Colleen Campbell speaks to her experience as a field researcher on the Eastern Slopes Grizzly Bear Project, collecting the locational data (among other things), and as a visual artist whose practice has been shaped by her fieldwork. Tina Loo discusses her experience using the data. Hers is a different kind of encounter, at once intimate and at a distance from the bears, but nonetheless productive of meaning.

We begin, however, with a brief overview of the history of animal tracking to put the locational data we use in context and to discuss the kinds of stories it makes possible.

Making Tracks, Finding Histories

Tracking animals has a deep history. A combination of inquisitiveness and necessity led early humans and their descendants to familiarize themselves with footprints, feathers, hair, and scat. An ability to read these traces of the animal past, or, more specifically, traces of animals who had passed by, was crucial to people in contexts where they were both predators and prey, where they needed to feed themselves and avoid becoming food.

If the necessity for such knowledge faded for some people in some places over time, the curiosity that fuelled its acquisition did not. The desire to know where animals go led to experiments in bird banding and fish tagging in the late nineteenth and early twentieth centuries. The shortcomings of these methods may, as Robert M. Wilson points out, explain the enthusiasm with which scientists in the second half of the twentieth century embraced radio-telemetry, a method to determine location from radio signals emitted by a transmitter worn by an animal.[8] Many hoped this technology, developed in the shadow of Sputnik and the context of the Cold War, would finally make wildlife legible.

As Etienne Benson shows, radio-tracking technologies, with their promise of transcending the limits of human observation, were embraced by many American scientists and the government agencies that funded them in the postwar period. Not only did they change the practice of wildlife science but they also transformed our relationship with wilderness and wildlife itself. As a result, it was not long before some biologists raised questions about the utility and impacts of these new tracking technologies. Olaus and Adolph Murie took issue with the grizzly bear research carried out by Frank and John Craighead in Yellowstone National Park in the 1960s and 1970s. For Olaus Murie, such technologies compromised what he called "wilderness wildlife": they were invasive, required handling the animals, and had no place in national parks. With echoes of Aldo Leopold's critique of "the gadgeteer," he argued that parks were places for "basic scientific research, with the least possible equipment. It should be for the kind of scientific study based on thinking, based purely on close observation, trying to understand the relations among various animal forms and the changing environment."[9]

Nevertheless, radio-telemetry technology persisted even when newer but more expensive technologies became available.[10] Such was the case for the Eastern Slopes Grizzly Bear Project (ESGBP). The locational data it generated charted the movements of a total of seventy-one collared grizzlies over an eleven-year period.[11] Carried out from 1994 to 2004 (inclusively), the Project brought together researchers from the University of Calgary, in partnership with a number of provincial and federal government bodies, environmental organizations, and the private sector. The researchers were particularly interested in bear demography, habitat quality and selection, population fragmentation, mortality, the needs of female grizzlies, and the specific as well as the cumulative effects of human development in the central Rockies ecosystem, a 40,000-square-kilometre area encompassing parts of Alberta and British Columbia, and within it, the Bow River watershed. More than 11,000 square kilometres in size, it includes half of Banff National Park and the Alberta provincial lands adjoining it, incorporating all of what's known as Kananaskis Country.[12]

While the project's scientists used the bears' movements to inform their recommendations about how the central Rockies ecosystem should be managed, we use them to show how locational data can be a source for animal histories. Thanks to field researchers like Colleen Campbell, we have more than 38,000 locations, showing where each tagged or collared animal went and, in some cases, brief comments from the trackers about what individual bears were doing or who they were with.

But data is not a story. How do you create one from all those latitudes and longitudes? In thinking about how to craft more "biocentric" narratives, the literary critic David Herman suggests that storytelling about non-human animals needs to "shift from the register of events to the register of actions."[13] History is organized around events and while an "event" can simply be an outcome, the way we define them is usually fundamentally anthropocentric. Events are often noteworthy—to us!—in some way; they may even be planned. An "action" carries no such valence: it is something that is done. Each of the data points we have records an action—a bear moving—taken by a particular animal and recorded by an individual tracker using radio-telemetry equipment.

In thinking about the meaning of all this movement—these actions— we were inspired by the work of Aaron Koblin, a digital media artist interested in visualizing data to say something about our relationship to technology. "Flight Patterns," his visualization of air traffic over the United States in a twenty-four-hour period, is especially useful.[14] One of the arguments it makes so powerfully is that movement makes space: as each day begins you see an increase in air traffic from east to west. That traffic is shaped by innumerable social, economic, and political relationships of different scales, from the individual to the global. What materializes from those relationships—captured in the movement of planes—is the continental United States.

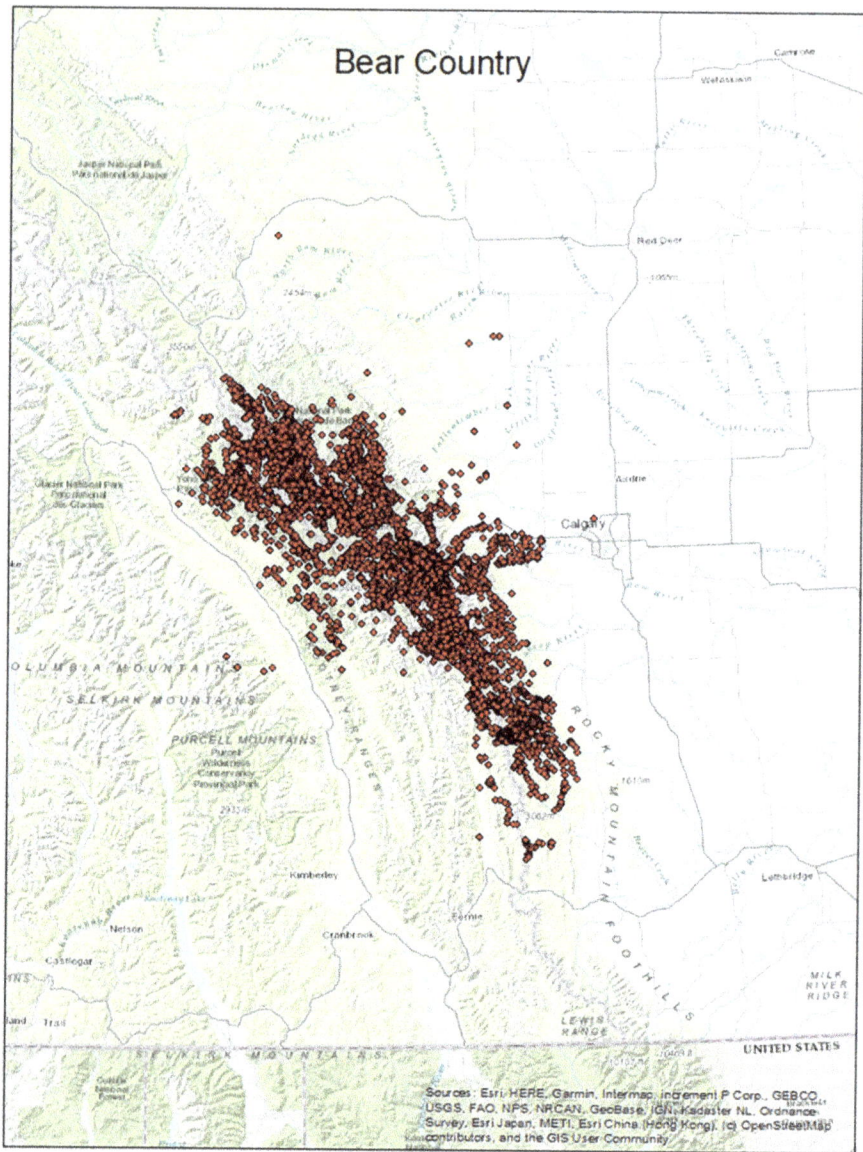

Fig 11.1 Map of Grizzly Country generated by plotting the locations of all the bears tracked by the Eastern Slopes Grizzly Bear Project from 1994 to 2004. Credit: Map generated by Tina Loo using Esri ARCGis. Map sources: Esri, HERE, Garmin Intermap, Increment P Corp., GEBCO, USGS, FAO, NPS, NRCAN GeoBase, IGN, Kadaster NL, Ordnance Survey, Esri Japan, METI, Esri China (Hong Kong), OpenStreetMap contributors, and the GIS User Community.

If movement makes space, then what materializes from the locational data gathered by the ESGBP researchers is bear country, the dominion of the eastern slopes grizzlies (Figure 11.1). Unlike Aaron Koblin's "Flight Patterns," the movement of bears does not manifest itself in an instantly familiar shape—and that, for us, is the point. Visualizing locational data with GIS "creates novel geographies and locales."[15] As Andrew Robichaud argues (Chapter 13), it shows us what we cannot otherwise see. The surprise the map elicits is its power; through the emotion it evokes, it has the potential to influence what we do. The unfamiliar shape of "grizzly country" underscores our status as outsiders. Despite the fact humans occupy parts of it, grizzly country is a foreign country; indeed, it is one we are oblivious to and our ignorance has worked to the detriment of its citizens. Now that we can see it, might we behave differently?

If air traffic in the US represents relationships and decisions made at multiple scales, ones shaped, for instance, by geography, infrastructure, and social, political, and economic relationships, then what explains the movements that make grizzly country? What can be said about the relationships and decisions that gave rise to the dominion of the bears?

Perhaps unsurprisingly, researchers with the ESGBP concluded that bear behaviour and movement are shaped by the quality of habitat and the seasonality of available food sources, something that brings them into the river valleys of the eastern slopes—and the lives of humans. As it happens, the valleys are also the very places that humans built their settlements, highways, railways, and recreational facilities, like ski hills and golf courses. Indeed, rather than deter grizzlies, these developments attract them: radio-telemetry shows that the bears were often found along rivers, roads, railways, and on ski runs and golf greens. These are all edge habitats favourable to the growth of a variety of berries.

Canopy forest cover restricts the growth of many foods that bears seek. Any conditions that bring light to the forest floor benefit the growth of berry bushes and many other foods that grizzlies favour. Fire breaks and burned areas, trails, roads, and railroads, campgrounds, logged areas, glades, meadows, ski runs, and towns all allow in light that promotes the growth of berry bushes. From Colorado to Alaska, buffaloberries (*Shepherdia canadensis*) are usually abundant in bear habitat. Other species that thrive in similar habitats include grouseberry, crowberry, wild strawberry, raspberry, wild blueberry, nodding onion, hedysarum, elderberry, cranberry, many kinds of sedges, and grasses. Bears seek them all; their movements track the availability of this forage. In the spring and early summer, grizzlies are often found at lower elevations, eating roots, graminoids (grasses and sedges), and forbs (herbaceous flowering plants). As this food becomes available at higher elevations, bears move uphill, and return to the valley bottoms in summer and early fall to take advantage of berry season.[16] In all, grizzlies forage on more than fifty plant species in the central Rockies, most of which grow in forest margins and open slopes.[17]

The central Rockies is part of a large range where bears rely on prodigious quantities of *Shepherdia canadensis* for the 20,000 to 30,000 calories of daily intake they need to prepare for hibernation. Research reveals that grizzlies will ingest 100,000 to 200,000 *Shepherdia* berries daily, as the crop ripens in the mid- to late summer.[18] When the availability of *Shepherdia* is compromised, bears get their calories from other plant species. In open spaces, like the verges of the roads and alpine meadows, they also dig for hibernating ground squirrels and marmots, and flip rocks looking for small rodents, invertebrates, and insects.[19]

While some human developments, like ski hills and golf courses, create environments favourable to the growth of food bears prefer, other developments constrain the animals' movements and fragment their habitat. The telemetry data showed that the grizzlies of the eastern slopes had larger ranges than their counterparts in British Columbia, likely because the habitat in the eastern slopes is poorer: they travelled more to get enough to eat.[20] But ranging widely increased the chances of encountering humans and human developments, especially roads.

For grizzlies, like for people, roads make movement easier, and because they do, bears, and especially female bears, tended to be attracted to them.[21] But the traffic on those roads also posed an obstacle—and a mortal danger.[22] Female bears of all ages and, to a lesser extent, subadult males, were found near roads and crossed them more often than adult males, regardless of the time of day.[23] The kind of road mattered: grizzlies selected low-traffic roads and avoided high-traffic ones when they could. Opened in 1962 and twinned within national park boundaries between 1981 and 2014, the Trans-Canada Highway in particular proved to be an especially challenging barrier to carnivore movement and a source of wildlife mortality. Over the course of the Eastern Slopes study, average daily traffic flows increased twenty per cent.[24] But it was not the only such high-volume throughway in the Central Rockies Ecosystem: as the Eastern Slopes Grizzly Project scientists observed, "[w]e know of no other area within occupied grizzly bear habitat in North America that has such an extensive network of high speed, high volume highways."[25]

In contrast to highways, railways seemed to be less of a constraint and more of an attraction to bears. The relative absence of humans and car and truck traffic offered grizzlies food and easy passage, particularly in mountainous terrain. Not only could they take advantage of the berries and other herbaceous plants that grew in the disturbed environment along the railroad right-of-way, but they also could avail themselves of the grain spilled on the tracks by leaky hopper cars and the animals killed by passing trains. Indeed, on the eastern slopes, where the best habitat happens to be used by humans, food found on and along the rail lines may be especially important to the health of individual bears, if not the population as a whole.[26]

The relationships that shaped the movement of bears through the Bow River watershed were thus ones they had with the immediate material environment, something that in turn was shaped by their sex, their place in bear society, climate, and the needs, desires, and economy of a growing human population. The area is an hour or two drive away from Calgary, which by the end of the study had a population of nearly one million. It also encompasses a major commercial transportation corridor, providing rail and road connections between the prairies, the Port of Vancouver, and Asian markets. In addition, the area is an international tourist and recreational destination, which includes multiple national and provincial parks, ski hills, hotels, and golf courses, as well as the towns of Canmore and Banff and the village of Lake Louise. The parts of the watershed that are not designated parkland are open to ranching and subject to resource extraction; specifically, logging, mining, and oil and gas development.

Given all this, if Karl Marx did animal history he might have argued that these bears experienced and made history under conditions that were not of their own making.[27] As the members of the ESGBP put it, the grizzlies inhabiting the Bow River watershed "live in one of the most developed and rapidly developing landscapes in which they still survive."[28] In their final report, the project's scientists noted survival rates of ninety-five per cent for female grizzlies and eighty-one to eighty-five per cent for males. In their view, these remarkable numbers were attributable to better management of human food and garbage beginning in the 1980s.[29] Given the continued development and human population pressures in the area, however, researchers considered the animals to be under stress. Maintaining their numbers would require further regulation and monitoring.

While these survival rates were certainly the result of effective human intervention, they were also a tribute to the ability of the grizzlies to deal with change, often within their own lifetimes and over generations. The animals moved around to exploit the caloric possibilities opened by ski hills, golf courses, campground developments, and rail traffic, and they negotiated the dangers presented by cars, trucks, and trains. Doing so was something bears learned from their mothers, with whom they usually stayed for two and a half years, and through their own observations and experience. For instance, researchers speculated that the large male grizzly known as "The Boss" (M122) grew to the size he did because he had learned to avoid trains, having once been grazed by one. That ability allowed him to feast regularly on the elk and deer carcasses he knew he would find by the tracks.[30] These animals knew, learned, and remembered things; they were and are knowledgeable.

We can thus think of locational data of the kind collected by the ESGBP as an expression of the "situated knowledge" possessed by the bears. It is knowledge that is located—"situated"—in the social, historical, and material contexts in which it was produced as well as the animals' sex, age, and personalities.[31] As the scholars of science and technology put it, "all forms of knowledge reflect the particular conditions in which they are produced, and at some level reflect the social identities and the social locations of knowledge producers."[32] In short, the movements of the eastern slopes grizzlies are a manifestation of their past experience and learning, of who they are. It is an artifact of their history, one that is entwined with that of the humans who live, work, and visit the central Rockies ecosystem as well as those who benefit indirectly from its development.

Not only can the locational data from the Eastern Slopes Project be a source for a population-level history of a particular group of grizzlies, allowing us to see how their collective experience is shaped by and entwined with that of humans, but it also has the potential to tell us about specific individuals. In other words, it is a source for biography. Animal biography has a long and contentious genealogy, dating back to the early twentieth century and the "nature fakers" controversy that pitted naturalist John Burroughs against authors like Ernest Thompson Seton and Charles G. D. Roberts, who had written enormously popular, sympathetic portraits of individual animals. The problem, according to Burroughs, was that they were "sham natural history," overly sentimental and decidedly anthropocentric. Since then, writers have struggled with how to tell animal stories from their point of view.[33] For filmmakers Leanne Allison and Jeremy Mendes, locational data offers a way to do so. They tapped into its biographical potential in their interactive documentary *Bear 71* (2012), which tells the story of one eastern slopes grizzly (F71) from her perspective.[34] From the time she was tagged until her death on the railway tracks, F71's movements were monitored—by wildlife personnel when she was near human-use areas, and with GPS and trail cameras. Images from the latter, combined with compelling data visualization of her GPS locations, reveal the stresses she confronted in the Bow Valley. At the same time, and with echoes of Olaus Murie's critique of the Craigheads' radio-tracking of the Yellowstone grizzlies, *Bear 71* serves as a critique of the surveillance that allowed her story to be told—and which envelops us all.

Even without the compelling trail camera trap images and the dynamic data visualization that animates *Bear 71*, we believe the locational information we have can reveal something of the social and, we argue, emotional worlds of individual animals. It is possible to see the relationships they had in which humans did not figure centrally if—again—we follow the advice of David Herman and others. In addition to calling for a "shift from the register of events to the register of actions," Herman argues that stories about animal life need more granularity and slower pacing. He, as well as Gordon Burghardt and Marc Bekoff, also urge us to practice a kind of critical empathy in writing animal stories, imagining "what it might be like" for them, given the particularities of their bodies and biology.[35] Doing the latter helps avoid anthropocentrism. Herman asks us to consider "If I were a member of species X, I would engage with the world along the following lines."[36] Only then might we capture animals' experience.

With all this in mind, meet bears F30 and F46, female grizzlies who lived with their families east of the resort village of Lake Louise in a region that included the ski area and the drainages of the Pipestone River and Baker Creek. It is one of four "hotspots," areas that sustain more females than might be predicted given the habitat.

Born in 1985, F30 was first collared in the fall of 1994. At the time, she was accompanied by three "young of the year," as biologists call cubs less than twelve months old: they were likely her first. She had a reputation among humans as a cranky bear, known to bluff charge people or vehicles that surprised her or got too close. Charging is an aggressive, but defensive action; it was a way for F30 to create enough space and time to get her cubs away, as was the case in mid-June of 1995, when she ran at a truck in the east parking lot of Whiskey Jack Lodge at the Lake Louise ski hill. After doing so, she veered off and chased her cubs into the trees and safety.[37]

While F30 was wary of humans, she and her cubs had good relations with other grizzlies, especially F46 and her young, with whom they were often seen. CM, another tracker with the Eastern Slopes Project, delighted in the relationship, noting that she spotted F30 in early July 1997 "with 3 cubs and with #46. #46 is with her cubs so there is a meeting of at least 7 bears going on!"[38] F46 was a year older than F30, and was collared a year later, in 1995. At the time, she had two yearling cubs, a male and a female. The male was fitted with an ear transmitter and became M45.

Colleen Campbell monitored F30 and F46 for eleven years during which they had two litters each; they were located by telemetry and observed in close proximity with their offspring numerous times during the summers. Their first litters of three and two cubs, respectively, were the same age and were observed playing together on several occasions.

In the summer of 1997, F30 was recaptured to replace her collar. Her cubs, all females. were still with her. They, too, were captured and given ear tag transmitters that identified them as F56, F59, and F60. The next summer, F46's other cub, a female, was captured and given an ear transmitter identifying it as F65.

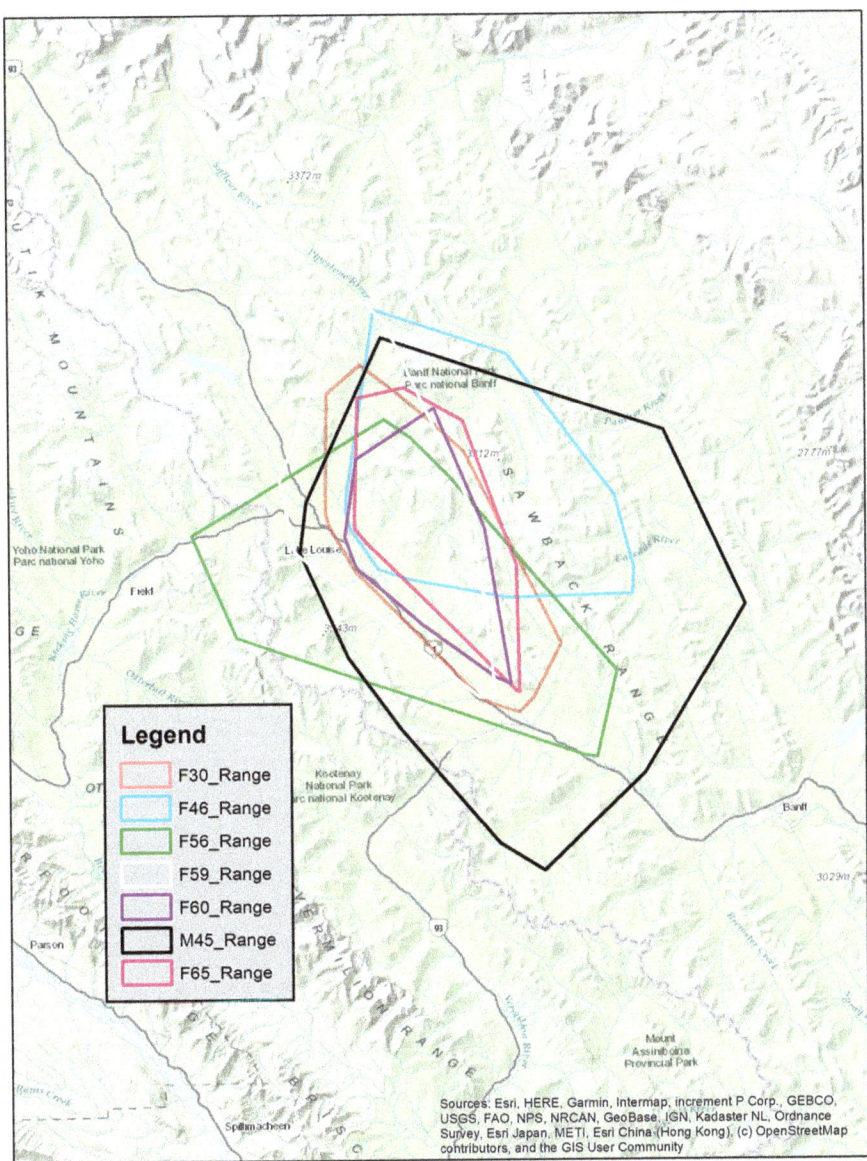

Fig. 11.2 The ranges of grizzly bears F30, F46, F56, F59, F60, M45, and F65 generated from the tracking data collected by the Eastern Slopes Grizzly Bear Project. Credit: Map generated by Tina Loo using Esri ARCGis. Map sources: Esri, HERE, Garmin Intermap, Increment P Corp., GEBCO, USGS, FAO, NPS, NRCAN GeoBase, IGN, Kadaster NL, Ordnance Survey, Esri Japan, METI, Esri China (Hong Kong), OpenStreetMap contributors, and the GIS User Community.

For the next number of years, these seven bears—F30 and F46 and their cubs F56, F59, F60, M45, and F65—shared overlapping home ranges that included the ski hill, Pipestone Valley, Baker Creek, and the mountain passes and lakes east of Boulder pass (Figure 11.2).[39] While it was not unusual for family groupings to be seen together, the data also suggest that grizzlies could form long-term relationships with unrelated animals of the same species. We know that male and female bears come together for the purposes of mating. But these associations are short in duration, counted in hours or days: the average length of M-F encounters was seventy-two hours, longer in "pre-berry season;" in other words, during breeding season.[40] Researchers also reported that same-sex encounters were usually between adult and subadult grizzlies, and were "significantly shorter" in duration, averaging twenty-two hours for F-F associations and fourteen for M-M associations.[41] What's interesting about F30 and F46 is that they were two adult bears who carried on their association—their friendship?—sometimes for days, and certainly over years.[42]

F30's and F46's second litters of three and one, respectively, were a year apart. F46 was cautious about her single cub being near the other cubs until hers was two years old and robust enough to hold its own playing with F30's three three-year olds. When they had no offspring, F30 and F46 were seldom in such close proximity. At the conclusion of the ESGBP study, monitoring ended; we never learned if these cubs might have grown to be "friends" as adult bears, as their mothers appeared to be.

Such friendly associations are not ones that non-scientists have paid much attention to when it comes to keystone predators like bears. Insofar as we see their relationships, it is usually the ones they have with their young. We often paint their interactions with other animals as competitive or adversarial, overlooking the possibility that the proximity of these animals to each other could be for companionship and play and not just utilitarian reasons like predation, procreation, and protection.

F30 and F46 were not particularly unusual. During early grizzly bear investigations in Yellowstone National Park, researchers observed a variety of relationships female bears had with their young cubs, some keeping them very close, others exhibiting less tight bonding. Females were also observed in the company of one or more other females with cubs, sometimes persistently over a season, and once, one female relocated her den before winter hibernation to within a short distance of the female with whom she had spent significant time during the summer. Additionally, four subadult males, three of them related plus one adopted into the same family, were observed travelling together for several seasons. Their relationship apparently bestowed on them greater status within their habitat than would be granted a single bear of the same subadult age.[43]

In addition to giving us insight into the relationships these animals may have had with each other, the movement data also lets us discern distinct behaviours and individual personalities. In general, male bears tended to have bigger home ranges than did females and this was certainly the case with the Lake Louise grizzlies. For instance, F46's cub M45 had a range of 1,435 square kilometres: this was more than five times larger than his sister's, F65, who ranged over a 284-square-kilometre area.

But there could also be a good deal of variation among members of the same sex. Grizzlies, like people, are individuals. Take F30 and her offspring, all females. Though F30 was not known to have taken her cubs across the Bow River, the Trans-Canada Highway or Highway 93N, all three of her offspring crossed on their own. F56 was especially adventurous: for three successive summers (1999 to 2001), she explored up into the Plain of Six Glaciers area and crossed Abbot Pass (2,925 metres) on at least two occasions. Why? If we were grizzlies, we would not be headed up that high if we were just hungry: there is very little food at higher altitudes. Could it be that she was possessed of a different personality, that she was more curious?[44] Or fun-loving? According to the notes accompanying the telemetry data, climbers reported seeing her in October 1999 at Abbot Pass "bum sliding down the Death Trap," one of the glaciers. Later that day, she was spotted again, this time at the teahouse at Lake Agnes, just above Lake Louise, a favourite destination of human day hikers (Figures 11.3 and 11.4).[45]

The locational data for F59 shows that for most of August 2002 she started moving big distances: on average, she moved twice as far every day that month than she did in July, nearly fourteen kilometres daily compared to just six. Moreover, her movements were not in one direction, but back and forth, all over the place. Why? After all, it was late summer and berry season, and if we were grizzlies, we would not be moving big distances every day. Instead, we would be focused on feeding, packing in the

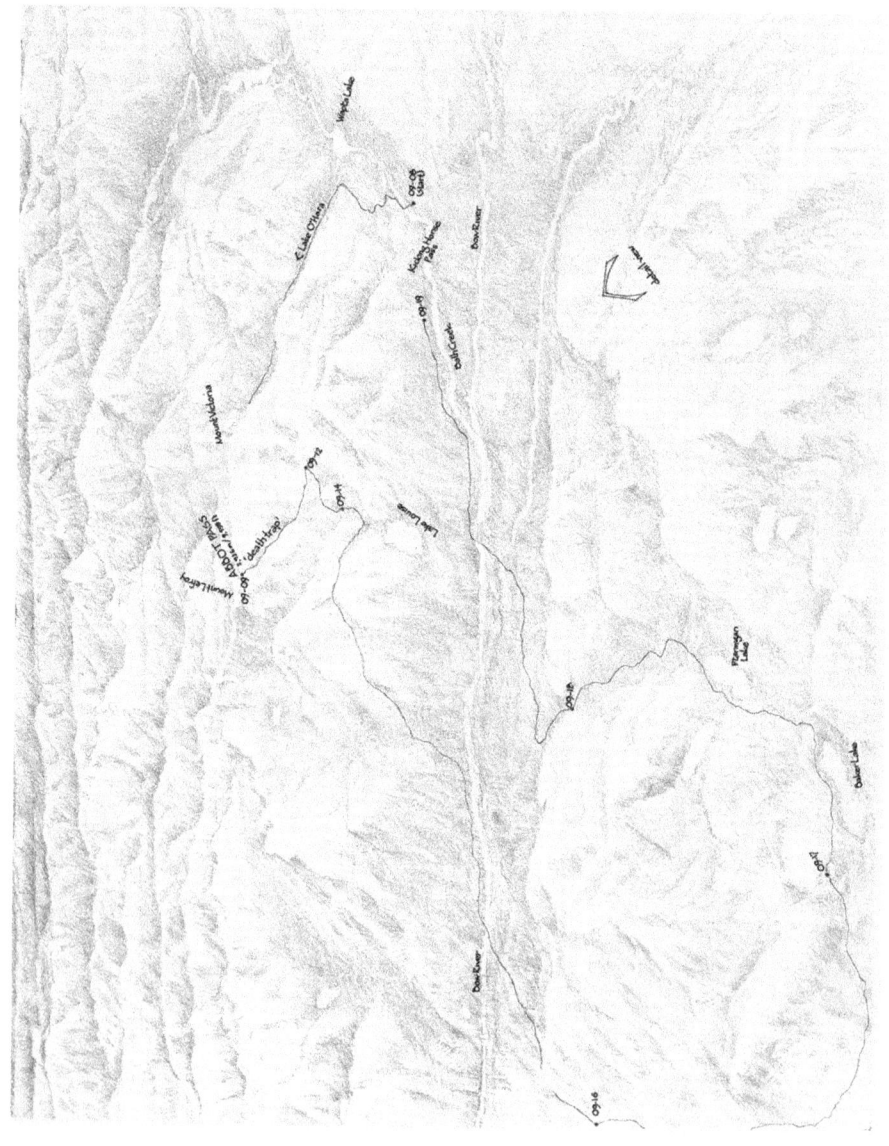

Fig. 11.3 F56 was wearing a GPS collar, which captured her approximate route. This map shows twelve days of travel from 8 September 1999 to 19 September 1999. Map by Colleen Campbell, 2020.

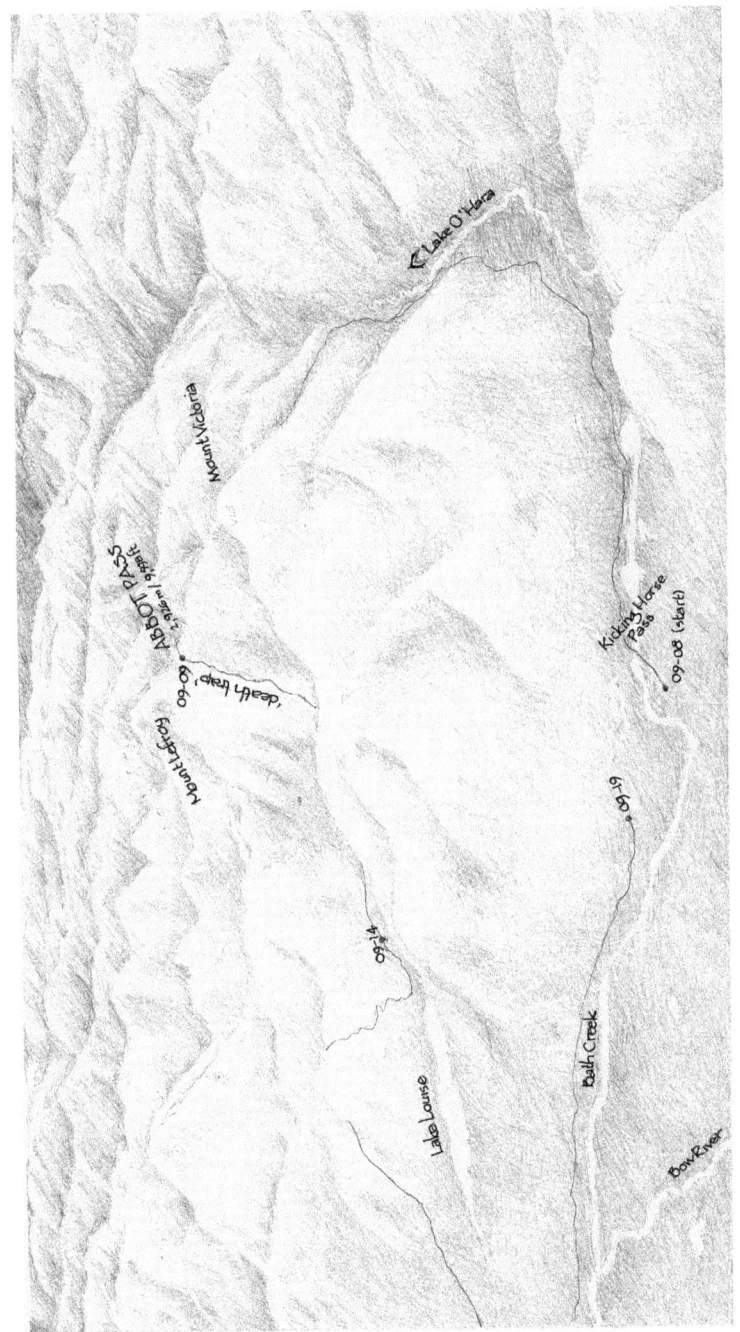

Fig. 11.4 Detail of F56's route over Abbot Pass and down the "Death Trap," during September 1999. Map by Colleen Campbell, 2020.

11 | Making Tracks

calories concentrated on the Lake Louise ski hill, in preparation for winter and hibernation.

But that is not what F59 was doing. As Colleen Campbell recalls, her movements in early August coincided with the disappearance of her cub, who was never located as far as we know. Could she have been looking for it? If so, it is another glimpse into the emotional lives of these animals. F59's movements let us add concern, anxiety, and love to curiosity and adventurousness as sentiments these grizzlies held and possible motivations for their associations and movements. In revealing these emotions and behaviours, the locational data allows us to move beyond a reductionist view of animals that sees them as life forms motivated only by the need to survive.

Of course, the bears did not just interact with each other; they also interacted with other animals. Observers saw grizzlies in the company of other animals, like wolves, elk, deer, geese, and—for the Lake Louise bears—Colleen Campbell.[46] Field researchers like Colleen were also a part of the lives of the eastern slopes grizzlies as much as they were a part of hers. She followed F30 and her family (as well as other bears) for more than a decade.

Colleen's experience, which she relates in the next section, reminds us that fieldwork can generate insights about the natural world and our relationship with it. As Richard White observed, people have historically come to know nature through labour, not just recreation, and what they come to know through work differs from the knowledge generated by play.[47] Colleen's wildlife work on the eastern slopes shaped her understanding of animals, the natural world, and her own place in it. The story she tells of encountering F30 departs somewhat from the usual stories of humans meeting other apex predators, like Val Plumwood's classic one, which emphasizes violence and the experience of being prey.[48] That said, like those stories, hers is still one that emphasizes how the knowledge that is produced by such encounters comes as much through the sensing body as the thinking mind. An awareness of that, as well as human vulnerability, can lead to an appreciation of connection and the more-than-human condition of our existence.

Ways of Knowing and Being through Encounter

My career as a field researcher started in 1991, with coyotes. Coyotes have small home ranges and hunt at any time, all year long. Each coyote—male, female, juvenile, breeding adult—is like a beautiful wild dog, and part of a family group. I loved searching for them. I was happy in the woods. During the summer of 1993, I monitored two grizzly bears. Each was often near a road, and I monitored them only when they were at risk of encountering humans, to try to maintain distance between people and the somewhat indifferent bears.

The Eastern Slopes Grizzly Bear Project started in spring of 1994. Bears range more widely than coyotes. The work shifted in complexity. Telemetry was the primary method of locating individuals, usually from the ground, occasionally from the air. We sometimes worked in the backcountry, collecting scat and hair samples (non-invasive ways to collect DNA) and identifying rub trees. Periodically, I was enlisted to track a mortality, possibly collect a carcass, and help with a necropsy. I assembled capture kits, entered or checked data, wrote reports, presented talks and, from time to time, proposed a research idea. The biologist for whom I worked generously encouraged each of us to expand our responsibilities. Eventually, most of us worked alone, most of the time.

Bears are seasonal and so was the work of tracking. Every spring, I was thrilled to hear the first "pings" of a functioning collar. For many years, the heartbeat VHF rhythm that primed my spirit for summer belonged to F30, while she was lingering near her den. Once she left her den high on a ridge, her signal would be lost in the convolutions of the landscape. I would have to look for her when I began my regular "commute" on foot from Temple Lodge to the lakes and ridges east of Boulder Pass (Figure 11.5). The work was predictable but there was no typical day. I started before dawn. Using telemetry, I would locate any bears I could find as I drove from Canmore to Lake Louise. Later, I would hike to Boulder Pass and beyond, the work directed by the activity of the bears and the weather.

The first spring hike to Boulder, relentlessly uphill for 5.2 kilometers, was brutal. I was an interloper and I always felt a little spooked working alone. My loud calls ("EH-OH") were effective. Even when there were two of us working together, we would broadcast our presence loudly, letting

Fig. 11.5 Colleen doing telemetry, ca. 1992. Photo credit. Mike Gibeau.

the bears know we were there. Most animals, including grizzlies, prefer to avoid humans if at all possible. I know of only one time a field researcher deployed bear spray during the years of the ESGBP work.

I explored—climbing ridges to listen for signals, following game trails, noting a scrape, a rub tree, plants, or watching a bear in an avalanche slope, perhaps five hundred metres away, doing work that bears do: digging, resting, foraging.

Each day yielded some tidbit, some experience to be treasured: cubs playing, a bear—once, two wolverines—sliding in the snow, hare tracks that disappeared at a junction with a bounding leap of a marten, astonishingly, a lynx and a wolf, each about one hundred metres away from me in opposite directions along the trail. I became absorbed in everything I observed, trying to decipher the ever-changing puzzles I encountered. I came to know the bears and coyotes that I tracked as discrete personalities, as unique as each of my human friends.

The early season unease dissipated a little with each hike to Boulder Pass. I was becoming used to being outdoors, comfortable knowing I shared the mountains with creatures I could not see. Every hour on the ground fed my imagination and what was initially "liking my work" became reverence for where I worked. I began to understand that everything "fit"—somewhere.

Beyond the fieldwork and research, I learned about these animals' entangled histories with us, about coyotes' 10,000 years as a disreputable god and grizzly bears' 35,000-year tenure as a solemn spiritual guide. Until a few hundred years ago, we humans generally understood and respected the wildlife around us. The characteristics of different species shaped the stories people told about them, ones that were devised to give each a "place" in our world and ours in theirs.

Currently, we have a conflicted relationship with both coyote and bear and nearly all others: raccoons, cougars, bobcats, ravens and magpies, sharks and seals. We do not want them in our gardens, yet we long to see them. Most of them terrify us, yet we leap from our cars to get a photograph when we see one along the roadside.

It was this understanding that prompted me to write about the eastern slopes bears. Through that effort, I realized that much of what I wanted to share could be more effectively conveyed in a series of drawings. After about thirty pages in my sketchbook, I planned and drew twelve large sheets chronicling the life histories of all the eastern slopes research bears. I included information about grizzly bears that predated the formal research and those that have been monitored since—to 2017—more than 150 different animals. In the drawings, the individuality of each bear can be easily apprehended, and the species—by analogy, all species—understood as comprised of unique beings, each with a personal life story. Perhaps this is a route to appreciating the intrinsic value of other species and of the spaces that they need to live and thrive (Figures 11.6 and 11.7).

I would like people who see my drawings to understand what I learned through fieldwork; namely, that humans have historically related to

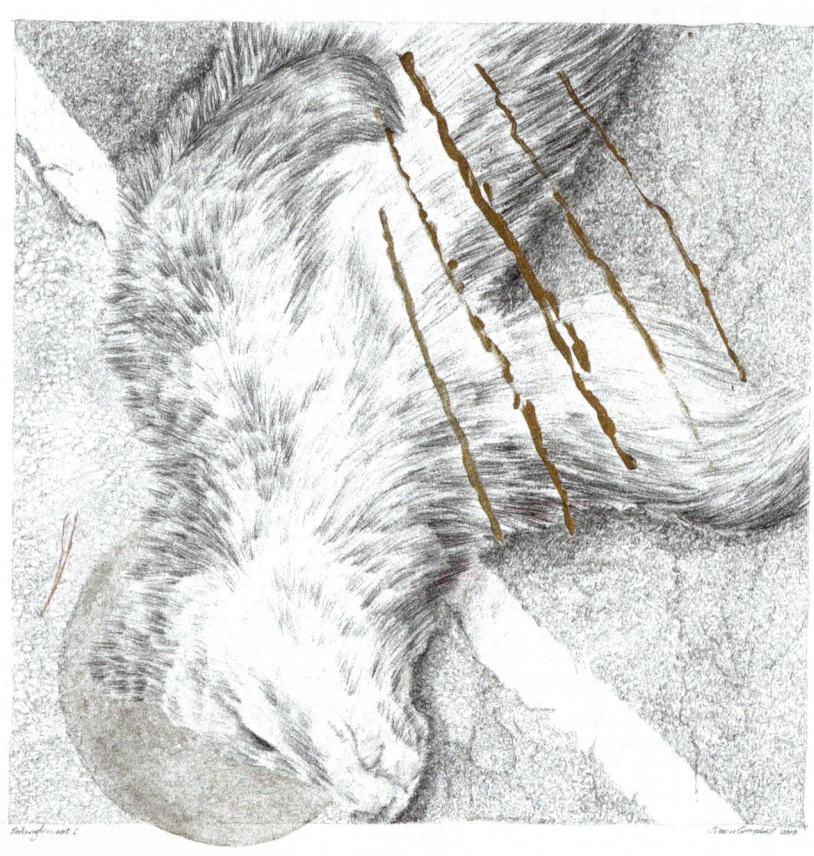

Fig. 11.6 Entanglement I, Graphite and watercolour on paper, 15.5" x 15.5", Colleen Campbell, 2019. Fear of living bears becomes lament, even outrage, when we kill one on the highways or the railways.

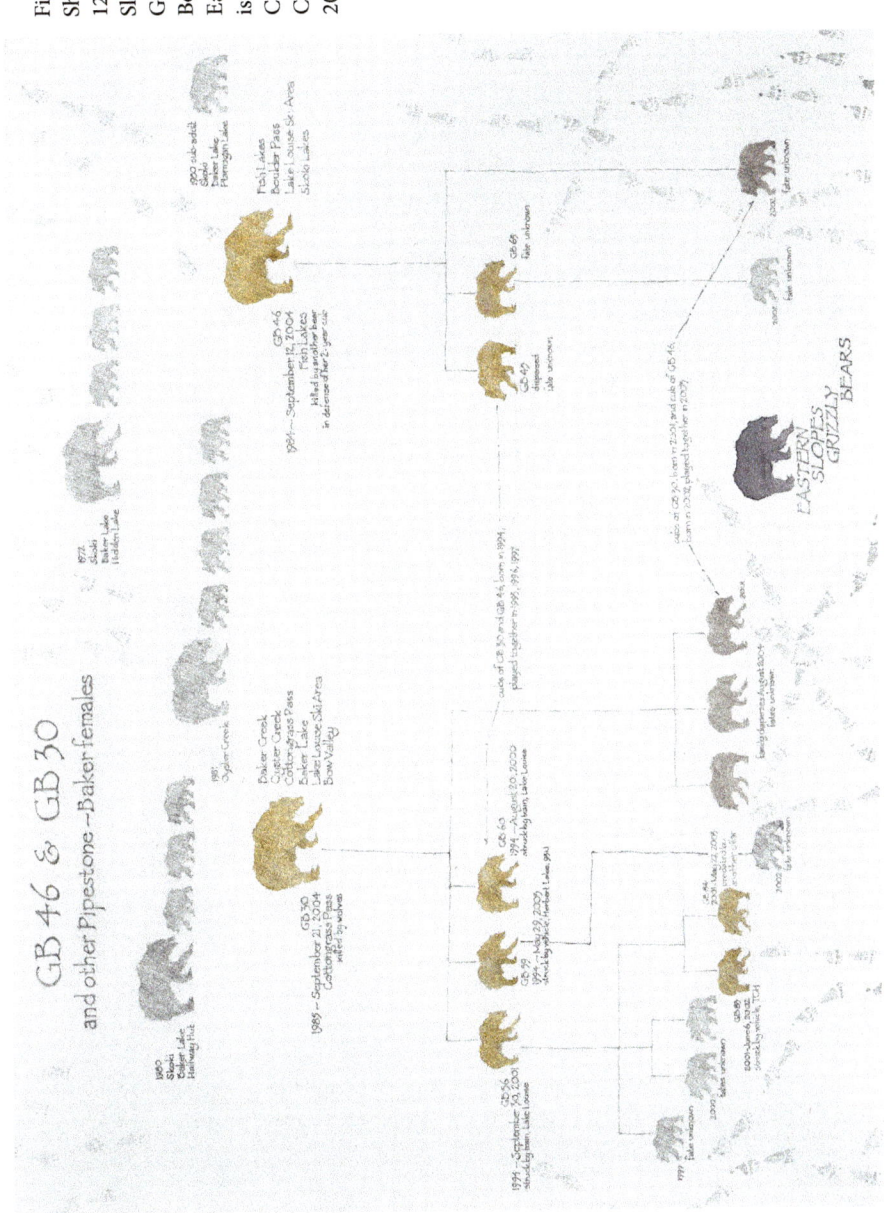

Fig. 11.7 Sheet #5 of 12, "Eastern Slopes Grizzly Bears: Each One is Sacred," Colleen Campbell, 2017.

11 | Making Tracks

wild animals through shared use of the same habitat with conditions—taboos—about how humans should behave. I made a lot of noise, never knowingly approached an animal, changed my path if I felt twitchy about something. Historically, there was a mutuality to the agreement, which humans apparently believed that the wild animals understood, as in the ancient story of a girl who married a bear, and a recent story of the protagonist tiger in Sasha Snow's and John Vaillant's accounts of a notable human-tiger conflict in Primoria, far eastern Russia, during the 1990s.[49] I want people to sense that, until recently, we did not see the world and everything in it "for our taking."

In the Bow Valley, where I live, we have been engaged in many efforts to coexist with the wild creatures around us.[50] We have changed our garbage management, worked to rid our neighbourhoods of bear attractants, such as fruit-bearing trees, fenced the highway, and built overpasses and underpasses for wildlife. We also have many NGOs offering adaptive educational programming so locals and visitors alike can learn to become "wildsmart." And, still, our relationship with other species and their habitat is very lopsided, dominated by human desire. Too often, our entanglements with other species are fatal for them (Figure 11.8). Our attitudes and desires are serious contributing conditions to the climate and environmental emergencies we face.

My twenty years of wildlife fieldwork and experiences, such as my encounter with F30 and her cubs, influence my research, persistently enter my studio work, and permeate the stories I tell when presenting to an audience. I share my belief that nature makes no mistakes and that we cannot enjoy our own species' health without a healthy world. We must value bears (and, analogously, all else) not only for the extrinsic benefits they may bring us through tourism and medical science—but also for their intrinsic qualities, as wild animals with a right to "place"—"bear country" and by analogy, all other "countries."

* * *

Late one August afternoon in 2004, I was tracking F30. She had moved nearly twenty kilometres east since early morning, staying out of sight as she travelled between the Bow River and the well-travelled secondary

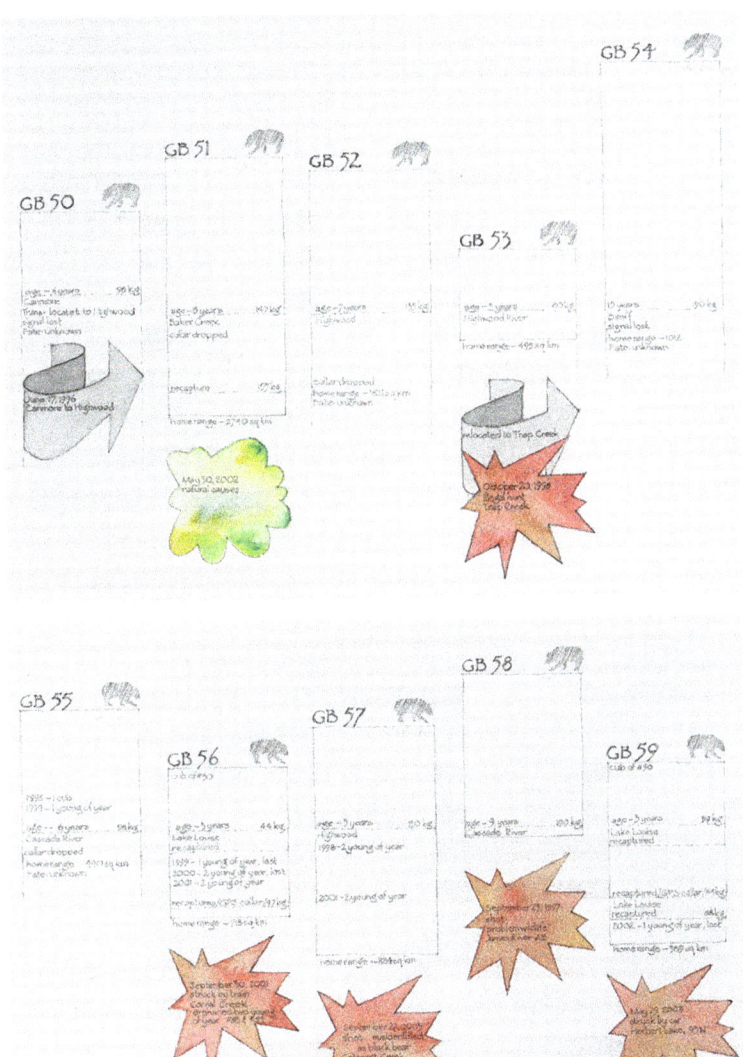

Fig. 11.8 Details of some of the lives described in "Eastern Slopes Grizzly Bears: Each One is Sacred," Colleen Campbell, 2017.

11 | Making Tracks

road. She was still keeping her cubs, now three years old, safe until the family eventually dispersed.

Shepherdia canadensis was abundant and F30 was following open forest edges along the rail and road, providing for herself and her three nearly grown cubs. Her signal placed her in the pinch where the train tracks lay between the river and a twenty-five metre escarpment that rises to the eastbound lane of a long split of the road.

At the top of the bluff, I pulled over to the grassy shoulder. The strength of the signal suggested I might see F30 and her family near the river below me. Nonetheless, I opened the hatch of my car to retrieve a portable antenna and compass so I could get a "fix" on her in case I did not make visual contact. The steady rhythm of pings originating from F30's collar was loud and I noticed that the attenuating lever was already toggled into position. "Attenuation" is a way of significantly reducing the volume to enable a tracker to isolate the direction from which the signal originates. My antenna was not connected, the signal was attenuated, the volume tuned as low as possible, and still the sound was too loud. The signal needle bounced repeatedly to the top of the scale.

I immediately realized that F30 must be very close. I did not anticipate that she was only a few metres behind me on the shoulder of the road, standing tall on her back legs and watching me.[51] Though she surely heard my car and the all the different clattery sounds of my work, F30 had topped the escarpment anyway—wild, beautiful, and perfectly "bear"— and was no more than six to eight metres away from me.

Having monitored F30 closely for nearly ten years. I had admired her countless times, most often through binoculars. In this moment, I could nearly touch her; she was balanced upright and facing me. I could see her nose twitch, testing the air for my scent; I could see the claws on her front feet, hanging relaxed at her sides, her ears directed towards me, and her hair quivering with the flex of her muscles as she subtly maintained her balance.[52] Magnificent.

Such moments distort one's sense of time. The whole experience lasted only a few seconds. I stood still and thought very calmly, "Interesting. I can do absolutely nothing to change this situation. She is right there." Those thoughts were followed quickly by "Hmm . . . bear spray is in the front seat of my car . . . and so is my camera." I felt no particular anxiety, no panic. F30 appeared to be studying me, just as I had studied her for the past decade.

Then she shrugged me off, dismissed me. F30 dropped to the ground and crossed the road, towards cover in the forest. Her three cubs topped the bank, in half-minute intervals, and behaved identically to their mother, standing tall on back legs to observe me and following her invisible footsteps across the pavement to disappear into the forest.

When I started working as a wildlife field technician, the work was straightforward; accurately locate an animal, record the data, find the next subject, day after day after day. Over time, I came to believe that when I closed the door of my vehicle to start walking into the wilderness, I was in someone else's home, often the "bear country" we identified earlier in this chapter. Acting persistently with respect and caution still guides me when I am on a trail. Not typically fearful, I have learned to turn around on occasion—at times in response to just a "shiver" or a sense in my spine, sometimes in response to an odd sound or a pile of fresh scat. I have learned to value my other senses, to trust my instincts—in many ways, to be the animal I am.

My experience is very different from that of Val Plumwood, who, while searching for a route through an unfamiliar waterway in her canoe, had a terrifying encounter with a predatory crocodile. I navigated ridges and trails with a detailed map in my mind and "knew" the bears I accidentally met at the crest of the escarpment. Though I was surprised by F30's proximity that afternoon, I had come to appreciate and respect her over the previous decade. I believe I was slowly habituated by time and my own caution to encounter F30 and each of her cubs—any one of which could kill me with a single swipe of a front paw—without panic.

* * *

Unlike Colleen, I have never encountered the eastern slopes bears in the flesh—but I have interacted with them in the process of analyzing the locational data collected by project members. My experience is a disembodied one, and my story is about the power of virtual encounters. In both of these ways, it runs counter to the emphasis in the literature: some of the most evocative and insightful work calls for taking the sensing body seriously in writing animal histories, both those of humans and non-humans, and it pays particular attention to what Ryan Tucker Jones calls "the living terrain of encounter."[53] Colleen's story of what she learned from her fieldwork and coming face-to-face with F30 is an example, though it differs from more conventional stories involving predators in that it does not involve an attack and near-death experience. Still, I would argue that despite these differences, my encounter was generative in ways similar to Colleen's.

I first encountered the grizzlies of the eastern slopes indoors, at the Whyte Museum of the Canadian Rockies, where Colleen's exhibit, "Eastern Slopes Grizzlies—Each One is Sacred" was on. I got to know them better when Colleen and I decided to collaborate on this chapter, and she shared the Excel spreadsheet containing all the locational data from the Project. To use it, I learned the basics of GIS and in the process became a tracker.

The process of "line tracking"—as the function on the GIS program I used is called—drew me into the lives of these animals. Though less embodied, it was a strangely intimate and even seductive experience. There were as many questions as there were answers; this despite arguments about modern animal tracking as an especially apt expression of human power over life in the Anthropocene. Seeing is not understanding: I knew where the grizzlies were at particular moments but I did not know more than that. And I had no idea of what was happening in the spaces in between data points.

Those questions speak to the power of data visualizations and, in my case, to the process of making them, to provoke an emotional response and potentially transform us. The maps and animations of movement make us marvel; they engage us. The questions that they cannot answer bring us up against our own intellectual limits, something that feeds and sustains wonder.[54]

Both Colleen and I have visualized the eastern slopes data differently, but in making tracks I have come to understand how doing so has the potential to cultivate what one scholar calls an "affective micropolitics of curiosity" in that space between seeing and knowing.[55] It is a desire to understand and learn rooted in humility. It is the kind of emotional engagement that can, bit by bit, shift how we see the world and, potentially, act in it.

Conclusion

As this story of the eastern slopes grizzlies has shown, locational data is a potential source for animal history. It can help us understand the lives of a population of animals as well as specific individuals. But it cannot be used alone. We have drawn on scientific studies as well as the observations of the human trackers who worked on the Eastern Slopes Project to help make sense of it. But more than other sources of information, animal stories require different narrative strategies and different ways of imagining, some of which we highlighted here; namely, the need to shift from events to actions and to practice a critical empathy, one informed by a knowledge of a particular animal's differences, by an understanding of its body, behaviour, and environment.

The kind of empathy required for more animal-centred stories can also come from encountering them—directly, as Colleen did, and indirectly, as in Tina's case. Both our encounters were generative: they made us more knowledgeable about the eastern slopes bears and, more broadly, they cultivated a particular disposition, one that helped us make sense of the movement data and write this grizzly history. They also speak to the curiosity that can come from entanglement, one that has the power to change how we are in the world.

NOTES

1. Thanks to Dr. Mike Gibeau whose work with grizzly bears is the source of data we used for this paper and for whom Colleen Campbell conducted many years of fieldwork; to Sally Hermansen, who helped Tina Loo learn ArcGIS; to Scott Jevons, GIS specialist, for his 3D maps which are the basis of the drawings showing the travels of GB F56; to Emily Wakild for her close reading of our piece and helpful suggestions; to Jennifer Bonnell, Sean Kheraj, Marcel Martel, and Jay Young who organized the "Traces of the Animal Past" conference at York University and to all the participants for their stimulating and generous engagement. We also benefited from the comments of two anonymous reviewers.
2. Erica Fudge, "A Left-Handed Blow: Writing the History of Animals," in *Representing Animals*, ed. Nigel Rothfels (Bloomington: Indiana University Press, 2002), 6.
3. Ann Laura Stoler, *Along the Archival Grain: Epistemic Anxieties and Colonial Common Sense* (Princeton: Princeton University Press, 2009). Although much humanistic scholarship has explored "the archive" as a place where knowledge is produced rather than found, it has often ignored the work of archivists in real archives—who have dealt

with such issues both theoretically and practically. See Michelle Caswell, "'The Archive' is not an Archives: Acknowledging the Intellectual Contributions of Archival Studies," *Reconstruction* 16, no. 1 (2016), https://escholarship.org/uc/item/7bn4v1fk.

4   Michel-Rolph Trouillot, *Silencing the Past: Power and the Production of History* (Boston: Beacon Press, 1995).

5   A few key works that have influenced us are Virginia DeJohn Anderson, *Creatures of Empire: How Domestic Animals Transformed Early America* (New York: Oxford University Press, 2004); Thomas Andrews, "Dying with their Boots On," in *Killing for Coal: America's Deadliest Labor War* (Cambridge, MA: Harvard University Press, 2008); Susan Nance, *Entertaining Elephants: Animal Agency and the Business of the American Circus* (Baltimore: Johns Hopkins University Press, 2013); and Brett Walker, *The Lost Wolves of Japan* (Seattle: University of Washington Press, 2005).

6   There's a taxonomic debate about grizzlies: some scientists see them as brown bears while others argue they are a subspecies of the brown bear called *Ursus arctos horribilus*. The information in this paragraph on the grizzly bear is from Robert E. Bieder, *Bear* (London: Reaktion Books, 2005); Charles C. Schwartz, Sterling D. Miller, and Mark Haroldson, "Grizzly Bear," in *Wild Mammals of North America: Biology, Management, and Conservation*, 2nd ed., ed. George A. Feldhamer, Bruce C. Thompson, and Joseph A. Chapman (Baltimore: Johns Hopkins University Press, 2003), 556–58; and Sarah Elmeligi, *What Bears Teach Us* (Victoria: Rocky Mountain Books, 2020), 20.

7   Henry Buller, "Animal geographies II: Methods," *Progress in Human Geography* 39, no. 3 (2015): 376.

8   "Comments by Robert M. Wilson," H-Environment Roundtable Review of Etienne Benson, *Wired Wilderness: Technologies of Tracking and the Making of Modern Wildlife* (Baltimore: John Hopkins Press, 2010), 13–14, http://www.h-net.org/~environ/roundtables/env-roundtable-3-1.pdf

9   On "the gadgeteer," see Aldo Leopold, *A Sand County Almanac and Sketches Here and There*. Special Commemorative Edition, with an introduction by Robert Finch (New York: Oxford University Press, 1989), 180. Olaus Murie quote from Etienne Benson, *Wired Wilderness: Technologies of Tracking and the Making of Modern Wildlife* (Baltimore: John Hopkins University Press, 2010), 61.

10 The key work on the history of animal tracking is Benson, *Wired Wilderness*. For a recent overview of tracking technologies see Roland Kays et al., "Terrestrial animal tracking as an eye on life and planet," *Science* 348, 6240 (2015), https://doi.org/10.1126/science.aaa2478.

11 Some eastern slopes grizzlies were fitted with GPS collars for a portion of the study period. There were an estimated one hundred grizzlies in the study area and at any given time, a third of them were collared and tracked by the Eastern Slopes Grizzly Bear Project.

12 The information about the ESGBP is from *Biology, Demography, Ecology and Management of Grizzly Bears in and around Banff National Park and Kananaskis Country: Final Report of the Eastern Slopes Grizzly Bear Project*, ed. Stephen Herrero (Calgary: Environmental Sciences Program, Faculty of Environmental Design, University of Calgary, 2005).

13 David Herman, "Animal Minds in Non-Fiction Comics," in *Animal Comics: Multispecies Storyworlds in Graphic Narratives*, ed. David Herman (London: Bloomsbury Press, 2018), 218.
14 Aaron Koblin, "Flight Patterns," https://youtu.be/ystkKXzt9Wk.
15 Nils Hanwahr, "Marine Animal Satellite Tags," in *Future Remains: A Cabinet of Curiosities for the Anthropocene*, ed. Gregg Mitman, Marco Armiero, and Robert S. Emmett (Chicago: University of Chicago Press, 2017), 93.
16 Schwartz, Miller, and Haroldson, "Grizzly Bear," 565.
17 David Hamer and Stephen Herrero, "Grizzly Bear Food and Habitat in the Front Ranges of Banff National Park, Alberta," *Bears: Their Biology and Management* 7 (1987): 199–213.
18 Arthur M. Pearson, *The northern interior grizzly bear Ursus arctos L.* (Ottawa: Canadian Wildlife Service Report Series Number 34, 1975).
19 David Hamer and Stephen Herrero, "Wildfire's Influence on Grizzly Bear Feeding Ecology in Banff National Park, Alberta," *Bears, Their Biology and Management*, 7A (1987): 179–86.
20 On the relationship between population density and home range size, see John A. S. Nagy and Mark A. Haroldson, "Comparisons of Some Home Range and Population Parameters among Four Grizzly Bear Populations in Canada," *Bears: Their Biology and Management* 8 (1990): 227–35.
21 Carrie L. Roever, Mark S. Boyce, and Gordon B. Stenhouse did a study that indicated that "bears were selecting roads and roaded habitat for travel." See their "Grizzly bear movements relative to roads: application of step selection functions," *Ecography* 33, no. 6 (2010): 1113–22.
22 Byron Benn and Stephen Herrero, "Grizzly Bear Mortality and Human Access in Banff and Yoho National Parks, 1971–1999," in *Biology, Demography, Ecology, and Management of Grizzly Bears in and around Banff National Park and Kananaskis Country*, ed. Herrero, 67. There are a number of other studies in this final report that speak to the relationship between roads and grizzly bear mortality.
23 Karen Graham et al., "Spatial and temporal use of roads by grizzly bears in west central Alberta," *Ursus* 21, no. 1 (2010): 43–56.
24 *Alberta Highways 1 to 986: Traffic Volume History, 1962 to 2017* (Edmonton: Alberta Transportation and Cornerstone Solutions Inc., 2017), https://open.alberta.ca/publications/traffic-volume-history#summary. Waller and Servheen estimated that the threshold for grizzlies crossing highways was one hundred vehicles per hour. Even at the start of the ESGBP, in 1994, volumes vastly surpassed that. John S. Waller and Christopher Servheen, "Effects of Transportation Infrastructure on Grizzly Bears in Northwestern Montana," *Journal of Wildlife Management* 69, no. 3 (2005): 997.
25 Stephen Herrero, "The Eastern Slopes Grizzly Bear Project and Science-Based Grizzly Bear Conservation," in *Biology, Demography, Ecology, and Management of Grizzly Bears in and around Banff National Park and Kananaskis Country*, ed. Stephen Herrero (Calgary: Faculty of Environmental Design, University of Calgary), 15.
26 Sonya Z. Pollock et al., "Spatiotemporal railway use by grizzly bears in Canada's Rocky Mountains," *Journal of Wildlife Management* 83 (2019): 1787–99, https://doi.

org/10.1002/jwmg.21750; and A. Gangadharan et al., "Grain spilled from moving trains create a substantial wildlife attractant in protected areas," *Animal Conservation* 20 (2017): 391–400, https://doi.org/10.1111/acv.12336.

27   The Marx quote in full is "Men make their own history, but they do not make it as they please; they do not make it under self-selected circumstances, but under circumstances existing already, given and transmitted from the past." See Karl Marx, *The Eighteenth Brumaire of Louis Bonaparte* (1852), https://worldhistorycommons.org/karl-marx-eighteenth-brumaire-louis-bonaparte.

28   Herrero, ed., *Final Report of the Eastern Slopes Grizzly Bear Project*, vii.

29   See David Garshelis, Michael Gibeau, and Stephen Herrero, "Grizzly Bear Demographics in and around Banff National Park and Kananaskis Country, Alberta," in *Final Report of the Eastern Slopes Grizzly Bear Project*, 26–49, and Stephen Herrero, "The Eastern Slopes Grizzly Bear Project and Science-Based Grizzly Bear Conservation," in *Final Report of the Eastern Slopes Grizzly Bear Project*, 6.

30   Carnivores in general are noted to be fast learners, and it seems that grizzlies learn to select their habitat from their mothers. See Colleen Cassady St. Clair et al., "Animal learning may contribute to both problems and solutions for wildlife-train collisions," *Philosophical Transactions of the Royal Society* B: Biological Sciences 374 (2019), http://dx.doi.org/10.1098/rstb.2018.0050; and Scott E. Nielsen et al., "Does Learning or Instinct Shape Habitat Selection?," *PLOS One* 8, no. 1 (2013), https://doi.org/10.1371/journal.pone.0053721. The information on "The Boss" comes from St. Clair et al., "Animal learning," 4. On how long grizzly bear cubs stay with their mothers, see Charles C. Schwartz, Sterling D. Miller, and Mark A. Haroldson, "Grizzly Bear," in *Wild Mammals of North America: Biology, Management, and Conservation*, ed. George A. Feldhamer, Bruce C. Thompson, and Joseph Chapman (Baltimore: Johns Hopkins University, 2003), 564.

31   Kristoffer Whitney, "Domesticating Nature? Surveillance and Conservation of Migratory Shorebirds in the 'Atlantic Flyway'," *Studies in History and Philosophy of Biological and Biomedical Sciences* 45 (2014): 84.

32   "Situated Knowledge," in *A Dictionary of Human Geography*, ed. Alisdair Rogers, Noel Castree, and Rob Kitchin (Oxford: Oxford University Press, 2013). Online edition.

33   On the "nature fakers" controversy, see Ralph H. Lutts, *The Nature Fakers: Wildlife, Science, and Sentiment* (Charlottesville: University Press of Virginia, 2011) and Lisa Mighetto, "Science, Sentiment, and Anxiety: American Nature Writing at the Turn-of-the-Century," *Pacific Historical Review* 54, 1 (1985): 33–50. John Burroughs' 1903 essay, "Real and Sham Natural History," is reprinted in *The Wild Animal Story*, ed. Ralph H. Lutts (Philadelphia: Temple University Press, 1998), 129–43.

34   *Bear 71*, directed by Leanne Allison and Jeremy Mendes (2021; Ottawa: National Film Board of Canada), film, https://bear71vr.nfb.ca/.

35   Quote is from David Herman, *Narratology Beyond the Human: Storytelling and Animal Life* (New York: Oxford University Press, 2018), 139. Gordon M. Burghardt argues for what he calls a "critical anthropomorphism" in his "Critical Anthropomorphism, Uncritical Anthropocentrism, and Naïve Nominalism," *Comparative Cognition and Behavior Reviews* 2 (2007): 136–38. Marc Bekoff argues that anthropomorphizing makes animal emotions accessible to humans, and doing so doesn't mean

discounting their different points-of-view. He believes it's possible to "biocentrically anthropomorphic." See his "Animal Emotions: Exploring Passionate Natures," *Bioscience* 50, no. 10 (2000): 867.

36 David Herman, *Narratology Beyond the Human: Storytelling and Animal Life* (New York: Oxford University Press, 2018), 139.

37 See spreadsheet entry for F30, 19 June 1995. F30 is also recorded charging vehicles on 10 June 1995 and 1 July 2002.

38 See spreadsheet entry for F30 on 6 July 1997. Also see entries for F30 on 7 July 1995, 14 July 1995, 30 June 2001, 2 July 2001, 3 July 2001, 7 July 2001, and 17 July 2003. In addition, these entries for F46 also record the proximity of F30: 26 June 1997 and 6 July 2001.

39 F30's cubs stayed with her for four years; F46's for five years. We are assuming the proximity of these animals to each other signalled a relationship. It's a valid one, at least according to Stenhouse et. al., who note that bears were seldom close unless they are associating in some way. See Gordon Stenhouse et al., "Grizzly Bear Associations along the Eastern Slopes of Alberta," *Ursus* 16, no. 1 (2001): 37.

40 Stenhouse et al., "Grizzly Bear Associations," 36–37.

41 Stenhouse et al., 36.

42 See footnote 38. In 2001, 30 and 46 and their cubs were together for over a week, from the end of June to early July, far more than the twenty-two hours encounters between female bears were supposed to last.

43 John J. Craighead, Jay S. Sumner, and John A. Mitchell, *The Grizzly Bears of Yellowstone: Their Ecology in the Yellowstone Ecosystem, 1959–1992* (Washington, DC: Island Press, 1995), 205–17.

44 On curiosity in black bears, see Ellis S. Bacon, "Curiosity in the American Black Bear," *Bears: Their Biology and Management*, 4 (1980): 153–57.

45 See spreadsheet entry for F56 for 9 October 1999.

46 For instance, the spreadsheet records that F46 and her cubs were seen in the vicinity of two bull elk and three mule deer on 8 July 1995 and that F30 and her cubs encountered a lone wolf while they were feeding on 8 August 1995. "All stood up and charged as the wolf skirted the group."

47 Richard White, "'Are you an environmentalist or do you work for a living?': Work and Nature," in *Uncommon Ground: Rethinking the Human Place in Nature*, ed. William Cronon (New York: W. W. Norton, 1995), 171–85.

48 The classic example is Val Plumwood, "Human Vulnerability and the Experience of Being Prey," *Quadrant*, March 1995, 29–34. Plumwood tells the story of being attacked by a crocodile while canoeing in Kakadu National Park in Australia.

49 Gary Snyder, "The Girl Who Married the Bear," in *The Practice of the Wild: Essays* (San Francisco: North Point Press, 1990); Catharine McClellan, *The Girl Who Married the Bear: A Masterpiece of Indian Oral Tradition* (Ottawa: National Museums of Canada, 1970); *Conflict Tiger*, directed by Sasha Snow (1997; Bristol: Sasha Snow Film Production); and John Vaillant, *The Tiger: A True Story of Vengeance and Survival* (Toronto: Vintage Canada, 2011).

50 See for instance, *Living with Wildlife*, directed by Leanne Allison (2018; Canmore: Front Range Films).

51 Often interpreted as threatening, standing is an expression of curiosity; it is a way for a grizzly to get a better sense of what is happening. See Stephen Herrero, *Bear Attacks: Their Causes and Avoidance* (New York: Nick Lyons Books, Winchester Press, 1985), 23.

52 F30's ears, as well as her upright stance, suggest she was curious. Like many animals, grizzlies' ears are good indicators of their state of mind. If the ears are back, the bear is indicating aggression. See Herrero, *Bear Attacks*, 219–20.

53 Ryan Tucker Jones, "A Whale of a Difference: Southern Right Whale Culture and the Tasman World's Living Terrain of Encounter," *Environment and History* 25, no. 2 (2019): 185–18.

54 Reflecting on the history of bear research and the power of telemetry to understand the species, biologist Cliff J. Martinka noted, "it seems to me that elusive knowledge provides another value—one of knowing that some mysteries continue to accompany a species of the wilderness." See his "Reflections on the Recent History of Bears," *Bears: Their Biology and Management*, 9, Part 1 (1994): 5.

55 Jamie Lorimer, "Moving Image Methodologies for More-than-Human Geographies," *Cultural Geographies* 17, no. 2 (2010): 252.

12

Spatial Analysis and Digital Urban Animal History[1]

Sean Kheraj

As several of the chapters in this volume illustrate, one of the primary challenges of historical scholarship on animals is making animals visible in historical records. People produce all traditional sources used in historical scholarship.[2] Of necessity, therefore, historians must find animals in the past through the eyes of people who wrote and thought about animals in the past. This is what geographer Chris Philo refers to as "the distorting lenses of historical documents written by humans."[3] Of course, these lenses have significant limits that constrain knowledge about animal histories. Our challenge is to illuminate where animals appear in inherently anthropocentric sources and find traces of animals in the past. Animal history applies an "animal lens" to the past to help reveal new insights and demonstrate the ways in which animals shape history.[4] To do so, however, historians first require methodologies to *see* animals in the past.[5]

Spatial analysis using Geographic Information Systems (GIS) software can be a powerful illuminant for animal history. It can bring animals into the foreground from sources that obscure their presence and influence. This new approach draws on the so-called spatial turn, which in recent years has influenced several subfields of historical scholarship. GIS allows scholars to translate textual spatial data into visual spatial data in ways that can reveal previously undetected and even unsuspected geographic relationships among people, non-human animals, and the ecosystems they share that are not obvious in the original sources. In doing so, GIS operates as more than just a visualization for presentation; it also becomes a tool of analysis.[6]

This chapter provides examples of the use of GIS in the analysis of the spatial relationships between human and non-human animals in nineteenth-century North American urban environments, just as Andrew Robichaud shows in his case study of San Francisco in Chapter 13. It argues that new digital tools and digitized historical resources now available to historians make it possible to yield significant historical insights into human-animal spatial relationships in urban environments through experimentation and simple play with digitized sources. All of this is now possible without the need to rely upon expensive multi-member interdisciplinary teams of scholars and technicians. Individual historians can generate meaningful visualizations and engage in spatial analysis with Web-based GIS tools and digitized historical records. This is possible due to a combination of factors that include the expansion of Web GIS applications, large-scale digitization projects, and crowd-sourced approaches to sharing data.[7]

To illustrate some of the ways in which historians can mobilize GIS and digitized historical sources to enhance the "animal lens" on the past, this chapter explores two case studies. The first case study examines the transformation of butchering regulations in the City of Toronto in the nineteenth century to understand the spatial relationships between urban development and access to butchered meats. The second case study expands the geographic lens on urban animal history to consider the Great Epizootic of 1872–73 and the interconnections among cities and the horses that powered urban transportation systems in nineteenth-century North America. In both case studies, I use ArcGIS Online as a platform for testing hypotheses about historical spatial relations between people and non-human animals in urban environments. This Web-based GIS tool by the spatial software developer Esri offers solutions for integrating digitized historical sources into maps for spatial analysis. It also supports crowd-sourced sharing of spatial data, which allows for iterative knowledge generation as historians build upon the work of other researchers and GIS specialists.

Butchering and Selling Meat in Nineteenth-Century Toronto

Before 1851, the City of Toronto prohibited the slaughter of live animals and the sale of butchered meats anywhere in the city outside of public market buildings. St. Lawrence Market, the city's first public market, was once the only place in the city where one could legally purchase fresh produce, including live animals and butchered meats (see Figure 12.1). Signed on 27 May 1834 by Toronto's first mayor (and future republican insurrectionary), the infamous William Lyon Mackenzie, By-Law 2 first established the rules and regulations that governed the city's public markets. Across fifteen different sections, this lengthy early by-law laid out the rules for the sale of meat and other produce in the city, limiting the sale of meats to licensed butchers.[8]

In a manner that was common in other North American municipalities, Toronto's public market by-law gave the city the power to regulate the sale of meat in order to achieve several goals.[9] First, public market by-laws provided a means to ensure the quality of food products. Market clerks and inspectors could check the products sold in the public market to verify that they had not been adulterated. This provided consumers with a degree of protection against unscrupulous sellers who might mix sawdust into a bag of flour or add weight to a cut of meat in order to raise the price. Second, this by-law offered a measure of protection for public health. The city required licensed butchers to furnish their stalls "with a plentiful supply of good meats" and prohibited the sale of "any unwholesome, stale, emaciated, blown, stuffed, tainted, putrid or measly pork, meat, poultry, or other provision." Third, public market by-laws established licensing fees that provided revenue to the city. Butcher's licenses were valuable, coveted commodities.[10]

Restrictions on the sale of live animals and butchered meats (along with other produce) created spatial relationships within the city that reveal some of the close connections between people and domestic livestock animals in urban environments. In an age before artificial refrigeration and railway deliveries, the urban food supply moved by foot and by hoof. Limiting the sale of butchered meats to public markets thus created geographies of access to food that influenced the development of the city. This chapter shows how GIS can reveal those relationships by mapping the

Fig. 12.1 Diagram of St. Lawrence Market, 1868. Source: By-Laws of the City of Toronto, 1834–1869. Toronto: Henry Rowsell, 1870.

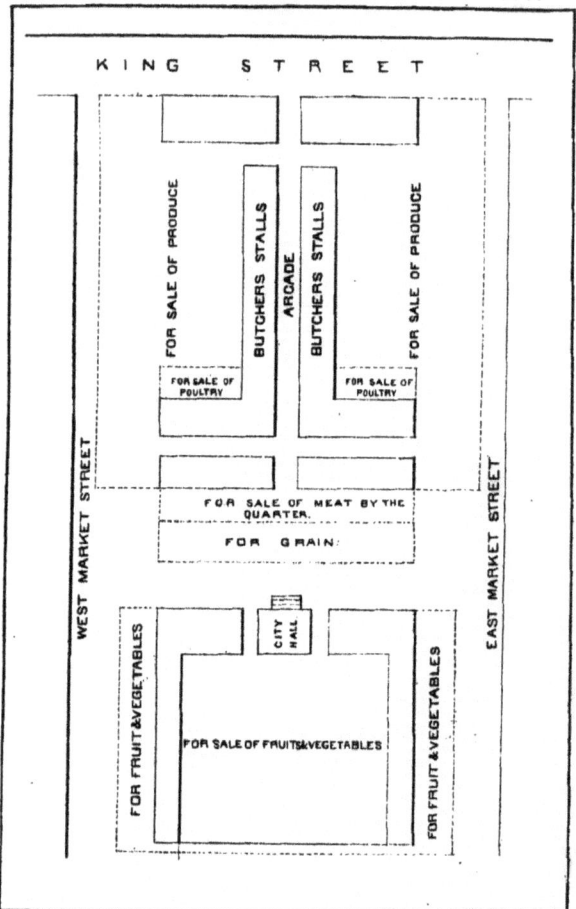

spatial distribution of food in nineteenth-century Toronto, allowing us to see the ways in which animals shaped the city.

For instance, in 1858, there were three public markets in the City of Toronto: St. Lawrence, St. Patrick's, and St. Andrew's Markets. Using circle vector layers with one-kilometre radii laid atop a georeferenced copy of W.S. Boulton's 1858 *Atlas of the City of Toronto and Vicinity*, it is possible see how much of the built-up portion of the city was within a one-kilometre walk from a public market (Figure 12.2). Georeferencing (or GIS rectification) is a process that reshapes a digital image and maps it to real-world coordinates. In this case, a user on ArcGIS Online has taken a digital scan of the 1858 atlas and altered its dimensions in GIS software to correspond with real-world coordinates of the streets and landmarks of the City of Toronto. In doing so, the one-kilometre radii vectors show which parts of the built-up city were within a relatively short walking distance from each public market. The most densely built-up neighbourhoods fall within a one-kilometre radius of at least one public market and imply a correlation between urban development and access to food. The map reveals that residents who lived in the sparsely settled areas north of College Avenue and west of Yonge Street lived furthest from the three public markets. The 1858 Boulton map shows this part of the city to have much less development.

The process of generating such a map even just a few years ago was considerably more labour intensive. A combination of improved Web-based GIS software, historical digitization projects, and data-sharing now make it feasible for solo researchers to compile such spatial visualizations in relatively short order. The underlying historical map was originally compiled and surveyed in 1858 by William Somerville Boulton and Henry Carew Boulton. This was the first large-scale map to depict the built environment of the City of Toronto.[11] Toronto Public Library scanned a high-resolution PDF copy of the thirty-sheet atlas, which is available to the public in its online catalogue.[12] In November 2017, an ArcGIS Online user georeferenced the image files of this atlas using ArcGIS desktop software and uploaded the georeferenced images as a sharable layer in ArcGIS Online, ESRI's Web-based version of its GIS platform. The three vectors with one-kilometre radii shown in Figure 12.2 were measured using the measurement tool in ArcGIS Online and laid atop the georeferenced map, which was inserted from the searchable database of shared layers. What would have once required a collaborative team of historians and GIS technicians to produce is now readily accessible to individual historical researchers to generate such maps for experimentation with spatial representations of different forms of historical data. In this example, the result shows what parts of the built-up portions of the city were within

Fig. 12.2 Map of one-kilometre radii from public markets in Toronto, 1858. Map Credit: Sean Kheraj, adapted from W.S. Boulton, *Atlas of the City of Toronto and Vicinity*, 1858.

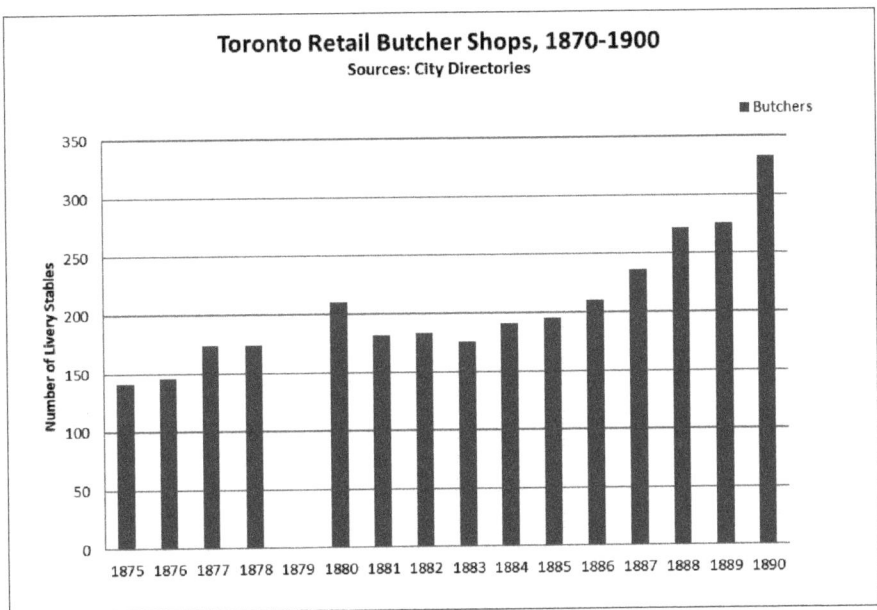

Fig. 12.3 Number of retail butcher shops listed in city directories in Toronto. Sources: Toronto City Directories, 1875–1890.

walking distance to access live and butchered animals for food. The results help to support the hypothesis that there was a relationship between urban development and pedestrian access to meats.

Online GIS tools can further be used to explore how those spatial relationships between Toronto residents and access to both live and butchered animals changed over the nineteenth century. In 1851, the City of Toronto liberalized its public market regulations to permit the slaughtering of animals at facilities elsewhere in the city, and in 1858, the city began licensing butcher shops outside of the public market buildings. The result of this change in policy was an explosion of butcher retailing across the city. Figure 12.3 shows the number of butcher shops listed in city directories from 1875 to 1890. These directories contain spatial data about the distribution of butcher shops in the form of street addresses, but those data are difficult to interpret unless they can be mapped. Once again, ArcGIS Online's repository of shared layers provides individual historical

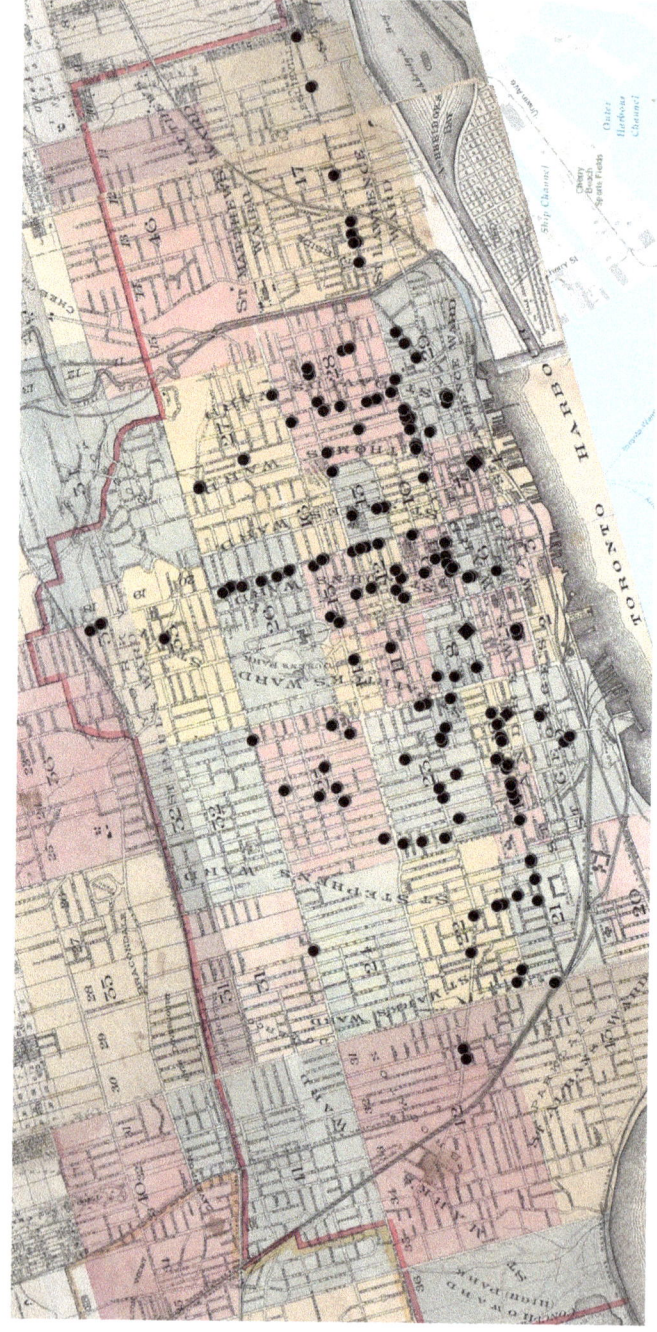

Fig. 12.4 Map of butcher shop locations in Toronto, 1890. Map Credit: Sean Kheraj; adapted from Charles E. Goad, *Insurance Plan of the City of Toronto, Ontario*, 1890.

researchers simple tools to begin to analyze spatial data to determine how butcher shops were distributed across Toronto in the past.

Figure 12.4 shows the locations of all butcher shops listed in the 1890 city directory. Once again, Toronto Public Library has digitized all the city directories in its collection for the period from 1833 to 1969, making this freely available on its website.[13] Each place marker is mapped to the address shown on a georeferenced copy of an 1889 fire insurance atlas of Toronto. This georeferenced resource was similarly uploaded by a user and deposited in the shared repository.[14] In this instance, geographers from the Department of Geography at University of Toronto scanned and georeferenced a copy of the original atlas from Toronto Public Library as part of the Georia Project, a joint initiative of l'Université Laval and University of Toronto. The Georia Project's long-term goal is to coordinate georeferenced databases of environmental, social, and health-related data in Canada "into on-line geographical information systems (GIS) that can be used by researchers and educators alike."[15] The process of plotting each place marker from the addresses listed in the 1890 directory is as easy as dropping a pin on Google Maps. The user can annotate each place marker too, which allows for additional historical context and referencing of source material. In this example, the interactive version of this map allows users to click on each point to see the name of the shop owner and the precise street address, as it appeared in the directory.[16]

As a tool of analysis, this spatial visualization reveals insights into the shifting landscape of animals, food, and transportation in nineteenth-century Toronto. When the city liberalized its regulations concerning butcher shops, the geography of access to butchered meats changed. Butcher shops appear to have spread rapidly in the period between 1875 and 1890 throughout much of the city, beyond the more limited setting of the three public markets. GIS allows historians to test theories about such spatial relationships. Figure 12.5 adds street railway routes to the map to test the hypothesis that butcher shop locations and transit were related. Visual analysis suggests that, as with other retailers, butchers tended to be located along the city's main street railway routes, particularly along Yonge Street and Queen Street, two of the earliest developed routes.

In summary, the GIS visualizations shown in Figures 12.2–12.5 partially illuminate one form of historical human-animal relation. I was able

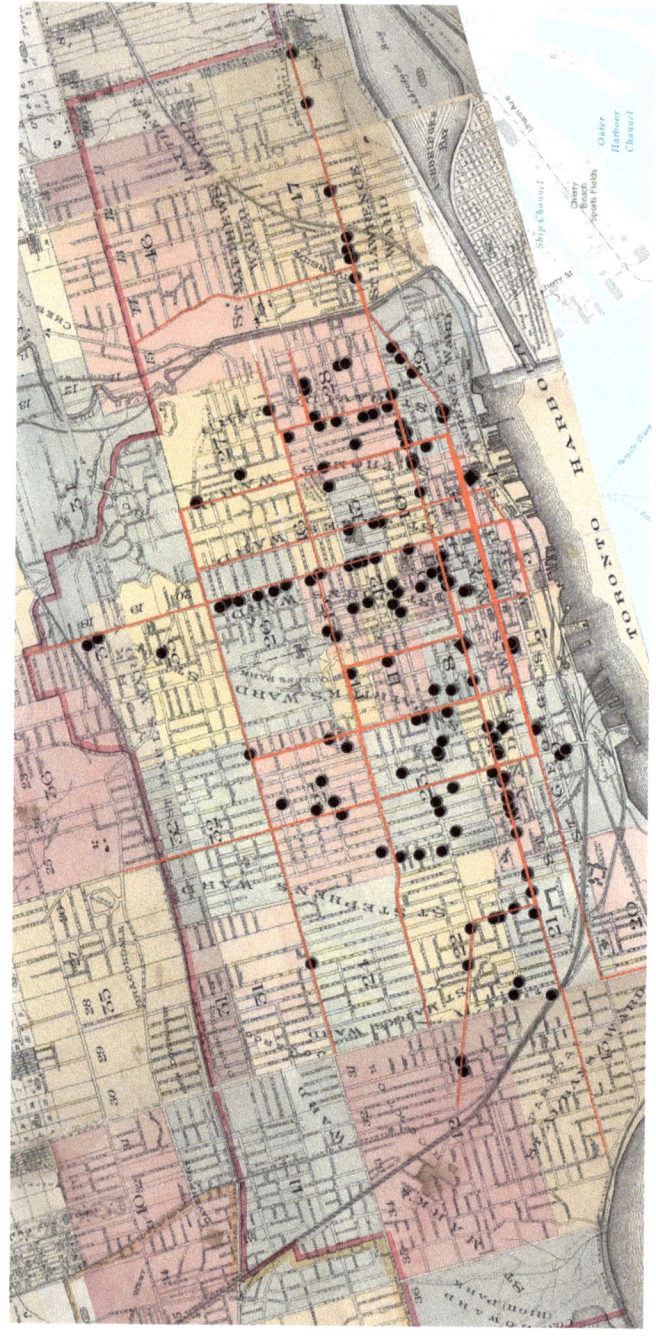

Fig. 12.5 Map of butcher shop locations in Toronto and street railway routes, 1890. Map Credit: Sean Kheraj, adapted from Charles E. Goad, *Insurance Plan of the City of Toronto, Ontario*, 1890.

to generate each map as a sole researcher to test hypotheses and analyze textual historical data in visual form. I am also able to share my maps and add my layers to the shared database for other researchers to use. Web-based GIS applications provide tools that remove the need for more complicated and resource-intensive computing software and hardware. The integration of shared resources in the ArcGIS Online platform allows users to leverage georeferenced digitized maps from other historical digitization projects. In doing so, the platform opens new possibilities for a wider range of historical researchers interested in exploring other aspects of the spatial relationships between people and non-human animals.

Reconstructing an Epizootic

The examples above show how historians of urban animals can use GIS to illuminate human-animal relations from historical documents at the scale of one city. The same tools can also highlight human-animal relations at the broader scale of urban networks. As the growing body of global scholarship in urban animal history has well established, industrializing cities of the nineteenth century were multi-species environments shaped, at least in part, by the exploitation of livestock animals for food and labour.[17] As Clemens Wischermann and Philip Howell claim, "the history of cities should now be unthinkable from the perspective of humans alone."[18] By the 1870s, these animals (and the supplies needed for feeding and sheltering urban livestock) also moved among cities in urban networks connected by railways. That movement of livestock and supplies linked the urban ecosystems of cities across North America, from Montreal to New York City to San Francisco.

No historical case study shows this better than the Great Epizootic of 1872–73.[19] In October 1872, an unknown illness struck the urban horse population of Toronto. According to firsthand reports, nearly every horse in the city appeared to be affected. Many believed the disease to be a virulent form of equine influenza. Within weeks, the disease spread to all major cities in the northeastern United States and Canada. By late winter 1873, horses in nearly every city in Canada and the United States had been affected by the epizootic. The Great Epizootic brought cities to a standstill as the sickness incapacitated hundreds of thousands of horses. Even though most horses survived, the temporary suspension of horse labour halted intra-urban transportation, including street railway services and the delivery of goods. The epizootic stranded commuters and left goods piled up at wharves and railway stations. It was made starkly clear how crucial horses were to the functioning of industrial cities in nineteenth-century North America.

But the Great Epizootic also revealed that the ecologies of North American cities were interconnected via animals and railways. Web-based GIS tools, shareable layers and GIS datasets, and large-scale digitization of historical newspapers make it feasible to visualize and analyze these spatial relationships among cities, horses, and railways. Figure 12.6 shows a map of every city in which horses were incapacitated by the Great Epizootic and the railway networks that connected Canadian and US cities. An animated version of this map shows the movement of the epizootic as it spread outward from Toronto (Figure 12.6).[20]

To create such a map, I analyzed an enormous digital archive of historical newspapers from several different collections. In Canada, there are many digital newspaper archive collections. However, the record of digitized historical Canadian newspapers is incomplete, fragmented, and difficult to access.[21] Canada lags behind the US, UK, Australia, and New Zealand in the digitization of historical newspapers.[22] There are few national newspaper digitization initiatives. Instead, most digitization projects focus on single newspapers or small collections of regional newspapers. Nearly all digital historical newspaper collections of Canadian newspapers are only available via paid subscriptions. Yet there are some significant collections that are freely available from public archives, libraries, and universities.[23] Digitized historical newspapers from the United States are more readily available. Substantial national collections from Library of Congress and private genealogy research companies cover newspapers from most regions of the US.[24] The newspaper record provides some of the best evidence to recreate the path of the Great Epizootic because they document when the symptoms of the disease became widely observable in the public. Each place marker on the animated map includes information about the approximate date that reports of widespread illness among horses appeared in newspapers from each city. Altogether, the map includes data from more than 480 newspaper reports and shows the arrival of the Great Epizootic in 164 cities between October 1872 and September 1873.

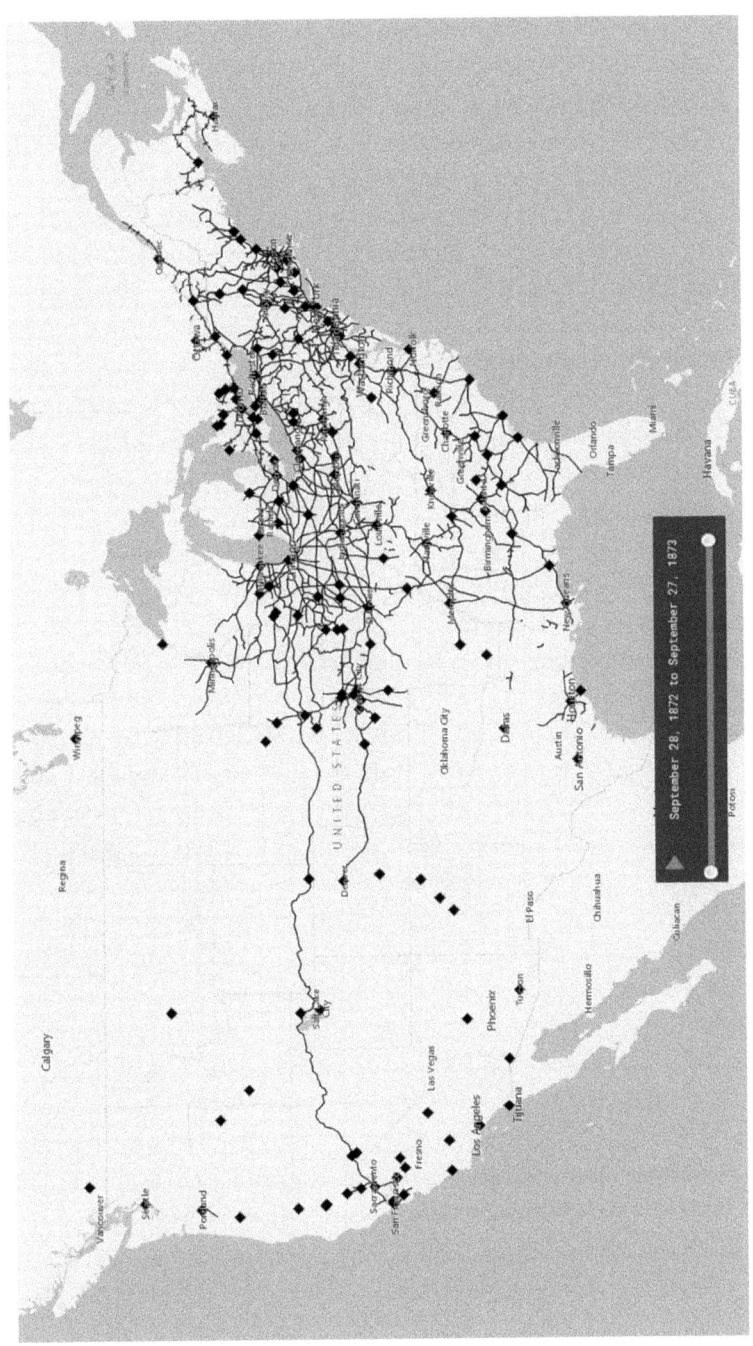

Fig. 12.6 Map of cities affected by the Great Epizootic of 1872–1873.

Once again, ArcGIS Online enabled the creation of this map and animated visualization. The simple place-marker tool (used to mark the locations of butcher shops in Figures 12.4 and 12.5) was used to annotate a base map of North American cities to indicate which cities had been affected by the epizootic and when the disease was first publicly observed. ArcGIS Online allows users to add a date-time field to make a historical GIS layer that is "time-enabled."[25] Such a GIS layer can then be added to a Web application template called "Time Aware" that animates GIS datasets by using the date-time field and a time slider.[26] For each city affected by the epizootic, the date-time field indicates the approximate date that reports first documented observations of symptoms among horses in the city. Both the place-marker tool and the "Time Aware" Web application template are relatively simple to use and do not require large-scale research teams.

To compare the movement of the epizootic shown in the time-enabled place marker layer of affected cities with the railway system, I added shared layers of historical GIS datasets of North American railways to the map. An ArcGIS user added a layer representing the railway network in the US in 1870 to the shareable database of layers in ArcGIS online. The dataset for this layer was created by a digital history project based at University of Nebraska, Lincoln, led by William G. Thomas III, Richard Healy, and Ian Cottingham called "Railroads and the Making of Modern America." This multi-authored digital history project "aims to collect and make available a wide array of materials to shed light on the ways Americans experienced the railroads in the nineteenth century."[27] By making their dataset open-source, it was available to be integrated easily into the time-enabled map of the movement of the Great Epizootic. A second layer featuring Canadian railways was created and shared by ESRI Canada Ltd. based on data derived from several historical atlases of Canada.[28] The addition of these two shared layers allows for comparative spatial analysis of the relationship between the movement of the epizootic and the North American railway system in the 1870s. Both historical railway GIS datasets were the products of multi-member digital history projects intended to share data to facilitate future research (much like Georia). The result is that these open, shared GIS datasets combined with Web-based applications make it possible for solo historical researchers to test theories and observe spatial relationships among people, non-human animals, and cities even on a continental scale.

Creating a time-enabled map of the movement of the Great Epizootic in a historical GIS tool like ArcGIS Online illustrates yet again how GIS can illuminate human-animal relations found in historical documents. Like the injection of a fluorescent dye into the bloodstream to highlight blood vessels for medical analysis, GIS highlights spatial and temporal data, making human-animal relations visible in ways that could not be accomplished solely by textual analysis of historical documents. The hundreds of newspaper reports that documented the arrival of the epizootic in Canadian and US cities in 1872–73 contain data about movement and time that cannot be seen unless it is mapped and animated. In doing so, the GIS visualization demonstrates how animal disease flowed through the urban network in a single common ecosystem. Horses working on the streets of Toronto could get sick and eventually infect horses on the streets of Oakland.

The application of GIS as a tool for studying the Great Epizootic not only adds broader scale to the "animal lens" for historians, but the use of time-enabled animation offers a way of observing change over time, fundamental to all historical analysis. The results produced unexpected findings that changed prior understandings of how this disease outbreak moved throughout North America. For instance, at the outset, I had expected to find out where and when the disease crossed the international border from Canada to the US. However, the evidence in the animation revealed that this was not a single event in a single place. Instead, the disease crossed back and forth across the border at least five times passing from Canada to the US and back into Canada at different points along the enormous border between these two countries.

Limits of GIS for Spatial Analysis in Urban Animal History

The examples above show exciting potential for the use of GIS in visualizing and analyzing historical spatial relationships among people and non-human animals in cities. The use of such powerful mapping tools, however, comes with certain caveats and cautions. GIS can be used as an effective tool of analysis for understanding spatial relationships and the shared datasets available to researchers make the use of GIS much easier than ever before. Interpreting spatial meaning from historical texts using GIS still requires skill, patience, and a critical eye. It also requires basic digital literacy and understanding of the processes (and limitations) of digitization of historical records.

Fundamental critical analysis skills are necessary for the evaluation of any shared datasets and GIS layers. When working with a repository of datasets like that available in ArcGIS Online, researchers must carefully choose sources from reliable and credible authors (as they would with the selection of any secondary research materials). Because the ArcGIS repository is open for any user to upload data, verifying the quality of the data is vital. In the examples above, I have tried to use datasets from credible academic research teams and GIS specialists. Basic research skills for evaluating quality and authenticity of sources then can allow animal history researchers to leverage the advantages of crowdsourced data sharing.

Transforming historical documents into digital objects and GIS visualizations also raises questions about how far researchers should go when manipulating data for analytical purposes. Robert Sweeny warns, "the act of warping abstracts the map from its original context. GIS rectification is one of the many ways that historical sources are made to be compatible with computers. It is a process . . . that facilitates ahistorical thinking; it can also allow us to see what might not otherwise be visible." Sweeny argues that GIS can remove documents from their historical logic. By this he means both the specific conditions under which a source was produced and the circumstances by which the source survived and was preserved into the present. Moreover, in the case of animal history, the logic of the sources is inherently anthropocentric. GIS can illuminate animals in the past, as I have argued here, but it may also obscure the human-centric vision of the sources themselves and the archival conditions under which they were kept as they are transformed from text to digital visualization. In the example in Figure 12.4, the map includes digitized and georeferenced copies of the plates of an 1890 fire insurance atlas for the City of Toronto. The place markers that sit atop that layer are a georeferenced representation of data from a digitized copy of a city directory. These documents were not originally meant to be used in this manner. Digitization and GIS make them legible to a computer and open possibilities for observing one form of human-animal spatial relationship. But this process also decontextualizes the fire insurance atlas and city directory from their own, independent historical logics. Fire insurance atlases were tools of trade for documenting and tracking insurance liability. City directories were commercial products and vehicles for advertising. Neither source was originally intended to reveal insights into how people and non-human animals shared space in the city. Choosing such sources and removing them from their original contexts might obscure omissions and silences in the sources. City directories capture geospatial data about animal trades in urban environments (dairies, butchers, tanners, livery stables, etc.), but they do not capture aspects of the place of animals in the informal economy of cities. Butcher shops were one place that residents of Toronto accessed fresh meat, but some urban dwellers still kept livestock in the city in the 1890s and slaughtered animals in their homes. Fresh meat could still be traded among neighbours in ways that are not captured in sources meant to represent the formal economy. And yet when cross-referenced using GIS, historians can, as Sweeny notes, see what might not otherwise be seen. Given the ongoing challenge of finding non-human animals in inherently anthropocentric sources, this kind of digital manipulation may be worthwhile, but it should be used carefully with a complete understanding of its limits and potential for misrepresenting the past.

In order to leverage new digital mapping tools and understand their limits, historians must possess at least some basic digital literacy skills. As Ian Milligan and others have warned, the revolutionary shift to digital information and online dissemination has meant that historians must acquire and teach new digital skills. "This does not mean abandoning traditional research methods," Milligan contends, because "historians will long continue to be masters of close reading and parsers of nuance and context—but it does mean that new skills to better contextualize and understand digital material are needed."[29] The resources used in the maps above do not consist of the impossibly large scale of the Web archives Milligan sees as a future challenge for historical researchers, but they do include the ever-growing archive of digitized historical documents available on the Web. Historians need some knowledge and understanding of the digital skills necessary to make use of that archive, including GIS skills.

While it is true that digital history scholarship often demands interdisciplinary collaboration, historians must also acquire the capacity to engage directly with digital tools in order to yield the full analytical benefits of a tool like GIS. Douglas Seefeldt and William G. Thomas see digital history scholarship requiring "interdisciplinary collaboration, the likes of which most historians have yet to embrace; cooperative initiatives that involve historians, programmers, information architects, designers, and publishers."[30] But historians cannot gain the same meaningful insights from GIS without direct engagement with the process of building digital maps; they cannot outsource that work entirely to technicians. Playing with digital maps, manipulating digitized documents, and conducting ad hoc experiments to test theories and hypotheses, I argue, are part of the analytical process enabled by GIS. It is akin to the ideas of William J. Turkel and Devon Elliot concerning "humanistic fabrication." They find that, "the present conjuncture—of making as a new social movement, of easy-to-use and freely available platforms that invite modification, of detailed online instructions for doing just about anything—makes it almost costless for historians and other humanists to research, teach, learn, play, and experiment with new technologies."[31] This is also true of GIS technologies. ArcGIS Online is one of a handful of new Web-based digital mapping tools that allow for the kind of play and experimentation that Turkel and Elliot argue can be applied to material production using 3D printing technologies. As the examples above show, playing with digitized sources using GIS can help make animals in the past visible to historians in new ways.

Play, in this instance, takes the form of an experiment to test a theory or hypothesis. In the examples above, the final outcome of each spatial visualization was not predetermined. Instead, they were the result of guessing, wondering, and then visualizing. What did the landscape of butcher shops in Toronto look like after the liberalization of public market bylaws? Can I see any relationship to the street railway system if I add another layer to the map? If I place time-aware markers on a map, can I see how the Great Epizootic spread from city to city? Will it show me when and where the disease crossed the international border? Tests, corrections, and iterations drive the process of using GIS as a tool for seeing animals in the past.

Conclusion

In his often-cited essay "Why Look at Animals?," John Berger acknowledges an immutable distance between people and non-human animals. An animal's "lack of common language, its silence, guarantees its distance, its distinctness, its exclusion, from and of man."[32] For the historian, that distance also spans the depths of time. To know animals in the past almost seems more impossible than knowing them in the present.

The most significant limit to the use of GIS for exploring historical human-animal relations remains that silence and the anthropogenic character of the sources themselves. In translating historical documents into digital objects and spatial visualizations, it is possible to see a version of animals in the past, but the illumination GIS provides merely casts different angles of shadows on thoughts, ideas, and language that people in the past used to interpret and understand animals. These digital tools must be used with a critical eye so as not to lose sight of the underlying evidence, which consists of fragments of human thought.

Still, GIS has much to offer animal history. In bringing human-animal relations to the surface of sources that relegate animal to the margins, GIS provides historians with new ways of seeing what might not otherwise be observed. By better understanding the relationships between people and non-human animals in space, we might learn more about how those relationships changed over time.

NOTES

1. The author would like to thank Jennifer Bonnell and Sandra Swart for their comments and feedback on this chapter. He is also grateful to all the participants of the "Traces of the Animal Past" conference held at York University in November 2019.
2. Beyond traditional textual sources, animal historians may also consider what Etienne Benson calls "material-semiotic traces of the past," a similar concept to the embodied sources produced by animals themselves that Sandra Swart describes in her chapter in this volume. See Etienne Benson, "Animal Writes: Historiography, Disciplinarity, and the Animal Trace," in *Making Animal Meaning*, eds. Linda Kalof and Georgina M. Montgomery (East Lansing: Michigan State University Press, 2011), 3–16.
3. Chris Philo, "Animals, Geography, and the City: Notes on Inclusions and Exclusions," *Environment and Planning D: Society and Space* 13 (1995): 677.

4   Joshua Specht, "Animal History After Its Triumph: Unexpected Animals, Evolutionary Approaches, and the Animal Lens" *History Compass* 14, no. 7 (2016): 328.

5   It is important to note that in this chapter, GIS analysis and techniques tend to privilege the visual over other senses. Indeed, the preceding paragraph is replete with references to sight, lenses, and vision as metaphors for generating knowledge about animal history. As other chapters in this volume show, however, sight is one among other senses that scholars use to generate new knowledge about animals and history. Sandra Swart (Chapter 1), in particular, points to some promising ways in which sound, touch, and even smell could inform analysis and interpretation of animal bodies as sources.

6   Jennifer Bonnell and Marcel Fortin, "Introduction" in *Historical GIS Research in Canada*, ed. Jennifer Bonnell and Marcel Fortin (Calgary: University of Calgary Press, 2014), xi; Richard White, "What is Spatial History?," The Spatial History Project (February 2010), https://web.stanford.edu/group/spatialhistory/cgi-bin/site/pub.php?id=29; Anne Kelly Knowles, "GIS and History," in *Placing History: How Maps, Spatial Data, and GIS are Changing Historical Scholarship*, ed. Anne Kelly Knowles (Redlands, CA: ESRI Press, 2008).

7   The examples of the use of GIS in historical urban animal history in this chapter rely on ArcGIS online, a commercial Web GIS product developed by Esri. Free, open source solutions are available from other developers, such as Geographic Resources Analysis Support System (GRASS), QGIS, System for Automated Geoscientific Analyses (SAGA) GIS, and others.

8   City of Toronto Archives (hereafter CTA). By-Law 2, "An act to regulate the Public Markets," May 27, 1834.

9   For more on the role of public markets in early North American cities, see Helen Tangires, *Public Markets and Civic Culture in Nineteenth-Century America* (Baltimore: Johns Hopkins University Press, 2003).

10 Tangires, *Public Markets and Civic Culture.*

11 Isobel Ganton and Joan Winearls, *Mapping Toronto's First Century, 1787–1884* (Toronto: Royal Ontario Museum and University of Toronto Library, 1984); "1858 WS Boulton: Atlas of the City of Toronto and Vicinity," Historical Maps of Toronto, accessed August 18, 2019, http://oldtorontomaps.blogspot.com/2013/01/1858-ws-boulton-atlas-of-city-of.html.

12 The catalogue listing for the PDF scan of this atlas can be found at https://static.torontopubliclibrary.ca/da/pdfs/912_71354_b594_br_fo_oss.pdf.

13 "Digital Toronto City Directories," Toronto Public Library, accessed September 25, 2019, https://www.torontopubliclibrary.ca/history-genealogy/lh-digital-city-directories.jsp.

14 "1889 Goad Insurance Plan of the City of Toronto" ArcGIS Online, accessed September 23, 2019, http://arcg.is/1bOnuT0.

15 "Georia: Georeferenced Databases for Accessing Historical Data", accessed September 23, 2019, http://mercator.geog.utoronto.ca/georia/home.htm.

16 To access an interactive version of Figure 12.4, visit: https://arcg.is/1qrCWq.

17 There now exists a broad international scholarship in urban animal history that highlights the degree to which industrialized cities were built to support livestock

husbandry and accommodate populations of a common assemblage of domestic livestock animals including cows, horses, pigs, and chickens. Some prominent examples include Andrea Gaynor, *Harvest of the Suburbs: An Environmental History of Growing Food in Australian Cities* (Crawley: University of Western Australia Press, 2006); Clay McShane and Joel Tarr, *The Horse in the City: Living Machines in the Nineteenth Century* (Baltimore: Johns Hopkins University Press, 2007); Peter Atkins, ed., *Animal Cities: Beastly Urban Histories* (Farnham: Ashgate, 2012); Catherine McNeur, *Taming Manhattan: Environmental Battles in the Antebellum City* (Cambridge: Harvard University Press, 2014); Sean Kheraj, "Urban Environments and the Animal Nuisance: Domestic Livestock Regulation in Nineteenth-Century Canadian Cities," *Urban History Review/Revue d'histoire urbaine* 44, nos. 1–2 (Fall/Spring 2015/2016): 37–55; Dean, Ingram, and Sethna, eds., *Animal Metropolis*; and Frederick L. Brown, *The City Is More Than Human: An Animal History of Seattle* (Seattle: University of Washington Press, 2017); scholars of contemporary urbanization have reached similar conclusions to the historical scholarship using a framework that blends urban studies and animals studies that Tora Homberg calls "zoocities" in *Urban Animals: Crowding in Zoocities* (London: Routledge, 2015).

18 Clemens Wischermann and Philip Howell, "Liminality: A Governing Category in Animate History," in *Animal History in the Modern City: Exploring Liminality*, ed. Clemens Wischermann, Aline Steinbrecher, and Philip Howell (London: Blomsbury, 2019), 1.

19 For a complete account of the Great Epizootic of 1872–73 and its effects on urban environments and horses, see Sean Kheraj, "The Great Epizootic of 1872–73: Networks of Animal Disease in North American Urban Environments" *Environmental History* 23, no. 3 (July 2018): 495–521.

20 An animated version of this map is available at bit.ly/greatepizootic.

21 Sean Kheraj, "Canada's Historical Newspaper Digitization Problem, Part 2," Active History, http://activehistory.ca/2014/02/historical-newspaper-digitization-problem/.

22 Richard A. Hawkins, "Digitised Newspapers" *Historical Insights: Focus on Teaching* (February 2011), https://www.advance-he.ac.uk/knowledge-hub/historical-insights-digitised-newspapers.

23 The largest digitized Canadian newspaper collections available by paid subscription include ProQuest's historical newspapers, Early Canadiana Online's periodical collection, and Newspapers.com. Some public archives, libraries and universities collections include the digital magazine and newspaper collection at Bibliothèque et Archives Nationales du Québec, the *British Colonist* collection from University of Victoria, the Simon Fraser University digitized newspaper collection, and Island Newspapers by the Robertson Library at University of Prince Edward Island. The most comprehensive index of digital historical newspaper collections in Canada is "Digitized Newspapers and Magazines" compiled by Kiera Mitchell, Brandi Adams, and Donica Belisle, accessed September 27, 2019, https://www.donicabelisle.com/digitizedhistoricalperiodicals.

24 For this map, I made extensive use of "Chronicling America" a mass newspaper digitization project of Library of Congress and GenealogyBank.com, a large private genealogy company that offers an extensive digitized historical newspaper

collection with access by paid subscription. See "Chronicling America" at https://chroniclingamerica.loc.gov/.

25 In order to activate the date-time field, users must first publish their layers as "Featured Layers."

26 For more information about Time Aware, visit https://arcg.is/0u1b9i.

27 "Railroads and the Making of Modern America: A Digital History Project," accessed September 27, 2019, http://railroads.unl.edu

28 "US Railroads 1870" ArcGIS Online featured layer, accessed September 27, 2019, http://arcg.is/08DTP00; "Canadian Historic Railways," ArcGIS Online featured layer, accessed September 27, 2019, http://arcg.is/1O0D4a.

29 Ian Milligan, *History in the Age of Abundance? How the Web Is Transforming Historical Research* (Montreal: McGill-Queen's University Press, 2019) 7.

30 Douglas Seefeldt and William G. Thomas, "What is Digital History?" *Perspectives on History* (May 2009), accessed October 18, 2019, https://www.historians.org/publications-and-directories/perspectives-on-history/may-2009/what-is-digital-history

31 William J. Turkel and Devon Elliot, "Making and Playing with Models: Using Rapid Prototyping to Explore the History and Technology of Stage Magic" in *Pastplay: Teaching and Learning History with Technology*, ed. Kevin Kee (Ann Arbor: University of Michigan Press, 2014), 176.

32 John Berger, *About Looking* (New York: Pantheon Books, 1980), 6.

13

Visualizing the Animal City: Digital Experiments in Animal History[1]

Andrew Robichaud

"Where did the cows go?" This was the seemingly trivial question that emerged as I stared at a computer screen that displayed a map our small research team had just created showing the locations of animal industries in nineteenth-century San Francisco. It was a question that unfolded a series of questions, and it was a pivotal moment in a research process that ultimately led to important findings about urban development, politics, and everyday life in nineteenth-century American cities.

To know where something happened is to begin a process of inquiry and exploration that may lead to an understanding of why and how it happened. Over the course of several years, from 2010 to 2015, I began an extended process of inquiry into where animals lived in San Francisco through a series of digital mapping and visualization projects. At times, the project felt like a fool's errand; at other times, mapping and visualization enabled moments of discovery that would not have been possible otherwise. Mapping and visualizing the animal city became an important way that I processed research for a dissertation and book project on urban animal life in nineteenth-century America. The visualizations ultimately led to several research breakthroughs, the publication of three online pieces, and important findings that would ultimately become part of the book *Animal City: The Domestication of America*.[2] This essay outlines some of the main contours of that research at the Stanford Spatial History Project and suggests how this type of digital and spatial history might be useful to other scholars of animal history, and to historians more broadly—particularly those working in areas where sources are limited or appear to be limited.[3]

The research for the book *Animal City* began with a relatively simple set of questions: What did nineteenth-century cities look like in their human and animal compositions? What can exploration of those changing environments tell us about environmental, urban, political, and social history more broadly? Other historians had blazed a trail in the field of animal history—largely a subfield of environmental history, but also coming from cultural, social, and intellectual history.[4] Some historians had already pointed to the centrality of animals in nineteenth-century cities, which contained a wide range of domesticated, semi-domesticated, and undomesticated species.[5] Charles Dickens described the "gentlemen hogs" he encountered throughout New York City in 1842, and countless other writers and artists depicted nineteenth-century American street scenes with cows, pigs, dogs, and other non-human animals at the centre of urban life.[6] In 2002, Theodore Steinberg summarized and built on some of the early literature of urban animals in a chapter called "Death of the Organic City" in *Down to Earth: Nature's Role in American History*.[7]

The descriptions offered by Steinberg and others—including Dickens—were enough to spark my imagination, but not enough to satisfy my curiosity. The picture of the animal city was incomplete. To say that semi-domesticated hogs, dogs, cattle, cows, and sheep inhabited nineteenth-century cities only gave the broadest outlines of what must have been a vivid (and pungent) reality of how humans and animals lived and interacted in cities. I wanted to spend more time on those city streets—in the alleyways, basements, and urban lots, and in the backyards, stockyards, and slaughterhouses, where animals lived and died. What was the experience of living in these cities? What were the conflicts that played out? What traces of this animal past still remain in our urban landscapes?

Uncovering this urban animal past also led to a clear question of change over time: What happened? What ultimately became of these animal cities and the many species that were once part of urban life? What happened from the time of Dickens (with his all-too-visible hogs) to the time of Upton Sinclair (with his largely invisible cows, pigs, stockyards, and slaughterhouse workers)? There was evidence of massive urban animal change, but no clear or complete explanation of what happened and why. Soon, it became clear that Americans had engaged in a complex remaking of their urban environments. Transformation of cities came not merely in the *subtraction* or restriction of particular species and animal businesses, but also in the *addition* of a growing set of relationships with animals that included pet ownership, animal entertainment, and zoos.[8] The transformation of the nineteenth-century animal city was, in many ways, about something greater, too: urban residents were at the forefront of new and modern landscapes and combinations of human-animal interactions.[9]

Since the "Animal City" Spatial History Lab project launched in 2010, there has been a wave of animal history scholarship—including several important and fascinating works on animals in nineteenth-century cities, which emphasized the significance of animals in understanding a wide range of urban, social, political, and environmental changes.[10] Additionally, a flurry of several new publications emphasized the importance of nineteenth-century animal protection and humane movements, and the political and cultural dimensions of Humane Societies and Societies for the Prevention of Cruelty to Animals, which actively and forcefully remade human-animal relationships in nineteenth-century cities.[11]

Seeing the Animal City

Historians seeking sources on the animal past face distinctive challenges, the most obvious being that animals leave no first-hand accounts of their experiences. They do not keep diaries or records, or write letters and memoirs that fill archives. This is to say nothing of the opacity of their very experiences living in the world—and our limited capacities as humans to understand those experiences—a topic that we humans will debate endlessly.

Nevertheless, sources on the presence, conditions, and experiences of many animals in nineteenth-century America are pervasive in more traditional sources, though these sources must be read cautiously and critically. There are ample travel accounts that describe urban animal populations, along with paintings, photographs, and sketches of features of the animal city. There are countless newspaper articles about nuisances and conflicts that arose because of animals in cities. There are court cases, public records of city and state governments, and records of numerous agencies and organizations tasked with policing various aspects of animal life and death in nineteenth-century cities (health departments, city pounds, parks departments, and SPCAs).[12]

But there were also many sources that seemed at first unusable, or of limited utility. What, for example, could be done with the hundreds of entries of animal businesses in San Francisco city directories? As I pored over the long lists of names and addresses in the Crocker-Langley city directories from the late 1800s, I could get a sense of the scale of the horse economy in San Francisco: hundreds of businesses listed under the categories "Horse Shoers," "Horse Clippers," "Bitters," "Stables," "Feed Stores," "Hay and Grain" stores, and more.[13] The directories also contained lists of businesses related to sheep ("Wool Pullers," "Wool Manufacturers," "Wool Graders and Packers," etc.), with other sources suggesting that live animals were likely present at some of the sites. There were milk cows at many of the city's "Milk Dealers" and "Wholesale Dairies," and livestock at many "Wholesale Cattle," "Wholesale Sheep," and "Wholesale Hog" businesses. Ultimately, these sources charted a human-centred commercial economy that was far from comprehensive in accounting for animal life. But the sources nevertheless contained valuable (though imperfect and incomplete) information on where animals lived and died in the city. What more could be done with this dense and flat collection of names and addresses? How could it be brought to life for historical scholarship?

The Stanford Spatial History Project (SHP) was essential in shaping how I came to think about these sources. With an existing interest in historical geography and environmental history, I was already accustomed to thinking spatially. But the intellectual community at the SHP cultivated an environment of collective intellectual exploration. In 2009, I was part of an experimental course called "Spatial History," taught by a team of historians and digital specialists who worked at the SHP.[14] A key part of the course was a collaborative group project that required learning basic skills in ArcGIS and Tableau. Students were supported by several staff members at the SHP lab space, which included a half dozen computers and appropriate software.

More than anything, spatial history became a way of seeing sources—a lens that I began to use to think about the possibilities of archival sources. Sources just needed a name, a date, and a location to be mappable—and once mapped, previously invisible spatial and temporal patterns might become visible; distances, densities, and networks could potentially be measured and analyzed. There was a sense of experimentation that came from this sort of inquiry—and that sense of experimentation was a stated purpose of SHP projects. An ideal project was not merely an "illustration" or a visualization of something that was already known, but instead should contain some degree of experimentation and some attempt to "see" sources in ways previously impossible. In this sense, a good data visualization could effectively *create* new sources for a historian to analyze, launching a dialogue or an iterative process of inquiry within a larger research project.[15]

City Directories

City directory data contained all three elements of a possible mapping project, along with an experimental quality of not knowing what our maps would ultimately look like. In an initial independent research project (with the help of SHP lab staff), I was able to map city butchers from 1860–1900—leading to a short online article about the transformation of San Francisco's butchering, livestock, and slaughtering landscapes over the course of those decades.[16] Though modest in scale, the project convinced me that if I could map the tens of other animal industries in San Francisco, I might get closer to *seeing* and understanding some of the geographical nuances and trends in urban animal life in nineteenth-century San Francisco. Did animal businesses cluster in certain parts of town? And how did these geographies compare to one another and change over time?

But the city directory data would first need to be entered and refined, and that was no small task. The Animal City project launched with a single undergraduate research assistant (RA) working about five hours per week on data entry (funded through a modest Stanford undergraduate research opportunity fund). The initial tasks for the RA were straightforward: enter the city directory data for each animal business into an excel spreadsheet that included the business name, the type of business, the year(s) it was active, and the addresses listed. Once we had addresses, the whole set could be processed through a free online geocoder that would create latitude and longitude points that we could then plug into ArcGIS and Tableau. (As Sean Kheraj's essay in this collection suggests, this process has become significantly easier over the past few years.)

But nineteenth-century addresses were not necessarily modern-day addresses. For example, 950 Brannan Street in 1870 might not be 950 Brannan Street in 2012. We had to pay attention to where and when the city made changes to its street numbering systems—information that was printed in the front matter of city directories. Some nineteenth-century addresses needed to be converted into twenty-first-century equivalents, and this took time. Furthermore, some addresses were vague (i.e. "Foot of Scott"), which required further research into topography, historical context, and sometimes an educated estimate to assign a point on a map. Figuring this out took some time, additional research, and data refinement, but ultimately it was a surmountable obstacle. Like any act of historical scholarship, mapping was also an act of interpretation, an attempt at objectivity in the face of sometimes-imperfect information.

But the payoff of mapping soon started to appear, even if finalized visualizations were far in the future. Even as we were refining data, we could already begin to see discernible spatial patterns in the distribution of animal industries that suggested some underlying patterns of urban human and non-human animal life. Butchers clustered near Mission Creek in the 1860s, then abruptly shifted farther south to Islais Creek after 1870, while a growing number of wholesalers began listing downtown "office" addresses. The wool industry clustered south of Market Street, near the wharves and depots where industrial goods changed hands—but also not far from the new slaughterhouse district known as Butchertown. The most spatially expansive features of the urban animal economy were those businesses related to horses, which spread out in a wide network across the developed city. The animal city was coming into sharper focus through mapping—and it was increasingly clear that there was not one animal city, but multiple animal cities.

But like any exercise in abstraction or representation, mapping could also mislead and obscure. For one, animal businesses were only one facet of urban animal life. They did not account for households that had one or two cows or pigs, or for small-scale or informal businesses not listed in city directories. What about the personal stable of a wealthy San Francisco gentleman? Or the cart mule of an Italian market farmer?[17] Furthermore, through mapping itself, the very uncertainty of our data was revealed. For example, city directories did not contain clear definitions of "Milk Dealers." The maps we made showed "Milk Dealers" occupying a geography that suggested that most did indeed have cows, but we could also safely assume (in the context of other sources) that a "Milk Dealer" in the heart of San Francisco's financial district was an office and did not have a herd of cows on site. The sources we had were primarily describing a human economy, and not necessarily the lives of animals. The maps we made (like any source) had to be critically and carefully read. Once mapped, we had to continue to read the sources against the grain, but they were now in visual form.

But what stood out from the maps we created were the clusters of "Milk Dealers" on the suburban fringe—sites that seemed likely to be actual dairy farms with cows. Even more, these fringe "Milk Dealers" appeared to be migrating over time.

It was the changing geography of these semi-suburban "Milk Dealers" that captured my attention. In particular, I noticed that, beginning in the 1880s, dairies in certain fringe parts of the city began migrating southward and westward—moving out of the neighborhoods in the eastern and northern parts of the city (the Potrero, the Mission, and Cow Hollow), and moving to neighbourhoods farther south (Figure 13.1). "Where were the cows going, and why?" Perhaps something was happening in the 1880s and 1890s to account for these geographic shifts, but what? City Directories tipped me off to the apparent movement, but could not explain why it was happening. More than providing a set of complete answers, mapping raised a new set of questions that I could then take back to other archival sources. In this sense, mapping animal industries was not so much an end in itself, but was instead part of an unfolding research process. It did not replace traditional research, but simply helped highlight certain questions.

Indeed, as I looked more closely at newspapers and laws from the 1880s and 1890s, I began to see stricter rules and enforcement of urban dairy practices. In the 1880s, the city government began cracking down on

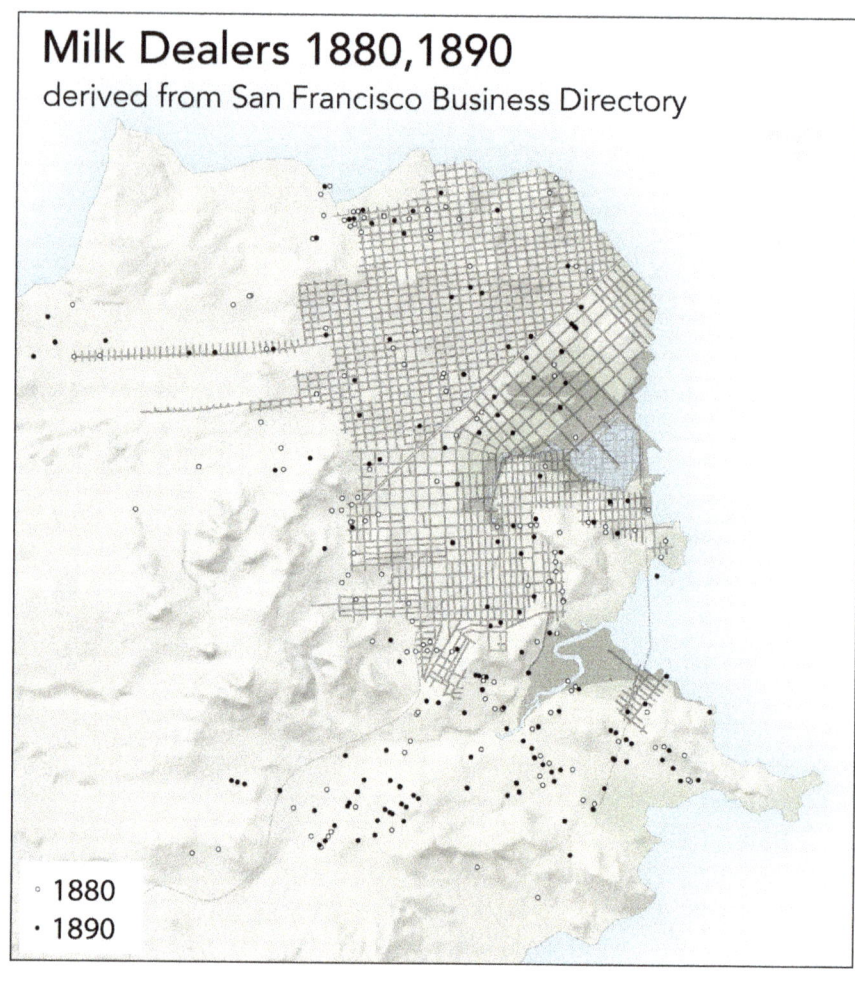

Fig. 13.1 Milk Dealers in San Francisco. Image and cartography by Erik Steiner, with research assistance from Liz Fenje, Stanford Spatial History Project.

small-scale urban dairies—particularly those that used the marshy grasslands of Islais Creek in the southeastern part of the city. Islais Creek was an expansive brackish marsh—one of the few wet, green, and grassy parts of San Francisco. But in the 1880s, San Francisco's city officials became increasingly concerned about the pollution filling the creek and marshes. As it turned out, the contamination of the creek and the adjoining marshes was part of another set of animal transformation in the city. In the 1870s, the city had ordered the removal of the slaughterhouses, hog ranches, stockyards, and tanneries to the southeastern shores of the city—a part of town that would become known as Butchertown. By the 1880s, the pollution from these animal industries was wreaking havoc on Islais Creek and the expansive marshes.[18]

The pollution of the creek had wider social implications. Since at least the 1870s, the grasslands around Islais Creek had been used as cow pastures, particularly for small-scale dairy farmers—most notably Italian immigrants. The pollution of the creek—combined with an apparent aversion to the immigrant farmers themselves—animated city officials to prohibit grazing cows in the marshes. In the 1890s, the city hired a full-time milk inspector, who spent his days on armed patrol, and who focused much of his enforcement on the grasslands around Islais Creek. The city also began a process of widely expanding what was called the "Two-Cow Limit" farther south, to encompass the Islais marshes (see Figures 13.2 and 13.3).[19]

The crisis over the Islais Creek cows revealed an interconnected web of animal life, death, and decay in the city, which came under greater governmental control and scrutiny in the 1890s. Would I have discovered this important phase of regulation had it not been for the mapping? Perhaps. But I might not have looked so closely. Mapping the dairy industry offered me a hint that there were big changes in urban dairy production in the last two decades of the 1800s, and refocused my attention on important periods and places of change. But, ultimately, it was more traditional sources and methods that explained and contextualized that change. In turn, the maps themselves—the changing geography of dairy production—also evinced the force of city policies.

City Ordinances

As the Two-Cow Limit suggests, there were also animals in city ordinances. But, like city directories, the data was flat and seemingly abstruse. Take, for example, the city's spatial restrictions on slaughterhouses. In 1864, a San Francisco ordinance prohibited residents from keeping more than five swine or slaughtering animals within an area delineated as follows:

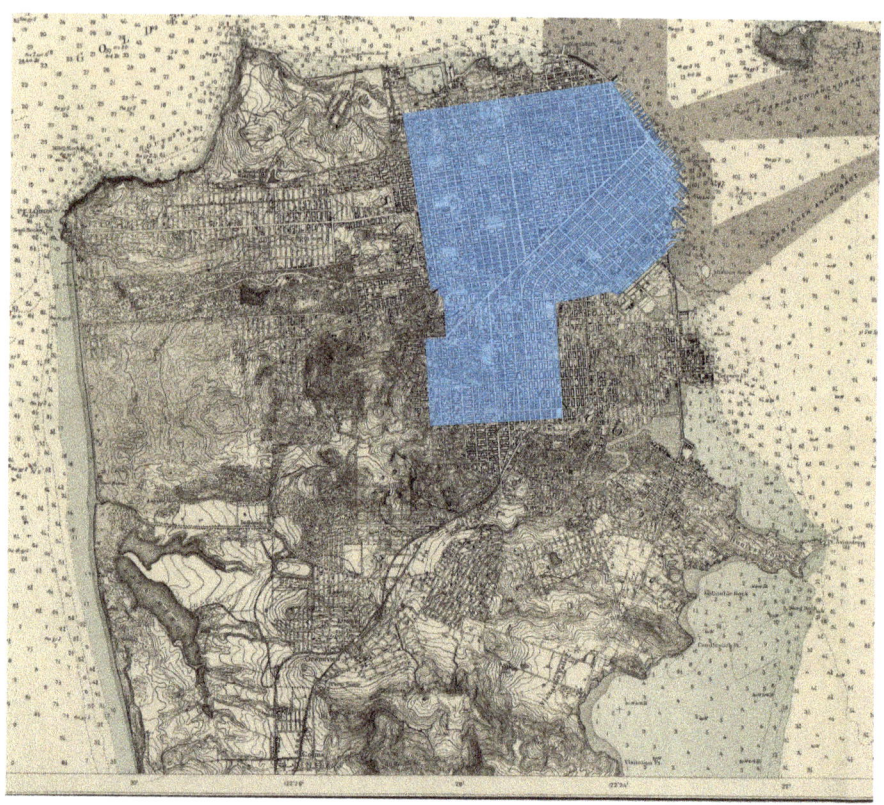

Fig. 13.2 and 13.3 Visualizations of San Francisco's "Two-Cow Limit" in 1887 (left) and 1905 (right). The Two-Cow limit allowed residents to keep no more than two cows in the area mapped in blue (with some additional restrictions). In 1910, the city extended the "Two-Cow Limit" to encompass the entire city and county of San Francisco. Liz Fenje and Mark Sanchez, Stanford Spatial History Project.

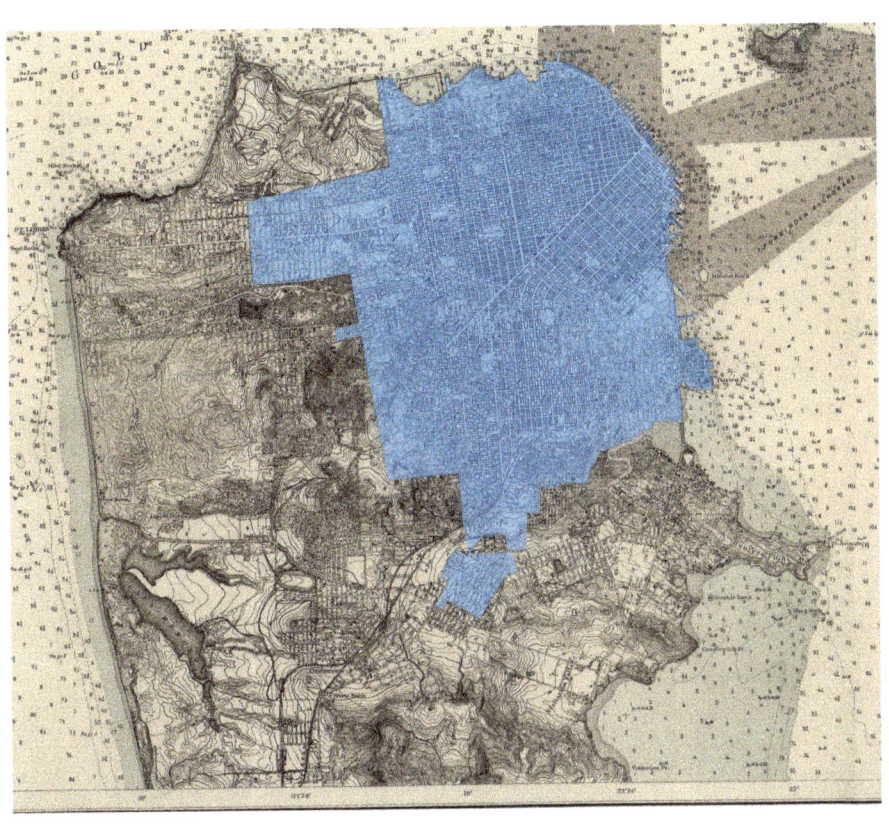

> Beginning at a point at the intersection of the Bay of San Francisco with the west line of Divisadero street; thence south along the west line of said street to its intersection with Ridley street; thence along the south line of Ridley street to Castro street; thence along the westerly line of Castro street to its intersection with the Charter line of 1851 of the City of San Francisco thence easterly along said Charter line to the deep waters of the bay of San Francisco.[20]

The ordinance was a jumble of words with little discernable meaning without visualization.

Like the dairy industry, the geographies of slaughterhouses, hog ranches, and stockyards were shifting, too. This was visible not only in city directories, but also in the growing number of municipal ordinances. Visualizing and mapping these early forms of zoning might offer a better understanding of how city officials were thinking about regulation, urban space, and urban development. To visualize these laws was relatively simple, but was nevertheless revealing of important shifts in how city officials were thinking about urban space, planning, and development. In this case, we had a sense of what mapping the laws would reveal; it was no big surprise what would come out of these visualizations. But the visualizations were a more direct and powerful form of communication—a *visual argument* that could more effectively express a trend than words, sentences, and paragraphs alone.

Tracing the evolution of slaughterhouse space also revealed an important shift in how city officials were thinking about animal nuisances, urban environments, and urban development. This became clear only through mapping. The early ordinances from the 1850s and early 1860s showed what was effectively a "negative space"—slaughterhouses could not exist in certain densely inhabited parts of the city. Over the 1850s and early 1860s, those ordinances continued to expand that negative space outward from the city centre. But in 1866, something shifted. The shape of the slaughterhouse space changed to create a confined and secluded area of dense animal populations and slaughterhouses. In 1870, the city confined the slaughterhouses even further, to a thirty-six-block area on the southeastern coast of the city, which opened up larger tracts of undeveloped land as part of a vision of permanent urban growth.[21]

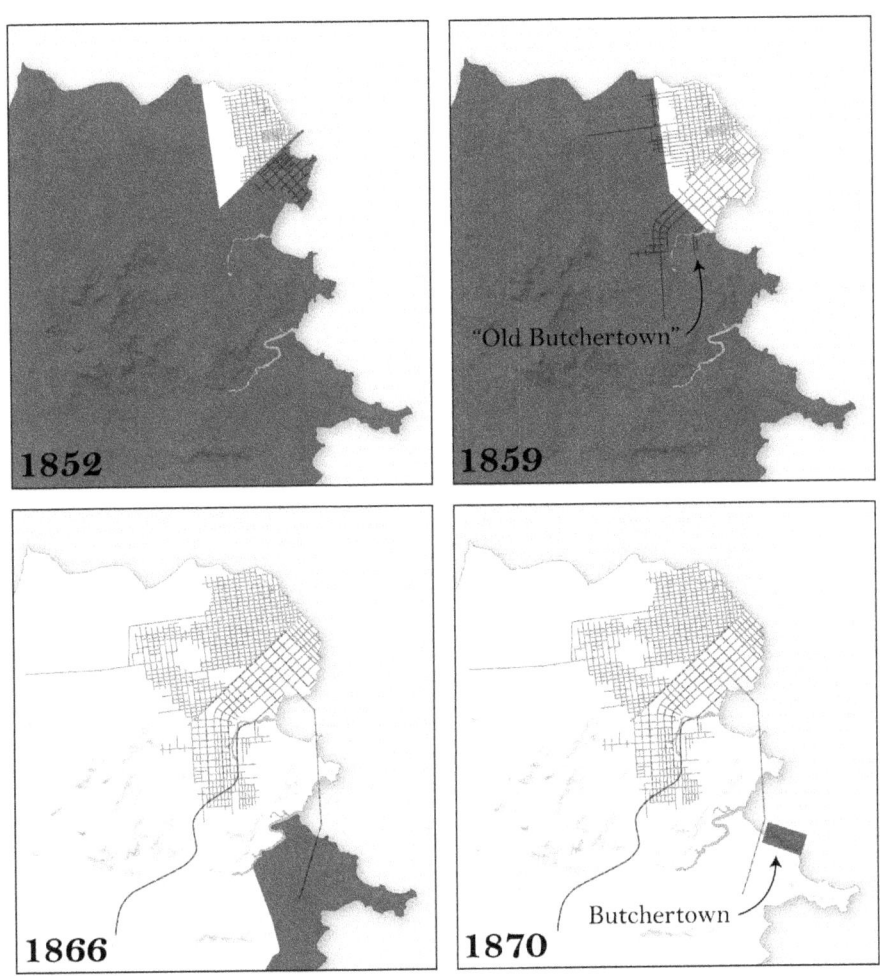

Fig. 13.4 Areas of permissible slaughter, according to San Francisco city laws. Visualizing these laws offered a powerful visual argument about the transformation of slaughterhouse and livestock landscapes in San Francisco. Image and cartography by Erik Steiner, with research assistance from Liz Fenje, Stanford Spatial History Project.

13 | Visualizing the Animal City   303

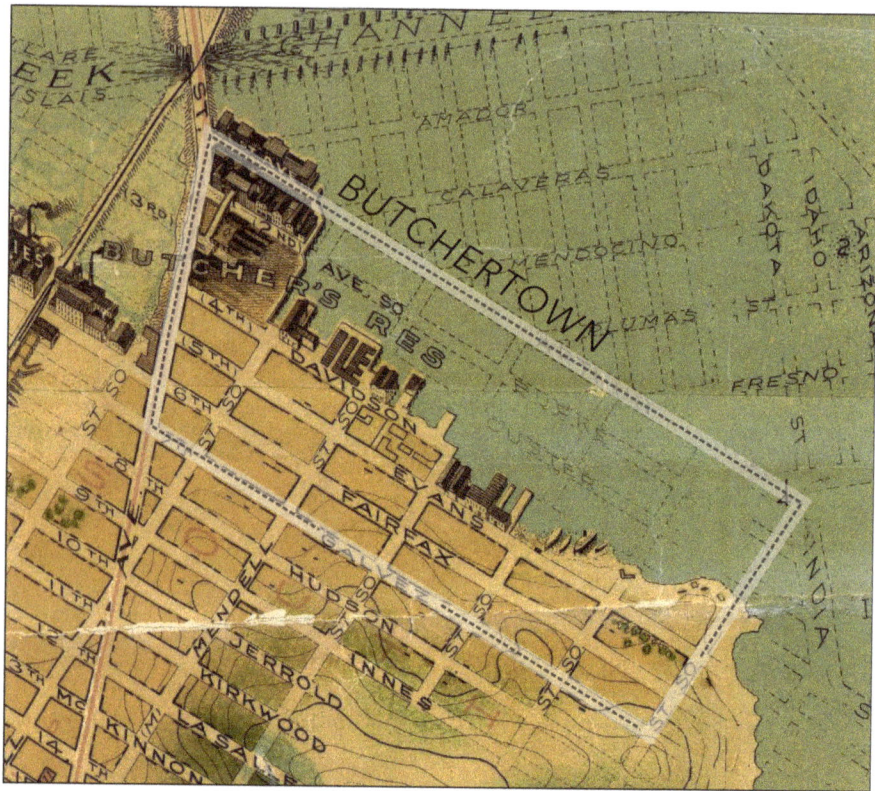

Fig. 13.5 The "Butchers' Reservation" (commonly known as "Butchertown") is shown here overlaid on this 1911 map. Map detail from August Chevalier, "The 'Chevalier' Commercial, Pictorial and Tourist Map of San Francisco From Latest U.S. Gov. and Official Surveys" (1911), courtesy of David Rumsey Map Collection. Cartography by Erik Steiner, Stanford Spatial History Project.

But the new slaughterhouse space was also designed to effect a certain environmental relationship. The 1870 "Butchers' Reservation" (Butchertown) appears in city ordinances as an area confined by a specific set of street names. Visualizing the extent of Butchertown using a map that showed the city's shoreline revealed an important feature of the space: half of Butchertown existed in the shallow waters of the San Francisco Bay. City officials sought to establish a particular form of environmental relationship between the slaughterhouses and the San Francisco Bay that would create a lasting and permanent solution to the slaughterhouse nuisance. But the waters of the San Francisco Bay could not keep up with the new scale of industrial waste, creating a new pollution problems that lasted into the twentieth century and beyond.

Animal Law Enforcement

Another important development in nineteenth-century urban animal life was the widespread establishment of Societies for the Prevention of Cruelty to Animals (SPCAs)—cultural, political, and legal institutions that first emerged in the United States in major American cities. San Francisco had been among the first SPCAs founded in the United States—established in 1868, only two years after Henry Bergh established the first American Society for the Prevention of Cruelty to Animals in New York City. In San Francisco, I had the good fortune of encountering an unprocessed and previously unused collection of San Francisco SPCA (SFSPCA) archival materials that had recently been gifted to the San Francisco Public Library. Within that collection were the bound diaries of San Francisco SPCA officers. These were law enforcement agents whose primary work was enforcing the expanding set of anti-cruelty laws in San Francisco, beginning in the 1870s. For historians of animals, these collections are valuable sources for understanding urban animal life, along with social relationships that were also being policed.

The officer diaries testified to the powerful police and law enforcement powers of SPCAs in the nineteenth century. Like many SPCAs, the San Francisco SPCA was an active and powerful corporation that acted as law enforcement and, effectively, as an extension of state government.[22] The SFSPCA ultimately employed a full-time officer to police the city, and the SFSPCA was legally entitled to collect whatever fines the court assessed for trial convictions. Those agents kept detailed diaries describing their daily activities and routes through the city—where they had made arrests, issued warnings, or simply observed animal suffering.

The diaries contained a wealth of spatial data embedded in the officers' daily accounts, often pointing to specific places where animals were found abused or suffering. But in certain ways, the diaries were also incomplete: they did not have reliable details about arrests or specific infractions—and they made no mention of prosecutions or legal outcomes. That information was, however, contained in a separate volume of "Prosecution Records," which was devoid of spatial data. Combined, these sources could be used to create some sense of the geography of law enforcement and arrests, which would offer a fuller picture of how the SFSPCA's power was exerted in real space. Were laws enforced evenly across parts of the city? Were the slaughterhouses and stockyards as policed as the horse stables and downtown streets? Were certain human and animal populations and geographies more or less surveilled and policed?

Tracing out and mapping every route would have been effectively impossible for our small research team at the Spatial History Project—and probably not worth the protracted and tiresome effort. But tracing out a sample of routes was possible—and we could focus on the routes that we knew had the greatest legal impact: those that resulted in prosecutions. A research assistant used the prosecution ledger to locate specific names and dates that could be matched with specific routes in the officer diaries. Using a feature of Google Earth, the research assistant then traced out the agent route as it was described in the diary. Those geocoded routes could then be overlaid on a map to show the routes of nearly two hundred cases that resulted in prosecutions. The map would give us a strong sample of where officers had travelled and exerted police power within the city of San Francisco.

The results from this visualization were somewhat surprising. The routes showed a density of enforcement routes in downtown San Francisco—near city markets where horses transported goods from market farms, and also in residential districts north of Market Street where families lived. There was also concentrated enforcement in some of the more industrial parts of town south of Market Street, and near the rail depots and wharves where horses carried heavy loads and where some livestock were unloaded from boats and trains and driven south to Butchertown. What was more informative, perhaps, was where SFSPCA officers *did not* travel, based on the sample of routes we mapped. In this particular sample, there was no trace of SFSPCA officers setting foot in and around Butchertown—where thousands of animals lived and died in the stockyards, hog ranches, and slaughterhouses. Why? Was the SFSPCA simply not interested in the cattle, pigs, and sheep in and around Butchertown, or in the milk cows and livestock that inhabited the city's suburban areas?

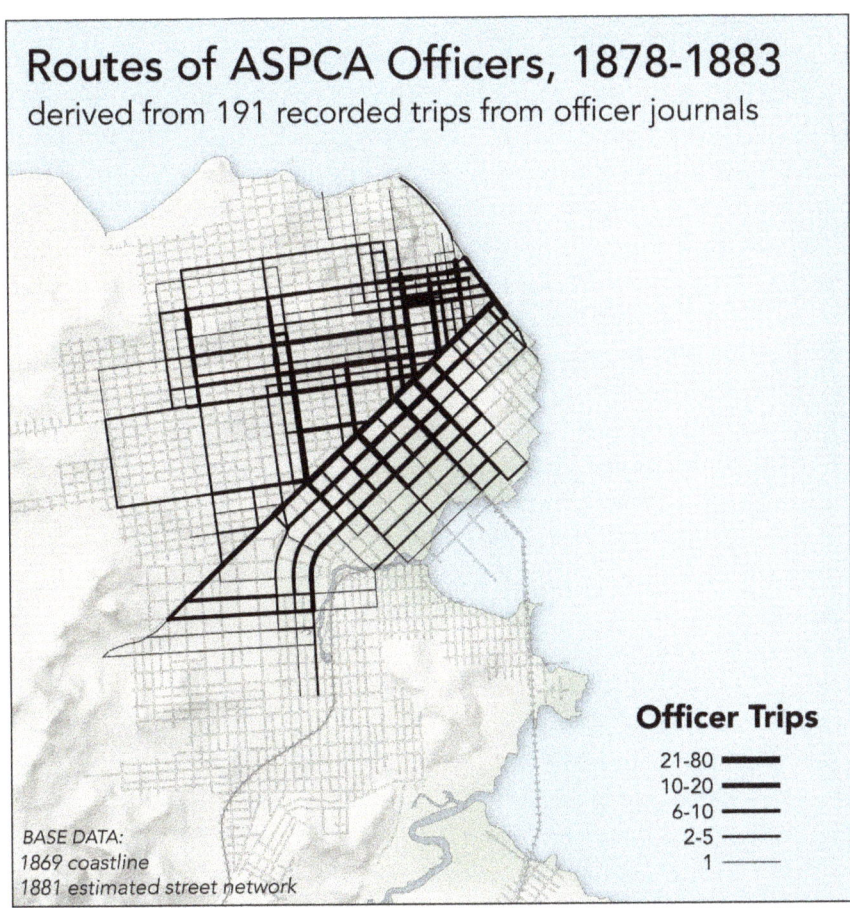

Fig. 13.6 This visualization was created using a sample of routes from cases that led to prosecutions from 1878–1883. This visualization allowed us to see the geographic extent and concentration of animal law enforcement. Research by Mark Sanchez and cartography by Erik Steiner, Stanford Spatial History Project.

This question of why the SFSPCA was so spatially limited ultimately became another research question that mapping posed but did not itself answer. Additional research revealed that there were a few practical limitations to the geography of SFSPCA enforcement. First, as officers made greater numbers of arrests, they were forced to appear as witnesses in court on most mornings. A trip to Butchertown required at least several hours—and often a full day for travel and observation. A second factor was that because the SFSPCA depended on fines collected from successful prosecutions, they favoured enforcing laws that would lead to this outcome. In short, there was less money to be made in Butchertown, where personal fault for animal suffering was often less easy to discern and prove. There were other reasons for the spatial limitations on SFSPCA power, but the intentional, legally made invisibility and distance of Butchertown was a key limitation when it came to enforcing laws. Increasingly, the geography of animal law enforcement overlapped significantly with human populations and the overlapping geography of horses in the city. Overwhelmingly, SFSPCA arrests related to the suffering of equine residents (and their human owners and observers) in downtown San Francisco.

In considering animal welfare as a means of social control, there was another part of town where I expected to see heavy SFSPCA presence, but where it was visibly absent: Chinatown. Our maps showed agents patrolling around the edges of Chinatown, but rarely within it. Prosecution and enforcement records also showed few Chinese names. The reason for the absence of the SFSPCA's presence in Chinatown is hard to pin down with any certainty. In some ways, the SFSPCA (which was largely—and probably entirely—white) seemed mostly uninterested in reforming Chinese practices when it came to animals. Perhaps reformers saw Chinese San Franciscans as beyond the circle of civilization that partly defined animal welfare movements of the period. Perhaps Chinatown was already under such heavy police surveillance that the SFSPCA did not see it necessary to police there.[23] Perhaps Chinese San Franciscans owned few horses and pets, which were increasingly the focus of SFSPCA officers.

But there is also some evidence to suggest that many SFSPCA members had a prevailing (though certainly condescending and demeaning) sympathy for Chinese immigrants—that many in the organization in fact sought to improve the wider treatment of Chinese San Franciscans, in part by reforming human relationships with animals. This came as many white Americans otherized and dehumanized Chinese immigrants more broadly, often comparing them to animals. Where Chinese San Franciscans do appear in SFSPCA records, they are at times objects of sympathy, not unlike the horses, dogs, and other animals the Society actively policed.

In one case, a San Francisco humane organization celebrated a boy who intervened to stop a child from throwing stones at a Chinese man.[24] This act of mercy stood in contrast to the wider, prevailing anti-Chinese racism and violence across the United States. Ultimately, however, the answer as to why SFSPCA agents did not spend much time in Chinatown remains elusive and perhaps multi-faceted. Nevertheless, mapping agent routes raised the question.

Mapping in these various ways was also useful in thinking about the legacies of nineteenth-century animal spaces. Understanding the geography of nineteenth-century animal landscapes had the potential to explain how certain parts of American cities developed over time, and how these invisible animal landscapes of the past continue to shape the way cities look today. Why was it that the areas devoted to stockyards, slaughterhouses, tanneries, and hog ranches in nineteenth-century San Francisco became an African-American ghetto of the twentieth century? Home Owners' Loan Corporation (HOLC) maps from the 1930s showed that the neighbourhoods in and around Butchertown were redlined—in large part because of their proximity to environmental conditions of concentrated animal life and death. "Occasional winds from the northeast bring obnoxious odors from stockyards and packing plants located in that direction."[25] The same was true of other neighbourhoods adjoining stockyard and slaughterhouse districts in other cities across the country. Nineteenth-century animal industry geographies had lasting effects—evidenced, too, in the property value maps that are now part of online real estate websites, suggesting that this past continues to shape the city and patterns of property values today. Understanding geographies of nineteenth-century animal life also shapes how I walk city streets—something I can now share with students in teaching them how to think about the construction of modern-day urban landscapes.

Conclusions and Questions

Most of the data visualizations from the Animal City project remain unpublished, stowed away in a cloud server. The findings were useful in terms of raising new questions, but the additional labour of refining and publishing them seemed to be daunting and of limited utility. In this sense, digital history might be closer to research that never appears in prose or in footnotes—or writing that is ultimately cut from a final draft. But there are traces of it everywhere. Digital analysis had an important place in building the foundations of the research that ultimately comprised the book *Animal City*—a book of narrative and analytical history that is not obviously built around digital mapping. Digital work informed a more traditional approach to writing and storytelling—scaffolding that was ultimately removed to reveal a structure more familiar to historians.

And though it is "research," digital work in many ways resembles teaching. Each of these projects had social, collaborative, and pedagogical elements. As a "primary investigator," I worked closely with one undergraduate research assistant at a time. For both of the students who worked on this project, digital work was an entry point into a wider inquiry on the topic. Both students sought to read books and articles on the topic, and asked incisive questions that could, at times, open up the research process further. "Why do you think there was a cluster of stables here?" one might ask. On one occasion, a student ventured into San Francisco and stood on the street corner that he had earlier read was the site of a brutal incident of horse abuse. There was multi-directional instruction at every turn—between the student, me, and the lab staff—where each person engaged the project through different forms of labour, knowledge, and expertise, and with varying perspectives that strengthened the whole of the research project. This sort of collaboration is all too rare in historical scholarship, which is usually a lonely and solitary endeavour. As this sort of digital scholarship becomes more manageable for individuals to do alone (as Sean Kheraj's essay in this collection suggests), what, if anything is lost in erasing the social and collaborative nature of digital history?

For all the energetic collaborative work, there were also unexpected challenges and frustrations. Studying the history of animals can be emotionally and mentally exhausting. I had become accustomed to spending my days reading reports of animals who suffered—horses beaten until their skin was raw or bloodied, or driven until they were hobbled or collapsed on the street. There were accounts of cattle with their "eyes punched out," of turtles strung together on their backs and kept alive in holds of ships to be sold alive in New York markets, and of sheep coming off trains and boats, prodded aggressively but unable to stand. As historians, we understand part of our work as bearing witness. But, at a certain point, I had forgotten just how bleak and dismal this animal history could be—and that an undergraduate new to the topic might find it overwhelming. A couple of weeks into a summer research job of recording spatial data from the SFSPCA officer diaries, an undergraduate working on the project told me frankly how distressing it all was. The student had just spent two weeks straight of his summer in Palo Alto reading and recording one case of animal suffering and brutality after another. Understandably, it was starting to take a psychological toll. We backed off and did other work for a while. But the conversation revealed to me an important part of both research and teaching that often goes unspoken: that we ought to be mindful of the heavy mental toll of doing research of any kind that requires the historian to take an unflinching look at the brutality and violence of the past. The violent history of human relations with animals makes animal history particularly vulnerable to such challenges.

In the end, mapping and visualizing aspects of the animal city did not contain a discrete set of answers and conclusions. A map can appear tidy and pat, but its construction and underlying data are messy and filled with human decisions and uncertainty at every turn. The conversion of human and animal lives into zeros and ones, dots on a map, was never a perfect translation. These Animal City mapping projects were as much starting points as ending points. But the process and conversations allowed for an extended meditation on the subject—the sort of long-term, internal processing most historians do—but one that activated visual and spatial thinking, and had social and collaborative components that made it distinct from the verbal, solitary, and intellectual work that dominates so much of traditional historical scholarship. For that reason, the exact payoff of the Animal City project is hard to define in metrics of publications, citations, and footnotes. It was part of a collaborative process of asking and answering questions that ultimately led to more questions and more research. Digital and spatial history never replaced more traditional forms of research or writing, but it did shape that scholarship in ways that were sometimes unexpected. The cows, it turned out, had something to tell when we were willing to pay attention.

NOTES

1. The author would like to thank Sean Kheraj, Jennifer Bonnell, and Catherine McNeur, along with the researchers and staff of the Stanford Spatial History Project—especially Erik Steiner, Jake Coolidge, Mark Sanchez, and Liz Fenje.

2. Andrew A. Robichaud, *Animal City: The Domestication of America* (Cambridge: Harvard, 2019). For the visualizations discussed in this article, please visit: https://web.stanford.edu/group/spatialhistory/cgi-bin/site/project.php?id=1047

3. For spatial history, see Richard White, "What is Spatial History," Stanford Spatial History Project (2010): https://web.stanford.edu/group/spatialhistory/cgi-bin/site/pub.php?id=29. See also Henri Lefebvre, *The Production of Space* (Chicago, Illinois: Blackwell, 1991).

4. For me, some early and influential works in animal history include Harriet Ritvo, *The Animal Estate: The English and Other Creatures In the Victorian Age* (Cambridge, MA: Harvard University Press, 1987), and *The Platypus and the Mermaid and Other Figments of the Classifying Imagination* (Cambridge, MA: Harvard University Press, 1997); Clay McShane and Joel Tarr, *The Horse In the City: Living Machines In the Nineteenth Century* (Baltimore: The Johns Hopkins University Press, 2007); Ann Norton Greene, *Horses At Work: Harnessing Power In Industrial America* (Cambridge, MA: Harvard University Press, 2008); Richard Bulliet, *Hunters, Herders, and Hamburgers: The Past and Future of Human-Animal Relationships* (New York: Columbia University Press, 2005); Jon Coleman, *Vicious: Wolves and Men In America* (New Haven: Yale University Press, 2004); Virginia DeJohn Anderson, *Creatures of Empire: How Domestic Animals Transformed Early America* (New York: Oxford University Press, 2004); Richard White, "Animals and Enterprise," in *The Oxford History of the American West*, ed. Clyde Milner, Carol A. O'Connor, and Martha A. Sandweiss (New York: Oxford University Press, 1994), 237–74. I recognize the importance of the use of "non-human animals" as part of a recognition that humans are, in fact, animals. But for the sake of simplicity, this essay uses the term "animals" in talking about "non-human animals."

5. For example, many urban waste and health histories include elements of animal history. See, for instance, Martin Melosi, *The Sanitary City: Urban Infrastructure in America From Colonial Times to the Present* (Baltimore: Johns Hopkins University Press, 2000); Joel Tarr, *The Search for the Ultimate Sink: Urban Pollution In Historical Perspective* (Akron, OH: University of Akron Press, 1996); and Charles Rosenberg *The Cholera Years: The United States In 1832, 1849, and 1866* (Chicago: University of Chicago Press, 1987).

6. Charles Dickens, *American Notes for General Circulation* (Paris: Baudry's European Library, 1842), 99–102. For visual art, see, for example, Neuville, "Bridewell, and Charity-School, Broadway, NYC 1808; James Kidder, *Boston Common 1829*; Unknown artist, *The Five Points* (painting) (1827), often attributed to George Catlin; Axel Klinckowström, *Broadway and City Hall, New York*, 1820; George Henry Burgess, *A View of San Francisco in 1850* (1878). See also Etienne Derbec and Abraham Nasatir, ed., *A French Journalist in the California Gold Rush: The Letters of Etienne Derbec* (Georgetown, California: The Talisman Press, 1864), 170.

7   Theodore Steinberg, *Down to Earth: Nature's Role in American History* (New York: Oxford University Press, 2002).

8   For pets, see Diane Beers, *For the Prevention of Cruelty* (Athens: Swallow Press Ohio University, 2006); Susan Pearson, *The Rights of the Defenseless: Protecting Animals and Children In Gilded Age America* (Chicago: University of Chicago Press, 2011). For late nineteenth century animal displays and entertainments, see Nigel Rothfels, *Savages and Beasts: The Birth of the Modern Zoo* (Baltimore: Johns Hopkins University Press, 2002); Elizabeth Hanson, *Animal Attractions: Nature on Display in American Zoos* (Princeton, NJ: Princeton University Press, 2002); Susan Nance, *Entertaining Elephants: Animal Agency and the Business of the American Circus* (Baltimore: Johns Hopkins University Press, 2013; Etienne Benson, "The Urbanization of the Eastern Gray Squirrel in the United States," *Journal of American History* 100, no. 3 (December 2013).

9   See John Berger, "Why Look at Animals?," in *About Looking* (New York: Vintage, 1980): 3–28; and Bulliet, *Hunters, Herders, and Hamburgers*.

10 See, in particular, Catherine McNeur, *Taming Manhattan: Environmental Battles in the Antebellum City* (Cambridge, MA: Harvard University Press, 2014), and "The Swinish Multitude," *Journal of Urban History* 37, no. 5 (2011): 639–60; Michael Rawson, *Eden on the Charles: The Making of Boston* (Cambridge, MA: Harvard University Press, 2010); Catherine Brinkley and Domenic Vitiello, "From Farm to Nuisance: Animal Agriculture and the Rise of Planning Regulation," *Journal of Planning History* 13, no. 2 (2014): 113–35; Frederick Brown, *The City is More than Human: An Animal History of Seattle* (Washington: 2016); Jessica Wang, "Dogs and the Making of the American State: Voluntary Association, State Power, and the Politics of Animal Control in New York City, 1850–1920," *Journal of American History* 98 (2012): 998–1024; and Etienne Benson, "Urbanization of the Eastern Gray Squirrel." See also Sean Kheraj, "The Great Epizootic of 1872–73: Networks of Animal Disease in North American Urban Environments," Environmental *History* 23, no. 3 (July 2018): 495–521; and "Urban Environments and the Animal Nuisance: Domestic Livestock Regulation in Nineteenth-Century Canadian Cities," *Urban History Review/Revue d'histoire urbaine* 44, no. 1–2 (Fall/Spring 2015/2016): 37–55; P. J. Atkins, ed., *Animal Cities: Beastly Urban Histories* (New York: Routledge, 2016).

11 Susan Pearson, *The Rights of the Defenseless: Protecting Animals and Children In Gilded Age America* (Chicago: University of Chicago Press, 2011); Janet Davis, *The Gospel of Kindness: Animal Welfare and the Making of Modern America* (New York: Oxford University Press, 2016); Jessica Wang, "Dogs and the Making of the American State: Voluntary Association, State Power, and the Politics of Animal Control in New York City, 1850–1920," *Journal of American History* 98 (2012): 998–1024;

12 San Francisco Municipal Reports, for example, contained annual reports from many of these departments, along with statistics on animals impounded, arrests made, etc. Animal lives are scattered throughout these reports, but not centralized in any one department.

13 For the centrality of the horse in nineteenth-century cities, see Clay McShane and Joel Tarr, *The Horse in the City: Living Machines in the Nineteenth Century* (Baltimore: Johns Hopkins, 2007); Clay McShane, "Gelded Age Boston," *The New England Quarterly* 74, no. 2 (2001): 274–302; and Ann Norton Greene, *Horses at Work: Harnessing Power in Industrial America* (Cambridge, MA: Harvard University Press, 2008).

14 The course was designed and taught by Richard White, Zephyr Frank, and Erik Steiner, with additional training and assistance from Whitney Berry, Mithu Datta, and Kathy Harris.

15 For other digital mapping projects that shaped my thinking of the possibilities of this work, see Brian Donahue, *The Great Meadow: Farmers and the Land in Colonial Concord* (New Haven: Yale University Press, 2004), along with his and other essays in *Placing History: How Maps, Spatial Data, and GIS Are Changing Historical Scholarship*, ed. Anne Kelly Knowles (New York: ESRI, 2008).

16 Andrew Robichaud and Erik Steiner, "Trail of Blood: The Movement of San Francisco's Butchertown and the Spatial Transformation of Meat Production, 1849–1901," Stanford Spatial History website: https://web.stanford.edu/group/spatialhistory/cgi-bin/site/pub.php?id=31.

17 Some of this smaller-scale data was, I was told, kept by the San Francisco water department, which recorded the number of animals in each household. But their archives were largely inaccessible and would have required an exceedingly tedious process of searching and requesting individual property records. Water departments in other cities may have more accessible records and might be of interest to animal historians. Sanborn maps also contain valuable data on stables and other built features of the animal city.

18 Robichaud, *Animal City*, chapter 3.

19 Robichaud, chapter 3.

20 "Official—Order No. 566," *Daily Alta California*, January 23, 1864, 6.

21 See Robichaud, *Animal City*, chapters 2 and 3. See also: Ted Steinberg, *Gotham Unbound: The Ecological History of Greater New York* (New York: Simon & Schuster, 2014).

22 Here my findings echo and build on the work of Jessica Wang, "Dogs and the Making of the American State."

23 Nayan Shah, *Contagious Divides: Epidemics and Race in San Francisco's Chinatown* (Berkeley: University of California Press, 2001).

24 "Does It Pay?" 1897 pamphlet, San Francisco SPCA, San Francisco Bands of Mercy, San Francisco Charities, Pamphlets, vol. 2, no. 7., The Bancroft Library, University of California, Berkeley. See also Robichaud, *Animal City*, chapter four.

25 Description from area "D16," Mapping Inequality Project: https://dsl.richmond.edu/panorama/redlining/#loc=5/39.1/-94.58

14

What's a Guanaco? Tracing the Llama Diaspora through and beyond South America[1]

Emily Wakild

Let us begin with Spook the llama. Spook lived in the animal enclosures at New York's Central Park Zoo in 1912.[2] Caretakers described Spook as a "morose, cantankerous" soul inhabiting the back of the deer range. Initially forlorn by this location, he looked out the back door at the road that circled past the pen. The busy street proved entertaining as it was full of noisy automobiles and anxious drivers honking. Spook watched the cars and, before long, learned to honk. Or so reported the head keeper at the zoo, Bill Snyder, who claimed "Spook thrust his head forward, drew back his lips so that his teeth were showing, and made a low and distinct sound like an automobile horn." Spook responded to honks, instigated them, and generally wreaked havoc distracting drivers with his uncanny honking. Complaints mounted and Snyder moved Spook upstate to a pasture along the river. Rather than live out his days peacefully, Spook observed the ships and soon learned to imitate boat whistles, restarting this cycle of imitation.

What does a historian *do* with an animal like Spook? What does this glimpse into a single llama's life provide? Is it merely a story, a fleeting source of entertainment? Or can historians use Spook, and animals like him, as sources for key questions about multi-species engagements and their significance? The patterns suggested by Spook's short biography illuminate the features of a modern llama diaspora. That is, since at least the 1530s, llamas and their kin have been in global circulation, attached to people and human interests, and carrying with them deep traditions of Andean practices. This circulation and movement—forced, retaining cultural indicators of identity (picture a llama in a *chullo* hat), and connected to sending and receiving communities—illuminates how multi-species assemblages build geographical footprints. It also suggests that even if historians have not written about them, the animals are always there, in the archives, in the stories, in human history. Although llamas have travelled, they have not really assimilated or become naturalized to new places; and there is no "invasive" llama problem. The idea of a diaspora, which has deep significance in Jewish, African, and Armenian histories, provides a useful concept for animal historians because it opens a path to examine the everyday existence of particular animal groups and the ways their evolutionary trajectory has been altered by diffusion. By considering animals as obvious yet as strange as llamas, diasporic thinking can reframe categories of animals from domesticated, threatened, endangered, or exotic species toward the ordinary and cumulative experiences of animals and the people who retain cultural knowledge about them

Spook and his kin raise issues of power, vulnerability, and agency in animal history. The regimes of compulsion—decades of capitalist and colonialist relations between the United States and Andean countries—partially explain what a llama was doing in New York. Spook's behaviour suggests he acted unexpectedly: he forced human handlers to adjust their thinking about his capacity, and in his mimicry of the world around him, he provided evidence of the ways humans have been involved in the lives of other beings, and vice-versa.[3] This does not exclude the perverse political, social, and economic incentives that placed limited value on the lives of not just exotic animals, but those who knew them well enough to control, breed, care for, and transport them. Perhaps this charismatic individual demonstrated autonomous intention—of the premeditated or rational sort—but more interestingly, his existence suggests ways other creatures become companions in a chaotic and unequal world. Spook's honking offers piecemeal resistance (through bonding and forming relationships) to a colonial regime that objectified animals in zoos. Whether or not llamas have had agency is less pertinent here than the ways llamas have and have not quite acclimatized to new habitats. They remain associated with their homeland; they remain exotic rather than quotidian. If the llamas themselves long for or feel connected to their ancestral territory, we can never know.

This chapter considers, unevenly, four camelid species native to the South American highlands (llama, alpaca, guanaco, and vicuña) and varied examples of human populations that accompanied them around the world. By drawing on literature of diasporic populations, this chapter examines two general movements that constitute the llama diaspora. The first movements, intellectual in nature, explain the existence of animals like Spook. Performance, entertainment, curiosity, ideas, and scientific descriptions uphold one set of forces that inspired animal movement. That is, by gifting and describing these animals, knowledge about their beings and about their products, uses, and qualities travelled the world. The second set of movements includes the physical and geographical movements of the animals—from wide open steppes into stone-hewn corrals for domestication, and from the steep slopes of the Andes to the mountain ranges of North America—where they worked as pack animals and companions of domestic sheep.

The key to an argument about an animal diaspora resides in concepts of movement, but it goes further. Diaspora is an orientation device (to borrow a term from Sara Ahmed) that allows us to trace genealogies of exchange and production across traditional lines, to examine how llamas inhabit spaces, and to trace what they are directed toward.[4] The physical and geographical movements of people with and near llamas reoriented the living animal bodies toward new experiences. Camelids' histories have travelled with them, although this has not generally been recognized—for instance, symbolic visual representations of camelids' histories are found in the ribbons and decorations that derive from Andean beliefs and traditions and that are tied into a llama's wool. By engaging larger diasporic processes, historians can reconceptualize shifts in economic transactions and cultural diffusion. Admittedly an imperfect and provocative fit, the idea of diaspora highlights the processes of intermingling—across cultures, across species, and across homelands. Recognizing the human pressures and affections exerted on other species through time and space more fully accounts for ways of co-existence in a multi-species world and methods for rethinking the multi-natural spaces that humans inhabit.[5]

Camelid Diasporas

Llamas have been transported around the world in vast numbers and with varying degrees of permanence. What these movements have meant, why they have occurred, and how they changed over time provides insight into how unique assemblages of life have been constituted over time. Keith Kenny argues that a diaspora should be seen "not as a social entity that can be measured but as an idea that helps explain the world migration creates."[6] Interpretations that imply the persistence of a homeland despite the scattering of peoples have given way to concepts such as transnational circulation, multi-directional flow, hybridity, creolized cross-cultural exchange, and global networked communities.[7] Nicholas Von Hear identifies three minimal criteria for diasporas: first, a population dispersed from a homeland to two or more territories; second, an enduring presence abroad; and third, a kind of exchange among spatially separated populations.[8] Llamas certainly qualify for the first two criteria, but the idea of exchange is more tenuous (although one might expand the concept of exchange to include cross-species exchanges, such as between guanacos and alpacas). Llamas have had difficulty naturalizing in new places without significant human time and investment. In part, this is because they are susceptible to diseases and to predators that also target flocks of sheep, for example. Llamas alone have no diaspora; but llamas deeply entangled with human populations do.

Here, interdisciplinary work on other animals helps develop these linkages. Anthropologist Laura Ogden suggests that considering the migration and (re-)settlement of non-human beings as "diasporas" illuminates the political complexities of loss and change. Concerned with the eradication of North American beavers introduced at the tip of South America, Ogden argues that reframing invasive species as diasporic populations alerts us to the emergence of identity, subjectivity, and experience.[9] This terminology brings attention to questions of belonging (which species belong where?) and also to origins (where and when have significant differentiations occurred?). Diasporas present complications with the commodification of

Fig. 14.1 Present-day range and approximate size of llamas throughout South America. Drawing by Colleen Campbell.

Fig. 14.2 Present-day range and approximate size of alpacas throughout South America. Drawing by Colleen Campbell.

Fig. 14.3 Present-day range and approximate size of guanacos throughout South America. Drawing by Colleen Campbell.

14 | What's a Guanaco?

Fig. 14.4 Present-day range and approximate size of vicuñas throughout South America. Drawing by Colleen Campbell.

certain species and impediments that arise from industrial production, such as genetic vulnerability and disease susceptibility. Furthermore, the idea of a diaspora directs attention to forced movement born out of the structural priorities of human populations and may highlight the uncertainty of a human-animal divide. As Bénédicte Boisseron points out, "exposing the arbitrariness of divides—whether based on race, gender, or species—is the root of any resistance against discrimination and oppression."[10] Boisseron provides useful ways for thinking through the implications of human-animal comparisons, especially those loaded with racial hierarchies, by shifting our focus to the inter-species alliances and intersectional encounters that open spaces for dual empowerment.

What's a Guanaco?

Camelids, like horses, originated on the Great Plains of North America forty to fifty million years ago but disappeared at the end of the Pleistocene, 10,000 to 20,000 years ago. Living South American camelids all belong to the taxonomic order Artiodactyla (even-toed ungulates), the suborder Tylopeda (pad-footed ungulates), and the family Camelidae. There are four separate species: the llama (*Lama guanicoe*), the alpaca (*Vicugna pacos*), the guanaco (*Lama guanicoe*), and the vicuña (*Vicugna vicugna*).[11] Early genetic work supported the suspected ancestry based on anatomical traits which showed that the guanaco was the ancestor of the llama and the vicuña of the alpaca, but recent studies reveal that the guanaco is also related to the alpaca. Llama mummies found in coastal Peru from 700 to 1,000 CE show a range of breeds and phenotypes that do not perfectly match today's constellation of species and breeds. Within a little more than a century of the 1532 arrival of the Spanish in the Andes, administrative documents report a population loss of up to ninety per cent of llamas.[12] This decline caused a bottlenecking event, associated largely with diseases introduced from European livestock, causing a significant "pinching out of variability and range" of camelids.[13]

Camelids have specific features that they share in common, and individual species have defining characteristics. All camelids have long legs and necks, complex intestinal systems, high crowned teeth, and nailed toes. One species can be distinguished from another by size, colouring, and range. Of the four species, only llamas and alpacas have been domesticated and no longer exist in the wild. Llamas are much larger than alpacas, have banana-shaped ears, and walk with their tails erect. Alpacas have long wool, spear-shaped ears, and do not raise their tails; they thrive in the arid steppes and plains at altitudes above 1,000 metres. Llamas and alpacas come in a range of colours and patterns, including white, brown, and black. Of the wild species, guanacos grow larger than vicuñas and inhabit lower altitudes ranging to sea level; both species have fawn-brown wool on their backs and white bellies. Llamas and guanacos are arid-adapted; vicuñas and alpacas remain water-dependent. All camelids are social animals, mark territory, defecate in dung piles, and form male-dominated "harems" or all-male groups in the wild.[14] All South American camelids can interbreed and produce fertile first-generation offspring. In 1998, the world's first camel-llama was born in Dubai.[15]

General consensus exists on the idea that llamas were first domesticated in the Andes around 4,500 BCE.[16] The study of domestication includes evidence from the zooarchaeological record, genetics of living and prehistoric camelids, and behavioural and biological data from living populations. Altering the relationship between humans and a non-human animal from predation to a symbiotic relationship results in genetic changes, structural modifications, and the emergence of new disease ecologies.[17] Reasons not to domesticate existed: for instance, vicuñas provided a stable, remunerative resource in ranges above fertile agricultural lands.[18] Overall, the vertical distribution of settlements in the Andes enabled by camelids took advantage of the upper limits of agriculture and led to prosperous trade networks and resource exchanges.

Camelid or llamoid species exist in a strange scientific place—in the middle of a number of categories. They are not the largest, the most widespread, or the most aggressive, prolific, or mysterious. Yet they are the only large mammal ever domesticated in the Americas.[19] They are also distinguished by what they are not (sheep, camels, horses). Llamas and alpacas are present—in petting zoos, multicultural fairs, dude ranches—throughout the US and Canada, although they are rarely the main attraction or the most common animals. Rather than displace or transform domestic livestock herds in North America and Europe, camelids have been grafted onto the same terrain, producing a novel cultural ecosystem that doesn't replace but only augments the pre-existing one. Llamas have entered into new arrangements, but at least for their human keepers, the species has never entirely abandoned its association with and concentration in its native Andean homeland.

Intellectual Movements

To know what a guanaco is, we must know those who have known it. Opening historical inquiry to animal knowledge widens the aperture of history itself. One way to trace the routes of animals is through the ways people have thought about them over time. Domestication is both a process and an idea, an intellectual experiment in shifting an animals' nature to serve humans that manifests in a physical process. Nerissa Russell, for example, has argued that the concept of domestication structures the thinking of researchers in the present and did the same for herders in the past because domestication has both biological and cultural components.[20] Scholars debate the appropriateness not only of the term, but also of the potential candidates for domestication. Consensus generally rests on animals with behavioural traits and social structures that make them adaptable, including characteristics such as diet flexibility and responses to humans that facilitate mutual relationships. Domestication is colloquially referred to as an event, but this connotation ascribes a fixity and permanence to a process that, as archaeologists and ethnozoologists explain, rarely has such clarity.[21] Just what domestication means and how it occurs is a topic of wide scientific discussion that I will not revisit here. What is unique about camelid domestication, however, seems to be the debates over how frequently and independently it occurred, the lack of availability of similar candidates in South America for potential domestication, and the missing rationale for domestication when compared with Eurasian animals.

Certain concepts surrounding llamas exist in the Andes among herders whose livelihoods depend on the animals. These include the animals as kin and part of a broader patrimony. In this setting, llamas belong not to the herder but to the *wamani*, who lives in the mountains nearest his corral.[22] *Wamani* are powerful supernatural beings that humans interact with and that must be placated to raise animals successfully. These beings can make a herd thrive and expand, but only through gifts and prayers. The process of giving respect may include a ceremony of renewal, where some llamas are dressed up like humans and some herders imitate llamas. Two animals may be "married" on a wedding bed; others may be made to imbibe alcohol or purified with a snow-like powder. Ritual obligations include the animals as members of the *allyu,* or place-based kin unit. Llamas were highly valued in pre-Columbian economies as gifts among kin or as grants from the more powerful. Their lungs and entrails were read for omens, potatoes were bathed in llama blood to bring about good harvests, and artistic representations on ceramics and stone indicated their important but ordinary existence.[23] Significantly, llamas have been and remain the only animal that can be consumed during solemn events, such as funerary rites, or during the religious celebration of Carnival. Llamas are offered to and symbolically consumed by mountain or Earth spirits (*Apus* or *Pachamama*). Wild animals, including guanacos and vicuñas but also deer, are notably absent from these cultural traditions.[24]

No intellectual exchange since domestication has more affected the llama than the arrival of Europeans in the Americas. The Italian sailor Antonio Pigafetta who sailed with Magellan is credited with giving the region of Patagonia its moniker and likely published the first written description of the camelids. He characterized the guanaco as a hybrid assemblage of recognizable parts from other animals, "the head and ears of a mule, the body of a camel, the feet of a deer, and the tail of a horse."[25] Spaniards frequently described them as awkward sheep. These descriptions and ideas became not only archetypes for understanding the relative physiology of the animals, but also passageways of knowledge transfer among networks of sociable scientists.[26]

Camelids figured in interesting ways—alongside extinct mastodons and giant ground sloths—in the debates over the supposed inferiority of American natures.[27] Chilean natural history expert and Jesuit priest Juan Ignacio Molina argued in 1776 that the South American camelids were "similar to but more elegant and better contoured than" camels. The camel, he explained "is a monster to tell the truth, compared to these quadrupeds." He reported that locals seemed to think they could live up to thirty years and described them as forming an intermediate gradation of beings alongside goats, deer, and camels.[28] Molina's work was a precursor for other scientists, including Charles Darwin, who described the guanaco as a "South American camel or an ass with a very long neck."

Darwin noted that the guanaco was timid, wild, and skittish, and that the guanaco's shrill whistle could be heard before the animals were seen. He observed trails beaten into hills by herds of up to 500 animals, yet, he erroneously claimed, the animals' curiosity would render them easily domesticated.[29] Molina's and Darwin's estimations differed but their ideas on camelids continued to shape scientific thinking.

The relationship between wild and domesticated fauna re-emerged in the first comprehensive survey of fauna of a South American country completed for the Argentine government in 1963. Juan Godoy, the lead scientist and author of this encyclopedic work, wrote that the camelids were most notable for the ways they prospered in the *altiplano* and desert conditions, where other livestock could not.[30] The resourcefulness of these animals in the Andes contextualizes their development and may help explain why they adapted so well to other places and landscapes.

What people thought about llamas exerted considerable influence on the products made of or provided by the animals. The wool, meat, milk, dung, bezoar stones (pebbles found in the gastrointestinal tracts, thought to contain medicinal or healing powers), and other products were believed to carry productive and reproductive energies. Wool is among the most charismatic of products and various arguments exist for justifying the high quality of camelid wool: finer than cashmere, it is known for its exquisite softness and warmth. More specialized applications of animal-derived products—such as the use of vicuña meat to cure hernias—arose in various places.[31] Llama meat, often dried and consumed as a type of "jerky" (*charqui*), accompanied potatoes as staples of Andean diets. Community herds of animals co-existed with individually marked and owned animals.[32] The absence of particular products has salience when considering the potential of diasporas to explain human interactions with non-human species. The geographer Daniel Gade examined reasons for why the llama remained "unmilked"—an oddity when compared to ox, cows, sheep, and other domesticated ungulates.[33] Gade argued that cultural prohibitions explain the absence of commercial enterprise in llama milk products and its cultural rarity among subsistence users. Archeologist Katherine Moore similarly notes that the lack of milking raises unique questions about the integration of agriculture and pastoralism, indicating a process with no close analogues elsewhere.[34]

Wild camelids are somewhat unique in that they can provide one of the more coveted products—wool—without compromising their wild station or necessarily sacrificing their lives. Collecting feathers, eggs, or dung is somewhat similar given the "free" status of these products, but wool is unique in that it must be shorn forcefully from the animals. Vicuña conservation challenges assumptions about the circulation of animal products and what makes animals wild.[35] Twentieth-century luxury demand for wool increased until vicuña populations dropped from an estimated one million animals across their entire range in 1940 to a nadir of 6,000 by 1965.[36] In response, Peruvian officials signed international treaties restricting trade (CITES), set up a territorial reserve, and enacted community development protocols to allow residents to sell vicuña wool upon population recovery. Results rapidly exceeded expectations and, within a decade, the pressures of animal abundance threatened the reserve's ecological viability. The Shining Path guerilla war disrupted the vicuña reserve in the 1980s allowing poachers to resume illegal harvests. When political stability returned in the 1990s, the national government revived conservation measures, especially the reserve and harvest restrictions. More than 350,000 wild vicuñas live in Peru today. The transformation of vicuña wool from a luxury item into a symbol of national pride and community development highlights the range of potential uses of camelid products. The surviving vicuña have been distributed across the Andes and some concern remains for the genetic weaknesses created through the near-extinction and regeneration of the population.

Llamas have been brought around the world for reasons of human entertainment. Historian Helen Cowie chronicles the first arrival of a llama in Europe, as a gift to the Holy Roman Emperor in 1558. Enthralled onlookers in the Dutch city of Middleburg examined the llama, along with armadillos and anteaters, and forced the revision of zoological classifications inherited from the Greeks and Romans.[37] Llamas inhabited zoos in London by the mid-nineteenth century, travelled with circuses, and became staples at county fairs. Performing in venues from museum dioramas to petting zoos, llamas radiated magnetism in their stoic stances, raised eyes, elevated ears, and revealing noises (think Spook). To be sure, llamas did not have a universal reputation for pleasant performances. P. T. Barnum's catalogue of animals noted in 1879 that "[w]hen irritated they eject the contents of their mouths upon the offending party; the substance discharged is exceedingly disagreeable."[38] Gift llamas abounded in some circles.[39] US Secretary of State William Jennings Bryan was sent a prize curly-haired llama by the mayor of Buenos Aires in 1914. The llama, along with five others, was ordered deported when found to contain hoof-and-mouth disease.[40] A similar incident occurred a year and a half prior when three llamas destined for a Kansas City zoo were found to have the disease. Argentine authorities refused to repatriate the animals, and the captain had them shot and thrown overboard; their bodies were found floating ashore in New Jersey the next day.

Physical Movements

If intellectual movements provide the backdrop for the diasporic shifts of llamas, physical movements are their corollary. In important ways, animals allowed the occupation and use of places that made little economic sense without them. In their evolutionary ranges, camelids link disparate parts of the continent—inhabiting niches in high-altitude mountainous areas and moving from the *puna* grassland into corrals toward domestication within those same environments. Rita López de Llergo noted that ways that camelids inhabited hostile, hard to reach landscapes that in turn led to isolated lives in the highland *puna* environment, where festivals were key social events that brought pastors into periodic contact with others.[41] Similarly, Javier Puente describes how a suite of animals, including sheep and camelids, turned high-altitude landscapes into domains of economic profitability.[42] Domestication has modern analogues, ones that raise important questions about how diasporic populations inhabit the Anthropocene. Regular discussions of hybrids—paco-vicuñas, for instance—allude to selective and continuing processes of interbreeding.[43] Domestication and transference or acclimatization are analogous but not equal processes. Nevertheless, attempts to re-situate llamas highlight the difficulties of secondary domestications. Acclimatization societies tried to bring the llama in large numbers to Australia in the 1860s. Their failure indicates the difficulty these animals had in establishing wild or feral populations in places where the Old World camel had no trouble.[44]

Llamas moved great distances for reasons of labour. Andean slopes meant difficulty transporting loads of cargo from cotton cloth to loads

Fig. 14.5 Theodor de Bry, Artist, *Americae: Nona y poftrema pars.* (Frankfurt: Matthew Becker, 1602). Llama detail from a set of twenty-five plates and captions, "IV. De indicis ovibvs, Metal-la ex montanis exportantibus." Book 1072068111, page 16 of the collection available through the Bodmer Lab through the University of Geneva, viewable online at: https://bodmerlab.unige.ch/recits-et-images/debry/#/grands-voyages/GVIX. Llamas depicted show character traits including stubbornness seen as lying down, docility to work in teams, and ability to carry loads from the mines.

of silver. Llamas helped. The Incas found this true along their intricate and expansive road system; the Spanish found it true for exporting and removing silver from high Andean mines, as depicted in the drawings of mining by Theodor de Bry from 1602. Beasts of burden are so called because they perform labour so that humans do not have to. This simplified transaction has near-universal appeal, leading to legal and juridical forms of property holding in some cultures.[45] Llamas have similarly been used to move people and goods in the Grand Canyon of Arizona, in the Rocky Mountains of Colorado, and in the Himalayas of Nepal.[46] Llamas and alpacas experienced a boom in population within the US during the

1980s and 1990s as they were bred on large farms and auctioned off to small farms to serve as pets, mascots, and even protectors of sheep, a role which they served poorly.[47] Llamas have certain evolutionary features that make them suitable for carrying loads in mountain landscapes. For instance, they are smaller and less destructive on trails than horses or mules, and their calm demeanors allow them to be transported on jet boats and planes for hunting expeditions.

Labour has embedded in its categorization an expectation of reward or coercion and an attachment to productivity. While the usefulness of camelids is apparent in historical sources, their resistance to labour, particularly the resistance of the alpaca, is also apparent. In this sense, labour is a movement of resistance and expression at the same time as it is something acted upon the animals. In this volume, J. Keri Cronin uses a 1916 painting to contextualize the juxtaposition of a dead pig lying frozen and prostrate in an outdoor winter scene with a grey horse labouring for humans centred in the frame. In addition to artistic depictions, scholars such as Massuni and Herzog have examined whether the efforts exerted by animals can be considered more than "normal" or reflexive and instead expressive.[48] In other words, does the work a llama undertakes to spit constitute an instinct, an act of expression, or labour on the animal's own behalf (labour in the sense of resistance)? In the same de Bry engraving (Figure 14.5) of the llamas carrying silver, an animal sits in resistance and must be cajoled into returning to work.[49]

Beyond labour as embodied work, labour as knowledge shaped llama populations because of the acute and special understandings that accompany animals. Laboured knowledge might include the descriptions of animal behaviour by scientists but also traditional ecological knowledge, such as how to convince a stubborn llama who has refused to keep working. Veterinarians, handlers, shepherds, packers, zookeepers, and others similarly develop hands-on, proximate knowledge of these animals and can themselves move in diasporas. Additional examples of laboured knowledge include H2-A visa recipients that come to the US to work shearing sheep.[50] These workers qualify for this exchange through their expertise shearing sheep and camelids in South America. On the other side of this labour exchange, starting in the 1960s, young adults from the US served as graduate students, peace corps volunteers, and agricultural specialists observing guanacos and vicuñas in South America, and they later used that knowledge to influence bovine grazing policies and the formal scientific study of camelids in the US.

Historical methods have the potential to chart wide-ranging contours of how humans have understood other animals and to suggest how these understandings influence the bodies of living beings. Brett Walker argues that the lens of intimacy provides a particularly compelling way for viewing animals because intimacy highlights the violence and transcendence of trans-species alliances.[51] What might we gain from knowing how animals have dispersed across the world? Patterns of knowledge, disease ecology, and economic interplay are a start. By highlighting ways of knowing—from biologists, veterinarians, entertainers, businesspeople, and pet-keepers—and embracing a transference of human cultural constructs to multi-species assemblages, we might begin to centre a synthesis that makes space for the personal and the perspectival. Considering diasporic experiences—knowing where and why all the llamas have gone and what they have done—opens up evolutionary processes to an intergenerational scale and causes us to pose ethical questions about species hidden in plain sight. That is, to focus only on llamas used in agriculture or commerce eliminates the space to consider that animals themselves, through a series of interactions, may have chosen cohabitation at various junctures.[52]

Although a llama imported to New York City may never return to its native Andean homeland, considering its life as part of a layer of connection with identifiable patterns emboldens a post-national geography. Attention to the interconnection of the processes that allowed an animal to become domesticated and then enclosed in an urban area provides insight beyond but inclusive of market-driven analysis. Recognizing the human pressures exerted on other species illuminates both the resilience and resistance of those animals. This line of thinking provides a sense of wonder for the past but also for the unknowable inner lives of animals. Diasporic conceptualizations similarly provide acceptance of a multi-species world where llamas may reside in our intellectual, physical, and geographical present.

NOTES

1 The author would like to thank Jennifer Bonnell, Sean Kheraj, Marcel Martel, and Jay Young for the inspiration behind the "Traces of the Animal Past" project and the invitation to contribute to it. Tina Loo and Colleen Campbell as well as conference contributors gave excellent comments that improved the essay, while Colleen Campbell provided elegant illustrations. Madisen Miller assisted with the initial research. The amazing Mavens collective of the Women's Environmental History Network gave constructive and critical feedback on the conceptual orientation of the ideas within.

2 "Park Llama Honked Just Like an Auto," *New York Times*, July 29, 1912.

3 Vinciane Despret, "From Secret Agents to Interagency," *History and Theory* 52, no. 4 (December 2013): 36.

4 Sara Ahmed, "Orientations: Toward a Queer Phenomenology," *GLQ: A Journal of Lesbian and Gay Studies* 12, no. 4 (2006), 543–74.

5 Patricia Marx, "Pets Allowed: Why Are So Many Animals Now in Places Where They Shouldn't Be?" *The New Yorker*, October 20, 2014. Marx takes an alpaca to a drugstore, and almost on an Amtrak train. See also the work on multi-natural traditions by anthropologists Eduardo Viveiros de Castro ("Perspectivismo e multinaturalismo na América indígena," in *A inconstância da alma selvagem e outros ensaios de antropologia* [São Paulo, 2002], 345–99) and Ricardo Cavalcanti-Schiel ("Las muchas naturalezas en los Andes," *Perifèria: Revista de Recerca i Formación en Antropologia* 7 [2007]).

6 Keith Kenny, *Diaspora: A Very Short Introduction* (Oxford: Oxford University Press, 2013), 1.

7 Graham Huggan, "Post-coloniality," in *Diasporas: Concepts, Intersections, Identities*, ed. Kim Knott and Seán McLoughlin (London: Zed Books, 2010), 56–57

8 Nicholas Van Hear, *New Diasporas: The Mass Exodus, Dispersal and Regrouping of Migrant Communities* (Seattle: University of Washington Press, 1998), 6.

9 Laura A. Ogden, "The Beaver Diaspora: A Thought Experiment," *Environmental Humanities* 10, no. 1 (2018): 63–85.

10 Bénédicte Boisseron, *Afro-Dog: Blackness and the Animal Question* (New York: Columbia University Press, 2018), xii.

11 Helen Cowie, *Llama* (Reaktion Books, 2017), 10–12.

12 Jane Wheeler, "Evolution and Present Situation of the South American Camelidae," *Biological Journal of the Linnean Society* 54, no. 3 (1995), 271–95; Jorge A. Flores Ochoa, *Llamichos y poqocheros. Pastores de llamas y alpacas* (Cuzco: Consejo Nacional de Ciencia y Technologia, Centro de Estudios Andinos Cuzco, 1988).

13 Katherine M. Moore, "Early Domesticated Camelids in the Andes," in *The Archaeology of Andean Pastoralism*, ed. J. M. Capriles and N. Tripcevich (Albuquerque: University of New Mexico Press, 2016), 20–22.

14 The southernmost reaches of the camelid's natural range include areas of Patagonia. Diego Rindel and Juan Bautista Belardi, "Mortandad catastrófica de guanacos por estrés invernal y sus implicaciones arqueológicas: el sitio alero los guanacos 1, Lago Cardiel (Provincia de Santa Cruz, Argentina)." *Magallania* 34, no. 1 (2006): 139–55.

15 Cowie, *Llama*, 26–27.

16 Moore, "Early Domesticated Camelids," 17.

17 Jane Wheeler, "On the origin and early development of camelid pastoralism in the Andes," in *Animals and Archeology*, ed. J. Cultton-Brock and C. Grigson (Oxford: British Archaeological Reports, 1984), 395–410.

18 See Bonavia "The Domestication of Andean Camelids," 144; and J. W. Rick, *Prehistoric Hunters of the High Andes* (New York: Academic Press, 1980).

19 Jared Diamond's chapter, "Zebras, Unhappy Marriages, and the Anna Karenina Principle: Why were most big wild mammal species never domesticated?," in *Guns, Germs, and Steel: The Fates of Human Societies* (London: Vintage, 1997). While the term "camelids" may not be a household name in English-speaking cultures, the animals called camelids are scientifically and culturally grouped as such throughout the Andes; recognizing one lends easily to recognizing another and though they can be differentiated, grouping them as camelids makes as much sense as would "horses" or "wolves" even though they span the divide across wild and domesticated.

20 Nerissa Russell, "The Wild Side of Animal Domestication," *Society & Animals* 10, no. 3 (2002), 285–302. The literature on domestication is vast though somewhat under-analyzed by historians. Most literature begins with and analyzes Charles Darwin, although more recent studies take up the idea of human domestication as well, Lorenzo Del Savio and Matteo Mameli, "Human domestication and the roles of human agency in human evolution, *History and philosophy of the life sciences* 42, no. 2 (2020): 21. For an overview of suitability toward domestication, see Diamond, *Guns Germs and Steel*, chapter 10; For a current overview, see Mary Ann Raghanti, "Domesticated species: It takes one to know one," *Proceedings of the National Academy of Sciences* 116, no. 29 (July 2019), 14401–3.

21 Duccio Bonavia, "The Domestication of Andean Camelids," *Archeology in Latin America*, (New York: Routledge, 1999), 130–47. For instance, dating domestication relies on changes in bone structure and concentration of animals, but it is exceedingly difficult to determine whether animals were domesticated in various places or if domesticated animals were moved into new sites. See Wheeler, "Evolution and Present Situation," 276.

22 Kent. V. Flannery, Joyce Marcus, Robert G. Reynolds, *The Flocks of the Wamani: A Study of Llama Herders on the Punas of Ayacucho, Peru* (New York: Academic Press, 1989), 25, 30, 37.

23 John V. Murra, "Herd and Herders in the Inca State," in *Man, Culture, Animals: The Role of Animals in Human Ecological Adjustments*, ed. Anthony Leeds and Andrew P. Vayda (Washington D.C: AAAS, 1965), 186.

24 Nicolas Goefert, "The llama and the deer: dietary and symbolic dualism in the central Andes," *Anthropozoologica* 45, no. 1 (2010): 25–45.

25 Cowie, *Llama*, 51. Quote in Cowie.

26 Patience A. Schell, *The Sociable Sciences: Darwin and His Contemporaries in Chile* (New York: Palgrave MacMillan, 2013).

27 Elizabeth Kolbert, *The Sixth Extinction An Unnatural History* (New York: Picador, 2015).

28 Juan Ignacio Molina, *Ensayo sobre la historia natural de Chile* (Santiago: Ediciones Maule 1810 [1987]), 289. He noted an additional Chilean species, the *chilihueque*.

29 Darwin, *Voyage of the Beagle*, 156.

30 Juan Carlos Godoy, *Evaluación De Los Recursos Naturales De La Argentina*: Tomo Viii Fauna Silvestre Volumen 1 (Consejo Federal De Inversiones. Buenos Aires: Consejo Federal de Inversiones, 1963), 171.

31 Adam Warren, "From Natural History to Popular Remedy: Animals and Their Medicinal Applications among the Kallaway in Colonial Peru" in *Centering Animals in Latin American History*, ed. Martha Few and Zeb (Durham, NC: Duke University Press, 2013), 124–48.

32 Murra, "Herds and Herders," 195.

33 Daniel Gade, *Nature and Culture in the Andes* (Madison: University of Wisconsin Press, 1994).

34 Moore, "Early Domesticated Camelids in the Andes," 17. Mare's milk has interesting cultural appearances but is also rarely utilized in South America. See John Travis, "Trail of Mare's Milk Leads To First Tamed Horses," *Science* 322 (2008): 368.

35 Emily Wakild, "Saving the Vicuña: The Political, Biophysical, and Cultural History of Wild Animals Conservation in Peru, 1964–2000," *American Historical Review* 125, no. 1 (February 2020): 54–88.

36 Antonio Brack Egg, "La situación actual de la población de vicuñas y recomendaciones para su manejo," 1980, Centro de Datos de Conservación, Universidad Nacional Agraria-La Molina, Lima, Peru; Kai Otte and Rudolf Hofmann, "The Debate about the Vicuña Population in Pampa Galeras Reserve"; and S. K. Eltringham and W. J. Jordan, "The Vicuña of the Pampa Galeras National Reserve: The Conservation Issue," in *Problems in Management of Locally Abundant Wild Mammals*, ed. Peter A. Jewell and Sidney Holt (New York: Academic Press, 1981), 259–90.

37 Cowie, *Llama*, 7.

38 P. T. Barnum, *History of Animals and Leading Curiosities and a guide to P. T. Barnum's Greatest of All Shows and Colosseum of Natural History and Art* (Courier Company, 1879), 15.

39 Juan Pimentel, *The Rhinoceros and the Megatherium: An Essay in Natural History*, (Cambridge MA: Harvard University Press, 2017).

40 "Llama for Bryan Ordered Deported," *New York Times*, March 16, 1914.

41 Rita López de Llergo, "Las regiones naturales del Perú: la Sierra," *Revista Geográfica*, *Perú*, 4, no. 12 (1944): 117.

42 Javier Puente, "Livestock, Livelihood, and Agrarian Change in Andean Peru" *Oxford Research Encyclopedia*, 2018, https://doi.org/10.1093/acrefore/9780199366439.013.501

43 López de Llergo, "Las regiones naturales del Perú," 117.

44 Harriet Ritvo, "Going Forth and Multiplying: Animal Acclimatization and Invasion" *Environmental History* 17, no. 2 (2012): 1–11.

45 Alan Mikhail, "Early Modern Human and Animal," in *The Animal in Ottoman Egypt* (New York: Oxford University Press, 2014), 19–37.

46 http://archive.nepalitimes.com/news.php?id=10815#.XY48C2Z7lPY

47 "U.S. llama population has dropped drastically. Where did they all go?" https://www.nbcnews.com/news/us-news/llamas-disappearing-across-united-states-n994181

48 Brian Massumi, "The Supernormal Animal," in *The Nonhuman Turn*, ed. Richard Grusin (University of Wisconsin Press, 2015), 2; Hal Herzog, *Some We Love, Some We Hate, Some We Eat: Why It's So Hard to Think Straight About Animals* (New York: Harper Perennial, 2011), 149.

49 Cowie, *Llama*, 57.

50 Teofilo Altamirano Rua, "Pastores quechuas en el oeste norteamericano.*América Indígena* 51(2/3): 203–222; Alison Krogel, "Quechua Sheepherders on the Mountain Plains of Wyoming: The (In)hospitality of U.S. Guest Worker Programs," *Journal of Latin American and Caribbean Anthropology* 15, no. 2 (2010): 261–88.

51 Brett Walker, "Animals and the Intimacy of History," in *The Oxford Handbook of Environmental History*, ed. Andrew Isenberg (New York: Oxford University Press, 2014), 52–75; Sandra Swart, "'But Where's the Bloody Horse?': Textuality and Corporeality in the "Animal Turn'," *Journal of Literary Studies* 23, no. 3 (2007), 271–92.

52 Michael Pollan's idea that plants have appended themselves to human desires has some sway here, *Botany of Desire,* (New York: Viking 2001) as does Edmund Russell's ideas on uniting patterns in biology and history, *Evolutionary History: Uniting History and Biology to Understand Life on Earth* (Cambridge: Cambridge University Press, 2011).

PART V:

Looking at Animals

Hidden in Plain Sight: How Art and Visual Culture Can Help Us Think about Animal Histories[1]

J. Keri Cronin

How can studying images of animals help us think about animal histories? While, of course, animals have been the focus of countless images throughout the history of art and visual culture, more often than not these images use animals as symbols of human ideas, politics, and culture. For instance, equestrian portraiture, a genre of imagery in which powerful leaders are depicted astride suitably powerful-looking horses, is intended as a tribute to the human subjects of these images—the horses are, for the most part, symbolic details intended to support this larger meaning.[2] Further, when we consider how images of animals have been collected, valued, and displayed, we are, of course, presented with a distinctly and unavoidably anthropocentric pattern. These images, in other words, were created, consumed, collected, and curated by humans. However, as Jay Young and Dolly Jørgensen have argued elsewhere in this volume, these anthropocentric patterns of collection and display can be interrupted by interventions and inquiries that destabilize expectations in museums, archives, and galleries. There is much potential for innovative animal history scholarship to take place when we revisit these histories and collections.

What can historical images teach us about the lives (and deaths) of non-human animals from previous time periods? Is there any value in turning to art and visual culture as we attempt to piece together their histories? In the following discussion, I argue that visual culture can be a very valuable tool in these endeavours. However, if we are going to consider how these kinds of visual texts can help us think about non-human animal histories, we have to also consider such things as the complex relationships that exist between material animal bodies and visual imagery. Further, we also need to be attuned to some of the methodologies used by scholars in the history of art and visual culture.

Art History Is (in Many Cases) Animal History

When we consider the plethora of imagery that we can draw on as we attempt to "trace the animal past," one of the first points to remember is that the history of art and visual culture is intertwined with animal histories on a very material level. For centuries, the production of art and art-making supplies has relied on the bodies (or body parts) of non-human animals. The literal entanglement of imagery and animal bodies goes back as long as people have been making pictorial records. For instance, throughout history, many pigments have been made from animal bodies: Indian Yellow has historically been made with concentrated cow urine;[3] Tyranian Purple was derived from shellfish (*Thais haemastoma* and *Murex brandaris*);[4] and the red pigment obtained from the body of an insect, known as the cochineal (*Dactylopius coccus*), continues to have widespread applications to the present day.[5] Likewise, paint brushes have been made with animal hair and many textile objects are made of wool derived from sheep and other animals raised for this purpose. Egg yolks have been used as binding agents in tempera paints, and egg whites (or, more specifically, the albumen protein contained within egg whites) were used in making albumen prints, an early form of photography. As the name suggests, another photographic process, the gelatin silver process, relies on gelatin (typically derived from animal bones) as a key ingredient. And, of course, we must consider the vellum and parchment derived from the skin of calves, sheep, and goats that has served as the surface material for countless manuscripts and works of art.

While this is by necessity a brief discussion of the complex histories of the use of animal bodies in the production of art, I mention it here because when we consider imagery as a source of information for learning about animal histories, we cannot forget this material connection between the processes of picture making and the bodies of so many animals. And yet it is easy to forget that these key "ingredients" were essential to the production of so many of the world's most revered cultural objects. This connection has become culturally invisible. We have become accustomed to not seeing this connection, and we typically view a painting, photograph, or a woven textile without seeing the traces of the animal bodies right in front of our eyes. In her discussion of medieval manuscripts, Sarah Kay describes this phenomenon as part of "the seemingly ahistorical existence of animals."[6] And this only increases as we look at and work with digital images. Of course, digitized collections have many benefits, including wider access and the preservation of fragile objects. However, looking at an image on a screen means we do not always have the opportunity to examine the material qualities of the picture. This means that it is more important than ever to be mindful of these connections.

Visual Analysis

In her study on the labour of horses in the United States during the nineteenth century, Ann Norton Greene talks about some of the difficulties in writing animal histories, including "keeping the animals at the centre of study."[7] What she means here is that it is important to go beyond the symbolic and cultural meanings that humans have attributed to animals. This is, of course, a central concern for all of us writing animal histories.

Echoing Greene's point, I want to emphasize the importance of keeping images of animals centrally focused if we are using them as part of our source material for writing animal histories. Images need to be taken as seriously as any other source or text. Images are not neutral "windows onto the past." Rather, images—be they famous works of art, snapshot photographs, or illustrated advertisements—are complex documents that require a researcher to pay close attention to such things as how the images were made, the context in which they were viewed, and how they continue to generate meanings. Further, images can wield a lot of power: they can both support and challenge dominant discourses. As Nicholas Mirzoeff argues, "visual culture is the relation between what is visible and the names that we give to what is seen. It also involves what is invisible or kept out of sight."[8] When we work with images as our primary source documents, we must pay attention to the multiple ways in which meaning can be created through our engagement with imagery.

So, how do we do this? What does this actually mean? Many scholars have not been trained in the methodologies that underpin history of art and visual culture programs and can, understandably, feel a bit daunted by this. If we have never stopped to take images seriously as historical sources, we may not be sure where to begin nor feel confident in our ability to work with visual material.

The first step in working with images is to conduct a visual analysis. Visual analysis is a key skill that students in history of art and visual culture programs learn in their academic studies. It is also a skill that should be practiced by anyone working with images as source material. Simply put, visual analysis is a deep description of the image under consideration. This seems like it should be a simple task, but it can be surprisingly challenging when we sit down to do it. We are surrounded by imagery in our day-to-day lives, but how often do we stop to really notice these images in detail? What do we see when we look at the image? What choices has the image-maker made? Which colours are used? Which materials? When I am teaching, I frequently give my students a few minutes to write a brief visual analysis of an image projected on the screen as a warm-up exercise. When we start to discuss their answers, it quickly becomes apparent that not everyone in the room has noticed the same details. As the discussion unfolds, some students add to their answers. Visual analysis requires deep concentration and critical engagement with the image under consideration, but ideally it also includes conversation and reflection. Regular practice can help deepen observational skills in a broader sense, and this is the primary reason that some medical programs now require their students to take courses in the history of art and visual culture.[9]

Visual analysis can also help us in our efforts to "trace the animal past." This kind of exercise can train us to look closely and critically at the representations of animals we are working with. For example, if we take a close look at Franklin Brownell's 1916 pastel drawing *Frozen Meat, Byward Market*, we can see the artist has included representations of a couple of different types of non-human animals in the scene. The artist has used compositional details to ensure that our eye is drawn to the frozen body of the dead pig laid out on the sled in the foreground of the image. The lines of the sled, the central placement, and the light-coloured pigment used to render this animal's body are intended to focus the initial attention of the viewer to this aspect of the picture. At the opposite end of the sled, we have a compositional detail that foreshadows the next step in this pig's journey—she will be rendered into cuts of meat, her body less and less recognizable with each violent slice. This, of course, is reinforced through the title given to the picture, *Frozen Meat*, although the actual moment of dismembering this pig's body is not represented here.

The loose application of the pastel pigment in this image coupled with the somewhat informal groupings of human figures gives this scene a casual, almost snapshot feel. This is very much in keeping with the Impressionist and Post-Impressionist styles of art-making that Brownell was drawn to in his career. This kind of art is intended to offer a "fleeting glimpse" of modern life, and certainly in a city like Ottawa the market square would be an excellent place for Brownell to find this kind of subject matter for his work.[10] This was a space that would be full of hustle and bustle, with conversations and commerce overlapping. In spite of the cold weather (as indicated by the rosy red cheeks and the layers of warm clothing worn by the people gathered in the market square), Brownell, in all likelihood, sketched this scene while outdoors at the market, as this was keeping with the practice of artists working to capture a "fleeting glimpse" of a scene such as this.

The pink, naked, scarred body of the pig contrasts sharply with the bundled-up human figures in this scene. The casual way in which the fully clothed human figures gather in conversation so near the body of this animal normalize this death. This is not a shocking scene for those gathered at Byward Market on this day; it barely even merits a second glance.

The hooves of the upturned pig's body also direct our eye toward two other non-human animals in this scene—two horses, both wearing harnesses and tack indicating their status as workhorses in this urban environment. The brown horse on the left side of the composition has been

Fig. 15.1 Franklin Brownell, *Frozen Meat, Byward Market, Ottawa* (pastel drawing, 1916). Source: National Gallery of Canada.

covered with a bright orange blanket, protection against the Ottawa winter chill. The grey horse in the middle of the picture, however, has not been given the same courtesy. I wrote about the tradition of equestrian portraiture at the start of this essay, about the symbolic equation of powerful leaders with powerful steeds. This is not the aesthetic tradition Brownell draws on here. In this picture, the horses are part of the everyday landscape of Ottawa, as they were in most urban centres in Canada in the early twentieth century.[11] These are but two ways that artists have represented horses throughout history, but at the risk of belabouring the point, I draw attention to the differences as a reminder that picturing non-human animals is a dynamic process that resists easy categorization.

In spite of the central placement of this dead pig, when we look around the composition, we can see that we are the only viewers paying any attention to this animal's body. Here she is rendered as simply another market commodity and not as an individual animal. But what if we wanted to know more about that particular pig? What if we wanted to know further details of her life and her death, details that this painting cannot immediately offer us? Likewise, if we wanted to know more details about the lives of the horses in this image, we may find ourselves coming up a little short if all we have to go on is this picture. Brownell's picture provides us with many visual details, but there is a lot this picture does not tell us. As art historian Patricia Johnston has argued that "visual images provide views of historical moments, but they are not transparent windows."[12] Many questions remain to be answered. Does this render imagery like Brownell's sketch useless for our understanding of animal histories? Not at all! Pictures like this can help direct the next phase of our inquiry—contextual analysis.

Contextual Analysis

When we are working with images as historical texts, visual analysis and contextual analysis must go hand-in-hand. Contextual analysis involves taking the detailed description generated in the visual analysis stage and using that as a launching point for specific and tailored research. As anyone who has tried to piece together the life story of an animal from a previous era is well aware, there are significant gaps in the historical record when it comes to individual details of animal lives.[13] So, where do we turn?

In addition to searching libraries and archives for texts and reports detailing things like the agricultural histories of Canada and specific references to this kind of economic activity in the Ottawa area at this time, we can also read about pigs—specifically, pigs who have been bred for human consumption. Farmed pigs have very different life histories than their wild ancestors, although as Brett Mizelle reminds us, they do have some common origins.[14] It would also be prudent to search for farming manuals and "how to" books for raising livestock from this era and location, similar to those Hodgins examines in Chapter 5. Local Ottawa newspapers might have a list of market prices. Archival documents from organizations such as the Ottawa Humane Society and the Canadian Society for the Prevention of Cruelty to Animals can also offer a glimpse into what counted as "cruel" or "humane" behaviour toward non-human animals in this specific context. As is the case today, these frameworks tended to be species-specific in the time period Brownell was painting. In other words, horses and pigs were not seen as equals in the eyes of the law nor of the officers tasked with preventing cruelty to animals. With this information in mind, the compositional relationships that exist between the two horses and the dead pig in Brownell's sketch become more complex than the formal arrangement of figures within the frame.

In addition to reading the history of human-pig interactions, we may also find books like Jeffrey Moussaieff Masson's *The Pig Who Sang to the Moon: The Emotional World of Farm Animals* to be useful in our contextual analysis. Granted, the cognitive ethology framework that Masson and others have taken in their studies of farmed animals in recent years was not a dominant way of understanding pigs when Brownell made this painting. And yet, when we are thinking about animal histories, this kind of information can play a useful role.

We may never be able to piece together the exact life history of this specific pig, and yet learning more about the ways in which she very likely lived and died does a very powerful thing: it transforms her from compositional detail to subject. Here, I would argue, the combination of looking at the image and reading these varied sources is key. If we were to just look at this image on its own, we would have many gaps in our historical analysis of the scene. If we were to just read about agricultural history or even the cultural history of human-pig interactions, we may still be thinking about these topics in an abstract manner. The image filters the historical and contextual information through to a specific narrative that invites us to consider the non-human animals within the frame in a more focused light.

Looking for Animals in the Archives

One of the reasons I use the phrase "hidden in plain sight" when talking about "tracing the animal past" has to do with how we encounter and interact with the visual history of animal lives. How, in other words, do we actually locate and access the material we are looking for when we visit museums, galleries, and archives? The history of human and non-human animals is intertwined in many ways and yet, as anyone who is interested in exploring non-human animal histories is acutely aware, the ways in which documents, records, and visual material in the collections of museums, galleries, and archives have been organized typically privileges the human over the non-human.[15] Further, catalogues and metadata often gloss over textual mentions or visual representations of non-human animals found within collections, which can make it challenging for historians to locate and work with this material.

Last summer I was working with a research assistant trying to find information about the animal workers who were an integral part in building the Welland Canals in the Niagara region of southern Ontario during the nineteenth century. We spent a lot of time in the archives, going through files looking for evidence of the lives and deaths of the dozens upon dozens of oxen, horses, and mules who were integral to building these canals.[16] We knew that these animals had been part of this project—the canals simply could not have been built without animal labour in this period—and yet there was, of course, no "animals of the Welland Canal" folder in the archives. That would have made our work too easy! We found brief references here and there, but it was only after several hours of digging that we started to find what we were looking for. My research assistant opened a file labelled "Construction and Management – Equipment" and it was here where we finally found multiple references to the animal labour used in the building of the first Welland Canal during the 1820s. This cracked our search strategies wide open, as we realized that we needed to be considering such keywords as "equipment" and "machinery" alongside the more obvious search terms and metadata. Now that we are aware of how this material is classified, it seems obvious, but this was not how we initially approached the archives. The animal workers were hidden in plain sight.

The material we found in this file included a diagram of an invention designed to make the work more efficient and to keep the workers (both human and non-human) safer as the enormous task was completed. As the first canal took shape, "thousands of tons" of excavated earth had to be hauled up the newly created banks to be removed.[17] This was incredibly difficult labour and "as many as ten yoke of oxen" were required in places.[18] However, this was also very dangerous work, and in response to a series of accidents in which human and non-human workers were injured or killed, new methods of working were sought. Eventually, the Board of Directors for the Welland Canal Company came up with a plan to "offer a reward of £125 to the person who would construct a machine that would remove the greatest quantity of earth in a given time, at the least expense."[19] The winning design was submitted by Oliver Phelps who explained how the machine worked as follows:

> A common wagon wheel fixed on an upright post, about seven feet from the ground on the top of the bank; a rope, with a hook on each end reaching from the bottom of the canal to the top, is fixed round this wheel which hooks on the back of the descending cart and to the tongue of the one below, so that the return team assists in pulling up the loaded one, thereby, in effect, reducing the ascent to a perfect level, as the loads are drawn up with more ease than they are removed from the level to discharge.[20]

This description was reinforced through a two-part diagram, one of the few visual sources we have available to us for researching the history of the first Welland Canal. When we do a visual analysis of Phelps' diagram, we can see that it is comprised of two separate but thematically related images. At the top of the diagram is a profile view of the canal as it might be seen by someone standing along the bottom of the ditch. On the far left we see three double teams of oxen yoked to wagons—the first two appear to have full loads of excavated earth heaped high in the carts behind them. Perhaps the third team is waiting for further material to be loaded. As our eye moves across the page toward the right, we can see an illustration of the crux of Phelps' plan being demonstrated. Here, as he described, we have two teams of oxen attached to a tow rope, which is, in turn, affixed around a wheel—one team goes up the embankment, the other returns down for another load. In both cases, the driver of each wagon holds a whip in his hand—the raised position of the whip indicates that the use of force to urge these teams on was a common enough occurrence to be included as part of the iconography of this diagram. The implicit violence toward the bodies of the animal workers here is normalized as part of day-to-day operations. At the top of this first diagram, we see yet another oxen team attached to an empty cart awaiting their return journey back down to the lower part of the work site.

The bottom half of Phelps' diagram shows the same process but from a bird's eye view. Here, we are to imagine we are hovering over the job site

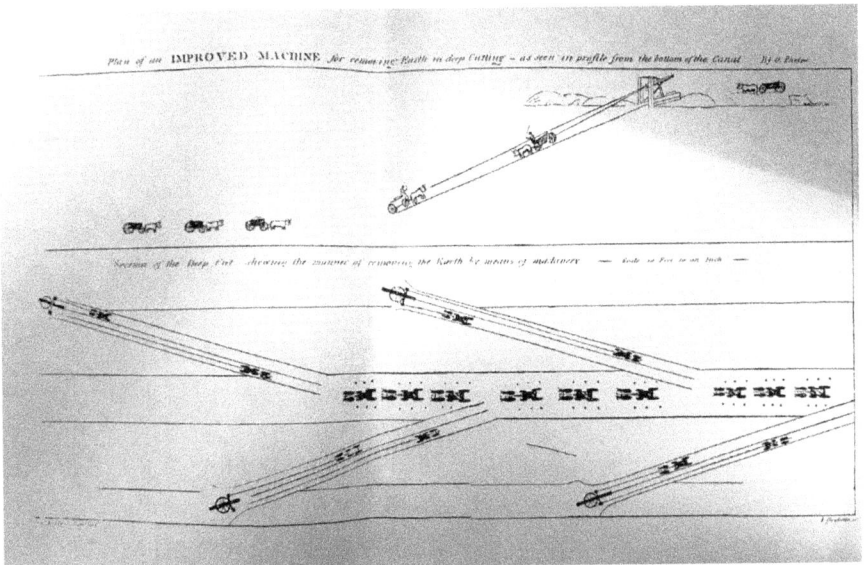

Fig. 15.2 Oliver Phelps' "Improved Machine" (ca. 1827). Source: St. Catharines Museum & Welland Canals Centre.

looking down at the work unfolding below. Once again, we see the teams of non-human animal workers engaged in the task of hauling wagons up and down the incline with the assistance of Phelps' invention, while other teams are lined up waiting for their wagons to be filled before being sent up the hill by their driver. The drivers (and their ubiquitous whips) are less visible from this vantage point, as are the bodies of the non-human animals hauling the loads. The small size of these workers in this representation stands at odds with the enormity of the massive construction project and the incredible physical exertion required by those working at the site, both human and non-human.

Phelps' method was, as Roberta Styran and Robert Taylor have noted, one of the many methods through which human and non-human animal labourers worked side by side to excavate and eventually build what would become the first Welland Canal.[21] And yet we have very few visual sources to draw on if we want to get a sense of what this labour actually looked like. The building of the first Welland Canal took place prior to the development of photography as a viable means of recording visual information. Further, the dirty, dangerous work of building a canal was not the kind of subject matter that easily lent itself to a commissioned painting in the nineteenth century, and as such, there is a "paucity of contemporary visual evidence" from this point in the project's history.[22] Therefore, surviving visual clues that we do have, such as Phelps' diagram, become even more significant as we try to piece together what the lives of these animals might have been like. However, at the same time, the lack of colour or of any other detail in this image isolates this representation from the project in which it was a part and, in many ways, conceptually separates it from what we know would have been a noisy, messy, difficult, and dangerous history. This is an abstracted diagram intended to showcase the mechanical ingenuity of its author, Oliver Phelps. The oxen so essential to this labour have been reduced to the status of mechanical equipment, much like the wagon wheel upon which Phelps' mechanism turned. This is reinforced by the filing system in which the diagram was archived. Like the Brownell picture, there are limits to what this image can tell us about what life was like for the non-human animal workers who helped build the Welland Canal.

What Do Pictures Want?

In both of these examples (Brownell and Phelps), we have images that were made to convey select pieces of information. For Brownell, the intention was to capture the dynamism of modern life in an urban centre in the early decades of the twentieth century. For Phelps, it was to illustrate the mechanical workings of his new invention in the late 1820s. These are two very different kinds of images made in different time periods under two very different kinds of circumstances and they rely on two very different methods of pictorial representation. In both cases, however, the non-human animal bodies were included as mere compositional details in the larger pictorial whole. If, in both of these examples, neither artist was driven by a desire to use their imagery as a way to convey detailed information about the animal bodies that feature so prominently in them, how do we, as historians looking to "trace the animal" past, work with this kind of visual material?

As is the case with any text or historical document, we need to be attuned to the various ways in which meaning can be derived from an image. My students are often surprised and frustrated to learn that there is no single "key" for them to use as they attempt to decipher an image ("but just tell us what the artist meant," they often implore when I ask them to analyze an image in class). I remind them that the intention of the artist is but one way in which an image generates meaning. The meaning of a picture is not static, nor is it handily embedded within an image for us to simply uncover. Rather, when we work with images, we need to consider such things as when the image was made, the types of technologies used, the intended audience, and our current context of viewing. It is also important to recognize that the background, socio-cultural position, education, and life experience of any individual viewer will also shape their understanding of any given image.[23]

The context in which an image is viewed can and does shape the meaning-making process. The members of the Board of the Welland Canal Company would have understood Phelps' diagram in a very different way than we are able to today. In the first instance, we have a group of people who would be scrutinizing the diagram with an eye toward making a very messy, expensive, and dangerous construction project go a little more smoothly. Those looking closely at Phelps' schematic diagram in the late 1820s knew what was at stake in a very visceral way. Perhaps they knew some of the workers (human and non-human) who were killed or injured in the construction. Perhaps they felt the financial pinch of a project not going according to plan on a personal level. Their intimate knowledge of the work site and its challenges meant that this image would resonate in different ways for those viewers than it does for us today.

What do we see when we look at a scan of Phelps' diagram on the monitors of our computers, tablets, and phones in the twenty-first century? What meaning can this image hold for us today? When I squint my eyes and try to make out further details in this image, I am acutely aware of all of the details this diagram cannot tell me. Are those horns of the oxen in the bottom register? Or is there a chance they are meant to be representations of the long ears of donkeys (another species of animals whose labour was integral to the building of the canals)? What did these animals eat? Where did they sleep? What was the process through which they were conscripted for this work? How long were their work days? Did any of them resist this work and exert a sense of agency that might be at odds with what their whip-wielding drivers wanted them to do? Like the Brownell example, it is at this point in our inquiry that the image guides us toward contextual research. This image contains less visual information than Brownell's painting does, but the process by which we can use the image to frame our research remains the same. Visual analysis is a key part of working with images, but as noted above, it must always be accompanied by contextual analysis. The images provide important clues for guiding our research inquiries beyond the frame of the picture.

We are asking very different things of these images than previous viewers might have, but here is the important part: neither line of inquiry is necessarily more correct than the other. In his provocatively titled book *What Do Pictures Want?: The Lives and Loves of Images*, W. J. T. Mitchell argues that images need to be understood as "as complex individuals occupying multiple subject positions and identities."[24] What Mitchell's thoughtful analysis makes clear is that when working with images we need to consider how they can potentially make meaning from a number of different angles and in a number of different spaces and moments in time. Further, Mitchell also stresses another important point, namely that what is excluded from an image can be as significant as what is included. Thus, he asks:

> What does this picture lack; what does it leave out? What is its area of erasure? Its blind spot? Its anamorphic blur? What does the frame or boundary exclude? What does its angle of representation prevent us from seeing, and prevent it from showing? What does it need or demand from the beholder to complete its work?[25]

In other words, where are the gaps in our knowledge? What are the limits of working with pictorial sources? How will we use these gaps and limits to further guide our research inquiries?

As I work with my research assistant to continue to try and piece together the stories of these non-human animal workers who were so integral to the building of the Welland Canal, we are mindful of how Greene describes working animals as "living machines" who "made many demands on people."[26] Just as Mitchell argues that as viewers we need to ask ourselves about the "needs" of an image, Greene reminds us that we need to consider what kinds of needs these non-human animal workers would have had and how the caregivers and co-workers who co-existed with them worked to meet these demands. There does not appear to be any central repository offering detailed information about the "living machines" who worked on the Welland Canal, but we do know that subcontractors—"often farmers who lived along the line of the canal and who owned ploughs, wagons, and teams"[27]—were a key part of this process. Hopefully, our ongoing research will give us glimpses into the relationships these farmers had with the non-human animals in their care. As we dig through these documents, letters, and records we hope to uncover information to help animate Phelps' diagram in new ways.

Conclusion

Visual culture can be an important tool in the toolkit of anyone looking to "trace the animal past," but it is important to understand that it also has its limits. To fall back on cultural clichés, such as a picture offering a "window on the past" or being "worth a thousand words," belies the complexity of an image as a cultural document. As this brief discussion has attempted to demonstrate, there are a number of significant ways in which visual culture is intertwined with animal histories—from the materials used to make images to the ways in which images can sanitize and normalize violence enacted on particular animal bodies. Images can also disrupt patterns of cultural invisibility and draw attention to some of the problems that might be entrenched in dominant ways of seeing and living with non-human animals. Detailed, descriptive visual analysis of imagery can draw our attention to aspects of a picture that we might not notice at first glance. It is, however, important to recognize that a single picture can never tell us the whole story, and that it is important to work from the image out as we seek further research. Visual analysis can help tailor our contextual research inquiries in important ways, and the two methods of inquiry necessarily go hand-in-hand. If we take images seriously—if we attend to Mitchell's plea to consider what images might need from us—they can be helpful as we seek to write more detailed animal histories.

NOTES

1. Thank you to Jennifer Bonnell and Sean Kheraj for inviting me to be part of the "Traces of the Animal Past" conference at York University in November 2019. This was one of the most intellectually enriching and enjoyable conferences I have ever had the pleasure to participate in. I am also grateful to the other participants for the rich discussions that happened at that event. I also want to thank my excellent research assistant, Alicia Floyd, who has been an incredible help on this and many other projects. I am grateful to my colleagues Lauren Corman, Kendra Coulter, and Barbara Seeber for the many enriching conversations about human-animal studies, animal advocacy, and animal histories we have had over the years. Finally, a big thank you to Laurie Morrison for, well, everything.

2. Perhaps the most well-known example of this is Jacques-Louis David's famous painting *Napoleon Crossing the Alps* (1801). In this painting, Napoleon—who famously did not enjoy sitting for portraits—is posed on the back of a spirited steed when, in actuality, we know from his journals that he made this crossing on the back of a mule. See Edgar Munhall, "Portraits of Napoleon, *Yale French Studies* 26 (1960): 3–20.

3. Kassia St Clair, *The Secret Lives of Colour* (London: John Murray, 2016), 71–73. See also Victoria Finlay, *The Brilliant History of Color in Art* (Los Angeles: J. Paul Getty Museum, 2014); Diego Tamburini et al., "New Insights Into the Composition of Indian Yellow and its use in a Rajasthani Wall Painting," *Microchemical Journal* 137 (March 2018): 238–49. In this article, the authors discuss the use of this colour in early seventeenth-century wall paintings in Rajasthan, India, as well as the use of this colour in Rajput-Mughal paintings dating back to the late sixteenth century.

4. St Clair, *The Secret Lives of Color*, 162. See also Dina Frangié-Joly, "Perfumes, Aromatics, and Purple Dye: Phoenician Trade and Production in the Greco-Roman Period," *Journal of Eastern Mediterranean Archaeology & Heritage Studies* 4 (2016): 36–56. In this article, the author discusses how places such as Beirut, Tyre, and Arados were important sites for the production of this colour as far back as the Bronze Age.

5. St Clair, 141–43. See also Elena Phipps, *Cochineal Red: The Art History of a Color* (New Haven and London: Yale University Press, 2010).

6. Sarah Kay, *Animal Skins and the Reading Self in Medieval Latin and French Bestiaries* (Chicago: University of Chicago Press, 2017), 2.

7. Ann Norton Greene, *Horses at Work* (Cambridge, MA: Harvard University Press, 2008), 7.

8. Nicholas Mirzoeff, *How to See The World* (Pelican Books, 2015), 11.

9. See, for instance, Casey Lesser, "Why Med Schools Are Requiring Art Classes," *Artsy* (August 2017), https://www.artsy.net/article/artsy-editorial-med-schools-requiring-art-classes; and Kate Wheeling, "How Looking at Paintings Became a Required Course in Medical School," *Yale Medicine Magazine* (Spring 2014), https://medicine.yale.edu/news/yale-medicine-magazine/how-looking-at-paintings-became-a-required-course/.

10. This is one of many images that Brownell made of the Byward Market area ca. 1916.

11. There is a significant body of scholarship on the multi-species nature of cities in previous historical eras. See, for instance, Diana Donald, "'Beastly Sights': The Treatment of Animals as a Moral Theme in Representations of London, c.1820–1850,"

Art History 22, no. 4 (1999): 514–44; Greene, *Horses at Work*; Katherine C. Grier, *Pets in America: A History* (Orlando: Harcourt, 2006); Hilda Kean, *Animal Rights: Political and Social Change in Britain Since 1800* (London: Reaktion Books, 1998); Sherry Olson, "The Urban Horse and the Shaping of Montreal, 1840-1914," in *Animal Metropolis: Histories of Human-Animal Relations in Urban Canada*, ed. Joanna Dean, Darcy Ingram, and Christabelle Sethna (Calgary: University of Calgary Press, 2017), 57–86; Sean Kheraj, "Animals and Urban Environments: Managing Domestic Animals in Nineteenth-Century Winnipeg," in *Eco-Cultural Networks and the British Empire*, ed. James Beattie, Edward Melillo, and Emily O'Gorman (London: Bloomsbury Academic, 2015), 263–88; Sean Kheraj, "Living and Working with Domestic Animals in Nineteenth-Century Toronto," in *Urban Explorations: Environmental Histories of the Toronto Region*, ed. L. Anders Sandberg, Stephen Bocking, Colin Coates, and Ken Cruikshank (Hamilton: L.R. Wilson Institute for Canadian History, 2013), 120–40.

12 Patricia Johnston, "Introduction: A Critical Overview of Visual Culture Studies," in *Seeing High & Low: Representing Social Conflict in American Visual Culture* (Berkeley: University of California Press, 2006), 1.

13 Two excellent examples of texts offering ways of thinking through these gaps are Susan Nance, ed., *The Historical Animal* (Syracuse: Syracuse University Press, 2015) and Joanna Dean, Darcy Ingram, and Christabelle Sethna, eds., *Animal Metropolis: Histories of Human-Animal Relations in Urban Canada* (Calgary: University of Calgary Press, 2017).

14 Brett Mizelle, *Pig* (London: Reaktion Books, 2011).

15 In recent years, there has been more of a concerted effort to start using archival collections to tell the stories of non-human animals from previous eras. The multimedia *Beasts of London* exhibition at the Museum of London and the *ANIMALIA: Animals in the Archives* exhibit at the Archives of Ontario are two recent examples of this shift in curatorial practices. For discussion of the *ANIMALIA: Animals in the Archives* exhibition, see Jay Young's chapter in this volume.

16 The first Welland Canal was built between 1824 and 1829; the second Welland Canal was constructed between 1841 and 1854; the third Welland Canal cut a significantly different route though the Niagara Peninsula and was constructed between 1872 and 1887; the fourth Welland Canal was built between 1913 and 1932. For more on the building of the canals as well as their precise routes, see Roberta M. Styran and Robert R. Taylor, *This Great National Object: Building the Nineteenth-Century Welland Canals* (Montreal & Kingston: McGill-Queen's University Press, 2012) and Roberta M. Styran and Robert R. Taylor, *This Colossal Project: Building the Welland Ship Canal, 1913-1932* (Montreal & Kingston: McGill-Queen's University Press, 2016).

17 Styran and Taylor, *This Great National Object*, 125.

18 Robert Stanley Taylor, "The Historical Development of the Four Welland Canals, 1824-1933," M.A. Thesis (University of Western Ontario, 1950), 26.

19 Styran and Taylor, *This Great National Object*, 125.

20 Quoted in Styran and Taylor, 137.

21 Styran and Taylor, 136.

22 Styran and Taylor, 134.

23 Students often struggle with this concept, so I refer them to the very thoughtful chapter called "Viewers Make Meaning" in Marita Sturken and Lisa Cartwright, *Practices of Looking: An Introduction to Visual Culture*, 3rd ed. (Oxford: Oxford University Press, 2017).

24 W. J. T. Mitchell, *What Do Pictures Want?: The Lives and Loves of Images* (Chicago: University of Chicago Press, 2005), 47.

25 Mitchell, *What Do Pictures Want?*, 49.

26 Greene, *Horses at Work*, 7.

27 Styran and Taylor, *This Great National Object*, 121.

16

Creatures on Display: Making an Animal Exhibit at the Archives of Ontario

Jay Young

"Hello human! You aren't the only species in the archives."

This simple but provocative hook, accompanied by a slideshow of vintage photographs, posters, and other visual records, welcomes visitors to the Archives of Ontario's onsite exhibit *ANIMALIA: Animals in the Archives*. Opened in December 2018 as the culmination of nearly two years of research and production, *ANIMALIA* draws on an array of records in the Archives' collections to show how non-human species are documented in an archival repository, and how animals are remembered in other memory institutions.

Whereas past exhibits at the Archives of Ontario commemorated specific, well-known historical events, *ANIMALIA* takes a different, unconventional approach. It argues for the importance of non-human species in Ontario's history by focusing on the records of five animal groups: fish, bears, dogs, horses, and birds. To foster diverse perspectives, the exhibit also features stories, records, and artifacts from other provincial memory institutions and organizations, including Deyohahá:ge: The Indigenous Knowledge Centre at Six Nations Polytechnic and the Royal Ontario Museum. In the months following its opening, hundreds of visitors—from

Fig. 16.1 Entrance to the Archives of Ontario's *ANIMALIA: Animals in the Archives* exhibit. Photo by author.

elementary students to seasoned researchers—have taken in the records and stories presented in *ANIMALIA*.

Animals have been interconnected with all human societies of the past, and so it is no surprise that they are an important aspect of public history. From living history museums to national parks, animals range from being front and centre or a secondary part of public history interpretation; they might be alive and require specialized veterinary care or be on display through taxidermy or photography and other forms of visual representation. At their best, public history projects communicate developments in historical research and introduce audiences to new ways of thinking about the past. Such is the case with successful public history projects about animals.

Surprisingly, only a handful of recent public history projects have focused on the role of animals within archival collections. As a historian trained in academia working in outreach at the Archives of Ontario, I had the experience of curating the *ANIMALIA* exhibit. Here, I want to reflect on some key considerations professionals at one GLAM (Galleries, Libraries, Archives, and Museums) institution faced as they created an exhibit about animal history for a broad public audience. I explore the exhibit's motivations, including the desire to reach new audiences who might have a greater interest in animals than history or archives per se. I then examine the research and content development process for *ANIMALIA*, with a focus on why the exhibit features particular animals, stories, and relationships, while excluding others. I also emphasize the importance of audience interactivity and strategies used to enliven two-dimensional historical records in a three-dimensional exhibit space. Creating an animal exhibit demands narrative choices about audience expectations, physical realities, and institutional dynamics.

The Terrain

The Archives of Ontario is the largest provincial archives in Canada and the premier source of information about the history of the land we now call Ontario and its people. Since 1903, it has been collecting, preserving, and making available the documentary heritage of the province. The Archives, part of Ontario's Ministry of Government and Consumer Services, is the official repository for records that document the decisions, functions, and activities of the largest provincial government in Canada. It also acquires records from individuals, businesses, and organizations that document significant political, economic, social, and cultural developments of Ontario. The Archives' vast collection includes 157,000 metres of textual records, 6.6 million photographs, 418,000 architectural drawings and maps, 84,000 library items, 39,000 hours of audio, video, and film records, and five terabytes of born-digital records. A wide range of researchers, from genealogists, students, and local historians to provincial policymakers, rely on our collections to better understand Ontario and its past.

At the Archives, we know that our records are more valuable if the public uses them. That is why the Archives has a robust outreach program, including facility tours, an active suite of social media channels, and educational programming for elementary, secondary, and post-secondary students linked to the provincial education curriculum. Exhibits—ranging from online, travelling, and onsite displays—showcase the work, collections, and services of the Archives of Ontario and tell innovative and unique stories from our holdings. At the centre of the Archives' exhibits initiative is the Helen McClung Exhibit Area, located within the Archives' public facility at York University in Toronto. This 185-square-metre space features permanent vertical and mobile horizontal cases, and movable display panels that enable flexible spatial arrangements. Since exhibits are typically mounted for a year or more, the Archives displays reproductions instead of original records. This ensures the long-term preservation of the original documents, which researchers can view upon request in the Archives' reading room. Admission to onsite exhibits at the Archives is free to the general public. Researchers, the York University community, and especially students and educators are key audiences for exhibits at our facility.

Before launching its *ANIMALIA* show, the Archives had mounted seven exhibits since its Helen McClung Exhibit Area opened in 2009. The three most-recent exhibits each commemorated an anniversary in Ontario's history: the beginning of the War of 1812, the start of the First World War, and the 150th anniversary of Confederation in Canada. *Perceptions of 1812: Identity, Diversity, Memory* highlighted records and stories in our collections about how the War of 1812 and its aftermath shaped the character of Ontario. *Dear Sadie: Love, Lives, and Remembrance from Ontario's First World War* explored the lives of four ordinary Ontarians who witnessed the conflict either on the battlefield or on the home front. *Family Ties: Ontario Turns 150* looked at how the experiences of four families living in Ontario around the time of Confederation intersected with larger trends of the era. These exhibits increasingly demonstrated the value of collaborating with other institutions, integrating diverse voices, highlighting captivating visual records and succinct textual interpretation, designing interactive activities to engage visitors, and directly aligning content with the provincial education curriculum.

As we began to plan our next project, the exhibit team at the Archives sought a new direction away from the anniversary model of past displays. We wanted greater freedom to explore a unique topic that had not been showcased at the Archives. At first, we thought big with current relevance in mind. We considered mounting an exhibit about the environment in some form, as climate change has made the natural world that sustains humanity a key issue for many Ontarians. Of course, "the environment" was too broad and impractical; we needed a more focused topic.

As with our last exhibit, *Family Ties*, the Archives collaborated with York University's public history program for an undergraduate student to work with the Archives—as part of their course practicum—to narrow the exhibit topic and explore whether we had records in our collections to make the topic feasible. A turning point came during an early meeting with our practicum student, Emma Kuzmaski. She suggested a focus on animal history. Along with her personal interest in other species, Emma was well-versed in the growing field of animal history, having enrolled in Sean Kheraj's upper-year animal history seminar at York. As soon as Emma shared her idea, I knew it was a promising one.

An animal exhibit offered many opportunities to showcase the Archives' government and private collections in a new way and engage new audiences. It enabled an exploration of environmental issues, but also of other political, social, economic, and cultural themes. The Archives constantly strives to interest those who might be unaware or even indifferent to our collections and services. To the general public, an animal topic could challenge the stereotype of archives as mere repositories of dusty, irrelevant documents. If animals intrigued prospective visitors, then they could be exposed to our records and hopefully the value and intrigue of archival collections. This would be especially true for the thousands of students who come through our doors for educational programming, who might have little interest in archives otherwise but who are are passionate about pets, wildlife, and other creatures. I envisioned young people adoring cute historic puppies, and thus becoming engaged with and learning from archival records—even if they did not realize it at first! An exploration of animals in the archives could be an effective topic to underline the historicity of everyday life: how continuity and change define our world, from the rise and fall of species' populations to the shifting practices of what animals we chose to keep as companions. Our current research audience, who often explore our exhibits during visits to our facility, would appreciate an introduction to the growing field of animal studies within the humanities. Ultimately, the topic rested on the element of surprise and a new way of looking at archives: other species are important to Ontario's pasts, and these histories are documented in our collections.

The Hunt

Once the exhibit team had initial support for the topic from management at the Archives, I continued the research process that Emma, our practicum student, had begun. In many ways, research for archival exhibits shares similarities with academic research. Exhibit creators often begin with a list of key questions that drive research, and then they search databases and view large amounts of records. Slowly, a skeletal narrative emerges, which leads to more concentrated research. Following discussions with archivists and other professional staff, I started to get a sense of promising collections to highlight in the exhibit.

When researching and conceptualizing a physical exhibit, however, curators must think in three-dimensions, which is different from a dissertation, journal article, or monograph. I am constantly considering the possibilities and limitations of the physical space, which is less of a concern when the ultimate product is pages of text. Similarly, we have learned from surveys and anecdotal feedback from previous exhibits that visitors prefer seeing more visual records and minimal interpretive text. Since our exhibit is free, "dwell time" (the length of time visitors spend inside the exhibit) is often short, so captivating visuals make a stronger impact than designs that are heavy with text. Our emphasis on dynamic visuals continued as we worked with Context Creative, our graphic design vendor responsible for the design of exhibit panels, wordmark (a text-based logo), and brand identity. We stressed an immersive experience filled with colour and other tactics that could energize the space for students and other visitors.

As my research progressed, an exhibit outline emerged. Initially, we contemplated different sections for various animal-human relationships, such as companionship, food, and work. Yet we felt this structure might cloud the narrative for visitors and lead to a repetition of species that fit within more than one category. Instead, we decided to focus on specific animal animal groups—a subtle nod to the spatial arrangement of zoos. Although any decision involves trade-offs, we felt our focus aligned best with our exhibit goals.

A key question remained: what animals would be featured, and how many? Which animals would be excluded? Mounting any exhibit involves choices, and some visitors might be unsatisfied. A major consideration was that the animals had to be well documented in our collections in order to showcase multiple record types. After all, creating greater public awareness of the records in our collections is at the foundation of our mandate. We also wanted to feature animals that represented varied relationships with humans, which translated to different motivations for their documentation. For example, animals living outside of captivity are typically documented in different ways in archival records than those with whom humans share companionship. Being a provincial institution of a large geographic territory, it was also important that we select animals found in diverse habitats across Ontario.

We decided to feature records and stories about five animal groups, an appropriate number based on the exhibit area's size and visitor enjoyment: fish, bears, dogs, horses, and birds. Admittedly, there was some debate about the inclusion of dogs and not cats, but canines won out. We simply had more, varied records of dogs in multiple formats than their feline counterparts. Dogs also allowed us to explore a greater number of human connections; in this case, their companionship and their significance as guide dogs, hunting aids, and other forms of work. Other animals chosen for the exhibit also promised an array of stories rooted in diverse relationships with humans. A number of factors influenced the animals that are the focus of the exhibit, from how comprehensively species are documented in our records to the ability to cover wide swaths of Ontario's geography.

The Specimens

The selection of specific animal groups and other considerations determined the stories we told, and those we excluded. A dramatic range of emotions marks the historical relationships between humans and other species. Given the Archives' role as a memory institution and a government organization, mounting any exhibit must be sensitive to our role as a public body and the expectations of our audiences, some of whom are young children. The unique nature of the visitor experience in our exhibit space also influences the subject matter. Most visitors see our exhibits as part of educational programming or a stop on a wider tour of the Archives' public facility, during which there is insufficient time to properly discuss and contextualize sensitive material. Our exhibit content does not shy away from exploring difficult moments of the past, but controversial topics must be approached delicately. *ANIMALIA* spotlights complex historical themes, like conservation, species extinction, animal welfare, animal labour, and hunting. One obvious exclusion is the massive impact of the livestock industry on Ontario's development, which is only highlighted indirectly in a handful of records scattered throughout the exhibit. This might at first seem like an oversight for a province whose capital city, Toronto, is nicknamed "Hogtown"; nonetheless, our exhibit team felt visitors—especially young students who make up a substantial segment of our exhibit audience—would likely be turned off by multiple visual records of holding pens, slaughterhouses, and other spaces related to animal processing. These tough choices made by the Archives of Ontario's exhibit team speak to the theoretical and practical challenges memory institutions face when creating animal history products for a wide public audience.

Stories in the exhibit examine the impact of humans on animal habitats, and the unpredictability of other species. A spotlight on sea lampreys in *ANIMALIA*'s fish section introduces these concepts and highlights how government records document ecological challenges. Lampreys are a parasitic invasive species to Ontario that kill their prey via a sucker-like mouth filled with sharp teeth. Originating in the Atlantic Ocean, they were first seen in Lake Ontario in the 1830s after completion of the Erie Canal. After expansion of the Welland Canal in 1919, the species spread to Lake Erie and eventually to the rest of the Great Lakes. By the 1950s, lampreys had devastated populations of lake trout, a popular species for commercial and recreational fisheries. One solution—mechanical barriers—did not work. By 1962, the lamprey crisis had subsided in the public's consciousness, following the application of a chemical that killed lamprey larvae. The story is told through photographs, graphs, slides, and other records from the Ontario Ministry of Natural Resources and Forestry's predecessors that bring awareness to the complex field of invasive species management. To help animate these records, the exhibit team commissioned a touchable

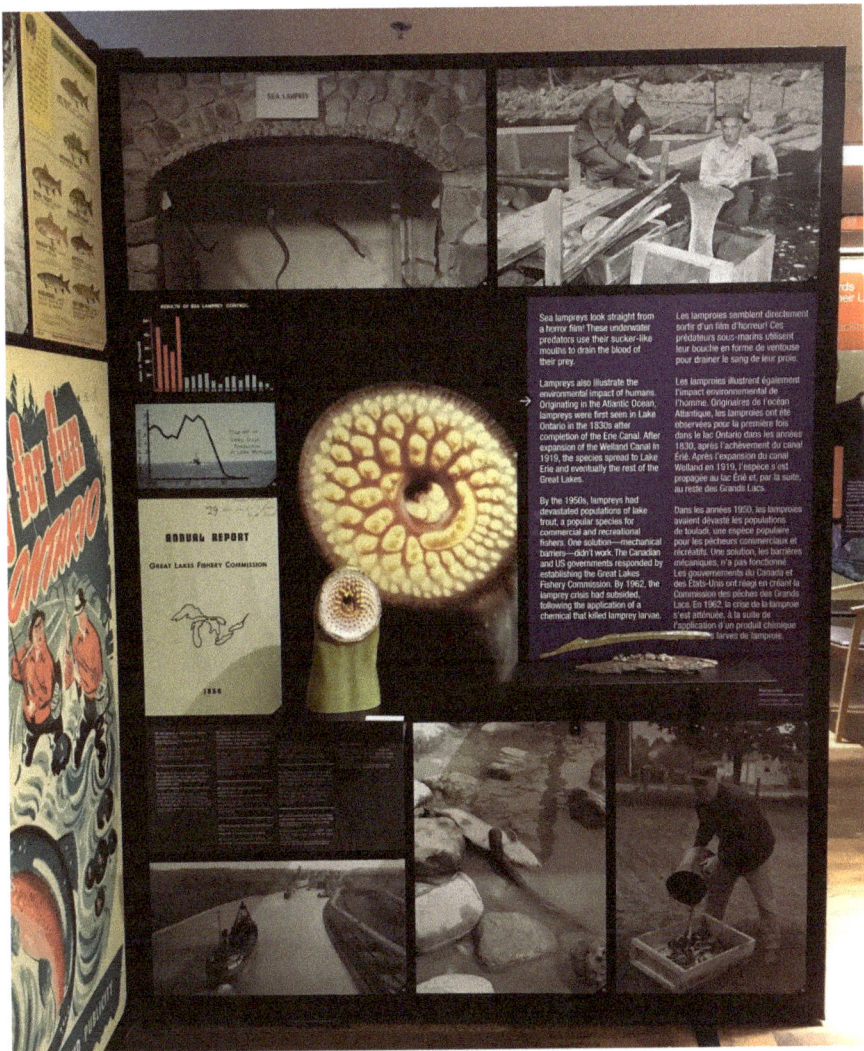

Fig. 16.2 Sea lamprey panel in the exhibit's section on fish. Photo by author.

three-dimensional model of a lamprey's ferocious mouth—a big hit with students!

Collaboration has been key to the success of *ANIMALIA*. Working with other institutions allows the Archives to enhance displays through

Fig. 16.3 G. D. Atkinson Flour & Feed: [street scene], Cornwall, Ontario, [ca. 1900], Marsden Kemp fonds, Archives of Ontario, I0013581.

artifacts, videos, and other sources and assets not present in our collections. Importantly, it enables the exhibit to include a wider range of voices and perspectives and leverage other institution-wide priorities. Doing so also brings further exposure to our collaborators and offers an opportunity for their holdings to be interpreted in a different setting with new audiences. The exhibit's section on bears features video of staff from Deyohahá:ge: The Indigenous Knowledge Centre at Six Nations Polytechnic in Ohsweken, Ontario, reciting stories that show how bears play a central role in many narratives of the Six Nations of the Grand River, shaping Haudenosaunee spiritual beliefs and illustrating their deep-rooted connections to the natural world. The Indigenous Knowledge Centre is collecting these stories as a way of preserving and nurturing Indigenous knowledge and wisdom. For the Archives, collaborating with the Centre has furthered our goal of working with Indigenous communities across Ontario. These videos—like display cases featuring horse-related artifacts from Black Creek Pioneer Village, a living history museum within walking distance of the Archives, and three specimens from the world's largest collection of passenger pigeons on loan from the Royal Ontario Museum—help us to show how animal memory is preserved in other ways beyond archival records.

The work of archivists and other subject-matter experts is another theme throughout the exhibit. One of my favourite records in *ANIMALIA* is a photograph from circa 1900 of a main commercial street in Cornwall, Ontario. In the foreground, a dog looks away from the camera. Inspired by Susan Nance's poignant discussion of the often hidden presence of other animals in archives, we feature a large reproduction of the photo in order to stress the process of archival research, and the essential role archivists play in describing collections to enhance their usefulness for current and future generations. "This photo prompts many questions about the place of animals in archives, and how they are present throughout the process of recordkeeping," notes interpretive text that accompanies the photo. We are neither aware if the photographer meant to document the dog (likely not), nor do we know much about the dog or its life. Luckily, when the Archives digitized the photo, staff listed "dogs" as a keyword for the record's metadata, which meant I was able to find this photo during research for *ANIMALIA* and include it as a useful—if ordinary—snapshot of one dog's experience in turn-of-the-century Ontario.

The Archives of Ontario believes that interactive activities help visitors better engage with content in exhibits that consist mostly of two-dimensional documents. Over time, our exhibits have increasingly featured elements involving touch, video, audio, searching, and trivia. Years of witnessing audiences of different ages, reading abilities, levels of historical knowledge, and other considerations have shown the Archives exhibit team that interactive activities make for a more active visitor experience. Engagement is the first step in inviting students to learn. Many interactives fill *ANIMALIA*. The exhibit team sought to design interactives that would be fun for visitors, but also introduce them to different historical and ecological concepts. One activity draws on information from a 1965 telephone survey report about dog breeds in the Archives' Elliott Research Corporation fonds (F 245) to urge visitors to think about continuity and change over time. An upright panel asks visitors to discover the most

Fig. 16.4 Interactive panel in exhibit's section on dogs. Photo by author.

popular dog breeds in 1965 and the most current data in 2017 via flip tabs. Not only does it prompt questions about sample size and data reliability, but also about why some breeds have fallen out of favour (Dalmatian) while others have remained on the list (golden retriever) or have become more popular (poodle and Shetland sheepdog). The exhibit's largest interactive feature is the last stop for many exhibit visitors. Oversized reproductions of historic photographs and artworks from the Archives representing diverse habitats within the province wrap across five large glass walls. Here, visitors are encouraged to draw their favourite animal in Ontario and place the paper sketch onto the animal's associated habitat represented on the wall. The interactive urges visitors to think about the diversity of animal life in the province, while giving them an opportunity to become part of the exhibit (and hopefully satisfying those who wish other animals were featured). Interactives bring archival records to life, increase dwell time, play to different learning styles, and foster a more immersive visitor experience.

* * *

Almost a year after its opening, *ANIMALIA* has shown many signs of success. The show has seen almost six thousand visitors, putting it on track to surpass attendance levels of previous exhibits at the Archives. Many visitors have left positive comments in the exhibit's guestbook by noting what they learned and why animals are important to them. Hundreds of elementary and secondary school students have explored the exhibit as part of a full-day field trip to our facility, in which they learn about archival records and Ontario's past. Educational programming at the Archives links to the exhibit's key themes, and students enjoy completing a "scavenger hunt" activity designed to teach them how to draw observational insights from the records, the accompanying interpretive text, and citations. An online version of the exhibit on the Archives of Ontario website, along with "micro-exhibit" content posted on our Twitter and Facebook channels, have also furthered the reach of *ANIMALIA* to thousands more people. As expected, our social media posts have promoted the exhibit to wider audiences, in part thanks to the many different animal-related days of significance (with accompanying hashtags) across Canada and the globe.

Admittedly, a small number of visitors have shared criticisms: in particular, the choice of dogs as an exhibit focus over cats (some in jest and others in seriousness), and the little space the exhibit gives to the role of livestock, animal processing, and related aspects in the province's history. Whereas some may see these silences as missed opportunities, they remind me of the choices curators must make when creating an exhibit within an institutional setting for diverse public audiences. Like any form of public history or cultural production, an exhibit cannot cover all aspects of a topic, especially one as wide as animal history. An exhibit about the documentary heritage of Ontario's slaughterhouses might have its time and place, but the exhibit team at the Archives of Ontario felt there were other topics that aligned better with our institutional context and promised greater appeal to our audiences.

The Archives exhibit team had to consider a multitude of factors related to audience expectation and engagement in the creation of *ANIMALIA*. The physical realities of the exhibit space, along with the Archives' brand and position as a government institution, also influenced key decisions about narrative, tone, and style. The exhibit has shown that the relationships between humans and other animals of the past is fertile terrain for public history projects. It has also demonstrated how exhibits and other forms of public history can take inspiration from emerging fields of academic study and translate research trends into products for popular audiences. In an era when some pundits have questioned new fields of research in the humanities, *ANIMALIA*'s greatest contribution within the academic realm might be how it shows such pursuits to be as enduring and relevant as ever.

17

Portraits of Extinction: Encountering Bluebuck Narratives in the Natural History Museum[1]

Dolly Jørgensen

Its snout is brightly illuminated against the stark black background. Its eyes reflect the light bouncing off the glass. It looks more grey than blue, but perhaps it would look more blue under a radiant sun, running across the plains. But it cannot run. It cannot even move—it is just a skin stretched out and mounted to resemble its former self. Of course, that makes it a perfect subject for a portrait; a portrait of extinction.

The taxidermied bluebuck (*Hippotragus leucophaeus*) I encountered at the Muséum national d'Histoire naturelle (MNHN) in Paris, France, is one of only four in the world. The bluebuck, an African antelope, was a victim of white colonization of the continent, only described by Western science in 1766 and extirpated by around 1800. The particular specimen on display is a portrait of the bluebuck—a remnant of a species which is long gone. Bluebucks exist only as representations of bluebucks.

Portraiture is an art form that takes on the Herculean task of revealing both the outside of an object or person and claiming to represent its internal essence.[2] The portrait prompts the viewer to use her imagination

371

Fig. 17.1 Bluebuck specimen on display in Muséum national d'Histoire naturelle (MNHN) in Paris, France. Photograph by author, July 2015.

to imagine the context beyond what is pictured—to visualize the world that the subject lived in. The portrait, then, both reveals directly and hints obliquely at its world.

Portraits are not reserved for individuals. As anyone who has appreciated Van Eyck's *The Arnolfini Wedding Portrait* (1434) or Rembrandt's *Night Watch* (1642) will know, portraits can also be a group affair. Whether there is one subject in the frame or several, Catherine Soussloff has argued that portraits are "pictures particularly indicative not only of an individual, but also of kinship and social status."[3] Portraits are about connections.

While art historians employ the term "portraiture" when discussing the representation of a person (or persons) in artistic form like a painting or sculpture, in this chapter I apply the concept of portraiture to animals in museums. This is not as great of a stretch as one might suppose. As scholars of taxidermy practice have demonstrated, considerable artistic skill goes into crafting animals put on display.[4] The taxidermy process involves separating skin from body, treating the skin to avoid decomposition and degradation, shaping a replacement body frame, replacing soft parts like noses and eyes, and then putting it all together into a thing that resembles the animal it once was. The physical body of the once-living animal is one element in the portrait, but it is not the whole image. When put on display, more things are added in the way of stands, labels, and cases—these identifying elements correspond well to practices in early modern portraiture which included names and even biographical stories on the canvas or the frame into which the art work has been placed. Because museums often have only one specimen of a species (particularly when specimens are rare, as they are with extinct species), a particular animal body on display with all of these accoutrements becomes a portrayal of the species as a whole.

Animal portraits encapsulate stories. As Samuel Alberti has argued, looking at museum objects allows us to see "relationships between people and people, between objects and objects, and between objects and people. We encounter not only collectors, curators, and scientists but also visitors and audiences. In this conception, the museum becomes a vessel for the bundle of relationships enacted through each of the thousands of specimens on display and in store."[5] The choices made for the display—from which specimens are collected to which specimens are selected for display to what positions animals are mounted in—all enact relationships.[6]

For environmental historians, this means that the museum is a place within which we can investigate the multi-faceted relationships of people and objects over time, including how stories of the past are communicated today. Environmental and animal historians have rarely engaged with natural history museums as places of environmental storytelling, although these museums include rich textual and physical material for analysis.[7] As Jay Young observes in Chapter 16 of this volume, "creating an animal exhibit demands narrative choices," and these choices deserve scrutiny. Historians of science and museum studies scholars, on the other hand, have been quite interested in the cultural contexts of natural history exhibitions, as well as tracing the histories of specimen acquisition.[8] There is an unexplored space of inquiry around how (and if) museums communicate animal histories—the historical interactions of animals as both individuals and species with others—in addition to typical displays of "natural history" which focus on the biological traits of animals and evolutionary development.

Because collected animal bodies are historical artifacts—and in the case of extinct animals, irreplaceable artifacts—when they are put on display they become interpretations of history. The history that is told in these public spaces does not come from an individual specimen alone; rather, it comes through relations in the museum, as noted by Alberti. A room with animals in glass cases is an archive of animal bodies, but it is also an archive of animal portraits. These portraits capture animals that can exist in our present only as representations. How each portrait is painted in our minds will matter to how we imagine them as they once were.

In this chapter I will examine three portraits of the bluebuck, one created by the MNHN in Paris, one by the Naturhistoriska Riksmuseet (NRM) in Stockholm, and one by Naturalis in Leiden to see how animals displayed in the archive of the natural history museum can narrate extinction. The fourth extant taxidermied bluebuck (and the only female specimen) is owned by the Naturhistorisches Museum Wien, but it is not on display, so it has not been included.[9] I am not writing an object biography of these specimens—although that could be done by examining how they were collected, treated, mounted, and displayed over time—but rather examining how they are shown to the visitor, frozen at one moment in time as a portrait of extinction.[10]

My method is one of encounter with the animal through display practices. The encounter with the museum specimen is an encounter with a physical object—a physical trace of an animal that once was living—in a specific context. Natural history museums have a long history of display practices, which involve putting animal remains in front of visitors.[11] Both in the collection of an object and its display, messages are communicated to the audience. As Hilde Hein observed, "[m]useums are actually warehouses of material things only superficially. At bottom they have always been reservoirs of meaning."[12] The representational practices of animals in museums—which animals are put on display and how they are displayed—connect (or disconnect) humans from those animals.[13] Museums are media spaces that create interaction between the audiences and the displays as well as among the visitors themselves.[14] In order to unpack the representational practices, meaning making, and media messiness of the exhibition of animal bodies, I adopt a critically situated, place-based, lived-experience method, which Duncan Grewcock has advocated for in museum studies.[15] The encounter with animal traces in the museum is a process—it unfolds through interaction and emotion. In this chapter I take the reader with me through this process of seeing bluebuck portraits.

Portrait 1: In Light and Darkness

The bluebuck (*hippotrague bleu* in French) at MNHN stands in a gallery dedicated to extinct and endangered animals. All of the glass cases are constructed with black frames, black backgrounds, and black bottom coverings. The labels are black with white print. Parts of the animals, especially the faces, are eerily illuminated with spotlights. The bodies are not evenly lighted and there is minimal ambient lighting in the room.

This technique of accentuating the difference between light and dark is known in art history as *chiaroscuro*. One of chiaroscuro's manifestations appeared in Dutch seventeenth-century paintings as the nocturnal scene lit by candlelight.[16] In these paintings, such as Dominicus van Tol's *Boy with a Mousetrap by Candlelight* (ca. 1664–65) and Gerrit Dou's *Old Woman at a Window with a Candle* (1671),[17] the candle makes the subject's face glow and slightly illuminates the surroundings to give a sense of the objects in the room. Working by candlelight stressed the virtue of using diligently one's mortal time, which can be snuffed out like a candle.[18] Rather than being portraits of a specific person, these seventeenth-century genre paintings depicted scenes of everyday life.[19] There are, however, serious limitations to reading genre paintings as historically accurate representations of the past; as noted by Wayne Franits, architecture, clothing, and other details in genre paintings can be inaccurate or incongruent with contemporary practice.[20]

The chiaroscuro portrait of extinction of the bluebuck created in the MNHN gallery draws the viewer into the details: the hairs lining up to follow the body's contours, the ridges on the horns repeating their pattern, the eyelids creating a double frame around the glass eye. But more than simply aesthetic, the chiaroscuro technique stresses the fleeting nature of life illuminated in this light. The label next to the body gives it historicity:

the bluebuck "was one of the first African mammal victims of the colonization of southern Africa. A small fearful animal, it was easy to hunt for meat, usually intended to feed dogs."[21] Life was fleeting for the bluebuck, which was not fleet of foot.

The room is filled with similar stories of the end: the New Caledonian rail that was "without a doubt the victim of hunting and animals introduced by humans"; the quagga that suffered "intensive hunting"; the Carolina parakeet whose extinction was "accelerated by hunting to supply the feather trade"; the passenger pigeon "relentlessly hunted"; and the great bustard that was "exterminated by hunters" in France. "Victim" is a word that appears in many of the labels, stressing the one-sided power relationship between human and animal in these cases. There is an underlying irony in these laments of hunting, which not only brought about the extinction of the species in question but also supplied the body now on display.

Although the gallery of extinct and endangered species at the MNHN contains many bodies and many stories, the chiaroscuro techniques make each appear to stand alone. The visitor is drawn to each body partly illuminated by light while partly concealed in dark. Yet these individual portraits speak to the same widespread phenomenon. They become genre portraits, a type that is repeated over and over again with the same aesthetic and the same basic message. It is a missive recounting the candles snuffed out too soon. Visitors are left in that darkness of extinction, with the anticipation that even those species on display that are not yet extinct soon will be.

Portait 2: Family Resemblances

Sweden's bluebuck (*blåbock* in Swedish) stands in a wall case near a corner on the first floor of the NRM. At its feet is a mounted thylacine and a small pile of Hawaiian tree snails. The bluebuck looks toward the adjacent corner case containing the extinct bird specimens: great auk, Mauritius starling, ivory billed woodpecker, passenger pigeon, huia, Cuban macaw, great moa (only a leg bone), and copy of an elephant bird egg.

Displays in natural history museums organize their specimens according to various principles. One way is taxonomic: all the birds together, all the land mammals together, all the marine mammals together, etc. The Naturhistorisches Museum Wien and the Natural History Museum

Fig. 17.2 Extinction cases that include a bluebuck on display in Naturhistoriska Riksmuseet (NRM) in Stockholm, Sweden. Photograph by author, May 2019.

in London follow this principle so that animals of the same type appear in the same galleries. Another common organization strategy is geographic. For example, the American Museum of Natural History in New York has a Hall of New York State Environment and a Hall of Ocean Life, both of which mix animals from taxonomic categories in order to show environmental connections. A third organizational principle is functional. The Horniman Museum and Gallery near London, for example, does this by grouping some animals with similar properties, such as wings (birds, bats, insects), and grouping others to show evolutionary variation, such as skeletal form.

The NRM has grouped the bluebuck along with the thylacine, Hawaiian snail, great auk, and others together because of one similarity: they are all extinct. This serves as a functional type or organization, like wings or hooves. These specimens make up a family of things related to one another through their non-existence. This kind of grouping—the extinct animal case—is a tactic used in other museums as well. For example, the Royal Albert Museum and Art Gallery in Exeter, UK, has one case in a wildlife room where they have collected all of their extinct birds and insects. But this is by no means the most common strategy: many museums spread out their extinct specimens into other groupings, such as the extinct birds in the Naturhistorisches Museum Wien, which are found randomly alongside common species, and the thylacine at the Smithsonian placed alongside existing Australian animals.

An understated sign inside the case near the bluebuck's back foot declares: "Displayed here are examples of extinct specimens. Some of them have been wiped out by humans, others due to natural causes."[22] But there is no indication of how each particular species died out, so the viewer is left to wonder if natural or man-made causes were in play for each. The bluebuck label only tells us that "the last bluebucks were killed in South Africa in 1800," a vague statement that is quite different from the MNHN one. The thylacine label likewise notes the last capture of a thylacine in the wild in 1933 and the presence of one in a zoo until 1936, but nothing is said about the deliberate program of extermination that brought about their extermination.[23] On the other hand, the great auk label does mention that the bird was "easy prey since it lacked the ability to fly," and the Cuban parrot story notes that it was "heavily hunted and young were captured as caged birds."

In a nearby display case, there is a grouping of species threatened with extinction. On this display's label, there is no doubt about the anthropogenic nature of extinction: "During the past 400 years, humans have drastically altered most of Earth's habitats. As a result, species are becoming rapidly extinct." An asp (a European freshwater fish), a Galapagos tortoise, and a gyrfalcon, among others, appear in this case. This group is related to the animals in the extinction case—there is an implication that they might have to be moved over in the future from the status of endangered to extinct. But they are a separate and distinct group at the moment—endangered is one thing and extinct is something else. This makes the presentation quite different from the MNHN room, which mixes endangered and extinct species haphazardly.

The mode of displaying extinction at NRM stresses kinship and status, as Soussloff pointed out is common in portraits.[24] Although they have individual labels, the specimens are not highlighted as individuals in spotlights; instead, they are associated visually and textually with each other. This gives them cohesion and provides extinction with a sense of scale at a glance. Yet unlike the MNHN display, which evokes strong emotional reactions with its chiaroscuro style, the NRM group portrait is rather flat with its evenly lit specimens standing in teal coloured cases with small off-white labels. The bluebuck is presented as an unremarkable member of the group called "extinct." Putting it together in this group creates an extinction family portrait.

Portrait 3: Pixelated encounters

RMNH.MAM.20681.b

Scientific name	*Hippotragus leucophaeus* Pallas, 1766
	Antilope leucophaea Pallas, 1766
Vernaculars	—
Vernaculars from associated taxon	blue buck (English)
Registration number	RMNH.MAM.20681.b
Source	Naturalis – Zoology and Geology catalogues
License	CC0 4.0
Institution	Naturalis Biodiversity Center
Collection name	Mammalia
Basis of record	PreservedSpecimen
Type status	Lectotype
Phase or stage	Adult
Sex	Male
Part	Skin
Preparation method	mounted skin
Number of specimens	—
Date	—
Collector	—
Locality	Swellendam
Site coordinates	—
Collectors field number	—

This is my initial digital encounter with RMNH.MAM.20681.b, the bluebuck held by Naturalis in Leiden.[25] Because this specimen is not on display in Leiden, the only way to see it without a special storage visit is to visit it online. Information about this animal has been entered into the BioPortal database, which catalogues Naturalis' holdings.[26] Here, the bluebuck has been converted into metadata: its scientific name, specimen number, sex, preparation, etc.

Even something as dry and potentially uninviting as the BioPortal tells a story. Literary scholar Ursula Heise has written about the construction of environmental narratives through databases like this one.[27] A key piece of information in this flood of data is that this specimen is the lectotype, which means that this individual is considered to be the representative specimen for the whole species of *Hippotragus leucophaeus*. The earliest known full-body image of a bluebuck, published in 1778 in G. L. le Clerc Comte de Buffon's *Historie naturelle, générale et particulière* and drawn by J. Allamand, was based on this museum specimen.[28] The database records "type status" because it gives the specimen a particular role for the scientific community. Any future newly-discovered suspected bluebuck specimens would be compared to this one to determine their legitimacy. Interestingly, there is no metadata for the species status; that is, there is no way to search the database for all "extinct" things, and there is nothing in the record that would tell an uninformed viewer that the animal was extinct. The database's narrative is not deliberately a story of extinction, although the reason I have found the specimen is because of its extinction.

After the metadata presentation, twelve photographs are linked to the RMNH.MAM.201681.b entry. These photographs together give a complete view of the specimen, including two whole body shots and close-ups of the head, neck, sides, legs, and rump. This photographic specimen display offers a view that the specimens described above do not: it allows the viewer to see all sides of the animal. In the museum cases in Paris and Stockholm, only one side of the bluebuck is visible—the other side faces the back wall of the case and thus is hidden from view. The Leiden images can be combined, at least mentally, into a 3D experience of the animal.[29]

Because each of these images is downloadable in high resolution (12 megapixels), as a viewer I can zoom in tightly. Using the fourth image on the second row, for example, I can see the individual hairs in the ears, the

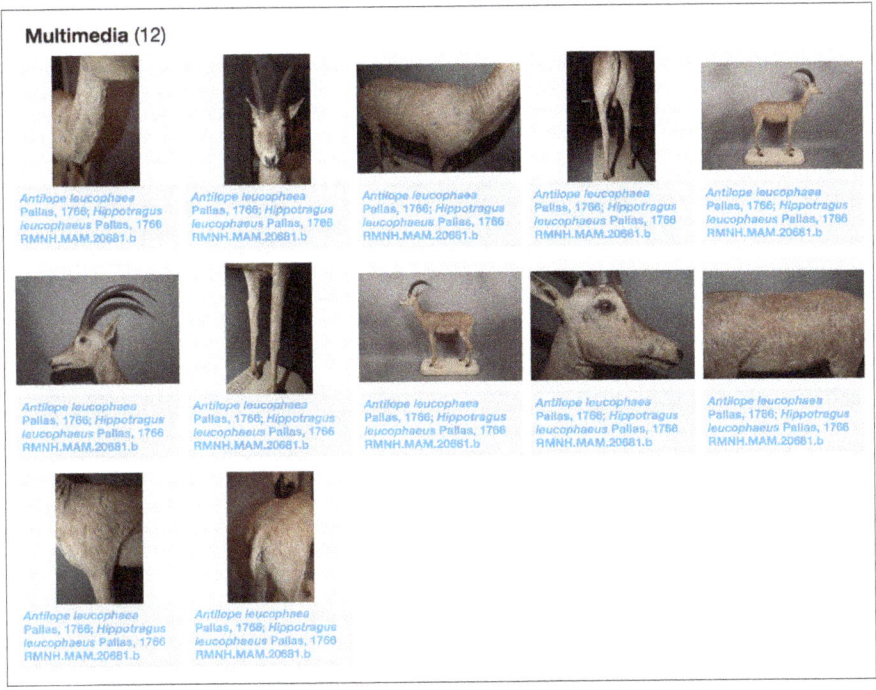

Fig. 17.3 Images of the bluebuck specimen held by Naturalis in Leiden, Netherlands, as documented in BioPortal. Images released into public domain by Naturalis under license CC0.

defined horn ridges, and even the holes and stitches in the skin created by the taxidermy process (Figure 17.4). This means that I can see details that are not visible if the specimen were standing in front of me behind glass.[30] A more intimate portrait of the bluebuck is available through this digital tool than in a museum gallery.

I am reminded by this viewing of the bluebuck about the PixCell series of artworks by Kohei Nawa. Nawa covers taxidermied animals found for sale online with variably sized beads to represent the pixels that the animal was first viewed as. As the artist says in a statement about his work, the PixCells produce "a magnifying and distorting lens effect occurring over all cell units."[31] When I encountered Nawa's works (two deer in different museum exhibits), the PixCells had indeed converted object into

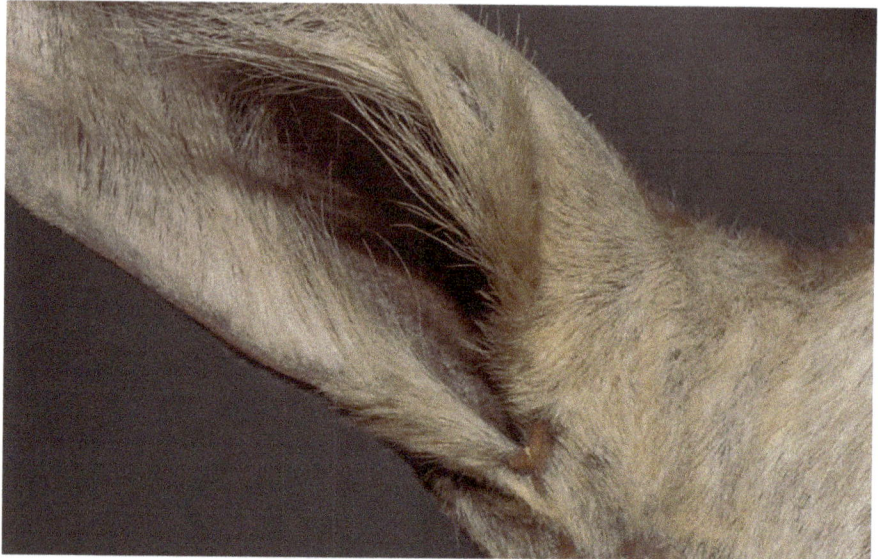

Fig. 17.4 Author-created close-up of image RMHN.MAM.20681.b_02 in BioPortal of the bluebuck specimen held by Naturalis in Leiden, Netherlands. Original image released into public domain by Naturalis under license CC0.

pixels, some of which were zoomed-in areas highlighting only a few hairs as if under a microscope. There is an uncanny feeling of seeing the animal parts very close-up while at the same time seeing the animal whole. This is precisely what the digital photographs of the Dutch bluebuck do. The pixilation allows the creation of a portrait at different zoom levels simultaneously.

Encountering a digital animal is not identical to encountering one as a physical object, but it is no less authentic an encounter. As environmental historian Finn Arne Jørgensen has argued, experiencing wildlife and environments through digital means is mediated by technology, but so is every other environmental encounter because technology always operates as a mediator of human experience of nature.[32] My encounters with the bluebucks at MNHN and NRM were also mediated by the glass of the cases, the labels next to them, the room's structures, and more. The museum database is no less an animal archive than the museum gallery.

Possibilities (and Limitations) of Extinction Portraits

At the beginning of this chapter, I noted that modern portraiture claims to present and represent both the external form of an object or person and its internal essence. How well do these three portraits of the bluebuck measure up?

They all represent the external form of the animal in that they all show a specimen that has been prepared to look like the bluebuck as it was when it was alive—or at least what someone thought it looked like when it was alive. The bluebuck specimens do look like the earliest drawings of the species, but that is not because the taxidermists did a good job; it is because the artist did: the earliest drawings were made from the prepared specimen, not the other way around. As far as we know the artists who produced the eighteenth-century drawings of bluebucks while they were still alive never saw one. Some of the taxidermy has stood the test of time more than others—both the Stockholm and Leiden specimens show their seams clearly. Of course, this could be thought of as a benefit to viewers who would be reminded by seeing the taxidermy remnants that the object before them is not a whole bluebuck but instead one that has been taken apart and then put back together far from its original home. Realizing the object's history can perhaps make us appreciate this extinct animal portrait as an artistic product.

The inside of the animal, its essence, is inconsistent in these portraits. There is some character description of the bluebuck in Paris: small, fearful, easy to hunt. Yet the taxidermied animal on display in MNHN appears to be the opposite—it looks quite regal and majestic. This is in contrast to the specimens in Sweden and the Netherlands which look rather frail. The portrait in Stockholm stresses the family status of the bluebuck as extinct, and the Paris exemplar's story also points out its extinction. "Extinct" is indeed one of the essential characteristics of the bluebuck. Yet, quite unexpectedly, the Leiden specimen's portrait does not make visible this characteristic at all. Nothing in this digital portrait would tell you that the thing you are looking at cannot be seen outside of a museum.

There is no single portrait of what a bluebuck was, or even of what it is today, in the archive of the natural history museum. It is an object of scientific curiosity in Leiden, a lamented victim in Paris, and a harbinger of extinctions-to-come in Stockholm. None of these are untrue, but they all seem incomplete taken alone. Perhaps brought together, they give us a fuller picture of the bluebuck and its extinction.

Natural history museums are being challenged in the twenty-first century to tackle the grand environmental challenges our age, including climate change and planetary mass extinction, in order to both educate the public and inspire action.[33] Yet part of moving forward is acknowledging the past. Portraiture as a genre connects the present to the past: each portrait crystalizes a subject in a moment in time and presents that to a viewer in some indeterminate future. How the portrait of extinction is constructed in the museum matters, because looking at a bluebuck is an encounter with a historical traumatic event. The bluebucks did not choose to "sit" for these portraits—instead, their lives were violently ended and their bodies set in a museum context. That trauma demands memory, acknowledgement, and mourning. Loss and mourning have the potential to do work for contemporary environmentalism.[34] The extinction of the bluebuck is a loss worth mourning—not as the universalizing trauma of the sixth mass extinction, but as a particular loss which "needs to be allowed this specificity if the loss is to have its full significance."[35] When I look at each bluebuck portrait, I am discovering irreplaceable lives.

Putting all three portraits together, we can create a composite understanding of the bluebuck as both a trace of the animal past in the archive and a portent for the future if ways of being in the world go unchanged. Museums themselves cannot change the bluebuck's extinction history, but the visitor to the gallery might become a "transformed witness: the observer transformed by their observation" through their interaction with this history.[36] As Jennifer Bonnell and Roger Simon have observed, exhibitions offering intimacy with "difficult" histories, such as extinction, challenge visitors "to ask what it means, in light of the experience of the past, to be what we are now (and, perhaps more significantly, how we might be in the future)."[37] The transformed observer has the capacity to change future stories. Presenting the bluebuck in the museum will not bring the animal back to life, but displaying a well-thought-out portrait of the bluebuck has the potential to communicate this animal's extinction history as something meaningful to the visitor. Through the encounter, the animal's history might move beyond the archive.

NOTES

1. This research was funded by the Research Council of Norway through the author's project "Beyond Dodos and Dinosaurs: Displaying Extinction and Recovery in Museums" (project number 283523).
2. For a general discussion of portraits and their functions, see Catherine Soussloff, *The Subject in Art: Portraiture and the Birth of the Modern* (Durham: Duke University Press, 2006).
3. Soussloff, *The Subject in Art*, 8
4. Merle Patchett, "Repair Work: Surfacing the Geographies of Dead Animals," *Museum and Society* 6, no. 2 (2008): 98–122; Rachel Poliquin, "The Matter and Meaning of Museum Taxidermy," *Museum and Society* 6, no. 2 (2008): 123–34; and Rachel Poliquin, *The Breathless Zoo: Taxidermy and the Cultures of Longing* (University Park, PA: Pennsylvania State University Press, 2012).
5. Samuel J. M. M. Alberti, "Objects and the Museum," *Isis* 96 (2005): 561.
6. Jane C. Desmond, *Displaying Death and Animating Life: Human-Animal Relations in Art, Science, and Everyday Life* (Chicago: University of Chicago Press, 2016), 6. For an idea of the entanglements in play, see also Donna Haraway's analysis of taxidermy, Carl Akeley, and the American Museum of Natural History, "Teddy Bear Patriarchy: Taxidermy in the Garden of Eden, New York City, 1908-1936," *Social Text* 11 (1984/85): 20–64.
7. Dolly Jørgensen, "Bettering Stories about Stories about Nature," *EcoZon@* 11 (2020): 200–7.
8. For a good overview of the historiography (although it is now somewhat dated), see Samuel J. M. M. Alberti, "Constructing Nature Behind Glass," *Museum and Society* 6, no. 2 (2008): 73–97. For more recent scholarship, see Karen A. Rader and Victoria E. M. Cain, *Life on Display: Revolutionizing U.S. Museum of Science and Natural History in the Twentieth Century* (Chicago: University of Chicago Press, 2014); the essays in Liv Emma Thorsen, Karen A. Rader, and Adam Dodd, eds., *Animals on Display: The Creaturely in Museums, Zoos, and Natural History* (University Park: Pennsylvania State University Press, 2013), as well as other work by Liv Emma Thorsen, including "Animal Matter in Museums: Exemplifying Materiality," in Hilda Kean and Philip Howell, eds., *The Routledge Companion to Animal-Human History* (Abingdon: Routledge, 2018), 171–95.
9. One picture taken by the museum is available online on their page introducing their zoological collections: https://www.nhm-wien.ac.at/forschung/1_zoologie_wirbeltiere/saeugetier-brsammlung. It is shown in ridiculously blue lighting that makes it appear bright blue.
10. For biographies of animals in museums, see Samuel J. M. M. Alberti, ed., *The Afterlives of Animals: A Museum Menagerie* (Charlottesville: University of Virginia Press, 2011) and Liv Emma Thorsen, *Elephants are Not Picked from Trees: Animal Biographies in Gothenburg Natural History Museum* (Aarhus: Aarhus University Press, 2014).
11. For histories of natural history collections and display practices, see Lorraine Daston and Katharine Park, *Wonders and the Order of Nature, 1150–1750* (New York: Zone Books, 1998); Rader and Cain, *Life on Display*; Tony Bennet, *The Birth of the Museum:*

History, Theory, Politics (New York: Routledge, 1995); and Anna Omedes and Ernesto Páramo, "The Evolution of Natural History Museums and Science Centers: From Cabinets to Museums to . . ." in *The Future of Natural History Museums*, ed. Eric Dorfman (London and New York: Routledge, 2018), 168–83.

12   Hilde S. Hein, *The Museum in Transition: A Philosophical Perspective* (Washington, DC: Smithsonian Books, 2000), 55.

13   For examples of animal display practices and representation, see Thorsen, Rader, and Dodd, eds., *Animals on Display*.

14   Anders Ekström, "Walk-in media: International exhibitions as media space," in *The Routledge Handbook of Museums, Media and Communication*, ed. Kirsten Drotner et al. (Abingdon: Routledge, 2019), 17–30.

15   Duncan Grewcock, *Doing Museology Differently* (Abingdon: Routledge, 2014).

16   For discussion of the theoretical and artistic basis of the technique in Dutch paintings at the time, see Ulrike Kern, *Light and Shade in Dutch and Flemish Art: A History of Chiaroscuro in Art Theory and Artistic Practice in the Netherlands of the Seventeenth and Eighteenth Centuries* (Turnhout: Brepols, 2014).

17   Junko Aono, "Boy with a Mousetrap by Candlelight" (DT-100), in *The Leiden Collection Catalogue*, ed. Arthur K. Wheelock Jr. (New York, 2017), http://www.theleidencollection.com/archive/; and Dominique Surh, "Old Woman at a Window with a Candle", (GD-103), in *The Leiden Collection Catalogue*, ed. Wheelock

18   Susan Donahue Kuretsky, "Light and Sight in Ter Brugghen'd Man Writing by Candlelight," *Journal of Historians of Netherlandish Art* 9, no. 1 (2017), https://doi.org/10.5092/jhna.2017.9.1.4.

19   Both portraiture and genre painting were interested in social milieu and employed many of the same conventions: David R. Smith, "Irony and Civility: Notes on the Convergence of Genre and Portraiture in Seventeenth-century Dutch Painting," *The Art Bulletin* 69, no. 3 (1987): 407–30.

20   For this critique, see Wayne Franits, *Dutch Seventeenth-Century Genre Painting: Its Stylistic and Thematic Evolution* (New Haven: Yale University Press, 2004).

21   Original labels in French. Translations by author.

22   This particular label is given in both Swedish and English. All other labels from this museum translated from Swedish by the author.

23   For the thylacine's history, see Robert Paddle, *The Last Tasmanian Tiger: The History and Extinction of the Thylacine* (Cambridge: Cambridge University Press, 2000).

24   Soussloff, *The Subject in Art*, 8

25   http://data.biodiversitydata.nl/naturalis/specimen/RMNH.MAM.20681.b. All data and images linked to the specimen in the database are given the CC0 licence allowing their full usage under any conditions.

26   https://bioportal.naturalis.nl. More than eight million objects were in BioPortal as of October 2017.

27   Ursula Heise, *Imagining Extinction: The Cultural Meanings of Endangered Species* (Chicago: Chicago University Press, 2016).

28 The image is found in Georges-Louis Leclerc Comte de Buffon, *Histoire naturelle, générale et particulière. Servant de suite à l'histoire des animaux Quadrupèdes*, suppl. 4: 151–53, 1 plate (Schneider, Amsterdam, 1778). For discussion of the history of bluebuck images, see A. M. Husson and I. B. Holthuis, "The Earliest Figures of the Blaaubok," *Hippotragus leucophaeus* (Pallas, 1766) and of the Greater Kudu, *Tragelaphus strepsiceros* (Pallas, 1766)," *Zoologische Mededelingen* 49, no. 5 (1975): 57–63. Many natural history drawings of the time were not drawn from animals in original habitats—artists often worked from animals in menageries, from mounted specimens or skins, or even from oral or written descriptions without having seen the animal in question.

29 BioPortal actually contains three-dimensional animated composite images of some of the extinct birds in the Naturalis collection, such as the Sharpe's rail (*Gallirallus sharpei*), which is the only extant specimen of the species: https://bioportal.naturalis.nl/multimedia/RMNH.AVES.87485_3/term=Gallirallus+sharpei+&from=2. Perhaps someday they will expand the three-dimensional images to include the bluebuck.

30 In contrast, Merle Patchett undertook a physical close-up investigation of the Naturalis bluebuck, which she documented in "Repair Work." Her project material is also available online at www.blueantelope.info.

31 The artist's statement and images of his PixCell series are available at http://kohei-nawa.net/works/pixcell.

32 Finn Arne Jørgensen, "The Armchair Traveler's Guide to Digital Environmental Humanities," *Environmental Humanities* 4 (2014): 95–112.

33 Felicity Arengo et al., "The Essential Role of Museums in Biodiversity Conservation," in *The Future of Natural History Museums*, ed. Eric Dorfman (London: Routledge, 2018), 92–96.

34 Sarah M. Pike, "Mourning Nature: The Work of Grief in Radical Environmentalism," *Journal for the Study of Religion, Nature and Culture* 10, no. 4 (2016): 419–41 and Thom van Dooren, "Mourning Crows: Grief and Extinction in a Shared World," in *Routledge Handbook of Human-Animal Studies*, eds. Garry Marvin and Susan McHugh (Abingdon: Routledge, 2014), 275–89.

35 Stephen Frosh, *Those Who Come After: Postmemory, Acknowledgement and Forgiveness* (Cham, Switzerland: Palgrave Macmillan, 2019), 21.

36 Hugo Reinert, "The Haunting Cliffs: Some Notes on Silence," *Parallax* 24, no. 4 (2018): 501–12.

37 Jennifer Bonnell and Roger I. Simon, "'Difficult' exhibitions and intimate encounters," *Museum and Society* 5, no. 2 (2007): 65–85.

Epilogue: Combinations and Conjunction

Harriet Ritvo

In a way it is odd that animals were ever considered either a new subject for historians or a peculiar one, although my own experience offers plentiful evidence that both understandings have been widely shared. After all, traditional archives are full of animals, as have been the societies that they—however imperfectly—reflect and preserve. But animals have tended to be segregated and subordinated in archives, often more so than they were in the flesh. For example, the Dewey Decimal System catalogues livestock under technology, along with other aspects of agriculture; alternatively, some archives silo such material in their economic or business history collections. Either way, cattle and sheep are isolated from other ungulates, as well as from any non-agricultural or economic contexts in which they may equally have figured. Institutions concerned with specific human-animal relationships have often preserved their own records, although not necessarily in a setting that is recognizably archival. Thus in the course of researching my first book, *The Animal Estate*, I consulted documents not only in libraries, but also at the desk of a vacationing dog club employee, in the office of a perambulating zoo director, and in a museum exhibit space amid a selection of other primates (my companions were stuffed). One consequence of the increasing recognition of the significance of animals as a topic of serious historical inquiry is that, since my first visits to them, each of these collections has been more conventionally housed and catalogued. Another, with broader implications, is that previously isolated sources and subjects are now (at least potentially) in conversation with each other. And as these rich archives have been recontextualized and repurposed, they have allowed historians to foreground the role that other animals have played even in histories that focus on humans, as they mostly do.

The most obvious effect of these changes (although it is also a cause) has been the development of animal history as a field or subfield or area of shared interest. The number and variety of contributions to this volume typify the way that our sense of possible subjects has expanded from a time when a study of animals in a given time and place could be considered a narrow topic, rather than a wildly ambitious one. In addition, the work collected here, which of course is only the tip of the iceberg, represents the culmination of a decades-long process of institutionalization, as evidenced by books and book series, journals and journal articles, conferences and conference panels, summer seminars, classes in course catalogues, and even graduate and undergraduate programs.[1] Alongside this subdisciplinary consolidation—and perhaps a still more persuasive indication of the vigour and appeal of the historical study of animals—has been the increasing integration of animal-related topics into so-called mainstream history, following a trail previously blazed by gender history, labour history, and postcolonial history, among others.

Inevitably, as has been the case whenever historians have extended their disciplinary boundaries, novel perspectives and topics have led to the reinterpretation of existing archives and to the exploitation of new kinds of archives. Historical work on animals has also required that historians engage with other fields of scholarship, especially in the life sciences, and with the expertise of the varied practitioners whose work requires constant and knowledgeable interaction with members of other species. Since many of the animal-related issues that historians explore have clear resonances with matters of current concern and debate, this work can also bring historians into contact with a range of non-expert (or at least non-professional) stakeholders, as well as with a range of non-human ones.

The animal turn in historical study thus reflects distinctively current preoccupations and methods, but previous periods saw many similar intersections of intellectual approaches and pragmatic claims to turf. The establishment of boundaries between different (though often allied) kinds of animals, whether expressed in vernacular terms or in the language of formal zoological taxonomy, sparked debates that were reflected in practice as well as in theory. Like the lines between kinds of animals, lines between language and practice tended to blur. That is to say, labels and connotations might remain stable, while denotations evolved over time.

In Britain, the absence of a definitive definition of "game," a category that has been chronologically volatile as well as socially contested, provides one example—although whatever its referents, the term "game" always connoted privilege. A 1717 edition of John Manwood's *Treatise of the Forest Laws*, originally written in the late sixteenth century and republished and revised many times into the early nineteenth century, listed deer among the animals for whom a forest was a "privileged Place"—meaning that only certain people could kill them. Among these allegedly privileged creatures, he included beasts of the forest (hart, hind [probably male and female red deer], and hare), beasts of the chase or venery (buck, doe [probably male and female fallow deer], and fox), and beasts and fowls of warren (hare, cony [rabbit], pheasant, and partridge).[2] (These categories recurred in most hunting guides, but, as is the case with the general category of "game," the species they included tend to vary somewhat.)

By the time that the *Handy Guide to the Game Laws* was published in 1905, emphasis (at least legal emphasis) had shifted from mammals to birds. Hares, rabbits, and deer received only passing notice, while the pseudonymous author's attention was more intensely focused on pheasant, partridge, grouse, woodcocks, snipe, quail, and bustards.[3] "Game" also existed in implicit opposition to the category of "vermin." Animals designated as "vermin" received no protection and could be killed by anyone licensed to shoot. This category also varied depending on time and circumstances. For example, an early nineteenth-century guide to field sports included foxes, which have often been heavily protected, along with badgers, martens, stoats, weasels, squirrels, wild cats, polecats, rats, mice, rooks, and sparrows under that rubric;[4] half a century, later a similar guide omitted badgers, squirrels, rats, mice, and wild cats, but included moles and additional birds of prey.[5] The Gun License Act of 1870 deployed the category without defining its contents, except to specify that rabbits were not vermin unless they were destroying crops.[6]

This trajectory suggests a shifting relationship between the economic significance of hunting (which primarily yields food) and its symbolic or aesthetic significance (which is concretized in other ways). Of course, both of these kinds of significance involve consumption, although of different kinds. Through all these vicissitudes, the deer—or, to be more specific, the stag (which usually meant the male of the red deer)—retained pride of place, at least in Britain. Landseer's portrait of "The Monarch of the Glen,"[7] distills the wild majesty attributed to these largest remaining representatives of the wild British fauna; it features a lone stag flaunting the twelve-point antlers that were characterized as "royal," posed against a romantically misty and mountainous Highland background. One of his descendants may have acted in *The Queen* (2006), where the current Elizabeth (as represented by Helen Mirren) feels an instinctive admiration and sympathy for him as, like Landseer's "Monarch," he stands in noble isolation against the Highland landscape. But what follows this transcendent moment ironically undermines it—she hears the gunfire of sportsmen and thinks that she has shooed the stag away to safety, but she subsequently encounters his corpse suspended upside down, being prepared for a less symbolic and more substantial destiny (as an article in *The Field* advised, "Hanging venison is the only way to get a really gamey finish to the meat"[8]).

Of course, even in his ultimate disaggregated condition, the stag will retain his aristocratic aura. Because of its relative scarcity or inaccessibility, or, to put it another way, because of its association with class privilege—as well as the complicated cachet of wildness—game has traditionally outranked the flesh of conventionally domesticated livestock. It has been prized for attributes, especially its strong taste, that are disparaged in lesser meats—which may be an example (one among many) of the way that abstract assertions of difference can overshadow any assessment of the quality or content of that difference, when the goal is to establish or emphasize hierarchy. Thus, the connotation of the adjective "gamey," whether considered in its literal or its figurative senses, can range from the most appreciative to the least, depending on the noun that it modifies. But with regard to the fruits of the hunt, it has invariably been positive. This has been the case even at the less majestic end of the game continuum—thus, hare was considered superior to rabbit, "being much more savory and of a higher flavour."⁹ But the preference was most forcefully enunciated with respect to the most imposing animals. For example, a plainspoken Victorian cookbook divided lovers of venison into two categories: those who "like it a little gone, and others a good deal. This state of putrescency is called by gourmands *haut gout*, high tasted; we should rather say at once, stinking."¹⁰

Although less impressive than the stag, whether in the field or in the kitchen, hares and rabbits similarly illustrated the way that characterizations of animals have been both synchronically contested and diachronically mutable. They did this jointly, in the form of leporides, which were alleged hybrids between the domesticated rabbit and the hare. Domesticated rabbits had existed in Britain for centuries (probably introduced by the Romans and then reintroduced from France during the medieval period—the long history of rabbit domestication remains controversial¹¹), and in the nineteenth century they were widely appreciated both as pets and as food. They were not, however, a major focus of interest among either agriculturalists or pet owners. One indication of this relative insignificance is the small part they and their fellow lagomorphs (members of the mammalian order that includes rabbits and hares, as well as, more remotely, picas) played in Charles Darwin's monumental two-volume survey, *The Variation of Animals and Plants under Domestication* (1868). The first volume, which is devoted to a species-by-species survey of domesticated animals and plants, includes a rather brief chapter on rabbits (for comparison, domesticated pigeons received two chapters and many more pages), and in the second volume, which treats scientific issues associated with domestication thematically, references to them pop up from time to time.

Within this relatively restricted compass, there are two mentions—widely separated and somewhat inconsistent—of hybrids between the rabbit and the hare. In the overview of domesticated rabbits in the first volume, Darwin speculated about a possible hare contribution to their ancestry:

> we may infer with safety that all the domestic breeds are the descendants of the common wild species [of rabbit]. But from what we hear of the marvellous success in France in rearing hybrids

> between the hare and the rabbit, it is possible, though not probable, from the great difficulty in making the first cross, that some of the larger races, which are coloured like the hare, may have been modified by crosses with this animal.[12]

This brief quotation alluded to several contentious issues faced by those concerned with the theory and practice of animal breeding in the nineteenth century, and although Darwin emphasized the difficulty of producing rabbit-hare hybrids, he did not express any explicit skepticism about their likely or even possible existence. That is, his use of "marvellous" was not ironic, although there is a certain carefulness or conditionality about the tone of the whole passage.

When he returned to rabbit-hare hybrids in the second volume, however, Darwin's attitude seemed to have altered somewhat. In the course of a general discussion of the impact of captivity on the fertility of wild animals, he noted that "[t]he common hare when confined has, I believe, never bred in Europe; though, according to a recent statement, it has crossed with the rabbit."[13] In the note supporting his newly qualified understanding of reliability of such accounts, he cited critical responses to the same French report: "[a]lthough the existence of the *Leporides*, as described by Dr. Broca has been positively denied, yet Dr. Pigeaux affirms that the hare and the rabbit have produced hybrids."

Many of Darwin's contemporaries shared both his interest in these alleged hybrids and his ambivalence about the possibility of their existence. Debate about the veracity or plausibility of claims to have produced leporides (as they were confusingly called, since the term "leporid" refers to members of the family *Leporidae* that includes rabbits and hares) rumbled on for years in Britain and elsewhere, and it was not confined within the scientific community. The *Cornhill Magazine* had reported in 1860 that a "M. Rouy [sic], of Angouleme, . . . each year sends to market upwards of a thousand of his *Leporides*";[14] according to the *Leeds Intelligencer*, this feat was made more impressive by the fact that "the two are violent foes: the rabbits always destroy the hares."[15] Four years later, the *Journal of the Royal Agricultural Society of England* published an elaborate account of M. Roux's [sic] techniques, along with reference to still less well documented accounts of rabbit-hare hybrids produced, also in France, as much as a century earlier.[16] In 1871 the *Church of England Magazine* weighed in, citing not only the skepticism of some naturalists, who felt that when alleged hybrid offspring were examined it became increasingly evident that "the efforts of the [paternal] hare fell far short of what had been attributed to him" and who also claimed, applying an unusual taxonomic standard, that when eaten, an alleged hybrid "did not appear to differ from a simple rabbit."[17] (It should be emphasized that these possessors of discerning palates knew what both rabbits and hares tasted like.) There was apparently a persistent popular audience for learned opinions on this topic; thus in 1872 the *Bath Chronicle* reported that, according to the *British Medical Journal*, the offspring of Guyot's "hybrids" bore a disappointing resemblance to ordinary rabbits.[18]

Although the *Encyclopedia Britannica* definitively announced in 1886 that the animals sold as leporides actually belonged to a large breed of rabbit often called "Belgian hares,"[19] that was far from the last word on the subject. As late as 1925 William E. Castle, a Harvard zoology professor who initiated the use of *Drosophila* (the fruit fly) in genetics research and wrote a book devoted to *The Genetics of Domestic Rabbits: A Manual for Students of Mammalian Genetics* (1930), felt called upon to publicly debunk the leporides in the *American Naturalist*: "We may accordingly relegate the hare-rabbit to the limbo of zoological myths, along with the unicorn and the sea serpent."[20] Belgian hares, however, have continued to flourish. At present, rabbit-hare hybridization has become a niche concern, which nevertheless continues to inspire such spirited denunciations as "a breed known as the 'Belgian Hare' is repeatedly alleged on the Internet as a 'hybrid between Old World rabbit and hare.' However, no valid primary report of this cross seems to exist (though the literature discussing this topic is extensive)."[21] Current Belgian hares remain taxonomically rabbits, but they have been increasingly bred to live up to their name in phenotype if not in genotype.[22]

In the middle of the nineteenth century, however, interest in the leporides clearly extended far beyond the ranks of pet rabbit fanciers or commercial rabbit breeders. Because (among other things) despite their obvious similarities, hybridization between hares and rabbits had proved challenging, reports of a possible breakthrough resonated with a range of other concerns about hybridity. That is to say, the reason that the leporides attracted such relatively widespread and sustained attention reflects their categorization—not as lagomorphs or leporids but as hybrids. And as hybrids in the news they were far from unique. The nineteenth-century British public flocked to admire hybrid superstars, such as the litters of lion-tiger cubs that had toured Britain in the 1820s and 1830s as part of Thomas Atkins' menagerie, but even relatively humdrum hybrids were considered worthy of notice. Zoo-keepers routinely produced (that is to say, encouraged the production of) hybrids between different bovine and simian species, the particular pairings determined primarily by which likely cross-breeders happened to be living in their cages and paddocks. So pronounced was the public interest in such combinations, that *Punch* was moved to satirize it in 1870: "The rhinoceros in Mr. LYON's menagerie last night presented the elephant with a fine foal. This is the first instance on record of a pachydermatous hybrid, which, should it fortunately survive, will doubtless prove no small attraction to zoologists."[23]

Miscegenation is almost but not quite a synonym for hybridization. The online versions of both the *Oxford English Dictionary* and *Roget's Thesaurus* acknowledge the relationship of these words, but apply miscegenation primarily to humans and hybridization primarily to animals and plants. In consequence, despite their significant overlap in denotation, the connotation of miscegenation has normally been negative, while that of hybridization has ranged from neutral to positive. But one of the things that makes animal history illuminating is the often unacknowledged or unconscious overlap between ideas about people and ideas about others. Understandings that have become unacceptable or fringe (or just inexpressible) with regard to humans can continue to be recognized, reified and, in many cases, enthusiastically enforced with regard to animals. The unalloyed descent required for most pedigreed breeds offers the clearest reflection of this tendency, but similar standards have been increasingly applied outside the breed book and the show ring.

For example, having teetered on the brink of extinction in the late nineteenth century, the American bison has become one of the success stories of species preservation. Although their free-ranging populations remain far below their historical maximum (in the tens of thousands compared to estimates as high as fifty million or more),[24] bison are now sufficiently numerous to be eaten undiluted as buffalo burgers or in hybridized form as beefalo (the name indicates hybrid descent from the American bison [*Bison bison*] and the domestic cow [*Bos taurus*]). But the relation of contemporary bison to the noble former inhabitants of the Great Plains is far from straightforward. The animals who end up in fast food restaurants and grocery stores come from domesticated stock, not from the wild herds that now roam many parks and preserves. But it appears that beneath their reassuring demographic success, even the apparently wild bison populations may be similarly compromised. That is, the impressive herds that wander around preserved and protected landscapes in the American West look and act like wild bison; they seem indistinguishable from the iconic beast who formerly adorned the American nickel. But many of those herds include individuals whose heritage also reflects contributions from domestic cattle; thus a 2013 article in the Sierra Club's glossy magazine pointedly celebrated the 3,700 Yellowstone bison as "free of cattle genes . . . our last wild bison."[25]

And although zoo caretakers once produced inter-species hybrids for the entertainment of the public, they are currently more likely to submit their charges to the machinery of pedigree. Studbooks have controlled the mating of zoo animals, especially if they belong to species that have become scarce outside of captivity, for more than half a century.[26] Paradoxically, since human control of reproductive choice is one of the standard criteria of domestication, this practice can make even tigers seem less wild. The standard justification for it is to maintain genetic diversity and to avoid the inbreeding that might otherwise weaken small captive populations. But it has also frequently been used to reify the category of subspecies (that is, in effect, to maintain racial purity). Both agendas mean that zoo animals whose parentage is unknown are precluded from breeding, and zoo animals whose parentage is deemed inappropriate may be sacrificed to eugenics, as was the fate of the unfortunate giraffe Marius at the Copenhagen zoo.[27]

Thus hybridization within and across species has raised concerns that resonate with debates in human political, social, and intellectual arenas, and with concerns of historians dealing with animal subjects in a range of other contexts. But some problems that confront animal historians also resist the expertise of specialists within whose field they also, albeit differently, fall. For example, much recent work in animal history attempts to take the experience and interests of other creatures into account, along with those of people. Of course, this is easier said (although very frequently said) than done, especially for historians, since, challenging as this problem is with regard to the present, it is much more so with regard to the past. Most animals communicate without recourse to human language, and even people who know individual animals well can have trouble understanding them. (The insights of researchers like Irene Pepperberg and Penny Patterson, who have been privileged to work with animals who possessed some command of English, are not easily applied to most inter-species relationships.[28]) A great deal of the evidence about the nature and experience of historical animals comes from the testimony of the people who observed them, interacted with them, and exploited them, and most of the rest comes from bones, skins, and other physical remains. (There is also abundant testimony from people who mostly imagined them, but this, even more than other apparently animal-related evidence, primarily offers information about people.[29]) Attempts to make room for animals by displacing people must struggle with the distortion and diminution that inevitably accompanies such filtering.[30] The stronger version of this agenda—the claim to give other animals a voice—is still more problematic, requiring a greater leap of both empathy and imagination.

Some of these difficulties are inherent in the term "animal" itself,[31] which refers to a category without clear boundaries. Biologically, it includes corals and starfish as well as gorillas and leopards; the contributions to this volume explore the experiences and impacts of species as disparate as elephants and flies. These creatures seem so different that the use of the blanket term "animal" to cover them all brings the term itself into question. Thus the elimination of the boundary that separates humans from animals seems to require the establishment of another or others, although the location of replacement boundaries is equally problematic. If no obvious gap can be discerned between most kinds of animals and those kinds most similar to them, large gaps emerge when very dissimilar animals are juxtaposed.

A similar tension surrounds the term "anthropomorphic," which eliminates the possibility of easy slippage between humans and members of other species. That is, calling something or someone anthropomorphic is seldom meant as a compliment, and this negative connotation assumes that the claim that humans and non-humans share perceptions, behaviours, and so forth, is inherently naive, sentimental or otherwise misguided. But like other assumptions, sometimes it is right and sometimes it is wrong. Representations like Edwin Landseer's *Wild Cattle of Chillingham*,[32] in which a stately bull looms protectively over a cow and calf, and *The Noble Beast*,[33] which foregrounds a stag accompanied by a doe and fawn, clearly deserve this critique, as do the Akeley dioramas in the American Museum of Natural History,[34] which present taxidermied rhinoceroses and giraffes in similarly improbable nuclear family groups. But it is hard to say the same of the many portraits and photographs that portray pets and children as part of the same social group. To describe that implied relationship as anthropomorphic is to erect or resurrect a barrier that may not have been perceived by any of the individuals involved. Thus, like "animal" or, even more, "the animal," the term "anthropomorphism" inherently privileges the problematic human-animal binary.

These scholarly challenges have recently been complicated by politics, academic and otherwise. Like humans, members of other species are vulnerable—in many cases much more vulnerable—to the systemic threats posed by anthropogenic climate change, as well as to the caprices of environmental regulation and deregulation. Intense commercial exploitation of natural resources, as well as the intense commercial exploitation of domesticated animals, remains the focus of heated controversy. At the same time, a few species have benefited, at least potentially, from enhanced legal status, a shift somewhat less robustly reflected in the range of consideration required when different species are used as experimental subjects. All these issues engage the expertise of scientists along with that of other stakeholders. Analogously, historians who wish to incorporate the experiences of members of other species in their accounts must be prepared to use evidence from outside the humanities—from fields like zoology, archaeology, geography, and genomics. While such incorporation will enhance the analysis of particular situations, it may pose a challenge to the apparent unity of the field—that is, as individual creatures or kinds become more fully realized, the differences between kinds may loom larger. But even if "animal history" turns out to be a label subject to radical taxonomic revision, alternative packaging should not diminish the vigour and significance of the scholarship it now contains.

NOTES

1. These have become too numerous to catalogue. For previous attempts to chronicle this development, see my "Among Animals," *Environment and History* (2014): 491–98; "The Animal Turn in British Studies," in *Proceedings of Anglistentag 2007*, ed. Klaus Stierstorfer (2008); and "Animal Planet," *Environmental History* (2004): 204–20.
2. John Manwood, *Treatise of the Forest Laws* (London: E. Nutt, 1717), 144.
3. A Solicitor, *Handy Guide to the Game Laws with Abridgment of the Acts Relating to Game* (London: Horace Cox, 1905), 4–5.
4. William H. Scott, *British Field Sports* (London: Sherwood, Neely, and Jones, 1818), 444–57.
5. John Mayer, *The Sportsman's Directory; and Park and Gamekeeper's Companion* (London: Simpkin, Marshall, 1845), vii.
6. *Handy Guide*, 34–35.
7. The original hangs in the Scottish National Gallery. https://www.nationalgalleries.org/art-and-artists/159116/monarch-glen.
8. "Hanging venison. How long is best?" *The Field*, February 11, 2016, https://www.thefield.co.uk/country-house/country-queries/hanging-venison-how-long-is-best-31276.
9. Thomas Webster and Mrs. Parkes, *An Encyclopedia of Domestic Economy* (London: Longman, Brown, Green, and Longman, 1847), 377.
10. *The Guide to Service:The Cook* (Londin: Charles Knight, 1842), 230.
11. Evan K. Irving-Pease et al., "Rabbits and the Specious Origins of Domestication," *Trends in Ecology and Evolution* (March 2018): 149–52.
12. Charles Darwin, *The Variation of Animals and Plants under Domestication* (1868) (facs. Baltimore: Johns Hopkins University Press, 1998), vol. 1, 109.
13. Darwin, *Variation*, vol. 2, 135.
14. "Studies in Animal Life," *Cornhill Magazine*, vol. 1, 1860, 604.
15. "Leporides," *Leeds Intelligencer*, May 19, 1860, 2.
16. "The Leporide," *Journal of the Royal Agricultural Society of England* 25 (1864): 265.
17. H. Whitehead, "Christianity and Its Scientific Opponents. No. IV. The Origin of Species," *Church of England Magazine*, vol. 70, April 15, 1871, 253.
18. "The Fate of the Leporides," *Bath Chronicle*, October 10, 1872, 7.
19. *Encyclopedia Britannica* (1886), s.v. "rabbit."
20. W. E. Castle, "The Hare-Rabbit, A Study in Evolution by Hybridization," *American Naturalist*, vol. 59, 1925, 282.
21. Eugene M. McCarthy, "Rabbits and Hares," *Macroevolution.net*, accessed May 5, 2022, http://www.macroevolution.net/rabbit-hybrids.html.
22. For example, the Belgian Hare Society of the UK consistently refers to them as rabbits and makes no claim to hybrid ancestry (http://www.belgianhares.org.uk/history-of-belgian-hares.html). They also point out that the rabbits who originated the breed came from Holland, not Belgium, and that the current breed was developed in England.
23. "Ordinary Occurrences," *Punch*, September 17, 1870, 123.

24 Bronx Zoo website: https://bronxzoo.com/things-to-do/exhibits/american-bison.
25 Philip W. Hedrick, "Cattle ancestry in bison: explanations for higher mtDNA than autosomal ancestry," *Molecular Ecology* 19 (2010): 3328–2225; *Sierra*, November/December 2013, 28.
26 Peter J. S. Olney, "Studbook," *Encyclopedia of the World's Zoos, R-Z*, vol. 3, ed. Catharine E. Bell, (Detroit: Fitzroy Dearborn, 2001), 1180.
27 The killing of Marius sparked a great deal of controversy. See, for example, Lars Eriksen and Maev Kennedy, "Marius the giraffe killed at Copenhagen zoo despite worldwide protests," *The Guardian*, February 9, 2014, https://www.theguardian.com/world/2014/feb/09/marius-giraffe-killed-copenhagen-zoo-protests.
28 Irene Pepperberg, *Alex and Me: How a Scientist and a Parrot Discovered a Hidden World of Animal Intelligence—And Formed a Deep Bond in the Process* (New York: MJF Books, 2008); Francine Patterson and Eugene Linden, *The Education of Koko* (New York: Henry Holt, 1988).
29 Harriet Ritvo, *The Animal Estate: The English and Other Creature in the Victorian Age* (Cambridge, MA: Harvard University Press, 1987), 232.
30 Thus Robert Delort, who highlighted this agenda in the title of his 1984 study *Les animaux ont une histoire*, produced a species-by-species account that did not fulfil his ambition: "to privilege the animal, and not the history," in *Les animaux ont une histoire* (Paris: Èditions du Seuil, 1984), 12. More recently (and successfully), Eric Baratay has similarly proposed "to detach history from an anthropocentric vision" (*Le point de vue animal: Une autre version de l'histoire* [Paris: Éditions du Seuil, 2012], 12).
31 Humans, of course, are also animals; I have not used "other animals" in this paper in the interest of euphony.
32 Laing Art Gallery, Newcastle: https://artuk.org/discover/artworks/wild-cattle-of-chillingham-northumberland-37231.
33 http://www.wikigallery.org/wiki/painting_201281/Sir-Edwin-Henry-Landseer/The-Noble-Beast.
34 https://www.amnh.org/exhibitions/permanent/african-mammals.

Contributors

JENNIFER BONNELL is an associate professor in the Department of History at York University. She is the author of *Reclaiming the Don: An Environmental History of Toronto's Don River Valley* (University of Toronto Press, 2014), which won the Canadian Historical Association's Clio prize and Heritage Toronto's best book award. Her new book project explores the relationships between beekeeping, agricultural modernization, and environmental change in the Great Lakes Region. For more on her work, visit https://jenniferbonnell.com/.

COLLEEN CAMPBELL worked 20 years as a field biologist, engaged in research focused on coyotes and grizzly bears. Field work overlapped with a long teaching career at Mount Royal University in Calgary and became the source of content for her studio practice as an artist. One drawing project "The Eastern Slopes Grizzly Bears: Each One Is Sacred" (exhibited at the Whyte Museum in Banff, Alberta, from October 2017 to January 2018) revealed key events in the lives of 87 individual bears studied during a 10-year research project and became the stimulus for her collaboration with Tina Loo.

JASON M. COLBY is professor of environmental and international history at the University of Victoria in British Columbia. His most recent book is *Orca: How We Came to Know and Love the Ocean's Greatest Predator* (Oxford University Press, 2018). He is currently researching for a new book project entitled *Devilfish: The History and Future of Gray Whales and People.*

GEORGE COLPITTS is an environmental historian at the University of Calgary. He is interested in relationships between human and non-human animals in colonial North America and recent times. He has published on animal history, the fur trade, conservation and the modern fur industry in Canada's north.

J. KERI CRONIN is a professor in the History of Art & Visual Culture program at Brock University. She is the author of Art for Animals: Visual Culture and Animal Advocacy, 1870-1914 (Penn State University Press) and the co-founder (with Jo-Anne McArthur) of The Unbound Project, a multimedia project celebrating women in animal advocacy (https://unboundproject.org/).

JOANNA DEAN is an associate professor at Carleton University in Ottawa where she teaches animal history. She is co-editor of *Animal Metropolis: Histories of Human-Animal Relations in Urban Canada* (2016).

JODY HODGINS is a PhD Candidate in the Department of History at York University where her research centres on histories of the environment, science, animals, and technologies. Her dissertation examines changes in the human-animal relationship over time by looking at animal health practices and the transition to professional veterinary medicine in rural nineteenth and early twentieth-century Ontario.

DOLLY JØRGENSEN is Professor of History, University of Stavanger, Norway. Her current research focuses on cultural histories of animal extinction and technologically-mediated relations between humans and animals. Her monograph *Recovering Lost Species in the Modern Age: Histories of Longing and Belonging* was published with MIT Press in 2019.

SEAN KHERAJ is an associate professor of Canadian and environmental history in the Department of History at York University in Toronto, Ontario and vice dean of the Faculty of Liberal Arts and Professional Studies. He is also director of the Network in Canadian

History and Environment and the author of *Inventing Stanley Park: An Environmental History* (University of British Columiba Press, 2013), winner of the Canadian Historical Association Clio Prize for best book in British Columbia history. His work can be found at https://www.seankheraj.com/.

TINA LOO is an historian at the University of British Columbia in Vancouver, where she teaches and writes about the environment and Canada. A member of the Royal Society of Canada, she is the author of a number of award-winning books and articles about subjects ranging from wildlife conservation and the impacts of hydroelectric development to forced relocation in Canada.

DR. LINDSAY STALLONES MARSHALL is an Assistant Professor at the University of Oklahoma which occupies land belonging to Hasinai (Caddo) and Kitikiti'sh (Wichita) peoples and originally shared by many Indigenous Nations – including Cáuigù (Kiowa), Nʉmʉnʉʉ (Comanche), and Na I sha and Ndee (Apache). Her research focuses on the creation and perpetuation of settler colonial public memory through history education. She also researches the environmental history of human-equine relationships with an emphasis on interdisciplinary and decolonial methodologies.

CATHERINE McNEUR is an associate professor of history at Portland State University in Oregon. She is the award-winning author of *Taming Manhattan: Environmental Battles in the Antebellum City* (Harvard University Press, 2014) and is currently writing a book about the lives, work, and erasure of Margaretta Hare Morris and Elizabeth Carrington Morris, under contract with Basic Books.

SUSAN NANCE is Professor of History and affiliated faculty with the Campbell Centre for the Study of Animal Welfare at the University of Guelph in Ontario, Canada. She is the author of various books about animal history, including *Rodeo: An Animal History* (2020).

HARRIET RITVO is the Arthur J. Conner Professor of History Emeritus at the Massachusetts Institute of Technology. She has written widely about the history of our relations with other animals; her books include *The Animal Estate: The English and Other Creatures in the Victorian Age*; *The Platypus and the Mermaid, and Other Figments of the Classifying Imagination*; and *Noble Cows and Hybrid Zebras: Essays on Animals and History*. Her current research focuses on wildness and domestication.

ANDREW ROBICHAUD is Assistant Professor of History at Boston University and author of *Animal City: The Domestication of America* (2019). His contribution for this volume is based on collaborative work he did as a primary investigator at the Stanford Spatial History Project and Center for Spatial and Textual Analysis.

NIGEL ROTHFELS is Professor of History at the University of Wisconsin-Milwaukee. He is the author of *Elephant Trails: A History of Animals and Cultures* (2021) and *Savages and Beasts: The Birth of the Modern Zoo* (2002), co-author (with Dick Blau) of *Elephant House* (2015), and editor of *Representing Animals* (2002). He is also General Editor of the book series Animalibus: Of Animals and Cultures, published by Penn State University Press.

SANDRA SWART is Professor and Chair of the Department of History at Stellenbosch University. She received her DPhil in Modern History while simultaneously obtaining an MSc in Environmental Change and Management, both from Oxford University. She focuses on southern African socio-environmental history, especially the shifting relationship between humans and animals as in her book, *Riding High – Horses, Humans and History in South Africa* (Witwatersrand University Press, 2010).

EMILY WAKILD is the Cecil D. Andrus Endowed Chair for the Environment and Public Lands at Boise State University. Her main academic research excavates documents, images, interviews, and fragments of the past to explain why and how large spaces for nature conservation emerged throughout the Americas. She is the author of *Revolutionary*

Parks: Conservation, Social Justice, and Mexico's National Parks, (University of Arizona Press, 2011) and with Michelle K. Berry, *Primer for Teaching Environmental History* (Duke 2018) both of which have been translated and published in Spanish.

JAY YOUNG holds a PhD in Canadian history from York University. From 2014 to 2020, he worked as an outreach officer at the Archives of Ontario.

Index

A

Ahmed, Sara, 317
Alberti, Samuel, 373–74
Allison, Leanne, 245
alpacas, 14, 318; as camelid species, 317, 323; colours and patterns of, 324; as domesticated, 323–24; throughout South America, 320; in the US, 330–31; as water dependent, 324; wool of, 324; in zoos, 324. *See also* camelids
American Bee Journal, 52, 62, 65
American Blue Cross Society, 142
American foulbrood (AFB): caused by, 59; control efforts, 63; destructive potential of, 59; hardiness of spores of, 61–62; impact on bee colonies, 59, 61; infections in 1880s and 1890s, 62; outbreak in 1870s of, 59; response to, 62; spread of, 53; virulence of, 63
American Journal of Agriculture and Science, 166–67
American Philosophical Society (APS), 161–64; *Proceedings of the American Philosophical Society*, 163
Anders, Frank L., 82
Andrews, Thomas G., 51; *Killing for Coal*, 51
animal advocacy movements, 91, 94
animal agency, 7–8, 25–26, 351; evidence of, 186, 316, 351–52; methodological challenges of, 15, 26; limited usefulness of questions of, 26, 49
animal bodies: in art production, 341; of bees, 53–54, 58, 67; of dolphins, 201; and embodied methodology, 23–24, 28–29, 41; exhibiting, 375; of greyhounds, 93, 108; as historical artifacts, 374; of horses, 34, 38, 41; and labour, 51, 348–49; of llamas, 317, 329; materiality of, 11, 14; and pigments, 340; reading of as sources, 8–9, 27, 67; and visual imagery, 340, 350

"Animal City" Spatial History Lab project, 293, 295, 309, 311
animal cruelty: and anti-animal cruelty, 137, 141, 146–48; and anti-cruelty advocates, 138; and anti-cruelty laws, 100, 305; and anti-steel trap leagues, 137, 142; in antivisection literature, 190; in the fur trade, 137–38, 144, 146; and horses, 81. *See also* animal rights; antivivisection movement; Societies for the Prevention of Cruelty to Animals (SPCAs)
animal health care, 117–19, 127–28, 131–32. *See also* animal health knowledge; animal health manuals; veterinarians; veterinary medicine
animal health knowledge, 117–19, 121, 127, 131. *See also* animal health care; animal health manuals; veterinarians; veterinary medicine
animal health manuals, 12, 117–20, 122, 126–27, 131–32. *See also* animal health care; animal health knowledge; veterinarians; veterinary medicine
animal historians: methods and challenges of, 5, 8–11, 13–15, 37, 305, 397; and other subfields of history, 22, 292, 373, 390; questions faced by, 3, 75–76; studying the recent past, 91, 112; as similar to other historians, 227–28. *See also* animal history
animal history: and anthropocentric sources, 120, 269, 284–85; and applying an "animal lens," 269–70, 283; and art history, 14, 340, 352–53; as emotionally exhausting, 310–11; field of, 3–4, 11, 15, 292, 361, 390, 399; locational data as a source for, 239, 263; methodological challenges of, 3–5, 9–10, 15, 200, 214, 269; methods of, 8–9, 13, 85, 239, 269; and oral history, 27, 29, 41, 97, 214; risks of, 8, 15, 73–74; scholarship, 293, 340;

409

animal history (*continued*) shortcomings of, 73–75, 284; so-called impossibility of, 4, 235; sources on, 236, 293–95, 305–6; urban, 269–70, 279, 283; and visual culture, 339–40, 342, 350, 353; writing of, 8, 341. *See also* animal historians
animal labour: and *ANIMALIA* exhibit, 364; and animal workers, 347–50; history of, 50–51; and honeybees, 12, 49–52, 66, 69; and horses, 279, 283, 341; and llamas, 329, 331; and oxen, 350–51; and Welland Canals, 347, 350–51; and working conditions, 50–51
animal protectors, 139–40, 142, 145, 147
animal rights: advocacy, 91; as a philosophy, 148; activists and groups, 148, 213
animal tracking, 237, 262
animal traps: and trappers, 138, 140, 143–44, 146–47; anti-trapping campaigns, 148; anti-trapping literature, 146–47; leghold traps, 137, 140–43, 145, 147–48. *See also* animal cruelty
ANIMALIA exhibit, 3, 5, 357–60, 367, 369–70; collections of, 14, 365–66; animals featured in, 363–64; development of, 359, 362–63 themes of, 364, 369. *See also* Archives of Ontario
Annales School, 35–37
Annesley, Lady Clare, 141
antelopes. *See* bluebucks
Anthropocene, 149, 262, 329
anthropomorphism, 74, 148, 398–99; pitfalls of, 10, 15; and animal stories, 142, 148–50; and US Navy Marine Mammal Program, 213
antivivisection movement, 13, 176, 186, 188, 190–91; Canadian Anti-Vivisection Society, 188, 190; Ottawa Anti-Vivisection Society, 190. *See also* vivisection
apex predators, 237, 252
apiaries, 58–61; and apiarists, 57, 66
archives: as repositories of evidence, 3, 361; animal bodies as archives, 23–24, 28, 36–38, 41, 93
— animals in: absence of, 138, 161; hidden nature of, 14, 138, 160, 175, 293; marginal nature of, 5, 316, 389; looking for, 7, 9, 176, 227, 345–47
creating one's own archives, 13, 95, 112; digital archives, 7, 12, 280; as human constructs 5, 10, 74, 76, 227; as privileging humans and the powerful, 75–76, 235, 346; as records of human agency, 92, 112; rural public archives, 120–21, 123, 126, 129; traditional archives, 12, 389, 218; voices not readily apparent in, 9, 92. *See also* Archives of Ontario
Archives of Ontario: *ANIMALIA* exhibit, 3, 5, 358; collections of, 14, 359, 361–63; and educational programming, 359–61; exhibit team, 360, 362, 364, 367, 370; as government institution, 359, 363, 370; Helen McClung Exhibit Area, 360; and interactive activities, 367, 369; as memory institution, 359, 363; outreach program at, 359; past exhibits at, 357, 360; and York University, 360–61. *See also* archives
Argent, Gala, 29
art history, 339–40; methodologies, 340; and portraiture, 371–73, 383–84
Audubon Society, 140

B

Banting, Frederick, 190–91
Barker, C. A. V., 126, 128
Barnes, Al G., 224, 226
Barnes, H. F., 168–69
Barnum, P. T., 328
Battle of the Greasy Grass, 75, 82–83, 85
Bear 71 [film], 245
bears, 13, 15, 21, 52; in *ANIMALIA* exhibit, 357, 363; and bear trackers, 239, 246; danger of roads to, 242–43; of the eastern slopes [Rocky Mountains], 241–42, 244, 255, 261–63; food sources of 241–43, 249; foraging of, 241–42, 254;
— grizzly bears: classified as endangered, 236–37; of the eastern slopes, 237, 241–42; female, 239, 242, 244, 248–49; F30, 246–49, 252–53, 258, 260–61; F46, 246, 248–49; as individuals, 249, 255; locational data on, 237–38, 249, 252; movements of, 14, 253; survival rates of, 244
and grizzly country, 240–41, 258, 261; habitats of, 238, 241–42; movements of, 239, 242–44, 249, 252; near golf courses, 241–42, 244; near railways, 241, 243–44; near ski runs, 241–42, 244; relationships among, 48–49; tracking of, 237, 253, 255. *See also* Eastern Slopes Grizzly Bear Project
beekeepers, 50, 66–67; and "reading" the bodies of bees, 53, 69; and bee forage, 52, 54, 68; and working environments for

410   Index

bees, 51–53; challenges of, 52–53; impact of American foulbrood on, 53, 65; livelihood of, 50, 54; and bee hives, 52, 55; records of, 52, 54, 68; responses to bee diseases by, 53, 61–63. *See also* honeybees
bees. *See* honeybees
Bekoff, Marc, 245
Bell, Dr. George, 120, 129–32; *Veterinary Medical Wonder*, 120, 129, 131
belt tackling, 127–28. *See also* horses
Benson, Etienne, 4, 121, 238
Benteen, Frederick, 83
Berger, John, 138, 287; "Why Look at Animals?," 287
Bergh, Henry, 305
Bert, Dr. F. A., 189
birds, 15, 376–78, 391; in *ANIMALIA* exhibit, 357, 363
Birke, Lynda, 93–94, 101, 106
Blackfish [film], 212
bluebucks: earliest known full-body image of, 380; extinction history of, 378, 384; as extinct species, 378–79, 383; metadata on, 380; at the Muséum national d'Histoire naturelle, 371, 375, 377, 382–83; at Naturalis, 381–82; at Naturhistoriska Riksmuseet, 376; portraits of, 375–76, 379, 381, 383; specimens of, 371, 380–81, 383; as victim of colonization, 376
Boisseron, Bénédicte, 323
Bökönyi, Sándor, 40
Bonnell, Jennifer: and Roger Simon, 384
book farming, 119, 162
Borst, Charlotte, 118
Botai culture, 38–39
Boulton, Henry Carew, 273
Boulton, William Somerville, 272–73; *Atlas of the City of Toronto and Vicinity*, 272
Brannaman, Buck, 77
Breck, Major Edward, 142
Brooks, J. Chadwick, 146
Brownell, Franklin, 343–46, 350, 352; *Frozen Meat, Byward Market*, 343
Bryan, William Jennings, 329
Bucephalus (horse), 23
Bucklin Banner, 223
buffaloberries (*Shepherdia canadensis*): as food source for bears, 241–42, 260. *See also* bears
bulls, 222–23, 229
Burghardt, Gordon, 245

Burroughs, John, 143, 245
butchering, 270–71; and butcher shops, 275–78, 282, 285–86; and butchered meats, 270–71, 275, 277, 285; and butchers, 271, 277, 295–96; and slaughterhouses, 292–93, 296, 299, 302–6, 309, 370

C

camelids, 317, 323; and animal labour, 331; as social animals, 324; domestication of, 325; features of, 323; histories of, 317; interbreeding of, 324; products of, 327–28; taxonomic order of, 323; wild, 328. *See also* alpacas; camels; guanacos; llamas; vicuñas
camels, 218, 220–21, 324, 329. *See also* camelids
Campbell, Colleen: "Eastern Slopes Grizzly Bears: Each One is Sacred" [exhibit], 257, 259, 262
Canadian Anti-Vivisection Society, 188, 190. *See also* antivivisection movement
Cartwright, R. G., 82
Castle, William E., 395; *The Genetics of Domestic Rabbits: A Manual for Students of Mammalian Genetics*, 395
Catlin, George, 79–81
cats, 107, 110, 178, 363, 370; domestic, 1–2
cetaceans, 15, 199–200, 202, 209, 213
Cheyenne (Nation), 82
circuses, 218–20; Al G. Barnes Circus, 223–24; historians of, 221–22; Howe's Great London Circus, 218, 222; M. L. Clark and Son's Circus, 218–19, 222–23, 228; Robert L. Parkinson Library and Research Center, 225; Sells Floto Circus, 217
Civil War, 82–84
Clark, Lee, 222–23
Clark, Mack Loren, 218–19, 221, 223
Cleator, Alice Jean, 139–40
Coates, Benjamin, 162
Coffey, Wallace, 80
Cold War, 199–202, 214, 238
colts. *see* horses
Comanche: horsemanship, 78–81; Nation, 75, 81; people, 79–80; teachings, 76, 79; wild horse capture, 75, 79–81
Conibear, Frank, 147
Connaught Laboratories, 7, 13, 176–78; Barton Avenue stable of, 176–77; guinea pigs at, 180–82; history of, 176; mice at, 182; public relations campaigns of, 182–83, 190;

Index   *411*

Connaught Laboratories (*continued*)
 publications of, 176, 180, 182, 186, 192;
 scientists at, 181, 189–90
contextual analysis, 345–46; relationship to visual analysis, 345
Cook, A. J., 63
Corbain, Alain, 29
Cottingham, Ian, 282
Cowie, Helen, 328
cows, 291–94, 297, 299–300, 306, 311; Two-Cow limit, 299–300
Cox, Lisa, 119
coyotes, 148, 253, 255
Craighead, Frank and John, 238, 245
Creighton, Emma, 101, 106
critical empathy, 245, 263. *See also* historical empathy
Crook, George, 83
Csordas, Thomas, 30
Custer, George Armstrong, 82–84

D

Daily Telegram, 137, 146
dairy industry, 299, 302; and milk dealers, 294, 297–98; farms and farmers, 297, 299; production, 299
Dakota (Nation), 77, 107
Darwin, Charles, 20, 327, 393–94; *The Variation of Animals and Plants under Domestication*, 393
Davis, B. J., 137, 146–47
de Bry, Theodor, 330–31
de Kruif, Paul, 189; *Microbe Hunters*, 189
deer, 244, 252, 392
Denison, Flora Macdonald, 188
Deyohahá:ge, 357, 366. *See also* The Indigenous Knowledge Centre
Dickens, Charles, 292–93
digital archives, 280
digital history scholarship, 286, 292, 309–11; digital skills and tools for, 270, 285–87
digital mapping and visualization, 291, 295–96, 302, 306, 309–11
digital sources, 10, 94, 96, 273, 285–86; and dogs, 95, 97, 101–2, 106, 111; and ethical considerations, 95, 97; as ephemeral sources, 94, 96; born-digital sources, 94, 97
digitization projects, 270, 273, 279–80, 284
digitized sources, 270, 277, 279–80, 284–86, 341
diphtheria, 13

dogs: adopters of, 99, 101–2, 104–5, 108–11; in *ANIMALIA* exhibit, 363, 367–69; behaviour of, 109, 111; bodies of as archives, 93; difficulty finding sources documenting the lives of, 92; dog tracks, 96–103, 111;
— dog-racing industry, 96–100, 102, 104–5; and anti-racing groups, 94, 100, 105; decline of, 98, 101; ties to organized crime, 98
— greyhounds, 12, 91–92; and digital sources, 95, 97; behaviour of, 105, 107–8, 110; betting on, 97–98; breeding, 92–94, 97–102, 104, 111; destruction of, 99–100, 102; history of, 97–98; and crates, 103–4, 108–10; lineages, 92, 101; needs of, 94, 106; racing, 92, 94, 98, 111; transition to family life, 94, 97, 101–2, 105–11
and kennel operators, 100, 102–3, 105; as laboratory animals, 190–91; needs of, 92; pit bulls, 91; puppies, 102; sighthounds, 97; trainers of, 91, 93–94
dolphins, 15; bottlenose dolphins, 13; and development of sonar, 201–2; and humans, 200–1; and US Navy research, 201; as pests, 201; scientific observation of, 201, 209, 212; military applications of, 202. *See also* Tuffy (dolphin)
The Dolphins That Joined the Navy [film], 204
domestication: and acclimatization, 329; as process and idea, 325, 329
Donovan, H. B., 180
Dorrance, Bill, 77–78
Dorrance, Tom, 77
Duffield, Deborah: and Sam Ridgway, 204; and Tuffy (dolphin), 204–6, 214; as distinguished marine mammalogist, 205

E

Eastern Slopes Grizzly Bear Project (ESGBP), 13–14, 237–39, 243–46, 248, 254, 263; beginning of, 253; conclusions of, 241; locational data generated by, 238, 241, 244, 261–62; observations of, 243–44. *See also* bears
elephants, 13, 15; from Assam, 228; circus elephants, 13; in classical times, 218; Diamond, 224; and elephant keepers, 218; Mena, 218–22, 228; Princess Alice, 217–18, 227; records of, 217; sold by Carl Hagenbeck, 228. *See also* Ned (elephant); Tusko (elephant)

elk, 244, 252
Ellard, Roland, 178
Elliot, Devon, 286
Elliott, Henry Wood, 145
embedded history, 28, 38, 41
embodied methodology, 23–24, 28. *See also* animal bodies,
Emmons, Ebeneezer, 168; *Agriculture of New-York*, 168
entanglement: as concept in animal studies, 237, 263; between human and other species, 256, 258
entomologists, 53, 65–66, 157–58, 168–69; advocacy for insecticides by, 64; records of, 67; responses to diseases by, 53, 61; and *Cecidomyia culmicola*, 169; and Margaretta Hare Morris, 161, 163, 166–69; and the Hessian fly, 158, 169
environmental history, 9, 51, 75; and environmental historians, 38, 373, 382
Evans, Bill, 202
Evans, Bryant, 207
Evans, Margaret, 126, 128
extinction, 41, 396; representations of, 371, 374, 383-84

F
farmers, 121–22, 124; and animal health care, 124–28, 130–32; and animal health manuals, 118; limited access to veterinary medicine, 122; understanding of animal anatomy, 124
Felt, Ephraim Porter, 168
Fenje, Liz, 298, 300, 303
Ferguson, Lynne, 77
Fijn, Natasha, 29, 39
fish, 363–65
Fisher, James, 119
Fiske, Minnie, 142
Fitch, Asa, 166–68
Fitzgerald, John G., 176, 180, 183, 186, 189–90
flies: *Cecidomyia culmicola*, 166, 168–69; *Cecidomyia culmicola* as misidentified Hessian fly, 159–60, 168; Hessian flies, 157–59, 161–64; larvae of, 158, 167; laying eggs, 157, 160, 163–65, 167; pupa of, 157, 166–67; wheat flies, 161, 166
Flores, Dan, 75
Florida Historical Society, 92
Flury, Henry, 142; "Lady in Furs," 142

Ford, Glenn, 204; in *The Dolphins That Joined the Navy*, 204
foxes, 148, 391
Franits, Wayne, 375
Fudge, Erica, 9, 235–36
fur industry, 138; critics, 138–39, 148; and anti-fur movement, 137–38, 148; fashion, 139–40, 143, 150; and fur boycotts, 137, 142; and fur-bearing animals, 139; furriers, 139, 145; growth of, 148; promoters, 138–39, 143, 148

G
Gade, Daniel, 327
Gagne, Raymond J., 169; *The Plant-Feeding Gall Midges of North America*, 169
game, 391–92
Gardenier, Andrew A., 124–25
Gaynor, Andrea, 9
gender: gender-based discrimination, 161–62, 168–69, 323; history of, 13, 26, 390. *See also* women
Gentile, John, 148
Geographic Information Systems (GIS), 7, 9, 14, 236; tracking bears with, 262; visualizing locational data with, 241, 262; and ArcGIS Online, 273, 275, 279, 282–84, 286, 294, 296; and digitized sources, 270, 286; and georeferencing, 273, 284; for animal history, 269, 286–87; potential for the use of, 269–71, 275, 279, 283–84, 287; spatial analysis using, 269–70, 275, 277, 283; limits of, 283, 287; visualizations, 270, 273, 277, 282–84, 286–87; Web-based, 270, 273
germ theory, 118, 127
Gibeau, Mike, 254
Gide, Andre, 23
The Globe [Toronto], 178, 181–82
Godoy, Juan, 327
Goodnight, Thomas, 138
Gray, John S., 83
The Great Epizootic (of 1872–73), 270, 279–83, 286
Greene, Ann Norton, 341, 352
Grewcock, Duncan, 375
Greyhound Racing Record, 93
greyhounds. *See* dogs
grizzly bears. *See* bears
Grumm-Grzhimaylo brothers, 37
guanacos, 14, 318, 325–26; as arid adapted, 324; as camelid species, 317, 323;

guanacos (*continued*) throughout South America, 321, 332. *See also* camelids
guinea pigs, 7, 13; breeders of, 179–80, 182; and cavies, 179–80; at Connaught Laboratories, 176, 178–82, 186; descriptions of, 183, 186; and diphtheria, 176, 183, 189; and their disappearance from records, 175, 183, 186–87, 191–92; as docile, 178–79, 190; as an expendable species, 189–91; as laboratory animals, 175–78, 180–83, 186, 191–92; as pets, 176, 178–79; prices of, 180–81; reproduction of, 180, 182; and vivisection, 187–88; and Voges holder, 186–87

H

Hagenbeck, Carl, 218, 221, 228
Haldeman, Samuel Stehman, 166
Hämäläinen, Pekka, 75
Haraway, Donna, 50, 52
Hare, Robert, 161–62
hares, 391, 393, 395
Harris, Thaddeus William, 163–64, 166–68; *A Treatise on Some of the Insects of New England*, 168; *Report on the Insects of Massachusetts*, 164
Haskett, T. H., 126–29
Healy, Richard, 282
Hein, Hilde, 374
Herman, David, 239, 245
Herrick, Edward Claudius, 163–64, 167
Hessian fly. *See* flies
historical empathy, 8–10. *See also* critical empathy
Hoare, Philip, 212
Hockenhull, Joanna, 101, 106
Hodgins, J. E., 126–29
Homquist, Captain Carl O., 207
honeybees, 12, 15; as agricultural producers, 54, 67; behaviour of, 53–54, 67, 69; declining forage sources of, 56–57, 68–69; and exposure to disease, 59, 67; foraging of, 52, 54; health, 12, 50, 54, 67; and insecticide poisoning, 63, 65, 67–68; keepers of, 50; labour of, 12, 49–50, 52, 66, 69; and risks of foraging, 53, 63–64, 67–68; robbing other colonies, 59, 62–63; as workers, 49–50, 67; working environments of, 52–53, 59, 65–66, 68
Hornaday, William T., 145

horses: agency of, 25–26, 30; in *ANIMALIA* exhibit, 363; Arab, 34; in art history, 339, 343–44; belt tackling of, 127–28; — bodies of, 23–24, 34, 41; as archives, 27–29, 32–33, 36–38
body language of, 29–32; branding of, 33–34; centring in history of, 12, 79, 84–85; colts, 33, 77; at Connaught Laboratories, 176–77, 182–83; dung of, 35–36; and domestication, 39, 80; domestic horses, 20–21, 37, 39; as expert communicators, 76, 78, 85; as fundamentally relational, 76–77, 85; gelding (castrating) of, 25, 33–34, 41, 127; and the Great Epizootic, 279–80, 282–83; hair of, 36, 41; and horse-centred analysis, 75–76, 82, 85; and horse-human interactions, 12, 76–77, 79–80, 82–85; mares, 32, 35; Mongolian horses, 30, 32, 34, 37, 39, 42; Przewalski's horse, 19, 20–21, 40–41; riding of, 26, 28–31, 40–41; stallions, 32, 35, 40–41; Thoroughbreds, 34; trainers of, 77, 80; volition of, 73, 75–76, 78–79, 82, 85; wild horses, 21, 40–41; wild vs domesticated, 41–42; and urban transportation, 270, 280, 283; labour of, 341, 347. *See also* takhis
Howell, Philip, 279
Hribal, Jason, 49–50
Hudson's Bay Company (HBC), 137–38, 140, 145–47, 149
humane societies, 99, 105; Ottawa Humane Society, 345; Toronto Humane Society, 147
Humphrey, Caroline, 33
Hunt, Ray, 77
hybridization, 395–97; and beefalo, 396; and rabbit-hare hybrids, 394–95

I

Indigenous histories, 75, 85
Indigenous knowledge, 12, 22, 41, 85; horsemanship, 75; dismissed, 74–75; failure to account for, 85; in a horse-centred analysis, 76; preservation of, 366
The Indigenous Knowledge Centre, 357, 366
Ingram, Darcy, 187
Internet Archive, 112
Isenberg, Andrew, 75

J

James, Chris, 80
John Lilly, 202; *Man and Dolphin*, 202

Johnston, Patricia, 345
Jones, Ryan Tucker, 262
Jones, Susan, 119
Jørgensen, Finn Arne, 382

K

Kansas State Archives, 92. *See also* archives
Kay, Sarah, 341
Kearny, Steven, 83; *The Cavalry Manual*, 83
Kenny, Keith, 318
Kheraj, Sean: animal history seminar at York, 361
khulans, 36–37
Khustain Nuruu National Park, 20–21
Kiefer, J. J., 168
Kimmerer, Robin Wall, 74
Kingston College of Veterinarians, 129
Kirk, Robert G. W., 181, 190
Klingle, Matthew, 191
Knight, Dr. A. P., 130
Knudson, Gus, 221–22, 225–26
Koblin, Aaron, 239; "Flight Patterns," 239, 241
Kramer, Max, 201
kulans. *See* khulans,
Kuzmaski, Emma, 361–62

L

Lakota: language, 73; Nation, 73, 82; people, 73; teachings, 73–74
Laut, Agnes C., 144–45, 147; *The Fur Trade of America*, 144
Lederer, Susan, 191
Lengkeek, Peter, 77
Leopold, Aldo, 238
LeSueur, Charles Alexandre, 159, 165, 167
Levi-Strauss, Claude, 24
Lilly, John, 201–2
Lister Institute, 180–81
Liverant, Bettina, 139
llamas: agency of, 317; ancestry of, 323; Andean homeland of, 325; and animal labour, 331; as arid adapted, 324; as camelid species, 317, 323; colours and patterns of, 324; and concept of diaspora, 14; and domesticated, 323–24; entanglement with humans, 318; and Europeans, 326, 328; as gifts, 329; in global circulation, 315–18, 328–29, 332; habitats of, 317; mummies of, 323; products of, 327; ritual role of, 326; throughout South America, 319; in the US, 330–31; wool of, 317, 324; in zoos, 324, 328. *See also* Spook (llama)
London Correspondence School, 117, 120, 126, 129; *The Veterinary Science*, 120, 126, 128
London Veterinary Correspondence School. *See* London Correspondence School
Long, William J., 142

M

Mackenzie, William Lyon, 271
Manwood, John, 391; *Treatise of the Forest Laws*, 391
Marchal, Paul, 168
Marengo (horse), 23
Marra, Kim, 31
Marx, Karl, 26
Masson, Jeffrey Moussaieff, 346; *The Pig Who Sang to the Moon: The Emotional World of Farm Animals*, 346
Matlass, David, 140
McKeon, Dennis, 103, 105–6
McLean, William B., 202
McShane, Clay, 51
Mendes, Jeremy, 245
mice, 178, 182, 391
Micklethwaite, F. W., 6
Milligan, Ian, 94, 285
Mirzoeff, Nicholas, 342
Mitchell, W. J. T., 352–53; *What Do Pictures Want?: The Lives and Loves of Images*, 352
Mizelle, Brett, 345
Molina, Juan Ignacio, 326–27
Möllhausen, Balduin, 79–81; *Diary of the Mississippi*, 79
Mongolia, 22–23, 29, 31; horse as national emblem of, 33; steppes of, 19; horse culture of, 3
Moore, Katherine, 327
Morris, David Copland, 149
Morris, Margaretta Hare, 13, 157–69; Asa Fitch, 166–67; and *Cecidomyia culmicola*, 169; and fly specimens, 164–67; as scientific artist, 161; of unknown fly by, 160–61, 164–66; erasures of, 160–61, 164, 169; reactions to findings of, 162–64, 166–69
Moses Brings Plenty, 77
Muir, John, 149; *Stickeen*, 149
Murie, Adolph, 238
Murie, Olaus, 238, 245

museums: Royal Ontario Museum, 357, 367; Whyte Museum, 262; C. A. V. Barker Museum of Canadian Veterinary History, 126; Circus World Museum, 225; American Museum of Natural History, 377, 399; Horniman Museum and Gallery, 377; Muséum national d'Histoire naturelle (MNHN), 371–72, 374–76, 378–79, 383; natural history museums, 373–74, 376, 383–84; Naturalis, 374, 379–82; Naturhistorisches Museum Wien, 374, 376; Naturhistoriska Riksmuseet (NRM), 374, 376–79, 382; Royal Albert Museum and Art Gallery, 378

N

Nadasdy, Paul, 11
Nance, Susan: 236; *The Historical Animal*, 5
Nash, Linda, 7, 68
National Greyhound Association (NGA), 93, 95, 97–102, 105–7, 109, 111
National Greyhound Hall of Fame, 92–93
National Sporting Library, 92
Nawa, Kohei, 381
Ned (elephant), 218; background of, 218–19, 222; and circus life, 220, 228; death of, 229; final years of, 228–29; historical records of, 220–21; joining Al G. Barnes Circus, 224; and Mena, 219–22, 228; name changed to Tusko, 224; stories of, 222, 227, 229–30; as Tusko, 224, 226–29; at Woodland Park Zoo, 229. *See also* elephants; Tusko (elephant)
New York Times, 137, 141–42, 212, 224
New York Women's League for Animals, 142
Nye, Elwood, 83

O

O'Gorman, Emily, 9
Oceti Sakowin, 73, 75, 77, 79
Ogden, Laura, 318
Olmstead, Alan, 59, 66
Olson, Kathryn, 138
Ontario Beekeeping Association (OBA), 52, 56, 62, 65
Ontario Ministry of Agriculture, 65; *An Act for the Further Protection of Bees*, 65
Ontario Veterinary Association, 118
Ontario Veterinary College (OVC), 117–18, 120–21, 129, 131
Ontario Veterinary Medical Association, 126
Ontario Veterinary Practice Board, 129

oral history: and animal history, 27, 29, 41, 97, 214; limitations of, 9, 13; and Indigenous knowledge, 22; and oral historians, 27, 31, 96; and oral tradition, 34; of horses, 22, 41
Ottawa Anti-Vivisection Society, 190. *See also* antivivisection movement
Ottawa Humane Society, 345
Our Dumb Animals, 10, 142–43
Owens, Trevor, 96
oxen, 347, 350–51
Oxford Handbook on the History of Medicine, 175

P

Padilla, Thomas, 96
Pahdopony, Juanita, 80
Panic of 1837, 157, 161
Paris Green, 64–65
Pasteur Laboratories, 180
Patterson, Penny, 398
Pearson, Susan, 8
Pellett, Frank C., 56
Pepperberg, Irene, 398
Phelps, Oliver, 348–51, 353
Philo, Chris, 269
Pigafetta, Antonio, 326
pigs, 292–93, 297, 306, 344–46
Pleistocene, 39, 323
Pliny the Elder, 200
Plumwood, Val, 252, 261
pneumonia, 124, 131–33
Powell, E. Alexander, 141
Proctor, Robert N., 176, 191
Przewalski, Nikołaj, 19
Przewalski's horse, 19, 20–21, 40–41. *See also* takhis
Puente, Javier, 329

R

rabbits, 142, 144, 391–93, 395
racial discrimination: 161, 169, 323
racoons, 148, 255
Rader, Karen, 182
radio-telemetry, 254; data, 239, 242, 249; equipment, 239; locating bears with, 241, 246, 253; as method of locating animals, 238; technology, 238
Reaves, John, 208
Reno, Marcus, 82
Retired Greyhounds as Pets (ReGAP), 107–8
Rhode, Paul, 60, 68

Ridgway, Sam, 202; and Deborah Duffield, 204; *Dolphin Doctor*, 213; *Mammals of the Sea*, 212; and Tuffy (dolphin), 203–6, 209–10, 213–14; and US Navy Marine Mammal Program, 202, 212
Ritvo, Harriet: *The Animal Estate: The English and Other Creatures in the Victorian Age*, 4, 389
Robert L. Parkinson Library and Research Center, 225
Roberts, Charles G. D., 245
Roberts, G. D., 142
Robichaud, Andrew: *Animal City: The Domestication of America*, 292, 310
Roosevelt, Theodore, 143, 227
Roscher, Mieke, 32
Ross, Wally, 203–4, 206
Rothfels, Nigel, 4, 138
Roux, Emile, 189
Ruhe, Louis, 219, 222
Russell, Edmund, 50
Russell, Nerissa, 325
Ryan, John M., 82, 84

S

Sagard, Gabriel, 1–3, 11; *Le grand voyage du pays des Hurons*, 2
Sale, Charles, 146
Sanchez, Mark, 300, 307
Sanofi Pasteur, 176–77, 184
Say, Thomas, 158–60, 163, 165, 167
Schiebinger, Londa, 176, 191
Seabiscuit (horse), 23
Sealab II, 199, 207–8, 214
Sealab III, 210
seals, 137, 140–41, 145, 255
The Secret History of the Mongols, 20
Seefeldt, Douglas, 286
Sellers, Chris, 66
sensory history, 24, 29, 34, 41
Seton, Ernest Thompson, 142, 245
Seventh Cavalry, 83–84
sharks, 199, 202, 207, 255
Shaw, David Gary, 4
sheep, 317, 324, 331, 340, 389
Sherow, James, 75
Simon, Roger: and Jennifer Bonnell, 384
Sinclair, Upton, 293
Sitting Bull, 77
slaughterhouses, 292–93, 296, 299, 302–6, 309, 370. *See also* butchering

Smith, Clinton, 81
Smith, John G., 65, 68
Smith, William F., 222
Snow, Sasha, 258
Snyder, Bill, 315
social history, 8, 25, 292
Societies for the Prevention of Cruelty to Animals (SPCAs), 8, 10, 141–42, 293–94, 305; American Society for the Prevention of Cruelty to Animals (ASPCA), 141; Canadian Society for the Prevention of Cruelty to Animals, 345; San Francisco SPCA (SFSPCA), 305–9, 311
Soussloff, Catherine, 372, 378
spatial history, 292, 295, 311. *See also* The Stanford Spatial History Project (SHP),
The Stanford Spatial History Project (SHP), 292, 294–95, 298, 303–4, 306–7. *See also* "Animal City" Spatial History Lab project; spatial history
Spook (llama), 227, 315–17, 328. *See also* llamas
squirrels, 149, 391
stallions. *See* horses,
Stanley, Agnes, 188
Stein, Charles A., 83
Steinberg, Theodore, 292
Steiner, Erik, 298, 304, 307
The Stockman Guide and Manual to Husbandry, 120, 122–25, 127
Stoler, Ann Laura, 235
Strunk, Simon, 175
Styran, Roberta, 349
Sweeny, Robert, 284–85

T

takhis, 20–21, 26, 36–37; food resources of, 36; as "free or spirit horse," 19; growing populations of, 37; interbreeding of, 39; narrative descriptions of, 37; and reintroduction to Mongolia, 20–21; and rewilding efforts, 39, 41; taxonomic position of, 37; as wild horses, 39, 41. *See also* horses; Przewalski's horse
tamaga, 32–33, 38
tamga. *See* tamaga
tamgha. *See* tamaga
Tarr, Joel, 51
taxidermy, 23, 138; practice, 373; process, 373, 381; and taxidermied animals, 371, 374, 381, 383

Taylor, Robert, 349
Terry, Alfred, 83
tetanus, 13, 176, 183
Thomas, Lynn, 26
Thomas, William G., 282, 286
Thompson, J. Gurnley, 121, 122; *The Domestic Encyclopedia of Facts or Farmers, Mechanics, and Household Manual*, 120–21, 123, 127
Toronto Humane Society, 147
Tortorici, Zac, 5
Townsend, Charles, 145–46
Townsend, Gordon, 57
Trouillot, Michel-Rolph, 235–36
Tuffy (dolphin), 13, 227; agency of, 200; background of, 199–200, 203–4, 207, 214; begins open water work, 206, 208; death of, 200, 210, 212–13; in *The Dolphins That Joined the Navy*, 204; evidence in archives of, 200; Deborah Duffield, 204–6, 214; recovery of ordnance by, 208; and oral history, 200; personality of, 204–5, 210, 214; and public interest, 199, 207; and Sam Ridgway, 206, 212, 214; and Sealab II, 199, 208; and US Navy Marine Mammal Program, 200, 203, 209
Turkel, William J., 286
Turley, James, 82–84
Tusko (elephant), 200; background of, 224; and Diamond, 224; final years of, 228–29; handlers of, 226, 229; name changed from Ned to, 224; as Ned, 224, 226–29; and rampage in Sedro-Woolley, 224, 226; sources on the life of, 226; stories of, 224, 227, 230; at Woodland Park Zoo, 229. *See also* Ned (elephant)

U

US Navy Marine Mammal Program, 199–200, 203, 209–10, 212–14

V

Vaillant, John, 258
Van Der Byl, Major Charles C.,
ventriloquism: as risk of animal history, 3, 8, 15, 29
vernacular knowledge, 37, 42
veterinarians, 122, 126, 131, 331–32; in rural areas, 117–19; and London Correspondence School, 126; view of animal health manuals, 117–18. *See also* animal health care; animal health knowledge; animal health manuals; veterinary medicine
veterinary medicine, 119; as costly, 117–18, 122, 131; demand for knowledge of, 119, 126; development of, 117; farmers' limited access to, 122; institutionalization in Canada of, 126, 129, 132; and Veterinary Science Association, 129; and veterinary training, 118–19. *See also* animal health care; animal health knowledge; animal health manuals; veterinarians
Veterinary Science Practice Act, 126, 129
vicuñas, 14, 324, 326; as camelid species, 317, 323; conservation challenges of, 328; throughout South America, 322, 332; as water dependent, 324; wool of, 328
visual analysis, 341–42, 345, 348, 352–53; and animal history, 342; defined, 342; relationship to contextual analysis, 345. *See also* contextual analysis,
vivisection, 187–88, 190. *See also* antivivisection movement,
von Hartenfels, Georg Christoph Petri, 218; *Elephantographia curiosa*, 218
Von Hear, Nicholas, 318

W

Wade, Evelyn, 178–79
Waite, Merton B., 66
Walker, Brett, 236, 332
Walker, Graham, 38, 40
Walton, Homer, 222
Wendake, 1–2
Wendat (people), 1–3
Weyodi (Comanche author), 81
White Hat, Albert, 73–74
White, Richard, 51, 252; *Organic Machine*, 51
Wilson, Robert M., 238
Wintermantel, Morris, 203–4
Wischermann, Clemens, 279
wolves, 236, 252, 254
women: and the American Philosophical Society (APS), 161; in the antivivisection movement, 188; and fur fashion 139–42, 144. *See also* gender
Wood, Forrest, 204, 208, 210
Woodcock Jr., William "Buckles," 218
Woods, Abigail, 119
World War I, 137, 139, 180, 360
World War II, 57, 140, 147, 181, 201
Worster, Donald, 38
Wright, Mabel Osgood, 143

X
Xenophon, 77–78, 80; *The Art of Horsemanship*, 77

Y
You, Chengcheng, 149

Z
zel lines, 26–27
zooethnography, 31
zoos: archives of, 218; Central Park Zoo, 315; in cities, 293; Copenhagen zoo, 397; and elephants, 226, 228; Hogle Zoo, 217; in Kansas City, 329; petting zoos, 324, 328; spatial arrangement of, 362; and takhis, 20, 41; and wild animals, 138, 220, 397; Woodland Park Zoo, 221, 225, 229

www.ingramcontent.com/pod-product-compliance
Lightning Source LLC
Chambersburg PA
CBHW041731300426
44115CB00022B/2971